The Un-Americans
Trashing of the United States Constitution in the American Press

By Thomas Bonsell

Country Cottage Publishing

© 1995 by Thomas Bonsell

All rights reserved. No part of this book may be reproduced or transmitted in any form by any means, mechanical or electronic, including photocopying or recording, or by any information storage or retrieval system, except as is expressly allowed by the 1976 Copyright Act or by the publisher. Requests for permission should be made in writing to Country Cottage Publishing, P. O. Box 1020, Wauna, WA 98395.

Publisher's Cataloging-in-Publication Data

Bonsell, Thomas
The Un-Americans: Trashing of the United States Constitution in the American Press

        includes appendix and index
        ISBN 0-9646768-9-3
        1. American journalism. 2. Constitutional law
        I. Title

Text edited by Linda Hinthorne-King

Manufactured in the United States of America
First Edition/First Printing

Table of Contents

Preface 1
Chapter 1 5
    Americanizing a World
    Reaching for the Stars and Stripes * A Perspective on Un-Americanism * A Prophecy Proven * Educators Fail Constitutional Test * Myths and Metaphors

Chapter 2 19
    Government to Have and to Mold
    Out With the Old, in With the ?? * The Agreement for Government * Four Citizens of Creation * A Different Source of Creation

Chapter 3 31
    Knowing America
    The Roots of the Nation * Limited Government * Source of the Elusive Rights * Speaking in a Different Tongue * Bashing the Supreme Court * "Original Intent" Fails Test of Logic * Beneficial Battle Over Bork * Kennedy: Better, but not Ideal ? * Views From Politicians * Extreme Views

Chapter 4 68
    Government as Power
    Power, Principles and 'Ocracies * The Fountain of Power * States' Wrongs, Not Rights

Chapter 5 85
    Powers That Be
    Principles Lost * Legislative Power * Legislative Limits * Presidential Powers * Judicial Powers * Principles That Made a Nation * A Miss by the Experts

Chapter 6 112
    Paring Powers
    But Who's Being Cut Out? * At War Over War * The People Giveth * Going to Extremes

Chapter 7 134
    Freedom Is
    An Argument for Nonpower * A Burning Controversy * To Amend or Not to Amend * Government Can Be Criminal * Easy Doesn't Do It

Chapter 8..**155**
    A Prized Possession
        The Bill of Rights * The First Amendment * The Second Amendment * The Third Amendment * The Fourth Amendment * The Fifth Amendment * The Sixth Amendment * The Seventh Amendment * The Eighth Amendment * The Ninth Amendment * The Tenth Amendment

Chapter 9..**218**
    Some Gospel Truths
        Understanding Needed * Without a Prayer * Tackling a Tough Issue * God in School * Holy Wars * Overcoming Overreaction * Christmas Spite * Taxing Problems * Revelations

Chapter 10..**260**
    Finishing Touches
        Creativity Lost * The Eleventh Amendment * The Twelfth Amendment * The Thirteenth Amendment * The Fourteenth Amendment * The Fifteenth Amendment * The Sixteenth Amendment * The Seventeenth Amendment * The Eighteenth Amendment * The Nineteenth Amendment * The Twentieth Amendment * The Twenty-First Amendment * The Twenty-Second Amendment * The Twenty-Third Amendment * The Twenty-Fourth Amendment * The Twenty-Fifth Amendment * The Twenty-Sixth Amendment * The Twenty-Seventh Amendment

Chapter 11..**304**
    Money: the Root of All Government
        A Mutual Dependency * Questionable Practices * Taxpayers' Nonrights * When All Seems Lost, Amend

Chapter 12..**321**
    Opinions and Other Biases
        Several Points of View * Citizen Involvement * Defending the ACLU * Bad Decisions * Fixing the Constitution * Opposition and Confusion

Appendix..**355**
    Constitution of the United States of America

Index..**375**

PREFACE

This book — a critique of the corporate publishing industry's ignorance of, or seemingly disdain for, the United States' governing principles — is written from the perspective of a newspaper editor who realizes the desire of many Americans to "take back their country" runs into an inescapable truism not widely recognized: most Americans don't understand much about what they wish to take back.

The book addresses opinions circulated in the mass media by individuals and institutions whose aims are to influence others. Those opinions are subjected to fair review and comment in the book by refuting the press, politicians and others who have appointed themselves critics of the United States Supreme Court while posing as experts to distort court decisions and the Constitution of the United States for political gain. The book praises those who have stood firm in defense of the Constitution when doing so was unpopular. And there have been instances in America's history when adhering to constitutional principles was unpopular and, at times, perilous.

Because the press has taken the lead in distorting the Constitution and court decisions, it's appropriate a journalist for 16 years — who studied the Constitution at Georgetown University Graduate School of Government — corrects the distortions. The author, also an intelligence analyst for nearly six years as a member of the United States Air Force Security Service and as a civilian at the National Security Agency, wrote the book to explain and praise the Constitution he defended.

This is not a textbook for law or political-science students – it would help as supplemental material – the purpose is to promote understanding of the United States system of self-government by concentrating on court decisions and on writings of the Constitution's creators. The material does draw on political-science and law textbooks but is presented in a clear-and-precise manner, as if it were a newspaper op ed column free of academic and legalistic jargon and phraseology that often obscure relatively simple concepts.

The book is for readers of editorial pages and the journalists who have misinformed them. It has value for attorneys, educators, politicians and students; especially students of journalism, political science and prelaw. It concentrates on areas of the Constitution Americans argue about the most and uses matcrial printed in the United States press (or broadcast) since the bicentennial of the American colonies' revolt against Great Britain.

The book is entirely pro-Constitution and pro-Supreme Court; the author is an unapologetic fan of the court. The material is presented on the premise that the court is never wrong — even when it makes a rare bad decision — court critics are seldom right.

THE UN-AMERICANS

The format of criticizing the newspaper industry was chosen because each critique shows the need and value of the book. Such need was demonstrated by an editorial in The Daily Oklahoman of Oklahoma City in the summer of 1993. The paper, questioning the fitness of Ruth Bader Ginsburg to serve on the United States Supreme Court because of her acceptance of abortion rights, asked; "Can *Roe vs. Wade* be defended on any constitutional ground?" This book says the answer is, "Yes." It's the anti-Roe position that can't be constitutionally defended. Roe can easily be justified on constitutional grounds by anyone who has studied the Constitution and who understands how the Constitution works — which evidently doesn't include those who determine editorial policy of The Daily Oklahoman. A strong constitutional defense of *Roe v. Wade* is in Chapter 10 of this book, and anyone who wants to make editorial policy for any American newspaper would be well advised to read it and make a concerted effort to understand it.

In the two centuries of the nation's existence there have been many excellent books concerning the Constitution. Unfortunately, they have been written by professors and lawyers, and do not appeal to most Americans because of writing filled with pomposity, verbosity and other barriers to understanding. Books and articles aimed at the majority of Americans have been written by politicians and journalists but were politically biased and, therefore, wrong; just as wrong as the columnists, editorial writers, publishers, editors and reporters criticized in this book.

This book won't make anyone a constitutional lawyer, but many people who claim to know the Constitution may find their knowledge incomplete or inaccurate. Readers should be able to use a new understanding of the Constitution to see what's important to the liberty of Americans — and the world — and what's political nonsense thrown about to advance someone's power, position or prestige. In order to preserve self-governance in the United States, Americans must learn its constitutional principles; this book is intended to facilitate that learning. Most importantly, readers should be able to adopt a profound appreciation for the Constitution and accept it as the only true patriotic philosophy for all Americans.

The book was written by an angry man; angry after devoting several years to intelligence work defending the United States only to see criminals leave prison — following sentences for felonies perpetrated for political purposes during subversive activities — being hailed as heroes, some given acting roles on television and/or jobs as radio talk-show hosts, plus book contracts from major American publishers. Other subversives have been proclaimed great American patriots for their crimes while given presidential pardons that amount to free passes around justice while American publishers

Preface

lust after their stories. A subversive who has gained fame and fortune through the customary book contracts and public appearances can then be nominated by a major political party to run for high office in the very government he subverted.

The author is angry at an American public which has become disgusted with what may be the finest governmental system ever created – the federal constitutional system. In an age in which blame usually is transferred to someone else, American voters express outrage at "politicians" for the problems of society. Whether it is the monumental federal debt, the costly solution to the savings-and-loan debacle, the highest crime rates in the industrialized world, failure to solve a health-care "crisis," a damaged environment that's dangerous to human health or other less-noticed problems the electorate voted for, incumbent officeholders are blamed even if they may be the ones working hardest to find solutions. Voters never blame themselves for voting for fairy tales (put forward by some politicians who often caused the problems with their programs or refuse to seek solutions lest they offend a special interest) while at the same time using the referendum process available in many states to enact laws that are blatantly unconstitutional which, in a fashion, is subversion.

The author, who has developed an expertise in constitutional law perhaps unsurpassed in American journalism, is angriest at a publishing industry that has its rights, freedoms and privileged position protected by the Constitution, and the people who defend that document, but publishes anti-Constitution ignorance in its books, just as newspapers do on their editorial and op ed pages. The publishing industry often criticizes others for doing what publishers do. Television is criticized for perceived shoddy treatment or cancellation of quality dramas such as *I'll Fly Away* and *Homicide: Life on the Streets* or light comedy as *Brooklyn Bridge,* but publishers are every bit as shoddy with their preference for trash produced by athletes, entertainers, criminals, subversives and famous fools.

Newspapers lead the criticism of television, then publish irresponsible political columnists who attack from positions of ignorance because it's thought they "elicit enormous reader response," while seemingly excluding whose who might show editorial policy to be faulty or un-American. In truth, there is as much competence and responsibility in television as in publishing and as much ignorance and irresponsibility in publishing as in television. Newspaper editors and publishers are political animals — much more political than they admit — and their political bent undermines any image of objectivity they try to impress on the public. Competent journalists, from obituary writers to political reporters, do their best to remain neutral — most do a fine job of that — but editors and publishers undo those efforts by accumulating as many former politicians or political aides and speech writers as possible to saturate editorial and op ed pages with editorials and columns that amount to little more than political position papers for former bosses of the journalist/politician and which level attacks on the politicians who replaced those bosses in public office.

And the author is angry about anti-Constitution propaganda dominating the recent phenomenon of talk radio and coming from people who have never served or protected the nation or who may have even subverted it.

Some materials in this book were included as insight or prediction long before they were validated by Supreme Court decisions, so they have been left much as originally written as illustrations of pro-Constitution material the publishing industry is reluctant to supply to American readers. Examples are in Chapter 9's observation that individual-initiated prayer at public schools is not forbidden; in Chapter 10, where it's explained why reverse discrimination in affirmative-action programs would not pass court tests, and in Chapter 12 which tells why the mention of God in the Pledge of Allegiance doesn't violate the Constitution, and why term-limit referendums for Congress are unconstitutional. The observations were made in the manuscript from a few months before the Supreme Court decided the reverse-discrimination issue to more than three years on term limits. Also included in this vein is the observation that property forfeitures in the war on drugs are illegal without a form of due process, though the court didn't require the full extent of due process (Chapter 8), it only required notification.

In recent years, some odd arguments have been featured in high-profile criminal cases (notably the Branch Davidian murder-and-conspiracy trial in Texas and the Randy Weaver murder trial in Idaho) which followed the deaths of federal officers who were killed while trying to legally arrest persons wanted on criminal charges. Defendants were found not guilty of murder on the grounds they were defending themselves or their property. After many years of the federal government being portrayed by its foes as a monstrous enemy of the people the argument that a person could open fire on law officials isn't too surprising. Hatred of the federal government — born in the 18th century to oppose the at-the-time unadopted Constitution of the United States — continues unabated by those people who detest the Constitution's principles of liberty for all, equality, human rights, due process, superiority of the national government, separation of church and state, restraint of police, regulation of commerce, or anything else that suggests a diminution of their exalted positions or opinions. Too often, that includes publishers and editors who control the information disseminated to America.

Chapter 1

AMERICANIZING A WORLD

REACHING FOR THE STARS – AND STRIPES

Monumental changes in the past few years have made it seem much of the world has tried to "Americanize" itself, by taking on the forms of the United States' governmental and economic systems. From Latin America and the Far East, to south-central Asia and Africa, to Eastern Europe and the Soviet Union, the evolution since the mid-1980s is to move away from dictatorial, one-party governmental systems into what may become permanent democratically based societies. Socialist nations Americanizing themselves have repudiated state ownership of their economies and have attempted to switch to market economies, although with great social hardship and deprivation for many.

The movement toward Americanization began slowly in unrelated nations such as Argentina, Pakistan, South Korea and the Philippines, then reached almost unbelievable momentum between 1989 and 1991 with abandonment of philosophies that controlled the Soviet Union and its allies for more than 70 years. When the Union of Soviet Socialist Republics ceased to exist at the end of 1991, that event signaled the permanency of Americanization.

Each nation was put on the road toward a democratically based governmental system by different reasons and events, but all seemed to be moving in the democratic direction, some just barely, others with zest and determination. The Philippines took the step toward Americanization with a military coup to oust dictator Ferdinand Marcos, South Korea put on a better image before the 1988 Summer Olympic Games, Argentina ousted its military dictators following their loss in the Falkland Islands war with Great Britain and Pakistan's dictator died in an airplane crash. With the ousting of the old order, each began what may lead to Western-style democratic governments and societies. These early transformations may have proved to the communist countries of Eastern Europe that there was nothing to fear from easing away from their doctrinaire rulership and taking on a more-open government.

Africa – historically controlled by tribal chiefdoms before three centuries of colonial dictatorships led to three decades of one-party rule learned from colonialism – took the path to democracy after the fall of communism left many states without superpower support. A few nations, such as Egypt, had been working toward democracy before the fall of Marxism. The Republic of South Africa swept out the old system and instituted democracy without delay in 1994.

It was as if much of the world was saying Americans knew all along what was necessary for the preservation of civilization. Away went monopolistic one-party political systems and in came promises of freely contested open elections. Out went the idea the ruling elite knew what was best for everyone and in came the willingness to debate and hear other ideas without threat of jail for those expressing opinions. And, as if on cue, Americans flocked to the newly emerging democracies full of advice and direction for the newcomers to the democratic arena. Former U.S. President Jimmy Carter was quickly on the spot in February of 1990 for what was considered Nicaragua's first truly free election, which resulted in the loss of power of the revolutionary Sandinistas a decade after they led the overthrow of the Somoza dictatorship.

At the same time, the Democratic and Republican parties had representatives in Poland to teach all they knew about democratic elections. Therein lies a problem. The problem is simply, while Americans are quick to tell others how to maintain a democratically based government and society, many are ignorant of their native society and government and often don't practice what they preach to others. The United States Constitution is bandied about as if it were a magical instrument that provides peace, prosperity, eternal tranquility, rights and privileges to everyone. Americans love to cite the Constitution as a legitimizing agent for all sorts of personal concepts and biased ideas. In reality, Americans know very little about the U.S. Constitution, and what they think they know is but a mythical extension of their opinions and perceptions.

A PERSPECTIVE ON UN-AMERICANISM

United States Supreme Court Judge Antonin Scalia, in the Northwest in the summer of 1988 to discuss the United States Constitution before a gathering of lawyers in Poulsbo, one of Washington state's superior seaside settlements, brought out a concept that's uniquely American and which helps explain the reason this book must exist.

He was reported by the Kitsap County (Wash.) Newspaper Group as saying, " 'We consider ourselves tied together not by genealogy or beliefs but by certain principles ... and ideas that are perceived to run counter to those principles which are embodied in the Constitution, are perceived to be un-American.' "

It's that definition of "un-American" used as the emphasis and title of this book. Scalia reportedly added that other nations or societies don't share with Americans the concept of "un." It was reported that Scalia said, "Labeling ideas as un-French or un-German means nothing ..."

Scalia's talk brought out several points which will be touched on in this book. He reportedly told the attorneys, "Basically, the concept of a limited federal government is not around any more." Of course that depends on how one determines "a limited federal government." Recent Supreme Court appointees – and that includes Scalia – have tended to rule in favor of governmental power whenever it conflicts with individual freedoms. When that happens, the federal government isn't limited. Scalia mentioned in his talk that the Constitution's Bill of Rights don't include an explicit right of privacy. Many people believe the Constitution does include a right of privacy, it just isn't listed. The Constitution also doesn't include a right of "singing in the rain" or "tiptoeing through the tulips," but Americans have such rights because rights exist in areas of human behavior in which government has little or no authority to act. And if the concept of limited government is ever to be taken seriously, it's up to Scalia and his colleagues on the Supreme Court to do the limiting by refusing to honor laws unconstitutionally enacted or actions illegally taken.

(Note that Scalia is called a "Supreme Court Judge, not Justice." That is because the Constitution specifically refers to its members as "judges," not "justices," as commonly believed by people who don't read the Constitution. But it does say "Chief Justice.")

Seemingly legitimate and acceptable ideas are commonly circulated throughout society as constitutional principles but are actually falsehoods – what Scalia referred to as "perceived to be un-American." These concepts come from all legitimate sources including presidents, senators and representatives, attorneys and judges, professors, journalists, the military and religion and other persons of high or low standing in society. In short, from everywhere.

These persons aren't un-American rabble-rousing subversives; they're merely ignorant of true constitutional concepts.

That ignorance is a threat to the continued existence of the Constitution and its principles that govern society. It should be obvious that a society's ideals and principles cannot be maintained if the population is ignorant of those facets of civilization – and that, sadly, is the state of 20th-century America – just when the rest of the world is looking to it for leadership.

THE UN-AMERICANS

After more than 200 years of existence, the United States' principles and ideals remain mysteries to nearly all Americans, and the most unfortunate part of this situation is many of those who know little or nothing about American concepts and standards are important in government, the law, academia and the press. We can forgive ordinary Americans for their lack of awareness, for they rely on this ignorant quartet for knowledge, but there's no overlooking the sins of omission of those four elitist groups for their "subversion by ignorance."

Understanding the principles and ideas of America requires understanding the Constitution – what it really says and means. Many people think that to understand the document, they need only listen to a president they support or some politician or political party – if they agree with the party line. Hardly anybody looks to the United States Supreme Court for enlightenment, and that is a shame for its decisions best explain our constitutional system of self-governance.

There's a logical reason for this. Presidents, governors, mayors, senators, representatives and other elected officials aren't required by Constitution, law or custom to know or understand anything about the Constitution or America's principles and ideals. And they usually satisfy that requirement well, for often they're little more than representatives of a political philosophy, movement or interest group. And when they represent their supporters – be it commerce, labor, religion, political party or prejudice – and fail to represent the well-being of the nation, their lack of knowledge about America's principles and ideals becomes evident.

Knowledgeable people look to the Supreme Court for understanding, and they look there for good reason. By custom the judges have always been attorneys, although the Constitution doesn't require them to be. Political scientists or philosophers may be just as effective as persons from the legal profession because the court is more a philosophical entity than a legal body. The selection process tends to weed out court nominees who are out of line with constitutional principles and allows through those of competence. Such competence isn't required of elected officials and usually isn't found there because they were elected by voters who haven't been taught those constitutional principles – a major flaw in the educational process of the United States. Unfortunately, the election process sometimes eliminates a true patriot in favor of someone whose political beliefs are more threatening to the Constitution than all the nation's foreign "enemies," and who was elected by appealing to the emotions of voters who know little about the Constitution. America's ideals get trampled in the process, as shall be seen throughout this book.

Sadly, Americans find more pleasure in bashing the Supreme Court for its decisions than in trying to learn from it or learning what those decisions actually said.

The United States has historically spent heavily and devoted considerable effort to protect the nation from being subverted by foreign powers thought to be out to destroy the nation. That assumption has been unquestioned by millions of Americans in government, the military and by ordinary citizens.

But there's one unescapable fact: no foreign individual or national power has ever subverted one single aspect of American social or governmental existence. All subversion that has taken place has come from within the country, and it has come from respectable members of society – no bearded left-wing radical hippies, no card-carrying commies or fellow travelers, no sin-infested Satan worshipers, no "outside agitators" have succeeded in subverting anything.

Subversion has come from conservatives on the right, liberals on the left and moderates in the middle; it has come from card-carrying Republicans and Democrats; it has come from the pious and trusted religious leaders in the churches and synagogues in all parts of the nation, and it has come from the "insiders" in all aspects of American life. And it has come for one reason and one reason only: most Americans haven't the faintest idea about what "this country stands for."

Rather than study and form opinions themselves many people in this modern world have turned to "experts" to tell them what to think. It's manifest in the nation's press where editors, publishers, columnists and editorial writers, feeling they have accumulated all the knowledge anyone needs from unknown and mysterious sources, assume they are so well qualified that they can tell mayors how to run cities, governors how to run states and, presidents how to run the nation. Journalists who have "seen it all" feel they "know it all," and as self-proclaimed "experts" they editorialize vehemently whenever a court makes a decision they don't understand – which is often – and they try to tell the court what sort of decision should have been made.

They could use their editorializing to explain what an important Supreme Court decision means to Americans. They choose not to do so. They are content to misinform their readers.

A PROPHECY PROVEN

Ignorance of their Constitution by Americans isn't unexpected and may not be an abnormal condition; it was foretold in 1819 by United States

THE UN-AMERICANS

Chief Justice John Marshall, who wrote in a landmark court decision, "A constitution ... could scarcely be embraced by the human mind. It would probably never be understood by the public" if it were cumbersome. The United States Constitution isn't cumbersome, but still it isn't understood by the public, because those claiming to be knowledgeable know very little.

Lack of understanding has been common during the past 200 years, but has become more evident in recent years, particularly since World War I, when Americans found a much-despised enemy in the communist movement. But in opposing what they perceived to be an un-American doctrine, some Americans became un-American themselves, quite often confusing valid constitutional principle with Marxist doctrine. But the saddest thing of all is that Americans have refused to make the effort to learn about the United States Constitution. And that doesn't stop many from trying to impress others with their "love of America."

Evidence of this presumptuous attitude is found in excerpts from a Denver Post editorial written in the mid-1970s just prior to the nation beginning a series of celebrations commemorating the bicentennial of the Revolutionary War, creating the nation, writing and adopting the Constitution and the adopting of the Bill of Rights. The Post wrote:

"Ours, to be sure, is an imperfect world. Four-fifths of its population dwells perpetually in the shadow of want, of hunger and of pestilence. One fifth has it made ...

"Americans, by and large, are among the 'haves.' Blessed by almost every resource known to man, inhabited by an industrious population, and possessed of governmental institutions that have passed the test of time, the United States is truly fortunate.

"Our founding fathers, not immodestly, understood all of this. And so they wrote into our Constitution the 'inalienable right' of every American to the pursuit of happiness. This was not a callous rejection of peoples less favored by fortune; it was simple acceptance of bountiful life as given.

"Now as then, the United States is the only country on the globe to make such a guarantee to its citizens; the inalienable right to the pursuit of happiness. In many parts of the world such a constitutional stipulation would seem impertinent."

What the Founding Fathers wrote into the Constitution or what guarantees they made are important points of the criticism of this editorial. The Post, decrying the harsh existence in much of the world compared to the quest of Americans for physical happiness, went on to say:

"And yet the suspicion grows that this frenetic activity isn't really providing the fulfillment our Constitutional writers had in mind. Even as our material possessions swell in number, our spiritual possessions seem to decrease. Do we still hold the same moral and ethical values as our forebears?

"If we do, why is our crime rate soaring, why are old people mugged on streets and women raped in parks? Why are we surly to our neighbors, wary of our politicians, and unwilling to defend our nation's role in world affairs? Why are our young people alienated from their elders, our minorities mistrustful of the majority and the poor ever hostile to the rich? "

The editorial, entitled *"The Pursuit of Pleasure,"* sounds good but isn't what it seems to be or purports to be. It was obviously written by an editorial writer and approved by newspaper executives who did not have the faintest idea what they were printing. It's a problem in American journalism that many people think their opinions are all that's needed to qualify them as "experts" on the United States Constitution or American ideals. That precisely is what is wrong with this editorial and with thousands of other editorials by hundreds of other newspapers.

The Post wrote, "And so they wrote into our Constitution the 'inalienable right' of every American to the pursuit of happiness." That statement is pure nonsense and totally inaccurate. It's obvious the quotation marks were used fraudulently for the Constitution doesn't include the quoted material or anything remotely resembling the statement. The writer and editors apparently assumed the phrase is in the Constitution, may have never read the document and don't understand it, just as Chief Justice Marshall feared more than 150 years earlier. The Post went on to say "... the United States is the only country on the globe to make such a guarantee to its citizens; the inalienable right to the pursuit of happiness." It's also obvious that since the Constitution doesn't mention "inalienable right," it cannot, and it did not, guarantee any such thing.

The newspaper's confusion over the Constitution may stem from the fact that the Declaration of Independence mentioned "certain unalienable Rights, that among these are Life, Liberty and the pursuit of Happiness." Because the Declaration of Independence says "unalienable Rights" and the Post said "inalienable right," that's evidence the writer and the editors didn't accurately quote that document either.

The Declaration of Independence and the Constitution have little to do with each other. The Declaration was written in 1776 to justify the American colonies' rebellion against the superior and, at that time, legal government in England. It's not a legal document and contains nothing that establishes a legal governmental body or entity. No person or organization is entitled to take any action, or prohibited from taking any action, because of the Declaration of Independence. It serves more as a motto or an idea for the United States, but has no legal authority. The Constitution, written in 1787, is a legal document and establishes all institutions of the United States government, either directly or indirectly. But it didn't become a legal document until it was ratified by nine states in 1788, 12 years after the Declaration of Independence. The Constitution establishes each branch of government, every power the government may use and empowers certain government officers with the authority to do certain things. It also places limitations on what government agents or institutions may do.

When the Post wrote, "And so they (our Founding Fathers) wrote into our Constitution the inalienable right ..." the newspaper was demonstrating further its ignorance about America.

The Declaration of Independence was written by Thomas Jefferson and ratified by the Continental Congress. When the Constitution was written 11 years later, Jefferson was the United States minister to France and had nothing to do with its creation, so he could not have written "into our Constitution the inalienable right ..." And of the 57 members of the Continental Congress who signed the Declaration of Independence, only six of them signed the newly created Constitution. So it's clear there were basically two different groups involved, and what one group thought or intended didn't necessarily determine what the other group thought or intended.

And when the Post wrote, "... this frenetic activity isn't really providing the fulfillment our Constitutional writers had in mind," it again indicates a lack of knowledge about the Constitution and its creation. Because the document's writers had to accept slavery in the South in order to get national acceptance of the Constitution, it is clear they didn't have in mind a utopian social order; they were trying to create a utile order. And that utile social order was intended to accomplish one thing and one thing only – survival of the nation brought into existence on March 1, 1781, by the Articles of Confederation.

Not knowing what the Constitution says or means is one form of journalistic sin when trying to influence or lead others. Another is almost knowing, but getting the words just wrong enough to make them misleading or inaccurate.

The Los Angeles Times did that with the following editorial comments reprinted in the Tacoma (Wash.) News Tribune in June of 1989:

"With its decision that the Constitution does not forbid execution of teen-agers and the mentally retarded, the Supreme Court has done violence not only to the Eighth Amendment, but also to the ability of Americans to stand unblushing among the civilized nations of the world.

Americanizing a World

"If the constitutional prohibition of 'cruel and unusual punishment' does not preclude (execution) of those who have attained a child's years or who never will attain more than a child's mind, it is difficult to determine what – short of drawing and quartering – it does forbid.

"Among the 159 members of the United Nations, only five others – Iran, Iraq, Pakistan, Bangladesh and Barbados – permit the execution of those whose crimes were committed before the age of 18."

While the writers and editors stood for an advanced moral position and a high degree of civilized behavior and thought, that fine attitude isn't the point. The only point with any validity is what the Constitution specifically says – and it doesn't say that "cruel and unusual punishment" is forbidden. It forbids "cruel and unusual punishments." This phrase from the Eighth Amendment may be the single most-misquoted clause of the Constitution. The lack of the "s" on "punishment" shows that the editorializers didn't read the Constitution before pretending to quote it. Journalists, of all people, should understand the difference in meaning that words, phrases and sentences have if but one letter is changed or if a hyphen is or is not used in compound adjectives. It's vitally important to know how to use the language to know what the Constitution says.

The manner in which the Constitution is supposedly quoted creates exactly what the editorial was railing about – difficulty, if not impossibility, in determining what the Constitution does forbid. It's not possible to determine what's forbidden unless the clause is accurately read, down to and including the "s" on "punishments."

This constitutional error is all too common; it's rare to see the proper phrasing from any source, including the legal profession up to and including the United States Supreme Court. What the "cruel and unusual punishments" clause really means is explored in Chapter 8.

It seems to be such a minor point that most people would think it not worth mentioning, but when it comes to determining or understanding a specific governmental power and the governing of more than 250 million people, precise meaning is required. No one can pretend, more than 200 years after the Constitution was written, that it's possible to read the minds of the men who created it to determine what they intended; we must take it for what it says, word by word, comma by comma and hyphen by hyphen.

At the beginning of the Iran-contra trial of former Marine Lt. Col. Oliver North in January of 1989, USA TODAY, the national newspaper of the Gannett Corp., presented its say on constitutional phraseology by declaring in an editorial, "The Constitution says North should be presumed innocent until proven guilty." Unfortunately, USA TODAY was only guessing about what the Constitution says, for it doesn't contain anything saying a person "should be presumed innocent until proven guilty."

The concept of presumed innocence is just that – a concept that predated the Constitution and had become a tradition and motto in most of America. Whether it was to be the American style of justice was to be determined by Congress, which was given power to legislate for the national government.

If USA TODAY were correct in its statement about what the Constitution means concerning presumption of innocence, the judicial code of Louisiana would have been declared unconstitutional long ago because that state uses the Code of Napoleon, which seeks to prove innocence. Louisiana's judicial code is just as constitutional as the judicial methods in the other 49 states, and USA TODAY editors simply didn't know what they were writing about.

Los Angeles Times Editor Shelby Coffey III was quoted by a USA TODAY reporter in 1990 as saying newspapers must not abandon their classic role of trying to appeal to mass readership. "Newspapers should be inclusive. We are an engine of democracy," Coffey said. Such positions are common in the journalism community. Many publishers, editors and reporters argue that they are the fourth branch of government, equal in importance with Congress, the presidency and the Supreme Court. A logical person needs to take such positions very skeptically. We have seen that journalists are no more qualified to comment on the Constitution than are any other persons. Some journalists seem to have the opinion that they needn't learn anything about the Constitution or even spend half an hour reading the document before "quoting" from it. Journalists are often unwilling to admit nonexpertise, and that indicates Coffey's metaphorical "engine" needs a major overhaul.

EDUCATORS ALSO FAIL CONSTITUTIONAL TEST

There are numerous people who seem to think they have some form of mystical ability to determine what "the founding fathers intended." But all too often they're like the journalists at The Denver Post, Los Angeles Times and USA TODAY who merely guess at what the Constitution says and means.

Such guessing isn't restricted to journalists. Educators also fall short of constitutional knowledge, as shall be demonstrated.

In 1989, USA TODAY published a series of tests to demonstrate the problems of education in the United States. The newspaper had the tests designed by specialists who held advanced degrees and high positions in gov-

ernmental education agencies. In tests dealing with U.S. government, the following questions were presented:
According to the Bill of Rights, which of the following is not allowed?
a) A trial by jury in criminal cases.
b) Testimony of witnesses who are related to the accused.
c) A trial held too soon after the defendant has been accused.
d) Cruel and unusual punishment.
The chief justice of the U.S. Supreme Court is selected by:
a) a national election with approval by a majority of state governors
b) a vote of existing Supreme Court justices
c) a constitutional amendment and presidential signature
d) appointment by the president with consent of the Senate

While the test designers were right in citing *d* as the correct answer to both questions, they were as guilty as the newspaper editorialists in failing to represent the Constitution faithfully, for as we have seen, the Eighth Amendment says "cruel and unusual punishments," and Article II, Section 2, and Article III, Section 1, specify "Judges" for the Supreme Court.

As for "The chief justice of the U.S. Supreme Court;" no such position is created by the Constitution. In Article I, Section 3, the office of Chief Justice is mentioned, but that in no way restricts the powers of that office to the Supreme Court. Educators should know that. When courts lower than the Supreme Court were created, the Chief Justice became the superior position by virtue of the Supreme Court having appellate, or superior, jurisdiction, as established by Article III, Section 2. Article VI says "the Judges in every state shall be bound" to the national law, and that little clause makes the chief justice the "chief justice of the United States," a far more significant position than "chief justice of the Supreme Court." That office has authority over every judicial action in the United States, whether in a federal court, state court, city or village court, because Article VI adds, "This Constitution, and the Laws of the United States . . and all Treaties made ... shall be the supreme Law of the Land; and the Judges in every State shall be bound thereby ..." No other judicial office can overrule, or in any way alter, a Supreme Court action. All other governmental bodies are likewise powerless in overruling judicial decisions, for the Constitution doesn't give judicial power to any other body. That makes the chief justice superior over all judicial matters. There was a time when "chief justice of the Supreme Court" was used, but "chief justice of the United States" has been used exclusively in judicial legislation since 1866.

Not knowing the difference between chief justice of the Supreme Court and chief justice of the United States seems to be a minor issue, but it does point out a serious problem – that is, many who profess expertise of the Constitution don't really know the document. What passes as knowledge is too often misconception and opinion. USA TODAY in January of 1984 made the statement that, "Ninety-nine chief justices have presided over the U. S. Supreme Court since its creation in 1789." That's wrong for the following reasons:

– The court was legally created June 21, 1788, when New Hampshire became the ninth state to ratify the Constitution. The court met for the first time Feb. 1, 1790.

– There were 15 chief justices by 1984, all others were associate judges.

– By 1984, more than 100 men and one woman had served on the Supreme Court.

Perhaps H. L. Mencken, the famed journalist of earlier in the 20th century, could understand better than others the condition of some important institutions in the United States. He described the press and academia thusly:

"Why presume so glibly that God who created the universe is still running it? It is certainly perfectly conceivable that He may have finished it and then turned it over to lesser gods to operate. In the same way many human institutions are turned over to grossly inferior men. This is true, for example, of most universities, and of all great newspapers."

MYTHS AND METAPHORS

Most Americans have the same problem with the Constitution as the journalists and educators just cited. Despite political harangues over court decisions and attempts to curb the court through unconstitutional means, the system seems to work quite well, as this book shall demonstrate.

Americans' concepts of the Constitution are usually based on myths and metaphors taken out of context to be used incorrectly and which have nothing to do with reality. These myths and misused metaphors are detrimental to the functioning of a responsible government and a just society.

Probably the most-widespread myth of the Constitution is the belief "the Constitution gives me the right ..." a familiar statement probably everyone has heard and uttered. As long as this myth is unchallenged, Americans' understanding of the Constitution will be incorrect.

It is commonly believed there is a "wall between church and state," the United States was begun as a "grand experiment" or it's based on some unnamed "Judeo-Christian principles."

It's thought and preached a person can't shout "fire" in a theater. In 1990, two writers of opposite political views cited that common myth in

Americanizing a World

"opposing view" columns in USA TODAY. A conservative, who formerly served in national office, wrote: "The right to intimidate, harass and extort money from your fellow citizens is no more the kind of speech protected by the First Amendment than crying 'Fire!' in a crowded theater is."

A week later, a writer of liberal persuasion wrote: "But just as free speech rights don't protect you when you holler 'fire!' in a crowded theater, they shouldn't protect those who use 'fighting words' or hurl inflammatory comments in a society already racially tense."

It's also falsely thought that "a clear-and-present danger" is all that's needed to invoke governmental action. Add to that the perceived prohibition of "taxation without representation," and the right of a trial by a "jury of one's peers," as USA TODAY claimed in a 1993 editorial. Equally false is the concept that the Constitution "guarantees" certain individual rights. Or that a wife can't testify against her husband in a criminal matter.

There's no requirement in the Constitution that the government "do the right thing," or enabling it to act when it perceives a "moral" need to do so. To "do the right thing" is a fine slogan; it's not a constitutional principle and there are no moral clauses in the Constitution. America as "the land of the free and the home of the brave" sounds fine in the national anthem and as a self-serving motto, but Americans aren't as free as they believe, nor as fearless, because when government power is in operation there's no freedom, and a fine Missouri maiden could scare the courage out of any brave American macho man.

What is true and will be shown throughout this book is:

– The Constitution gives to the government, not to the citizens.

– The "wall between church and state" is only a metaphor supposedly created by Jefferson in a letter that defined his understanding of the Constitution. No one knows if he originated the expression or heard it from one of his contemporaries.

– The Founding Fathers drew knowledge of constitutions from the states then practicing representational government with legislative, executive and judicial branches.

– The United States is based on the political theories of John Locke, a 17th-century English philosopher, who advanced ideas of government with three branches, a system of checks and balances and who refuted rule by divine right.

– Of course a person may shout "fire" in a crowded theater. What Supreme Court Judge Oliver Wendell Holmes really said was "free speech would not protect a man in falsely shouting fire in a theatre and causing a panic." That expression demonstrated his belief that there is no absolute to freedom of speech, because there were conditions presented by Holmes: the shout of fire must be false and a panic must ensue. No panic, no prohibition or punishment. Truth of the shouted statement is a valid defense even if a panic occurred. And, the case involved powers of government during war.

– Holmes also was responsible for the "clear-and-present danger" statement, but he didn't intend it to justify any or all government action. It was his way of determining if a legitimate government power took precedence over an individual's rights when the two appeared to clash.

– "Taxation without representation" was a rallying cry for a bunch of New Englanders who sought a reason to rebel against the rulership of England in the 18th century. It is nowhere to be found in the Constitution, even though many people try to invoke it to oppose legal governmental action.

– A trial by a "jury of peers" is likewise not in the Constitution. What is found is, "Trial ... shall be by Jury ..." (Article III, Section 2), "a speedy and public trial by an impartial jury ..." (Sixth Amendment) and "trial by jury" (Seventh Amendment).

– The only guarantee mentioned in the Constitution is "The United States shall guarantee to every state in this Union a Republican form of government ..." (Article IV, Section 4).

– Nothing is said about who can't testify in trials. Wives (or husbands) can be protected by law from being forced to testify against the other.

Almost everyone has opinions as to why communism that controlled much of the world for three-fourths of a century was a dismal failure while democracy, American-style, stays strong despite many problems. Communism, after all, promoted itself as the only hope for equality and justice, while American-style democracy can't control its citizens. Everyone seems to be going off in different directions, doing what he or she wishes for selfish reasons and determining individual values and morals, a pattern that should be more divisive than cohesive. Perhaps it's that communism could never decide how much freedom to allow its citizens – so it allowed very little – while American democracy lasts because people correctly decided in the 18th century how much freedom to surrender to the government by way of the Constitution. It's the freedoms Americans didn't surrender that seem appealing to the many nations of the world trying to Americanize themselves. Understanding how that freedom is preserved under a constitutional system is the one export the United States should be willing to give freely and without conditions.

Chapter 2

GOVERNMENT TO HAVE AND TO MOLD

OUT WITH THE OLD, IN WITH THE ???

With much of the world trying to dress in a wardrobe of Americanization, it's important to remember what's being sought is of utmost importance. All governments exist for much the same reasons – protection, civilization, prosperity, control – and governments must exist regardless of how people feel about them. It doesn't matter if one believes mankind was evicted from the Garden of Eden and left on its own to search for a way back to paradise or hit the ground with a civilizing thump after falling from the metaphorical tree of prehistoric animalism to evolve into its modern form. Modern mankind is here and needs governments, if only to prevent self-extinction. Governments of all forms exist to some degree to battle against that threat of extinction, even though not as wisely as most would hope.

Though some nations seeking Americanization may be more advanced now than they were when their recently rejected governments took power, that slight improvement has been inadequate – Marxism did eliminate the unacceptable tsarist system of terror in Russia but communism's terror made it equally unacceptable. Communism's only redeeming value may be that it broke the grip of tsarism and occupied the years required to give thoughts of democracy a chance to take root. Military juntas have been equally as unacceptable to modern men and women who think for themselves, as were theocratic dictators in the self-proclaimed Christian nations of medieval Europe. Governments of all kinds had been tried until England and the United States evolved into the present form of democracy, and that "accident" seems to be what much of the world wants.

It would be nice to think humans began working toward modern civilized governments because of well-thought-out principles, but such thinking would be unrealistic. Governments that have been created, used and rejected weren't philosophical creations. Many came into being because there were bullies who felt they had to be in control and were better suited than everyone else to exercise authority. They would seize power by sword, separating head from body of persons who wouldn't submit. The winners in such struggles would set themselves up as kings, princes, dukes, earls and

THE UN-AMERICANS

other titles and force others to view them as "royalty," or something superior to all other humans. Their concept of royalty is, of course, ridiculous, but the world accepted it for centuries.

The idea there are superior beings is the basis of most governments. Military men seize power while claiming only they can rule and maintain order, and people who disagree with that assumption are quickly dispatched with the modern "swords" of the state. Theologians, who claim to possess a direct communication with the "God of the universe," throughout history have used similar arguments to grab power and control society. The despotic theological state has been displaced in modern Western societies, so now theologians try to control governments with influence rather than the direct power of a few centuries ago.

Modern movements have also borrowed from the royal concept of power and control. When corrupt or unpopular governments are overthrown, little really is changed or improved. Most revolutionaries are not philosophers or deep thinkers so they base their revolutionary governments on the only governmental form they understand: the deposed power under which they developed their governmental concept. That was evident after the Russian Revolution of 1917. When revolutionaries finished disposing the tsarist regime, they had little concept of how to install their "workers' paradise," so they merely became a new royalty. It wasn't long before Communist Party leaders began enjoying exalted positions and special privileges as did the royalty they executed a few years earlier. Being a Bolshevik was similar to being a noble in the tsarist regime, and party membership was considered to provide a special ability to rule; a competence lacked by those not in the party. Likewise, when third-world colonies gained independence from European powers in the 20th century, they often took on the autocratic form of the departed economic government, rather than the representative forms of governments the colonialists, such as Great Britain, had at home. Some people were thus "owned" by their fellow countrymen, as they had been by the European masters. Military juntas of the Western Hemisphere, likewise, could not move away from the concept that military men were the only ones in society with the patriotism, sophistication, mentality and ability to govern. And, whenever an attempt was made to institute a representative form of government, the military would soon overthrow the new government and return to a dictatorship.

These governments have all taken individual power from the citizens in order to maintain superordinary positions of the so-called elite. It doesn't matter if this occurred on the basis of royalty, theology, the military or socioeconomic theories such as Marxism or fascism. The governments were

Government to Have and to Mold

basically the same, having only a "difference of degree, not of kind," a phrase often used by Supreme Court Judge Oliver Wendell Holmes to avoid unnecessary arguments on obvious differences or similarities, whether they be minor or major.

Such governments appear to be what those people seeking Americanization are rejecting in numbers unparalleled in human history. They probably will be somewhat successful in getting rid of the old order, but what will they be putting in its place? What may be a more-important question is, "Will Americans be of any help, or will they hurt, in assisting this transformation considering their confusion about the United States Constitution?"

THE AGREEMENT ON GOVERNMENT

At most schools of government, it's taught that the Constitution of the United States is a contract between Americans and their government. The concept of a constitution as a contract seems to be supported by history, taking form in early England with the practice of writing down important deals or transactions. Scholars have traced this practice back to the years prior to the Norman Conquest of England in 1066. A constitution as a contract evolved over time through several documents and practices, including the coronation oath, Charter of Liberties (1100), Magna Charta (1215), the Provisions of Oxford (1258) and the Confirmatio Cartarum (1297).

These documents contained characteristics of constitutionalism in that they attempted to bind ruler and the ruled with certain obligations to each other. Going into specific detail about these historical documents is something that should be left to the scholarly works of academia, this book is concerned with an easy-to-understand examination of the United States Constitution. A small amount of historical knowledge of England's development of constitutional thought helps demonstrate that the founders of the United States weren't embarking on some grand experiment of government about which there was no knowledge or expectations; they knew fairly well what they were doing and where they were going. Those who appreciate their creation believe what they had in mind is what we have today.

"Covenant" may be a better word than "contract" even though they are very close in meaning. A contract would require one party make an offer and a second party accept it. The government cannot be a party to such a contract because it didn't exist at the time the contract was created; it came into existence by means of that creation. A contract can be made only by "competent parties." A covenant, as used in the Bible, is applicable to all. So, the concept professors at the finest universities teach isn't exactly as it

THE UN-AMERICANS

should be – it should be taught the Constitution of the United States is a covenant among all Americans, not a contract between the citizens and government. It's important to view the Constitution as an agreement Americans made among themselves to better comprehend the arguments being made throughout this book.

The human race existed long before the invention of government, or the need for government. In a time without government, each person was forced to act as a government in his or her territory. Being an individual government carried with it the duty of making law, enforcing law and carrying out judgment. While these actions would occur at the moment needed, they were in fact, governmental functions and each person was a sovereign authority over a claimed territory. A family or clan would resemble a federated nation in which several governments existed together, each with authorities and functions. The territory changed from time to time as individuals or groups moved about, but the rule of the individual reigned. An individual decided what actions were not permissible (legislative power), who enforced the rules (executive power), and how violators were dealt with, including punishment (judicial power). And they protected their territory from others (war power). That's basically all there is to government.

But there came a time when human relationships were much more complicated – mostly because of population increases – and the sovereignty of the individual had to give way to the sovereignty of a group. While the concept of the contract or covenant probably didn't exist among primitive tribes, a covenant is precisely what they created. Each person surrendered the four powers to the group to be exercised by a select few for the benefit of the many. One set of laws would bind the many into a communal tribe whereas a system in which each person had a personal set of laws would destroy the community.

That's obvious; what isn't so apparent is that each person, by continuing to live in the community and to abide by the rules of that community, was agreeing with the terms of the governmental covenant. There need not be an awareness of that agreement; it had to exist in order to keep the tribe intact.

If an individual refused to give up any or all four of these governmental powers, he or she would be a violator of that covenant. A family could continue to exist as a lesser government, exercising powers in areas not given up to the tribe. A person could, of course, regain all four powers and use them as wished by simply leaving the jurisdiction of the tribe, becoming an individual nation on his own. These conditions still exist today – showing just how little mankind has advanced throughout the history of making gov-

Government to Have and to Mold

ernment – but with virtually no area of earth free of governmental authority, powers reclaimed by leaving one group would have to be surrendered to the sovereign group in a new area.

After the individual surrenders these personal powers to the government, the powers are to be used for the benefit of the individual and for the benefit of the community. No one should be expected to give up these natural powers only to be enslaved by those who are entrusted to exercise authority. Because the powers of each individual are equal to powers of everyone else, government must view each person under authority of those powers as being equal to all other persons. One type of person doesn't surrender a superior form or amount of power and shouldn't expect a superior form or amount of privileges or protection from the government. Some ancient people seemed to understand that concept much better than many modern people.

Modern man's misuse of what should be evenly administered power can be seen in virtually every area of the world. It should be obvious to all that the United States, which likes to exalt itself as champion of liberty and justice, has a history just as sordid as other nations, the main difference being that the United States has made attempts to correct its misuse of powers. When abducted Africans were brought to the colonies as slaves, beginning in 1619, they were stripped of their powers by their captors and received nothing from society in return. They were expected to obey the laws of society, but weren't benefited or protected by any law. The same has been true over the years for other groups because of their nationality, race, religion, or social status.

Those persons who are authorized to use the group's powers are to use only those powers given to the group. They should not go beyond those powers in order to control society or members of society who are unpopular or despised; the unpopular and hated surrendered the same powers as the popular and the admired. Under dictatorial regimes based on royalty, religion, race, military might or communist or fascist doctrine, those in control strip all power from the people – just as the slave dealers did – and return to the population only what they wish, not motivated by any concept other than their biases or opinions.

When the group's legitimate authority exercises the collective powers justly, the individual is expected to acknowledge that authority and refrain from acting counter to the just powers. That's the basis of civilized society. Of course, there will be some who won't recognize the surrender of their power and will continue to act as if they were independent of the governmental covenant. Some are branded "criminal," others "subversive." They become targets of government, and criminal law comes into being to challenge them. This law isn't intended to change the behavior of these people, but to give government authority to act against them.

The individual exercises civil or human rights in those areas where there's no law. Liberty is having those rights. Civilized society is always struggling to balance governmental power with individual freedom, and for this reason it was illogical in the past to label the West "The Free World," while maintaining the Eastern Bloc nations of European and Asian countries to be enslaved. Liberty involves much more than having a government acceptable to the American mind. There was only a difference in degrees of freedom and governmental power; those who obeyed all the rules and supported the rulers in the Eastern Bloc were "free," those who wouldn't go along with the rulers weren't free. But that also applies to the Western World; and, throughout history there have always been mavericks who don't go along with the rulers' leadership. The Soviet Union, until its demise, had ordinary people who longed for the return of a Stalinist-type regime, which they wouldn't have wanted had they felt enslaved during Stalin's dictatorship. Many Russians still want Stalinists to regain power in the struggling Russian democracy.

The rights of freedom needn't be named, listed or otherwise enumerated for government authorities to recognize them. The entirety of human existence can be called a right – the right to exist – and all behavior or other modes of being are rights. The right to think, the right to know, the right to learn and the right to be who we wish to be or to love whom and what we wish are rights; and they needn't be written down. If those people who work in government – they aren't the same as the government – wish to exercise power, they need to have permission to do so. Not authorization from other members of the governmental apparatus, authorization from those who empowered the government to act: the citizens. This concept isn't of modern origin, it came from the ancient Romans' idea the state was "ras publica," a public thing, and the people were the source of law and authority.

That concept does pose a bit of a dilemma for some religious folks who say they don't have the authority to give power to the state for it isn't their power to give; only God has the authority to rule. But by living in the society in which they do live, and by refraining from making and executing laws, they are tacitly accepting the conditions of the social covenant. If they accept the covenant by not leaving, they are part of the government, whether they admit it or not. In societies in which the individual has no say about the taking of power and in which the individual is prevented from reclaiming power by leaving, the argument might be valid, but has no validity in the self-governing representative democracies of the modern Western world.

FOUR CITIZENS OF CREATION

To illustrate the concept of government as an agreement among citizens rather than a contract between governors and governed, we look to a mythical group consisting of a man living north of the river, a man living south of the river, a fool on the hill and the farmer in the dell. These four, in theory, can exist peacefully in the same area without need of government. They would exercise authority over the territory in which they live, being in effect, sovereigns of their territory – such sovereignty is government. Each person would decide what conduct was permissible and what conduct wasn't permissible in his territory. Each would reserve to himself the authority to enforce those rules and to take action against any violation of those rules by any of the other three. He would also decide upon guilt or innocence and the punishment the violators deserved. That would be exercising the three branches of democratically based governments: the legislature, the executive and the judicial.

Each person also would make all decisions about what action was best for his territory in regulating for improvements or preservation. Each would determine what action was necessary in dealing with his neighbors, whether to wage war or to have friendly "foreign relations." And each would have the power to decide who could enter the territory in peace and who wasn't permitted in. In short, each of these persons acts as a bona fide government.When relationships became more complicated through such things as population increase, a need to roam farther in search of necessities or the need to co-operate for advancement of civilization or to protect a common territory, the people had to bind together under some form of an agreement.

This is the social covenant that's common in all modern self-governing societies. It's the first principle of the United States Constitution, and it got its start in primitive societies. It has never been recognized by dictatorial governments. It was recognized early in American history but seems to have become an alien concept in modern America as reaction to "collectivism" undermines the unity of society and nation.

When the man north of the river, the man south of the river, the fool on the hill and the farmer in the dell unite, they each surrender some of the powers they had used to rule their own territories. Their powers are put into a metaphorical "pot" to be used when and as forcefully as needed to benefit the four. They may select one or more of the quartet to exercise that collective power, but those selected are required to recognize from where the power came, and it came equally from each of the four. When one of the four tries to claim a superiority of some kind, he's subverting the principle of equality. And when government allows a special form of administration for some privileged people, it's subverting itself. Such concepts aren't in the United States Constitution and are therefore what Supreme Court Judge Antonin Scalia referred to as "un-American."

Any differences between our four citizens aren't recognized by the social contract. If they were all of the same race, religion, origin or social status, there would be no differences and no need to mention it. In primitive societies there were no differences, and all could exist within the social covenant. Those who couldn't recognize the authority of the covenant over their behavior only had to leave and live alone, join other groups or form new groups.

That's an option no longer. Therefore it is important to recognize that if the man south of the river were of a different race, he was still an equal in the formation of the covenant. He would have to receive the same benefits and protections the covenant offered, he couldn't be judged less worthy that the other three. The same principle would hold true if the visionary "fool on the hill" were female, gender or sexual orientation having absolutely no bearing on the agreement. She was also an equal partner to the covenant and therefore must be an equal recipient of its benefits. Should the farmer in the dell be of a minority religion or no religion at all, he also was an equal creator and was likewise entitled to equality under the covenant's laws. Belief isn't germane to surrendering of personal sovereignty.

The dictatorships of royalty, theology, politics or the military have all failed to acknowledge the existence of the equality covenant. And when some claimed a "divine right to rule," their actions were thought to be taken under the guidance of God and therefore to be judged only by God. If God didn't prevent any action, it was argued those actions were permitted by Him and therefore couldn't be made illegal by mankind. That explains why priests and ministers and kings and queens under a "divine right to rule" were much more blood thirsty than nontheological despots. Adolf Hitler, who came to power with approval of European religious leaders, based the Holocaust on racial and religious, not political, grounds. Since the days of Mohammed, Islam has accepted to a "divine right to rule" which precludes any deviation from Allah's "commands," and Allah's commands are what ever the "prophets" say they are.

Democratic-type societies have a difficult time developing in the Mideast because there's no room for the covenant between men; that would require usurping Allah's authority. For some Israelis, Jehovah's covenant for a "promised land" makes them unwilling to try to live peacefully with Arabs. It has been thought since the advent of religion that people choosing their rulers was as absurd as people choosing their prophets. By that reasoning, religion created the autocracy which led to all types of dictatorships.

The development-of-government story couldn't be told without the story of religion. Both Biblical and secular history relate the tale of Babylon developing as a city containing a partnership of government and religion, a situation that existed throughout history and was instituted in the Western world by the Roman Empire. Such partnerships have kept mankind subordinated to the elite and the powerful. But religion also has been responsible for the long process that led to the separation of church and state in some lands, even though that separation hasn't been easy to maintain and may not be completed. Religion also helped lead mankind to the United States Constitution.

Dictatorships reject the covenant just by the manner in which they come into existence: with the sword and gun and dead opponents. Those who would stand up in opposition to the seizing of authority are dispatched with no concern for the morality of the act. Under the covenant, authority isn't seized by the powerful; it's surrendered by tacit agreement. For that reason, there's no danger in some people opposing or resisting government. The main danger to the covenant arrangement is the misuse and usurpation of government authority.

A DIFFERENT SOURCE OF CREATION

The "freedom" westerners think they enjoy today is a contrived concept. It exists in bits and pieces. Total freedom has given way to civilization and government in differing degrees, in different areas and in different times and has become a relative concept; there's more freedom in some areas than others. There was a time when man was truly free, but that ended thousands of years ago with the development of powerful kings and kingdoms or powerful priesthoods. Often the two were combined with a king being deified, something that exists today in slightly different form. A nation that claims to represent God on earth is practicing this modern theocratic kingdom, much to the dismay of its neighbors and the world, and making the innocence of Eden an impossibility.

The United States' version of constitutional "freedom" wasn't secured by the Revolution of 1776, as Americans like to deceive themselves into believing. It actually took root during the "English Revolution" from 1628 to 1689 in England. The was quietly begun in 1628 after the House of Commons drew up the Petition of Rights that said royal prerogative couldn't touch the property of Englishmen. But King Charles ignored it and tried to rule on his own. He dismissed judges who didn't interpret law to please him and imprisoned some leaders of Commons. He ruled without Parliament for 11 years but had to reconvene that body in 1640 to raise money for his war with the Scotch. Reconvening Parliament was the beginning of Parliament's rise to power, for it voted for a redress of grievances, not money to fight the war.

Parliament was again disbanded by the king but had to be recalled months later because of Scotch successes in the war, and money was desperately needed. But Parliament, rather than give what the king wanted, virtually took over control of the government and refused to go home. It arrested and executed the king's chief councilor, enacted laws providing regular meetings of Parliament and prohibiting its dissolution. It abolished the Star Chamber and other seats of royal power, and demanded control of the militia.

When Charles attempted to arrest Parliament leaders, war broke out. Oliver Cromwell, who was first elected to Parliament in 1628, led his New Model Army in Parliament's cause. Following victory by Cromwell, what was left of Parliament (after many members were expelled and sent home) convicted Charles of treason and beheaded him in 1649. Parliament then established the Commonwealth with three resolutions: 1) the people were the source of all power, 2) as representatives of the people, Commons held supreme power, and 3) laws enacted by Commons didn't need consent of either king or House of Lords. There were movements among middle-class Puritans for freedom of religion for themselves. Others wanted that freedom extended to more than just the Puritans and even went so far as to propose separation of the church and the state.

Cromwell expelled Parliament in 1653 because of the members' failure to give way to the more-representative Parliament the army demanded. Cromwell then controlled Parliament through his council of the army. Officers of the army then wrote a constitution called the Instrument of Government, under which Cromwell took the title of Lord Protector.

Other attempts to work through parliamentary governments failed. Parliament did draw up a new constitution called the Humble Petition and Advice, but Cromwell continued to rule as a military dictator. After Cromwell's death in 1658 his son, Richard, took over as ruler but couldn't cope with the struggle for power between Parliament and the army. He resigned in 1659, which paved the way for King Charles II to be restored to the throne in 1660. He was succeeded by James II in 1685, but by 1688 James had displeased the English nobility who invited William of Orange to come rescue England. William came and James fled to France without a fight.

Government to Have and to Mold

Parliament in 1689 drew up the Revolution Settlement with the terms:
– The throne was offered to William and his wife, Mary.
– No taxes could be levied by the throne.
– No standing army could be maintained.
– No laws passed or suspended without consent of Parliament.
– Parliament should be held frequently, election to it and debate in it should be free of any interference.

For the first time, principles of constitutional government were spelled out. Freedom of religion followed that same year and freedom of the press came a few years later.

This wasn't a truly democratic revolution because there were no efforts to extend political rights to, or improve social conditions of, the common people; liberty and equality weren't advanced; only the triumph of Parliament was assured and only a small number (wealthy) were represented in Parliament. But it was a beginning, and it was the system under which the citizens of the 13 American colonies were governed until they rebelled nearly a century later, at which time it was these principles they used to set up a sovereign national government. They didn't have a grand scheme or a god-inspired experiment in mind – they did what they knew – and it took them two attempts to come up with the United States Constitution. And the two tries indicates the willingness to admit that there was no American "genius" involved; it was trial and error, then another try.

As for the claim that the United States was a creation of the 13 colonies, the argument of Sen. Daniel Webster of Massachusetts in 1830 ought to settle the issue. In a reply to another senator, Webster said, "... I hold it to be a popular Government, erected by the people; those who administer it responsible to the people; and itself capable of being amended and modified, just as the people may choose it should be ... It is not the creature of the state governments.

"This government, sir, is the independent offspring of the popular will. It is not the creature of State Legislatures ... the people brought it into existence, established it, and have hither to supported it ..."

Webster wasn't expressing a lone opinion, he was in tune with reality. In 1795, Supreme Court Judge William Paterson wrote, "What is the Constitution? It is the form of government delineated by the mighty hand of the people ..."

In a historic case in 1819 (*McCulloch v. Maryland*), Chief Justice John Marshall wrote, "The Convention which framed the constitution was, indeed, elected by the state legislatures. But the instrument, when it came from their hands, was a mere proposal, without obligation, or pretensions to it. It was reported to the then existing Congress of the United States, with a request that it might 'be submitted to a convention of delegates, chosen in each state by the people thereof, under the recommendation of its legislature, for their assent and ratification.' This mode of proceeding was adopted; and by the convention, by congress, and by the state legislatures, the document was submitted to the people. They acted upon it, in the only manner in which they could act safely, effectively, and wisely, on such a subject, by assembling in convention." Marshall went on to say it mattered not that they assembled separately in their respective states, there being no compelling reason for one huge assembly rather than several smaller ones. And an assembly in a state in no way created an action by state government, the action was by the people.

Marshall and Paterson, who were prominent citizens at the time the Constitution was created, knew what it was and how it was to affect the nation. They worked for adoption of the new Constitution. Marshall was a member of the Virginia ratifying convention. Webster was considered a leading constitutional authority of his time and the attorney who successfully argued the McCulloch case. So, when these three early experts on the Constitution say it was the creation of the American people, it was the creation of the American people.

Other early Americans recorded specifically from where government power came. The 1776 Virginia Constitution, which served as a model for the federal Constitution, said in section two of its Bill of Rights, "all power is vested in, and consequently derived from the people ..."

The final point in this argument concerns what the Constitution says and what it doesn't say. The first and last clauses of the Preamble state clearly, "We the people of the United States ... do ordain and establish this CONSTITUTION for the United States of America." It says, "We the people ..." It doesn't say, "We the states ..." or "We the nobility ..." or "We the elite ..." It says, "We the people ..." It doesn't say, "We the businesses ..." or "We the churches ..." or, "We the intelligentsia ..." It says the people establish the Constitution; it doesn't recognize any other source as the establishing authority.

These citations should settle the issue that the people of the United States have entered into a covenant among themselves to form the present national government, covenants for their state governments, and covenants for local governments. There's no elite governing class, no divine right to rule and no "higher law" taking precedence over the Constitution.

Chapter 3

KNOWING AMERICA

THE ROOTS OF THE NATION

Perhaps the greatest confusion Americans have about their Constitution concerns the idea that it and the government were founded on religious. When Sen. William Armstrong, R-Colo., introduced a resolution in Congress to proclaim 1983 "the year of the Bible" he was careful to accompany his resolution with the statement that the United States was created on Biblical principles, a belief shared by the majority of Americans. It's common to hear and read that the nation was founded on "Judeo-Christian principles." That's a favorite phrase of newspaper columnists, religious practitioners or politicians looking for votes. It has become so common that it isn't questioned; just taken for granted.

Somehow Americans have come to believe the United States is "under God," a motto so accepted it found its way into the Pledge of Allegiance, just as "In God We Trust" adorns the nation's currency. A Republican Party activist in the state of Washington, who said he was involved in the conservative Christian movement, told the Seattle Post-Intelligencer at a 1986 party convention, "We believe our country was founded as a Christian nation and we've drifted from what the Constitution intended. Separation of church and state is not mentioned in the Constitution."

That's a freely used concept often present at political events (especially elections); in the daily American press, in magazines, in pamphlets, on television shows of all kinds from news shows to documentaries to purely entertainment; in Congress, the statehouse or city hall; in casual conversation and in speeches. These statements are accepted by many without question and taken for granted that they have some factual basis, but are merely assumptions which would surely surprise the men who created the Constitution, those who ratified it and those men and women who interpreted it in court decisions. The founders apparently were unaware they were creating a "Christian" nation, government, Constitution or any other religiously based entity. The history of discrimination against Jews in the United States would indicate the "Judeo" portion of the "Judeo-Christian principles" assumption isn't practiced by many Americans.

In The Federalist Papers, a collection of newspaper articles written by three of the nation's founders – Alexander Hamilton, John Jay and James Madison – supporting ratification of the Constitution, the United States wasn't called a "Christian nation," nor was it proposed the Constitution would make it a "Christian nation." The Constitution was written to create a republican form of government with all its powers coming from the people. That means a republic based on democratic principles. Madison said in Federalist No. 39 that a republican form of government wasn't enough because several unsatisfactory nations had republican governments. Why it's important to view the United States as a republican form of government based on democratic principles can be seen by looking at other republics.

Nazi Germany was a republic based on fascist principles. The failed Soviet Union was a republic based on Lenin's interpretation of Marxist principles. China is a republic based on Mao's interpretation of Marxist principles. A republican form of government based on democratic principles is what the founders intended the United States to be and, that is precisely what the founders created. During the deliberations at the Constitutional Convention, the phrase "the state of nature" was often uttered. "The state of nature" is considered by some Christians to be anti-God.

When people refer to Biblical or Judeo-Christian principles being the foundation of the nation, they fail to specify the principles they are speaking of. If some of those mystery "principles" were enumerated, they might not be so exclusive to Christianity and Judaism. They may also be embraced by other religions and found in the holy writings of Islam, Buddhism, Hinduism, Shintoism, or any pagan theology. Some of those unspecified principles may also be discovered among agnostics and atheists. We cannot know how much overlapping of principles there may be, because those who claim such things never seem to list the principles of which they speak.

It's illogical for a person to dismiss the "separation of church and state" because it isn't written in those words in the Constitution, but to accept the idea that "… our country was founded as a Christian nation …" a phrase equally absent from the Constitution. The First Amendment does a good job of describing separation of church and state. It isn't necessary to qualify that amendment with words that might state, "This amendment separates church and state."

"What the Constitution intended" was that the United States be founded in such a way that Christianity and Judaism could be practiced without governmental interference or assistance, just as could Islam, Buddhism, atheism or any other religion, nonreligion or antireligion. Allowing the free exercise of the main religions doesn't create a nation based on those religions. If government were meant to have power to assist or interfere with the practice of religion, that power would have to be mentioned or implied somewhere in the Constitution, for the only powers the federal government may have must be given it through the Constitution.

Christianity did contribute to the creation of the United States Constitution, although unwillingly and unintentionally. To understand Christianity's contribution we need to go back to Western Europe around the 10th century when the Roman Catholic Church exercised nearly all authority over a loose-knit society. Catholicism, which had been made the recognized religion of the Roman Empire in the fourth century, held together civilization by being, by far, the most-advanced institution on the continent. The merchants and craftsmen of the time were interested in trade and did a great deal of traveling in pursuit of business. The peasants had land to cultivate. Church leaders were permanent residents of the land the governed. As the only group with education being important to their profession, the clergy was better equipped for rulership. But there was no democracy – that isn't a Christian principle just as authority elected by the people isn't a Christian principle.

In his book, *Freedom in the Western World,* Herbert J. Muller wrote, "Throughout Western history until this century, the major established churches did not lead the struggle for freedom, but on most fronts offered the most stubborn opposition to it. They authorized the persecution of Jews, infidels, heretics, dissenters, freethinkers. On principle, they denied freedom of conscience, freedom of speech and press, so long as they had the power to do so. They fought the unorthodox theories of science, the main agent of emancipation."

By denying what we today call "civil rights," the established churches unwittingly created freethinking and dissension, which ultimately led to freedom and the Constitution of the United States. Church leaders, possibly unable to distinguish between Biblical fact and Biblical metaphor and allegory, were teaching what appeared to be contradictions of faith. They would tell their followers:

– Man was created in God's image but man is an unworthy fallen creature;

– Man must love God, but man must fear God;

– God is good and merciful, but God is jealous and wrathful;

– Eternal bliss awaits mankind, but man must endure depravity;

– The world was created for man out of God's goodness, but the world was the devil's possession and was to be despised and fled.

– Man should respect himself, but man should loathe himself;

– Life is sacred, but life is wretched and vile and a testing ground;

– Man should love his neighbors, but hate infidels and heretics;

– Life on earth is immensely important, but the life to come is all that matters.

The medieval mind recognized such teachings, taken literally, to be confusing. People therefore began to think and choose for themselves, which ultimately led to scientific curiosity to explain what religion didn't, or couldn't, explain.

Professor Muller wrote, "... Christianity promoted freedom because it never achieved the unity, certainty, and fixity that it always aspired to ..."

The Protestant Reformation of Martin Luther and John Calvin was a revolt against the authority of the Catholic Church, and revolt against authority led to further thoughts of democratic freedoms. Calvin and Luther also had high regard for education, which made Protestantism more open to new ideas and ultimately to ideals of freedom of thought, speech and the press, and most importantly, to the concept that humans could choose their leaders.

The concept for separation of church and state that so many people in the United States can't find in the Constitution comes directly from Christianity; it just took nearly two millennia for the thought to sink into the human mind. And it comes much in the form of a commandment, not a "neat idea" that might be attempted or merely considered. The separation was ordained by the Bible when Jesus Christ said, "Render to Caesar the things that are Caesar's, and to God the things that are God's." According to the King James version of the Bible, the question asked had been, "Is it lawful to give tribute to Caesar, or not?"

Many people like to edit the Bible to make that passage read "pay taxes," but that isn't what the King James version says and the King James has been the Bible most used in Western civilization since 1611, the one the Founding Fathers would have been familiar with. Christ's answer to the question wasn't restricted to any single thing. He didn't say to render taxes, or to render one thing, a few things or most things; he said "the things," a phrase that would be all-inclusive. That is, every thing that belongs to Caesar must be rendered to him, and that includes recognizing his civil authority over the population and his control of the state. That means everything that belongs to God must be rendered to Him, and that includes recognizing His spiritual authority and His control of the church. By dividing "the things" of Caesar from "the things" of God, Jesus was specifying a break from the traditional way of sharing of authority. He didn't say, "Render to Caesar some things that are God's, and to God some things that are Caesar's."

His commandment leaves no room for combining those "things," nor does it endorse dual authority. There's no principle in Christianity for "checks and balances," and laws aren't written by representatives elected by the faithful. Other Biblical references indicated to Christ's followers that they were to be no part of the world, which means spirituality is to be no part of Caesar's government. Christ also said his Kingdom was not of this world. Such pronouncements didn't necessarily mean believers were to drop out of society, because other commandments demanded that they obey and respect secular authority, nor were they to abandon the world, because "God so loved the world, that he gave his only begotten Son ..."

If a modern-day Christian fails to recognize the separation of church and state, she or he is mentally subverting the Constitution and subverting the Bible, for Christ didn't leave an opening for Caesar and God to share authority. Caesar (*kaiser* in German and tsar in Russian) is represented to this day in governmental form throughout the world; in Washington, D. C.; in statehouses, county seats and city councils; by school boards, military forces and police departments. Religionists who proclaim themselves to be American patriots are denying Christianity, because Christianity is international, with no alignment to any secular nation. A true Christian must be a "patriot" of all lands and swear allegiance to all the earth.

When church leaders were the ruling civil authority of Western civilization, they were subverting this Biblical principle. The Constitution writers recognized that, and so purposely withheld from government the authority to exercise civil power over religion.

The Constitution also specifies in Article VI that "... no religious Test shall ever be required as a Qualification to any Office or Public Trust under the United States." That clause definitely creates the principle of separation of church and state. Refusal to accept that principle of separation is "un-Americanism" under Justice Antonin Scalia's definition, and membership in a legitimate American political party doesn't negate a person's un-Americanism.

For guidance, the founders looked to John Locke, who in 1669 wrote a constitution for the proprietors of the Carolina Colony in North America. That constitution was never put into effect, but Locke's value as a political thinker had been recognized. He later offered his views in "Two Treatises of Civil Government" (1690), in which he dismissed the theory of divine right of kings to rule. He said sovereignty didn't belong to the state, but to the people, and the state is supreme only when it's bound by civil or natural law. He advanced theories of natural rights, property rights of the people, and the duty of government to protect those rights. He also advanced the idea of rule by the majority, or with consent of the majority. He was the father of a three-branch government consisting of legislative, executive and judicial branches, with the legislature being the most powerful in a system of checks and balances. The checks and balances were brought about by giving each branch specific powers, some of which would negate actions of the other branches. He strongly believed in freedom of religion and took seriously Christ's commandment to separate church and state.

These principles are all found in the United States Constitution, just as most, or all, were found in the constitutions of the colonies. It wasn't a great gamble or experiment on the part of the Founding Fathers when they wrote the United States Constitution, they had seen these principles in action in the colonies. These principles are easy to find and list, unlike the unspecified "Judeo-Christian principles" some persons link to the creation of the nation.

What a handful of Puritan pilgrims had in mind when they came to the New World has nothing to do with the founding of the United States. The Pilgrims who came to New England were years behind the Spanish colonists who founded Saint Augustine in what's now Florida, in 1565, and the English who settled on Roanoke Island off the coast of present-day North Carolina in 1585.

Nor were the supposed religious aspirations of the Pilgrims evident in the first permanent settlement – Jamestown – in 1607. That Virginia settlement was established for trading and colonization of North America. Some colonies were later founded by religious sects on religious doctrine, and had state religions early in their existence. But that concept changed – or should have changed – March 4, 1789, when the United States Constitution went into effect as the public authority of the nation. Anything that existed prior to the adoption of the Constitution had to conform to its new rules. That didn't happen automatically, for it would have been virtually impossible to negate 170 years of law and practice to instantly create everything anew. Most existing law was perfectly fine, some wasn't, and legislatures and courts had the task of eliminating the offending statutes and practices, a process that continues to this day.

It would be painful for persons who fancy themselves patriotic Americans and faithful Christians, but refusal to admit separation of church and state appears to be "un-Americanism," and using political or governmental icons, such as flags, in worship of God could be rendering to God things that are Caesar's.

Many Christians take separation of church and state seriously, and recognize that God must control the church, the state must not; and the state governs politically, God doesn't. The principle of separation of church and state is that religion can't govern and government can't worship, just as Jesus Christ commanded and the First Amendment to the United States Constitution specified. Our Founding Fathers – some of them devout religionists – understood this well, so they wrote the Constitution for a republican form of government based on democratic principles, not on "Judeo-Christian principles."

LIMITED GOVERNMENT

When Justice Scalia mentioned the concept of limited government not being around anymore, he wasn't completely accurate. The concept is much alive for many people; it's the practice that seems not to be around anymore. And this concept is worth exploring, because "limited government" may mean different things to different people.

Many people claim there's been subversion of the principle of "limited government" as they attack the national government for the taxes it levies and the money it spends on various programs. They may a lament lack of "limited government" while they criticize the number of federal employees or laws enacted. Absence of "limited government" is cited when some regulation they dislike begins to affect them.

"Big government" is named as the culprit by those who claim to be speaking for "limited government." But limited government has nothing to do with the size of the government, how many people it employs or how much it takes in taxes. Limited government has nothing to do with the number of laws or the extent of their objectives. The concept of limited government has never been intended to mean a small and ineffectual government, unable to render protection to certain groups or individuals. It was never meant to restrict governmental taxing and spending. It was never meant to prevent government from assisting some, or all, of its citizens.

Some Americans say the United States government has but one function; defense of the nation, with all other functions belonging to the states or local governments. But that isn't what the Founding Fathers said when they wrote the Constitution. It's clear from the Preamble what the intentions and purposes of the new government were to be.

The Preamble states, "We the People of the United States, in Order to form a more perfect Union, establish Justice, insure domestic Tranquility, provide for the common Defence, promote the general welfare, and secure the Blessings of Liberty to ourselves and our Posterity, do ordain and establish this CONSTITUTION for the United States of America."

There are six definite objectives of government in the Preamble and numerous powers in the body of the Constitution empowering the government to carry out its functions. It should be obvious that the six objectives could cover the entire scope of human existence in the United States. That doesn't suggest the founders were intent on creating an ineffectual national government that could do little. Ineffectual government was what they were trying to get rid of; the Articles of Confederation adopted after the Revolution had proved to be too weak and ineffectual.

Hamilton, in 1787, wrote to the Americans about what he perceived to be limited government. He said in Federalist No. 78, "By a limited Constitution, I understand one which contains specified exceptions to the legislative authority; such, for instance, as that it shall pass no bills of attainder, no ex-post-facto laws, and the like." There are many limitations on the government in the original Constitution, and many more were added with the Bill of Rights and other amendments.

Very few additional powers have been added to the Constitution, and most of those added were given to Congress to protect citizens against misuse of power by other branches of government or from lower governments. Examples are the powers of Congress to protect voting rights from state or federal interference, the power to eliminate slavery, and the power to protect civil rights from state subversion. By such amendments, the Constitution is much more limited now than it was when first adopted. Hamilton could have mentioned two additional types of limitations:

(1) By giving specific powers to specific branches of government, other governments or branches of the national government are prevented from duplicating specific acts. That delegation of power limits to one place, for example, the law-making function. The President may not legislate; that's limited to Congress. And states may not enact laws in areas where the federal government has sole authority.

(2) Government can't act in areas in which it hasn't been granted the power to act. The "wisdom" of legislators doesn't matter; the only thing important is constitutional authority. Felix Frankfurter, who served as a Supreme Court judge from 1939 until 1962, often said the Constitution doesn't contain a solution for every problem. His meaning was simple; government can't do as it wishes, it can only do what it is authorized to do.

One reason "limited government" seems to have disappeared is America has undergone monumental changes since its creation. For example: Congress was given the power "To regulate Commerce with foreign Nations, and among the several States, and with the Indian Tribes." That power hasn't changed since it was written; commerce has changed.

In the late 18th century there was little commerce between nations and between the states. Most business was localized and therefore subject to regulation by local governments. Today there's little commerce that is only local. But the same limitations on Congress that existed in the 18th century still exist today, one of them being that Congress may not regulate commerce that's strictly intrastate.

But for most Americans, the limitation of the national government is real; their main contact with the federal government is with the Postal Service and the Internal Revenue Service. When one begins a private business, that contact is greatly increased, just as it is if one enters military service or commits a federal crime. It's at state and local levels that Americans experience the most governmental interference in their lives.

In his essay, Hamilton was arguing for the power of the Supreme Court to reject laws not properly based on a constitutional power. He was leaving instructions to Scalia and his colleagues to do the limiting of government by judicial decree when the other branches of the federal government or local governments exceed their authority. When the Supreme Court declares a law or act unconstitutional, it's reminding the other branches of government about limitations.

It's this function in government that the Supreme Court serves best and for which it should be appreciated. There's a possibility government and humans cannot coexist peacefully, because the history of government has been the state against the individual in a battle of power versus rights. In most cases, when a legislature enacts a law, it's a limitation on rights of someone. When the executive branch enforces law, the individual is stripped of freedom.

It's up to the court to step in, when asked, to serve as an arbiter and to determine if government action is superior to rights or rights superior to government power. Too often, the court has been severely criticized when it ruled. Usually the criticism has been unwarranted and totally mistaken, for the court has a history of being the most true of any branch of government to the Constitution and sympathetic to the citizens. When the court has been mistaken, it has admitted error and corrected its mistakes – few as they have been. When it's accused of being mistaken, usually the critics are mistaken.

A great debate throughout the history of the court has been over the ideology of its members. Some people want only those who espouse a so-called "conservative" viewpoint, while others want "liberals." It may be most people can't tell the difference between the conservative and the liberal. Oliver Wendell Holmes was accused by many court critics of being a liberal, but scholars of the court view him as a typical aristocratic New England conservative. His "sin" was that he wouldn't place his political views over the Constitution. He would admit the power of government to do many things he might oppose politically. Louis Brandeis was a liberal, but he and the conservative Holmes agreed on virtually every decision because the Constitution, when read correctly, transcends all political biases. William O. Douglas was accused of being a dreaded "liberal" on the basis of three supposed passions: preserving the Constitution as he perceived the founders created it, conserving the environment of God's blue earth, and adoring a pretty young woman. The first is a conservative position, the second should be, and the third is just good common sense.

The only ideology that should matter is constitutional ideology, something that does seem at times to take an inferior position to the conservative-liberal arguments.

When Brandeis was appointed to the court in 1916, it was said he created the "Jewish seat" and would bring a Jewish viewpoint to the court. Thurgood Marshall's 1967 appointment was expected to give a "Negro viewpoint," as a "woman's viewpoint" was expected from Sandra Day O'Connor's appointment in 1981. But the three stayed away from such biases and mainly presented constitutional viewpoints.

Columnist Carl T. Rowan, writing a rousing newspaper endorsement of the O'Connor nomination for the Supreme Court said, "It is precisely because women are 'different' that they deserve a voice in deciding what is right or wrong, just and unjust, wise and foolish." Women certainly do deserve a voice in what concerns us all, but to assume providing a forum for all viewpoints is a function of the Supreme Court is foolish. The Supreme Court doesn't decide justice or injustice; it decides constitutionality. It doesn't determine wisdom or foolishness; it decides legality of governmental action, the right or wrong of government, not right or wrong of a person.

How a proposed judge views the function of government under the Constitution is what matters most. Some think government must be restricted to the "letter" of the Constitution to do only those things it's authorized to do. Others think government has "inherent" powers and can do as government authorities wish, except what's expressly forbidden. The first viewpoint would be one concerning "limited government," Scalia's lost constitutional principle. The second position seems to be what is most wanted by government leaders and a large part of the public. But for most of the court's history, something between the two perspectives seems to be the norm.

SOURCE OF THE ELUSIVE RIGHT

People like to claim a right to do something, say something, believe something or be something. What constitutes a "right" has been determined to be human conduct government is powerless to prohibit, but many people

Knowing America

are confused about where rights originate. Americans will use terminology such as "God-given," "natural," "human" or any other word to suggest origin.

Even those people supposedly in a position to know better have little knowledge to impart on this subject. The following quotes demonstrate the problem that supposedly knowledgeable persons have with the concept of rights.

– A spokesman for the International Anti-Euthanasia Task Force at the University of Steubenville (Ohio) wrote in a guest column of USA TODAY in 1990, "The law of the land has never yet bestowed a special right to kill on those whose claim is love. Nor should it do so."

– A USA TODAY editorial in 1990 made a similar statement when it tried to explain the Bill of Rights. The newspaper asked, "Do you like to say what you want when you want? The First Amendment gives you that right.

"Do you think you should be able to worship any god you wish in any way you wish? The First Amendment gives you that right, too."

– In 1984 the Sunday Seattle Times quoted a judge of the Washington State Supreme Court as saying, "Federal constitutional rights only set a floor below which states may not go, and don't pretend to set a limit on what rights a state can grant its citizens."

– In describing a congressional hearing on the proposed Equal Rights Amendment, columnist George Will wrote in 1983, "(Utah Republican Sen. Orrin) Hatch's point, which Massachusetts Democrat Sen. Paul) Tsongas unwillingly confirmed, is that ERA bestows a right without identifying it."

– The Denver Post reported in a 1975 Associated Press story that, "Supreme Court decisions and federal laws enacted since the start of the 1960s have given public-school students new legal rights."

Those quotes were made over a 15-year period, but they are essentially the same statement, nothing has been learned or changed about Americans' knowledge of their rights. All five statements made important and intelligent observations concerning the subjects they were addressing, but all made assumptions about "rights" that were totally false.

The first quote assumes rights come from the supreme law of the land, that is, the United States Constitution. The Constitution doesn't grant rights.

USA TODAY was wrong about the First Amendment and the Bill of Rights. The Bill of Rights does not create rights to give to United States citizens.

The Washington Supreme Court judge was correct in pointing out that state constitutions may restrict state and local government power much more than does the federal Constitution. He was wrong in assuming that amounts to granting of rights by the states. Rights do not come from state governments.

Will, an intellectual conservative, was correct in seeing the ERA didn't specify a particular right. But he was wrong in saying the ERA "bestows a right." Rights do not find their roots in constitutional amendments.

The Post and Associated Press were correct in noting that the relationship between schools and students had changed. They were wrong in assuming those changes involved rights newly created by laws or court decisions. Rights existed long before government or courts were created.

Our four mythical creators – the man north of the river, the man south of the river, the fool on the hill and the farmer in the dell – had all the rights that God or nature bestowed on them long before they created the covenant of self-government. They were free to do as they wished. That was their right. They weren't prevented from exercising their rights of freedom until they gave up some of those freedoms to form the governmental covenant. That's why there are no such things as "constitutional rights." There are God-given rights; there are human rights; there are natural rights; there are civil rights; there are no constitutional rights. As discussed earlier, Americans are the source of governmental authority; they surrendered their private powers, by means of constitutions or charters, to empower all their governments. That surrender created constitutional powers, not constitutional rights. The Constitution only acknowledges the existence of certain rights, it doesn't create those rights.

An argument can be made that the Constitution acknowledges two types of rights – neither granted by the Constitution. When this book mentions "rights" it will concern "privileges and immunities" mentioned in Article IV, Section 2, and in the Fourteenth Amendment. A privilege is a right existing in areas controlled by regulation. An immunity is a right not subject to regulation.

For example, a person may obtain a vehicle of any type for personal use. That acquisition isn't subject to governmental control other than what contract law might impose. The state may make no laws governing the possession of a vehicle that was legally obtained. Ownership is, therefore, a right of immunity. But, when that vehicle is used on public roads or property, it becomes subject to whatever regulations government is empowered to make. That means no one has an absolute right to drive or possess a driver's license, the state has made driving a privilege right. Privilege rights exist where government regulation exists.

SPEAKING IN A DIFFERENT TONGUE

Lack of knowledge about American principles has created a form of bilingualism in the United States. In addition to their customary English, Spanish or other native language, Americans have developed a second language that's used throughout the land and ties Americans together as one nation by transcending regional dialects. Some use it as if it had great meaning.

That language is "Sloganese." Americans like to speak and think with slogans which can lead to problems because slogans mask ignorance rather than reveal knowledge.

A popular slogan in the 20th century has been to "get the government off the peoples' backs." Others cite "the rule of law," "law and order," or "drift and decay."

Add to those, "kicked God out of our schools," "forced busing," "fought and died for Old Glory."

Then there are the slogans of "love of country" and "America, love it or leave it."

To understand the harm of "speaking Sloganese" one only has to look to the multi-billion-dollar failures in the savings-and-loan industry that came about trying "to get the government off the peoples' backs." The people didn't have the government on their backs; government was on the backs of the industry in the form of regulations and was there to protect the people. Removing regulatory action didn't "get the government off the peoples' backs" it put the government on their backs in the form of taxation to pay for the fiasco caused by refusal to enforce regulations. The Founding Fathers gave to the government power to regulate commerce for good reasons, and the crisis caused by unregulated businessmen should be proof of the founders' wisdom. The "rule of law" or "law and order" are equally unrelated to freedom; they often are used to eliminate freedom. Law is government power in action, and should be used only when necessary. The evil of "law" should be evident by events of the 20th century. The killing of millions of people by both Adolf Hitler and Joseph Stalin was done under the authorization of law – they didn't kill outside the law of their regimes.

The "eviction of God" from the schools isn't true, and is dealt with in detail in Chapter 9. "Forced busing" could be called "forced equality" or "forced constitutionalism" and be accurate. While some think Americans "fought and died for Old Glory," others might say they "fought and died" for freedom, or for family and nation, or for the Constitution. One person's perception of what's important to fight for isn't necessarily another person's perception. And no one is so wise as to dictate that fighting for Old Glory is more important than fighting for freedom or for the Constitution.

As for the slogan "America, love it or leave it;" one could plead, "Americans, learn our democratic principles."

BASHING THE SUPREME COURT

Learning about America's principles may be too difficult for some who assume their opinions are superior to those principles. And when the Supreme Court makes a decision that offends those opinions, the Court comes under attack; a popular pastime for most of the nation's history. The court usually seems to stay above the criticism and isn't easily swayed, which is a positive for it. Chief Justice John Marshall's observation that the public couldn't understand a detailed Constitution underscores the attacks: the assailers don't know the Constitution, and have failed to understand the court's decision. Instead of learning, the critics attack with no ammunition other than their opinions.

This criticism doesn't make sense. The court judges begin consideration of a case by reading the briefs detailing both parties' arguments. Both sides to the controversy are given time to present arguments, and the judges question the presenters to clarify points in their arguments. The judges and their clerks then research past judgments, and debate all points of view. Only then is a decision made, a decision that has taken a considerable amount of time, research and debate to reach.

On the other hand, news-industry critics usually have only a few years' experience reporting on local criminal courts. Writing and editing a few stories on torts and misdemeanors don't qualify journalists to comment on constitutional law. Criminal law and constitutional law are two different "dogs," as dissimilar as a Chihuahua and a Saint Bernard.

Decisions aren't made off the top of the judges' heads; they come after considerable deliberation. Critics launch an attack upon hearing of a decision; no impartial hearing of both sides of the argument, no research, no debate and, most importantly, little knowledge of constitutional law. The attack is immediate and loud; and usually wrong. The critics usually ignore the constitutional question, though the court always makes its decision on the constitutional question.

A few illustrations on this point.

In 1989, the Public Broadcasting Service (PBS) presented a television program called *Visions of the Constitution*. On the program, a narrator, who was identified as a college president and former law professor, said the

Supreme Court declared the death penalty to be unconstitutional only to later reverse itself and approve the death penalty. That's nonsense. The Supreme Court had never declared the death penalty unconstitutional. What the court said will be covered in more detail in Chapter 8. The narrator also claimed that in the much-criticized Dred Scott decision of 1857, the Supreme Court declared black slaves to be "nonpeople." That, likewise, is nonsense. The Supreme Court never said that. The Dred Scott decision may prove to be more important than court critics think, and its contributions to the civil-rights victories of the 1960s and '70s will be discussed in Chapter 12.

The court was attacked by The Denver Post for a minor 1979 decision that said government had no obligation to open pretrial proceedings to the press when the defendant asked that certain evidence be excluded and some statements be suppressed in a criminal case. In a critical editorial, the Post said, "The issue before the court was not fundamentally a press issue – it was a citizen issue. Yet the court paid lip service to the larger principle and chose to center its concerns on whether the press treats criminal defendants fairly in pretrial coverage."

How the press treats defendants had nothing to do with the constitutional issue; the constitutional issue almost always concerns government power, and it certainly did in this case.

Later that summer, another Post editorial attacked the judges for trying to clarify the decision. The judges were accused of being "confused," when in reality, the critics were confused. And it was the press' confusion that required some justices to speak out. Journalists could have made an effort to understand the decision but chose to put biased interests above constitutional principles that were involved. The most-important matter in this situation was the relationship between a murder defendant and the state, which was trying to deprive him of his freedom or his life. Critics of the court missed the point. Criticism came from a newspaper already shown to have misquoted the Constitution and displaying ignorance about the origin of individual rights. So it tried to lecture the Supreme Court on the Constitution, and on rights of public and press.

The right of Americans to question or criticize Supreme Court decisions should never be eliminated, but those people who wish to disseminate criticism through a privileged manner of communication – the airways or the press – have the obligation to know what they are talking or writing about. When they criticize from ignorance, the "engine of democracy" sputters and dies.

INTENTIONS OF THE FOUNDERS

Many critics of the Supreme Court cite the "intentions of the founders" when opposing a court decision or resisting governmental action or law judged by them to be proper. Critics say the founders' intention is the only thing the court can consider when making a decision, but if that were the case, governing a modern America would be extremely difficult, if not impossible. No one can read the minds of the framers of the Constitution to determine their intent about specific laws or actions because the framers were not concerned with specifics of law. They were concerned with writing a document that gave powers to the national government. That was the intent. That was the result.

If those who claim everything must agree with the framers' intentions were to have their way, the United States would have a difficult time indeed. To understand that point, we compare the framers' work with modern reality.

In Article I, Section 8 of the Constitution, the founders wrote that Congress shall have the power:

"To raise and support Armies ...

"To provide and maintain a Navy;

"To make Rules for the Government and Regulation of the land and naval Forces."

Article II, Section 2, adds:

"The President shall be Commander-in-chief of the Army and Navy of the United States, and of the Militia of the several States when called into the actual Service of the United States."

We know that was the founders' intentions because that is what they wrote. People who would restrict the authority of the United States to "the founders' intentions" would have to dismantle the United States Air Force because the founders didn't intend for Congress to have the power to create an air force, fund it or make laws governing it. Nor did they intend to have the president serve as commander of an air force. We know what they intended because we can read their intentions concerning only "land and naval Forces." The modern nation would certainly be restricted in defending itself without the Air Force.

The country probably couldn't have a space program or regulate the airways to protect radio and television broadcasting. Those things operate on technology that could never occur to the founders, so they couldn't have intended that the federal government have the authority to cover such areas. In spite of exceptional intelligence, Benjamin Franklin probably couldn't envision a rocket blasting off from a Florida space center on a mission to the edges of the galaxy. He and his colleagues therefore couldn't propose any constitutional intentions for a space program. Franklin probably couldn't even envision Florida.

Could the founders foresee a reason to include in the Constitution a power to promote modern medical science when they could never anticipate the scope of technical miracles made in the past 200 years? The only intent they had for science was to provide for patent protection of inventors' "discoveries." (Article I, Section 8.)

Congress was given power to establish "Post Offices" and what the Constitution called "post Roads" but that wasn't intended to provide the extensive interstate highway system we have and need today. The founders intended to have roads for riders or horse-drawn carts for mail delivery; they in no way envisioned our modern high-speed automobile and truck traffic. They likewise couldn't have envisioned the railways and airports the nation relies on.

Much criticism of the Supreme Court centers on decisions it has made about state powers in the operation of the public schools. Many people, who don't care for decisions concerning racial equality and segregation, or religious practices and authority over students, claim the founders didn't intend the Constitution to be read in a manner supporting such decisions. In 1985, Justice O'Connor, writing on some religion cases, observed that public education didn't exist when the First Amendment of the Constitution was adopted, so how could the founders have had any specific intentions on the matter?

There was no way for the Founding Fathers to foresee the damage industrial advancement has done to the environment, therefore they couldn't have intended a power for ecological activities. But we have a system of national parks, monuments and recreational areas, which helps make living more pleasant and much of nature's wonders have been saved, possibly for all time. The founders were living in a time when environmental awareness wasn't the concern it is today. If we were to restrict ourselves to their intentions, we would have little or no flood control or electrical production at federal dams, and we wouldn't be concerned with saving endangered animal species or protecting the environment. Such needs weren't anticipated by the founders, but they provided power for them to be addressed.

By giving Congress authority to raise and support military forces, the Constitution implies a power for any type of military force Congress deems necessary. And the authority to support space programs, medical research, modern transportation or other unintended activities, such as intelligence agencies, can be found in various areas of the Constitution, although not explicitly stated. To require everything to be specifically named would be unrealistic. For that reason, the only intentions of the founders that matter are the powers they intended government to have and the powers they intended government not to have. And those intentions are spelled out in the Constitution.

When people get hung up on the founders' intentions, they tend to read the Constitution backwards. They concern themselves with what is written about a particular right or action of the individual, and not about what the government's powers are in relationship to our rights. An example of this "backward reading" came in a 1987 guest column in USA TODAY. The column, written by the executive director of the Center for Judicial Studies in Washington, D. C., said, "The job of judges should be to find out what was intended by those who wrote the Constitution or statute and decide accordingly."

That is nonsense. The job of the judges should be to find out what governmental power was used to create law or authorize governmental action. And, if there was no legitimate power, there can be no legitimate statute or action.

The columnist also wrote, "... neither abortion nor any alleged right of privacy is anywhere mentioned in the Constitution."

The assumption being that there is no right of privacy that sustains abortion rights. That conjecture comes from misreading the Constitution. The only valid issue is governmental authority because the people give power to government through the Constitution; therefore, it's the powers granted that must be "mentioned" in the Constitution not the rights that are free from regulation. The critic should have looked for power to regulate, not a right to be free of regulation.

That principle was explained by Chief Justice Marshall. He wrote in 1819 (*McCulloch v. Maryland*), "This government is acknowledged by all to be one of enumerated powers. The principle, that it can exercise only the powers granted it, would seem too apparent ... that principle is now universally admitted." That principle has never changed; but is no longer universally admitted, especially by those who don't understand constitutionalism.

Critics of Constitution and court use the "intentions" subterfuge to try to add legitimacy to their political positions. The man quoted above was opposed to abortion, but couldn't find a constitutional position to support his politics. He, therefore, called upon unspecified "intentions of the founders" to help him out. Imagined "intentions," not surprisingly, will always coincide with the political agenda of the person referring to them. And two persons can claim to know opposing "intentions" in their battle with each other.

One of the founders – Madison – argued in Federalist No. 38 that the Constitution wasn't perfect and implied future Americans could make refinements as the need arose. His point was that power to accommodate changing conditions and concepts can be added through the amending process included in the Constitution; and that's a hint not to rely on "the founders' intentions" because their concepts may not reflect later needs. The founders never intended to lock the nation into 18th-century notions, and people who resort to "the founders' intentions" for ammunition for their politics are simply "speaking Sloganese."

One of the founders' intentions was noted by Jay in Federalist No. 3 with the assurance the "best men" would consent and be appointed to serve the government under the new Constitution. That doesn't appear to have happened.

'ORIGINAL INTENT' FAILS TEST OF LOGIC

During the administration of Ronald Reagan, Attorney General Edwin Meese publicized that regime's philosophy of "original intent." It would be presumptuous to assume Meese was speaking for himself, because one would think that as a licensed attorney from the state of California he would understand the Constitution better than his statements suggested. As a political subordinate, he would be required to subjugate himself to people of superior position but inferior knowledge. Meese, nevertheless, in 1985, criticized the Supreme Court for invalidating an Alabama law providing for daily moments of silence in public schools "for meditation or prayer." There's no way to an original-intent theory in that case – according to Justice O'Connor's observation – because there was no public-school system in 1789, when the Constitution became law of the land, or in 1791, when the Bill of Rights was added. So how could the framers have had any intentions about what public schools could or could not do?

Meese pinned the administration's position on the argument that nothing in the original Bill of Rights was intended to restrain state powers. That's true, but it missed the point. An important original intent of the Constitution's founders was that the people of the United States could change their covenant as they wished: to add or subtract powers, and restrain or abolish government at their will. They wished a change in 1868 with the adoption of the Fourteenth Amendment. That amendment says explicitly,

THE UN-AMERICANS

"No state shall make or enforce any law which shall abridge the privileges and immunities of citizens of the United States ..."

But, did the creators of that amendment intend it to apply the Bill of Rights to the states? The chief proponent, Rep. John A. Bingham of Ohio, in 1871 said the "original intent" of the amendment was to extend the Bill of Rights to state action. He was quoted as saying the amendment was to "vest in Congress a power to protect rights of citizens against the States." He added that court judges "had been powerless to enforce the Bill of Rights" in a case against a state, and the amendment he wrote was intended to give Congress and the Supreme Court the power to apply the Bill of Rights to state action. That was the "original intent" of the Fourteenth Amendment, and if Meese and the Reagan administration were truly serious about "original intent" they wouldn't have questioned the Supreme Court.

The founders feared permanent professional armies, so they made provisions for militias of the states to be called by the national government when needed. Armies were originally intended to be temporary creations. That's why Article I, Section 8, restricts funding of armies to no longer than two years. If the Reagan administration had been consistent on original intent, it might have sought a reduction in the military forces, not the buildup it did seek. Because it perceived a foreign military threat, the Reagan administration ignored "original intent" of the founders concerning a professional army and only cited "original intent" in areas where it couldn't have its way.

It's puzzling that people who can't find a separation of church and state, or a right of privacy, and don't understand the principle of limited government, can find a doctrine of a permanent "original intent."

The silliest constitutional position from the Reagan administration was that a Supreme Court decision applied only to the case on which it was based. That position ignored the concept that each case is intended to examine the legality of a governmental law or action. If the Reagan position were to be adopted, there could hardly be equal protection of the law, a constitutional principle. Should a law be passed to confiscate all private property, only those persons who could afford to take a case to the Supreme Court would have their property rights protected. That situation would, in effect, make a government power illegal to people with wealth to resist government action, but acceptable to persons or groups that couldn't afford legal action. That wasn't an original intent of the founders. It should be clear that adherence to a doctrine of original intent is an idea contrary to the principles embodied in the Constitution. According to the definition supplied by Justice Scalia, a Reagan appointee, ideas of original intent and unequal application of power should be "perceived to be un-American."

BENEFICIAL BATTLE OVER BORK

A battle between contrasting views of the Constitution was fought in the summer and fall of 1987 after President Reagan nominated Federal Appeals Court Judge Robert Bork for a position on the Supreme Court. The battle concerned whether government has power to do what it wishes except what the Constitution prohibits or whether the powers of government are limited to those given to the government by the people.

Bork was credited with having excellent legal credentials and was presented as a man who personified the Reagan administration's legal theories. He obtained his law degree from the University of Chicago and had been a law professor at Yale University. He was a self-proclaimed "originalist" who adhered to the "original intent" doctrine widely accepted by political conservatives.

Bork, who was nominated July 1 and rejected by the Senate Oct. 23, was described by all – even his political opponents – to be a man of brilliant legal scholarship who prided himself on his ability to adhere to the legal precedent. When his defeat came by the widest margin in history, his political allies railed against what they called a "lynch mob" or "special-interest groups" and "political pressure." President Reagan accused special interests of a "campaign of disinformation and distortion." Bork was quoted by the Associated Press as saying he was "glad the debate took place because there is now a full and permanent record by which the future may judge not only me but the proper nature of a confirmation proceeding."

Of those statements, Bork's was the only one that has any value in the understanding of the United States Constitution. The other statements must be dismissed as purely political rhetoric. It wasn't differing views about politics that caused Bork's defeat, it was differing views between Bork and the majority of the senators about the Constitution.

The defeat of Bork didn't damage the nation, as many politicians would have liked others to believe. It may have strengthened the nation, because it did present both constitutional views, and it forced another choice of less controversy, a conservative judge who was acceptable to nonconservatives. The selection process seems to force politicians to settle for less-controversial people. It's rare when an extreme view of the Constitution is ever represented by its judges. There's never been a Marxist or a fascist on the court. There's virtually no way a socialist or a monarchist could ever be confirmed; the selection process will never allow that. Extremism in the administration and in the Congress is more likely, and has been more frequent.

THE UN-AMERICANS

Whether Bork held extremist views, as his opponents claimed, or was a "moderate centrist," as his supporters claimed, isn't the issue. If he were an extremist, the United States has a large extremist movement calling itself conservative, because Bork's views find wide acceptance on the political right.

Bork had a broad background of private practice in Chicago and New York, and experience as solicitor general in the Richard Nixon administration's Justice Department. He gained fame for firing Watergate Special Prosecutor Archibald Cox Oct. 20, 1973, an act that didn't endear him to many Americans. His "excellent legal credentials" were of little concern in this matter; he needed excellent constitutional credentials, and the two aren't the same things.

Bork's statement concerning the confirmation procedure is valuable in assessing some statements made by his supporters. One supporter, attorney Bruce Fein, wrote in a USA TODAY column, "The Constitution envisions but a cameo confirmation role for the Senate, to check only for incompetence, cronyism, corruption, or moral turpitude." That is not true. The Constitution envisions nothing of the sort. It says the President "... shall nominate, and by and with the Advice and Consent of the Senate, shall appoint ... Judges of the supreme Court ..." That's all the Constitution says on the matter; it doesn't put any qualifications or limitations on the power of the Senate, and it doesn't give the President any duty or privilege other than nominating. The Constitution mentions nothing about "incompetence, cronyism, corruption or moral turpitude." It doesn't say a nominee needs to have any qualifications or be free of any weaknesses. The Constitution doesn't require a nominee to be a judge or an attorney. He or she need not be a law-school graduate, a college graduate or even a high-school graduate. Nor does a nominee need to be a United States citizen or even an adult. Senators can accept or reject a nominee on any basis they wish, because the Constitution doesn't place any restrictions or qualifications on either the Senate or the nominee. The only statement in the Constitution that pertains to qualifications says, "The Judges, both of the supreme and inferior Courts, shall hold their offices during good Behavior ..." That applies after a person becomes a judge, not before. And the Constitution doesn't define "good Behavior." Congress would define that because it has the power to remove the judges in impeachment proceedings.

Some supporters of Bork argued that the senators couldn't take into consideration the judge's ideology, but had to restrict their voting to his legal credentials. These supporters were strangely silent about where in the Constitution they found such restrictions. They were silent because the

Constitution says nothing of the sort, and they were substituting their opinions for the principles embodied in the Constitution. The objective of the Constitution is to have a selection process in which the President and the Senate would co-operate in the choosing of court judges. It has worked well for it has kept extremists off the court, and has made the Supreme Court the most-trustworthy branch of government and the best friend the individual has in Washington, D. C.

Understanding the Constitution can be enhanced by examining some of the opinions attributed to Bork, and which caused him to be rejected for the life-time appointment.

Reliance on legal precedent is an excellent philosophy for a lower-court judge, a law professor, a practicing attorney or a Justice Department official, but it isn't acceptable for a Supreme Court judge. The Supreme Court doesn't follow precedent; it sets precedent for others to follow. The court is to decide what hasn't been decided; the final arbiter to conflicting arguments. It doesn't decide guilt or innocence of individuals; its power is to decide the appropriateness of government action or law. If it followed precedent, it would have no work because there would be no precedent to follow. If it went along with other courts' decisions, it wouldn't be supreme. A Supreme Court ruling is precedent.

In addition to "original intent," Bork advocated the principle of "judicial restraint." That philosophy has flaws, the most obvious being that when the courts restrain themselves in deciding between individual rights and government power, the rights die. When there's "judicial restraint," there's often no restraint of legislature or executive, and if they were expected to restrain themselves, there would be no "checks and balances." The Supreme Court has served the nation well in restraining governmental assault against citizen freedoms, not restraining itself from protecting the citizens. This is a legacy of two centuries that Americans should embrace and cherish, not reject. "Judicial restraint" is an argument against limited government. It's used by government officials wanting to restrict or control the citizens. To understand the result of "judicial restraint," one only has to study Nazi Germany, Stalin's Soviet Union, Communist China or myriad dictatorships around the world.

There's nothing in the Constitution establishing "original intent" or requiring "judicial restraint." On the contrary, the Constitution seems to be saying just the opposite. Its amending process of Article V is a rejection of an original intent. Its judicial power in Article III, Section 2, doesn't restrain the courts for it says, "The judicial power shall extend to all Cases, in Law and Equity, arising under this Constitution, the Laws of the United

THE UN-AMERICANS

States and Treaties made, or which shall be made, under their Authority; – to all Cases affecting Ambassadors, other Public Ministers and Consuls; – to all Cases of admiralty and maritime Jurisdiction; – to Controversies to which the United States shall be a Party; – to Controversies between two or more States; – between a State and Citizens of another State (repealed in 1798); – Between Citizens of different States; – between Citizens of the same State claiming Lands under Grants of different States, and between a State, or the Citizens thereof, and foreign States, Citizens or Subjects." That passage says "all Cases" three times and "Controversies" twice. It doesn't contain a single statement to make someone believe "judicial restraint" is a constitutional principle.

When Bork argued that judges cannot protect rights not found in the text of the Constitution or in the intentions of the founders, he was wrong. That concept can only be held by suggesting there are no rights of freedom, only privileges the government hands out to the citizens. The concept that government is the source of rights is embodied in dictatorial societies, not free societies. It was a concept that colonists rebelled against in 1776. A proponent of limited government would argue that judges cannot protect or recognize powers of the state not found or implied in the Constitution, the opposite of Bork's position. The majority of Supreme Court judges have decided controversies through the years by searching for a constitutional power, and it's a principle that appears to be the "original intent" of the founders.

In his confirmation hearings, Bork rejected the idea of a constitutional right of privacy, even though he endorsed the desirability of privacy, and indicated the only privacy rights detectable in the Constitution are in speech, religion and in the protections against self-incrimination and unreasonable searches and seizures. That position is reading the Constitution backwards, upside down or inside out. The right of privacy, existing since the beginning of the human species, is to be found in all areas of human conduct except where government has legal power to intrude.

Bork, who once argued against a decision voiding Connecticut's prohibition of artificial birth control, told the hearing, "It's a little hard to locate something about contraceptives in the Constitution." The Constitution not mentioning contraceptives should have been evidence the founders didn't think it was government's business to regulate in that area. How the creators of the Connecticut covenant covered the matter is a different argument, but even their creation had to conform to the United States Constitution, more so after adoption of the Fourteenth Amendment. It's hard to understand how some members of the covenant could empower a governmental creation regulatory authority over sexual practices of others. If a person has no authority over a particular behavior of others without government, he or she cannot give a power to government to regulate that behavior when creating the state. Bork asked, "Suppose a senator introduced a bill that said every man and woman and child in this country has a right of privacy. Period. I don't think that bill would go anywhere until he had to tell everybody exactly what that right of privacy protected. Did it protect incest? Did it protect beating your wife in private?"

That argument missed the point of a privacy right because all governments have "police power" to protect persons from unwanted or unsought actions of others. Police power, without question, would be used to punish wife beaters or those who force incestuous attention on victims. A privacy right would never negate a proper use of the police power or any legitimate power. Adherents of the privacy right have never advocated it as a protection of criminal behavior.

Other controversial Bork views were that the First Amendment protects mainstream political speech, but doesn't extend to subversive or obscene speech; and women have no constitutional protections against laws that discriminate against them. The first position is misreading the First Amendment, the second is misreading the entire Constitution.

There's nothing in the First Amendment that puts limitations on freedom of speech or makes a distinction between different types of speech. The First Amendment doesn't specify "political speech," or "subversive and obscene speech," and it doesn't offer partial or incomplete protection. There are always people who wish to limit or prohibit speech by others, something that couldn't be surrendered in the covenant among neighbors, and something the First Amendment is intended to prohibit. The man north of the river couldn't regulate the speech of the man south of the river, so he would be unable to cede to government the power to do what he couldn't do without government. For someone who prided himself on sticking to the letter of the Constitution and using the framers' text as a guide, Bork fell far short of those goals. Like all rights, free speech is intended to be universal except where government has power of regulation. An example of this would be Congress' power to regulate interstate commerce and the states' powers to regulate intrastate commerce. Commercial speech is subject to control through regulation – that much is beyond argument. No one should argue for total freedom of speech in making sales promises or creating contracts. The control of false commercial promises is certainly within the regulatory authority of both the national government and the state governments.

THE UN-AMERICANS

Fraud committed with speech or criminal conspiracy are certainly subject to punishment under governmental police powers. It's up to an accuser to prove that "subversive" or "obscene" speech are similarly subject to regulation by government.

The argument that women have no constitutional protection against discriminatory laws is likewise lacking in substance. There are many persons sharing that thought with Bork, but they fail in offering any constitutional evidence to support their position. They are wrong, because the Fourteenth Amendment requires "equal protection of the laws," under state jurisdiction, and that's a constitutional protection for women; the protection against discrimination Bork couldn't find.

Constitutional protection under federal jurisdiction is implied. A careful reading of the Constitution fails to detect anything that would suggest that the powers of the federal government can be administered in different manners or with different force against different persons for any reason. In fact, the Constitution seems to imply that powers are to be administered equally. There's no suggestion that governmental powers may be applied differently to persons of differing sexes, ages, education, mentality, races or social positions. The Constitution suggests that powers of government are not applied to men differently than they are applied to women. The Preamble says, "We the people of the United States ..." It doesn't say, "We the male people of the United States ..." That statement indicates women were equal with men in surrendering of rights during creation of the governmental covenant.

The fact that women didn't participate in politics in the 18th century doesn't mean they had differing rights. Women tacitly agree to obey the laws and mores of the society, just as do men. And they should expect an equal standing with men under the laws. There's no difference in government powers on account of sex embodied or implied in the United States Constitution.

While most of Bork's views may be constitutionally sound, those mentioned are not. None reflect principles found in the United States Constitution, but the refutation of them can certainly be found in, or implied by, what the document says. And it was the adherence to these unconstitutional positions that caused the Senate to reject Bork for a seat on the court. It was these political views – not "political pressure" or "special-interest groups" – that caused the Supreme Court position to be filled by Anthony Kennedy rather than Robert Bork. The rejection of Bork was certainly not because of "disinformation and distortion," as President Reagan's political hyperbole claimed.

Knowing America

KENNEDY: ACCEPTABLE BUT NOT IDEAL?

When the Reagan administration settled on Kennedy, the court got a judge that was acceptable to a broader spectrum of the nation even though his views differed little from Bork's. It's still too early to judge how Kennedy, a judge from the West Coast's 9th U. S. Circuit Court of Appeals, compares to the judges of the past, but some concepts he held, or were attributed to him, before his confirmation seemed reassuring. His statement concerning equality in public education was that the decision rejecting segregation had only one problem, "... it wasn't decided 80 years earlier."

A principle he articulated, and which seems to be forgotten in government circles, came in a 1984 speech in Sacramento, Calif. He said, "The Constitution cannot be thrown about as a panacea for every social ill." That statement seems to agree with Frankfurter's idea that the Constitution doesn't contain a solution to all problems. But it's the meaning intended that's important.

Advocates for "limited government" or "limited constitution" would hope he meant that government cannot rely on an unspecified universal power to do whatever lawmakers want to do, but are restricted to those powers the founders intended government to have. A true belief in "original intent" should mean that judges would pay close attention to the powers specified in the Constitution of the United States and in the constitutions of the states. But Kennedy doesn't appear to support that concept. His position that Americans' rights under the Constitution are limited to the original intent of the document's founders appears to reject the principle of "limited government" in favor of a principle of "limited rights." To limit rights to an original intent would suggest the founders wanted an unspecified universal power that would – without the Bill of Rights – allow any government action, with the only citizen rights being those mentioned in the original Constitution. The original document only cited the rights to be free from bills of attainder and ex post facto laws; to hold copyrights and patents; a jury trial, and the right to enjoy the privileges and immunities of all the states under state jurisdiction.

There's also an implied right to hold public office. The original rights mentioned in the Constitution that many political conservatives would honor are few, and the founders left no record anywhere to indicate they intended rights to be nearly nonexistent.

To settle this matter, one must look to what the founders did when creating the Constitution. If they intended government to have a universal power, they would have made just that one grant of power and specified some limitations. The founders didn't do that. They listed the powers the government might exercise; they listed them one by one, clearly delineated and, in some cases, very limited and specific. The founders' original intent wasn't to limit rights to those specifically mentioned in the Constitution; their original intent was to limit governmental powers to those specifically mentioned or implied.

Kennedy said the courts should defer to the political branches of government unless the Constitution mandates otherwise. But it appears the Constitution does mandate otherwise. Its grant of judicial power (Article III) that extends "to all Cases, in law and Equity, arising under this Constitution ..." coupled with the peoples' First Amendment right "... to petition the Government for a redress of grievances" indicates that all actions by all political branches of government are subject to judicial review. An individual with a complaint determines if political actions should be contested in court. The court should never refuse to consider an individual's petition on the grounds that it doesn't want to get involved or is deferring to a political branch of government. That would be denying the right to petition the government; a most-precious right that isn't recognized in most of the world, and which could be the most-valuable right of all.

Supreme Court Judge Harry Blackmun supported the people – not the political branches of government – when he told a New York Times interviewer in 1983, "One has to be aware that human beings are involved in these cases."

He was recognizing the importance of not viewing the individual as being inferior to other entities or interests. "Maybe I'm oversensitive, but these are very personal cases. We're dealing with people – the life, liberty and property of people," Blackmun said. In a way, he said the concern under the Constitution must be for the individual because that's where the judges' authority has root – it didn't come from kings, state governments, corporations, churches, special or privileged classes – and it's the individual's concerns that must be considered.

Former Justice William Brennan added to that in 1986 when he opined that the United States doesn't yet provide justice to all. He called for broader protection for citizens, a concept often rejected by political spokesmen. That protection is precisely the importance of the Supreme Court. It often stands between the individual and political opportunists who enjoy their power, and will use it against anyone, for any reason, at any time, and who would prefer they were free to do as they wish. And it's the independence of the court that protects the individual, not deference by the judicial system to political branches of government.

Knowing America

The Supreme Court is often accused of overstepping its authority; but the accusations come from the same political opportunists who misuse their authority, and the complaints are usually political rhetoric. A judge of moderate political views was Potter Stewart, and his assessment of the Supreme Court contradicted critics' views. "If the court does more than decide cases, then it's going to get itself into trouble, I've never seen it it do that ..." he told USA TODAY in 1984. Deciding cases is the function of the Supreme Court – it must decide cases the people ask it to decide. It must not step back and let a political entity run wild with legislation; it must not practice a "judicial restraint" that would deny a citizen's right "... to petition the Government for a redress of grievances."

Stewart's concept of an ideal judge was, "One who, when you read his or her opinions, you couldn't tell whether it was a man or woman, or a white person or a nonwhite person, or a Catholic or a Jew or a Protestant." That's a view this book is intended to promote.

When a president nominates prospective judges, he tries to select those who hold his views. Then he assumes the new judges will allow him to do as he wishes, giving a judicial stamp of approval to his political actions. Presidents have often received something opposite of what they expected, and the nation has gotten outstanding judges. Those who have been major "disappointments" often have gone on to be the judges of note who contributed the most to national progress. Oliver Wendell Holmes could be the most obvious of these.

Presidents usually don't understand the Constitution, and they delude themselves into thinking the Constitution respects their judgment, which they assume to be beyond question. But the judges usually do understand the Constitution and aren't subject to be swayed by politics.

A common recent concept in selecting judges is to get those who "interpret a law, but don't create new laws" or "legislate from the bench." Columnist Will claimed judges legislate in an April, 1994, article by writing, "The court has become ... a superlegislature doing what it believes other legislatures, because of their obtuseness or cowardice, have neglected to do." He added, "They (the justices) are not rendering decisions based on a search for the Constitution's determinable historical meaning. Rhetoric about the 'living Constitution' is a license for justices to legislate."

The Supreme Court has never legislated, despite what some ill-informed columnist thinks. That's what Justice Stewart said, and that should become evident by the end of this book. The court, of course, must decide the cases before it. It doesn't create the cases, or the situations or laws that give rise to those cases. It cannot decide a case, and then allow a governmental entity found guilty of misusing its power, or using a power it doesn't have, the luxury of continuing in its villainous ways. The court has the authority to order an end to illegal governmental action, because that's part of judicial power and that's what the Constitution embodies in the Supreme Court. Court decisions are administered in the form of orders. A court doesn't allow the state to accept a decision, it orders acceptance. When the court orders a rectifying action on other branches of government, it's not creating new law, it's ordering compliance with existing law; the Constitution of the United States.

Accusing the court of "making law" is nothing more than "speaking Sloganese," and is not a valid argument. It is usually biased political hyperbole trying to hide the unconstitutional action of the political branches of government. When the Supreme Court was voiding segregation laws, it was accused of making law. That accusation wasn't true. The court was merely ordering subversion of the Constitution to end. Requiring obedience to the "supreme Law of the Land" isn't making law, it's ordering legal government behavior.

After retiring from the Supreme Court, Chief Justice Warren Burger proposed the creation of a center for constitutional studies. "It would attract scholars and political leaders from all over the world," he told USA TODAY. A problem with Burger's proposal is where does he propose to find enough instructors for such a center? He can't get many from the media or political branches of government. That should be obvious by now. There's enough disagreement and lack of knowledge about the Constitution in education and the law to make those fields questionable as providers of instructors. Americans must learn about the Constitution themselves before they try to teach it to others.

With the disintegration of communism in Europe, the United States has been receiving students and scholars, political leaders and journalists to study America's constitutional democracy. Considering the lack of American constitutional knowledge, one can only offer: "Lots of luck, Europeans."

VIEWS FROM POLITICIANS

Ideally, judicial and political branches of government would understand the functions of the others, and would co-operate in all their endeavors. The Supreme Court seems to understand functions of the legislature and executive better than they understand the court, which may be because of a higher level of education in the judicial branch. Freedom from political elections – where judges don't have to worry about pleasing a sizable portion of an electorate that doesn't understand the Constitution – enables the court to work on behalf of the public's best interest, and the nation keeps functioning. A national goal should be to make it function better, and that could happen if all Americans made the effort to understand the Constitution.

Before his election in 1980, Reagan railed against the Supreme Court for what he called "abuse of power." That "abuse" was probably nothing more than deciding a controversy to Reagan's dislike. His plan after election, Reagan said, was to appoint judges "who respect and reflect the values and morals of the American majority." That statement shows a lack of understanding about the court, for its job isn't to reflect the values and morals of the American majority. Its values and morals are usually much higher, and its function is to respect and reflect the principles of the Constitution. The court's job is to judge conflicts between citizens and government; values and morals have nothing to do with that. The court doesn't make judgments on the basis of political slogans, it decides all contentions before it according to principles of the Constitution. Reagan took office on an oath to "… preserve, protect and defend the Constitution of the United States." Nowhere in that oath is there a promise to learn or respect the Constitution, and Reagan – upholding a tradition of political office holders – apparently did neither.

Another Reagan complaint was the court would "override public opinion," which was nothing more than political sloganeering. If public opinion was all that mattered, the nation wouldn't have Supreme Court judges; it would rely on poll takers. And if the Founding Fathers wanted the court to reflect "public opinion" they would have stated something to that effect in the Constitution. The Founding Fathers apparently wanted the Supreme Court judges to make knowledgeable constitutional judgments based on their skills as jurists; skills few other persons – especially actors – have. Remember, the great Chief Justice, John Marshall, felt in the early 19th century that the public probably couldn't understand the Constitution if it were cumbersome. He was right. Presidents also often can't understand the Constitution when it isn't cumbersome. Therefore, neither presidential opinions or the opinions of the public should be factors in a decision on constitutional interpretation.

When he had finished his eight years in office, the President praised himself on his "Reagan Revolution," but that revolution hadn't made much difference in constitutional interpretation. Presidents seldom get their political slogans accepted by the court, and the people benefit because of that. In his final address from the White House, Reagan said "… I hope we have once again reminded people that man is not free unless government is limited. There's a clear cause and effect here that is as neat and predictable as a law of physics: as government expands, liberty contracts."

Such a fine political statement must be tempered with the observation that most of Reagan's Supreme Court nominees held to the philosophy that the court must practice judicial restraint and defer to the political branches of government. That practice would assure expansion of the political portion of government, which would constrict liberty. It was Reagan's appointee, Justice Scalia, who conceded that the concept of a limited federal government seems to be passe.

This observation isn't intended to question domestic or foreign policies of the Reagan administration, only its constitutional understanding. There is ample evidence that the Reagan administration worked almost universally for expanded governmental power, not less. And expanded power is putting the government on the peoples' backs, not "protecting individual freedom from government intrusion," the reason Reagan often gave for becoming involved in politics in the first place.

Appealing to the electorate's lack of constitutional understanding isn't limited to one administration or one political philosophy. George Bush showed in the 1988 presidential election that campaigning against constitutional principles of the United States may be more productive to a candidate than endorsing those principles – something that says much about Bush's political acumen and the electorate's constitutional ignorance.

William Safire, a conservative New York Times columnist and former speech writer in the Nixon administration, summed up that thought in one sentence in a 1988 column. He wrote, "Bush has come off the floor with an uncharacteristic snarl, seeking the approval of 'Reagan Democrats' by flag-waving – making an issue of the Pledge of Allegiance (and inferentially, school prayer) – and slyly suggesting that a concern for civil liberties is un-American."

Such a campaign strategy did work in getting Bush elected, but it did nothing to teach respect for the Constitution and American principles. Bush, seeming to allege opponent Michael Dukakis to be less than patriotic for vetoing a Massachusetts Pledge of Allegiance bill similar to what was declared unconstitutional nearly 50 years earlier, taught the wrong thing. It also was a backdoor attack on the earlier Supreme Court for protecting the liberties that should be available to all Americans. The truth of the Pledge of Allegiance controversy will be detailed in detail in Chapter 7. The truth of the school-prayer issue will take up a significant portion of Chapter 9.

Misusing the Constitution for political gain isn't new or restricted to any level of government. Shortly after the Reagan administration took power in 1981, concern about terrorism and law and order prompted moves to increase governmental authority, not restrict it. These concerns manifested themselves by:

– A proposal was made by the Central Intelligence Agency for a "presidential order that would grant broad powers to the U.S. intelligence community to spy on Americans here and abroad," according to the Newhouse News Service. The proposal would have removed a need to show probable cause for wiretapping abroad and for clandestine entries in the United States and abroad. Newhouse reported it would have reduced procedures to protect privacy rights.

– Also proposed at that time, was the re-establishment of the House Un-American Activities Committee which joined Sen. Joseph McCarthy in his "investigations" of the 1950s. Rep. Larry McDonald, R-Ga., was reported to have said he "wanted the revived committee to investigate domestic terrorism as well as 'subversives' in anti-nuclear groups and leftist political parties." McDonald didn't say anything about "subversives" in pronuclear groups and rightist political parties. The push for revival of the committee (disbanded in 1975) and the Senate subcommittee on internal security (abolished in 1978) was begun by the conservative Heritage Foundation of Washington, D. C., in a matter of days following Reagan's election in 1980. According to the Associated Press, the research group "called for ending restrictions that ban mail openings by the FBI, require prior approval from the president and attorney general before the FBI can conduct break-ins, and only permit investigation of political groups when they are suspected of criminal activity." Only groups from the left were singled out for tighter surveillance even though they weren't suspected of criminal actions.

– Reagan's administration sought to "outlaw journalists" identifying intelligence agents; even if the agents' identities were already known.

– The CIA and Federal Bureau of Investigation proposed that intelligence agencies be exempt from the Freedom of Information Act.

– Reagan also pardoned two FBI agents who had been convicted of common crimes committed while in the employ of the government, and which they thought were part of their job.

The administration obviously felt it needed these new powers, and many others it argued for over the years, in order to carry out its duties, but they were all designed to increase the power of government and reduce the amount of freedom available to the individual. They weren't designed "to get the government off the peoples' backs."

Some people question the legality of intelligence agencies, but their

THE UN-AMERICANS

existence and operation can be tied to national defense or the foreign-affairs power shared by the president and Congress. The key word that would define their function and authority is "foreign."

There's no constitutional authority to be used over "subversives" in the anti-nuclear movement or in leftist political parties while excusing their counterparts on the right. There's nothing in the Constitution that would indicate Congress should regulate, or the president should control, the patriotism or lack of patriotism on the part of any citizen, a vital point in Bush's distortion of the Pledge of Allegiance stand of Dukakis and in flag-burning court rulings. People who protest governmental action are in no position to subvert the nation because they have no power. Their protest is proof they lack authority and influence. They cannot, therefore, be subversives. Real Americans know that. The true danger to the nation is by "subversives" who serve in the United States Congress or the administration, in the several statehouses, city halls and on school boards and regulatory bodies. They have the power to do real subverting.

A strange argument arose in 1983 when Congress was debating whether to make the birthday of the Rev. Martin Luther King Jr., a national holiday. There's no constitutional criterion concerning creation of holidays, so Congress could make its own determinations, because it wasn't guided or restricted by any consideration other than its own desires. Sen. Jesse Helms, R-N.C., expressed opposition to the proposal on two grounds: 1) "We need more productivity, not more leisure time," and, 2) King was accused of having a Marxist philosophy and was attacking the United States when he was fighting against racial discrimination by government entities.

The first point is valid. Congress has the power to make rules for the functioning of government and it can regulate interstate commerce; so it surely has the power to create a holiday and apply it to the federal government and most business. And rejecting the proposed holiday was a valid prerogative. Helms' second point was confusing. True American patriots know King was fighting against state-sponsored racial discrimination. There's nothing in the Constitution that sanctions racial discrimination, or sexual discrimination, or social discrimination, or regional discrimination, or national-origin discrimination, or religious discrimination, or any other type of discrimination. Discrimination, therefore, is subversion of constitutional principles. King was displaying a constitutional philosophy and was attacking subversion of the United States. Helms – who pretends to find anticommunism or anti-Marxist clauses in the Constitution when others find nothing of the sort – made it clear in this instance that he opposes anyone who makes an effort to fight subversion of the United States Constitution.

Helms' attitude was shared by the late Federal Bureau of Investigation leader, J. Edgar Hoover. It's now common knowledge he tried to discredit King, and show that "communists" were taking over the civil-rights movement. Hoover acted as if he thought those who embraced equal rights were trouble makers, if not subversives. By using the FBI for more than 40 years as a personal secret police against those who had differing philosophies of government, Hoover acted as a barrier to understanding the United States Constitution. His use of the FBI in an attempt to discredit and smear others should be viewed as un-Americanism, for there's no constitutional authority for the government to discredit and smear. Hoover apparently had no idea of true American ideals and standards, and his so-called patriotism was merely a charade. Patriotic conservatives, such as Justice Holmes, always allow others the same rights to hold personal political thought, and they don't proclaim their thought as the only legitimate thought.

Perhaps it's a sign of advancing political maturity that the majority of Americans are rejecting the thinklessness of Hoover and Helms, and are openly accepting the constitutional principle of equality of all people. It's an insult to patriotic Americans for Helms to suggest to them that equality, justice, freedom and respect for the individual are only Marxist or communist principles. They are principles of the Constitution of the United States, and people who work to preserve these principles are not subversives, they are genuine patriots. The real subversives – and un-Americans under Justice Scalia's definition – are those who would deny equality, justice, freedom and respect for the individual.

EXTREME VIEWS

Distortions of true patriotism by political leaders should never be used as reasons to explain the proliferation of hate groups, both of the right and the left. The politicians don't create the thinking that extremists espouse, but their political distortions of the Constitution create a shield for those out of touch with reality to hide behind, and they provide slogans and idioms where clothes of respectability can hang. Richard Butler, pastor of the Church of Jesus Christ, Christian, and leader of the Aryan Nations of Hayden Lake, Idaho, tried to wear those clothes of respectability in 1985 when he wrote an opposing view to a USA TODAY editorial. In his article trying to justify his group's racial position, Butler penned, "... the Declaration of Independence and Constitution of the USA became the organic law in perpetuity for their white racial 'posterity.' Thus was created a government of organic law and not of men or men's opinions."

He added later in the column, "The 'we the people' in the Constitution's preamble were and are the Aryan or white race of people who became the lawful de jure citizens of this new national state for our race.

"Our present generation of white Aryan people living in the USA and the free, white immigrants constitutionally admitted are the only lawful de jure citizens as the posterity of those who framed and adopted our Constitution."

Butler would have been more accurate if he had written "your Constitution" because he indicates with these statements that he, in no way understands the United States Constitution, just as he doesn't understand the teachings of Jesus Christ or the Bible.

The Preamble of the Constitution, as has been said earlier, doesn't put any qualifications or disclaimers on just who "the people" are. If it doesn't exclude any person or group of persons, it must include those persons. It doesn't reject any American for it says, "We the People of the United States ..." It doesn't say it applies only to Aryan or white people. It doesn't say, and the founders never implied, that it applies to only one race or one group.

Knowledge about American history should have revealed to Butler that many colonists – especially those in the north – were utterly repulsed by slavery and racism, many had freed their black slaves. Those blacks and their descendants were allowed to became citizens of the colonies in which they lived. By being citizens of Massachusetts, New Jersey, Pennsylvania, New York or any of the other colonies, they were included in the phrase "We the people of the United States." They were just as much part of "the people" as Madison, Jay, Hamilton, or any of the other white founders. The founders didn't exclude blacks, or any other nonwhite race, in the phrase "We the People;" it refers to all United States citizens.

If Butler had read the Constitution, he might have found power for Congress "To establish an uniform Rule of Naturalization." That clearly means that Congress makes the rules about which immigrants can be admitted as "lawful de jure citizens" of this nation. Immigrants who qualify for admission under congressional law, qualify under the Constitution. That's the true meaning of "constitutionally admitted." And it applies to Africans and Europeans, Asians and Latins, Arabs and Indians. It applies to everyone, and distortions of the Constitution can't change that.

Whether Butler's ideas find much support in the nation isn't important here. The only concern is that his concepts, while not far removed from thoughts by some people who hold legitimate positions on all levels of government, are clearly counter to the constitutional principles of the United States. They could be the most-obvious "un-American" ideas of all under

Scalia's definition. And they cannot be included in the concept of a great American covenant, because all Americans are parties to that covenant.

Many people in the United States intelligence community or armed forces may have no more understanding of the Constitution than do journalists, politicians or the average citizen. They may have never seriously studied the Constitution, or even read it, but they know it's what they are defending. They weren't recruited or hired by their agencies to defend Butler's philosophies. They aren't fighting his war. They toil behind their big gray desks or go about their James Bond imitations daily with the understanding it's for the United States and its Constitution, and most accept Supreme Court decisions defining constitutional principles, regardless of their personal political opinions.

Butler's position isn't new or much different than many ideas that have been around since the birth of the nation. It's only one of the latest, and like those of past years, it won't get much support because there are too many true Americans – of all races – to combat the misrepresentations. Like other distortions, Butler's position was born of ignorance and lack of the effort needed to learn the Constitution. Butler might like to convince many Americans that his racial opinion is really patriotism, that his views of what America stands for are accurate and unique.

Many people who know nothing of American principles will proclaim their patriotism, and try to prove that allegiance by waving the American flag. But waving a flag will in no way make a patriot out of a bigot or racist than wagging a tail will make a dog out of a cat.

To assume that persons with differing political views are "subversive," as Representative McDonald did, is absolutely ludicrous. Subversives are those who would distort or destroy the Constitution for any reason and by any means. Subversives don't need to be on the extreme left or right; they can subvert the Constitution from the middle of the political spectrum just by being totally ignorant of that document and having power or influence to create great damage. They do much more harm than extremists, who have no power or influence to accomplish anything subversive. Being a patriot isn't a series of physical acts, such as waving a flag, singing an anthem or reciting a pledge or oath. True patriotism is learning, understanding, accepting and living by the principles of the United States and its covenant. Those principles are found in the Constitution; and they don't include racism.

Chapter 4

GOVERNMENT AS POWER

POWER, PRINCIPLES AND 'OCRACIES

There's really nothing to government other than application of power. Power is government, and government is power over the individual or institution. With no power there would be no government, and without government there would be no power to control or protect the individual. Absence of government power would be absolute freedom, but such freedom wouldn't be in the best interest of the individual. In the Federalist Papers, Alexander Hamilton argued for adoption of the Constitution on the basis that it amounted to "the safest course for your liberty."

He was correct, of course. The thought of total freedom may seem appealing, but such totality is only an illusion because the free individual knows that freedom can be taken by others at any time, unless there is the power to protect that liberty. Hamilton's argument was that without the government created by the Constitution, the liberty of Americans could be taken from them with ease, therefore government is a necessity. Some people believe it's possible to live without government, or the least amount of government imaginable, but that's not true. Strong government is often desirable to weak government – it's the type of government that insures liberty, not the size of government. To empower government to protect liberty does require a reduction, or elimination, of some freedom of the individuals.

There's nothing mystical or esoteric about the powers of government. Government is a creation of humanity, and is to serve humanity. Government isn't an institution alien to the individual, it's an extension of the individual, and draws its authority from the individual. In order to serve society and the individuals of that society, government must have the power and authority to do what it was created to do.

It's the source of that power that seems to confuse to many Americans. As has been shown, some people have little knowledge of the source of their rights. Some people attribute the origin of rights to governments, constitutions, political bodies, laws, court decisions or other unspecified sources. That confusion also reigns in the minds of many concerning the source of governmental power.

Government as Power

For thousands of years, humans have assumed that certain superior people have an innate ability to rule society. The elite were thought to possess a special talent of understanding and, as such, had authority to rule, and no one was allowed to question those assumptions. Such an attitude may stem from the paternalistic pattern of life prevalent in nearly all societies. That attitude was then incorporated into government.

Throughout history, numerous forms of government have been tried, beginning with the family, followed by the clan and the tribe. These evolved into simple organized governments which changed, advanced and developed into the superstates of today. Political scientists have applied names and descriptions to all types of government, but all contain traits and principles of the others, making labels almost meaningless.

Mankind has resorted to aristocracies and monarchies, autocracies and plutocracies, oligarchies, democracies, bureaucracies and theocracies. There have been kingdoms, fiefdoms, principalities, empires and republics. Man has used authoritarianism and totalitarianism. There have been authoritocracies, mediocracies and ochlocracies, also known as mobocracies. Often governments act like idiotocracies when the world could use a few savantocracies. Before there was government, there was anarchy.

To understand constitutional powers of the United States, one must consider the powers exercised by other forms of government. Instead of the similar and overlapping forms of government just mentioned, the list has been reduced to five – all based on the source of their governmental powers. The types of government are:

THEOCRACY: A religion-based government. Its authority to rule and its governmental power is said to come directly from God. Power is exercised for the "glory of God" by people "chosen by God." No human questioning of that authority can be allowed because imperfect human beings must be obedient and subservient to the perfect God and His divine rulership. Rebelling against the theocratic system – regardless of the severity of that rebellion – has been regarded throughout history as rebellion against God, and has been punishable severely. God pronounced the death penalty on Adam and Eve for rebelling in the Garden of Eden: Therefore Christian theocracies inflicted death on humans with ease. That's God's punishment, they argued. The people who control God's power, and conduct His earthly concerns, are said to be chosen by God and called to His service; that's the reason their ministry is a "calling."

God's chosen servants can't be questioned or opposed because that's questioning and opposing God. A theocratic system cannot contain such constitutional principles as free and contested elections, or freedom of speech and religion. There can be no petitioning the government for redress of grievances and no contested trials, for God or his ministers would never charge an innocent person with a crime, and no one could have a grievance about God's just pronouncements.

ARISTOCRACY: A government based on the premise that power and authority come from an elite class of people who are superior to all other people. Government power is exercised for the benefit of the elite by members of the elite. Aristocracies are governments with royalty as a ruling class. All power is the personal property of lords, sheiks, dukes, emirs, earls, sultans, barons and other such titled people, who exercise power of rulership over their personal lands and subjects. Power could be obtained in a number of ways, including selection, conquest and assumption. When a national government is needed, elite people give power to a kingdom headed by a member of their class, and power is an inheritance of those born into the ruling establishment. Aristocracies usually develop and evolve with theocracies, for God is cited as giving legitimacy to the system. Supporters of aristocracies have argued throughout history that God chooses the rulers, and gives them rulership authority, by determining their fate. His choice, it's said, is born into the ruling elite. God chooses His kings, queens and other luminaries in this manner. This system, like its theocratic cousin, allows no questioning of its power or authority because that also would be anti-God.

Because the best people are selected before birth to be born a noble, any opposition to them would come from unchosen "inferior" people. And "inferior" people can be dealt with in any manner God's "superior" people choose.

AUTOCRACY: For present purposes, autocracy will be defined as a system in which power is considered an automatic feature of government, with power coming from the state, to be exercised for the benefit of the state, by people chosen by the state. This system features "inherent" powers government gets from itself, or creates for itself. Powers are universal, to be used as the state wishes, when it wishes, in any way it wishes, without restraints or challenge.

The system uses a special group of people deemed best qualified to rule. That group forms the government, and can use state power in any manner it deems necessary. Qualifications to be a member of the ruling group aren't inherited, such as in an aristocracy, but can be acquired by several methods. Party membership, education, wealth are some sources of qualifications for power, which can be gained or lost by the competence or incompetence of the individual. The individual can gain a superior position through applica-

Government as Power

tion and work, but must be accepted by those in power. Such were the systems of Nazi Germany and the communist nations of the world. Power isn't the property of individuals; it belongs to the state that represents a group or community. Communism taught that power belonged collectively to the entire community, to be exercised by the "qualified" few, for the benefit of the group. Fascism taught that power was held by those within a select group, such as a "superior" race, to be exercised by and for that group.

Like the other systems, opposition to the power of the government isn't allowed because the opposition would be by those who hadn't earned power and approval. The opposers are looked upon as being enemies of the special group and, by inference, the state.

MILITOCRACY: This is a term invented especially for this study. It's a system in which power is seized by force and exercised by the conquering military. Other systems, such as aristocracy and autocracy, take power from the people by force – though they never admit it – but power isn't retained in a military establishment. In a militocracy, the armed forces are deemed to be the source of government power and authority because of their patriotism and duty as protectors of society. A militocracy doesn't allow opposition or questioning of its authority because that would be considered unpatriotic. It does not pass on power through inheritances of class, wealth, race or any method used by other systems. It resembles the theocratic and autocratic dictatorships in that one can become a power holder by entering the power structure and earning advancements, with authority being accumulated as one gets higher. Militocracy is similar to its predecessors in that a special group of people is deemed to be best qualified to administer power and authority. These people are considered to be the source of power and, as in the other systems, they are to be served by government. Ordinary persons are left out because they weren't the sources of government power. Thus the civilian population is considered potential enemies to be controlled by any means possible.

DEMOCRACY: The system the Founding Fathers chose when they wrote the Constitution. In this system, power is freely given to the government by the individual, even if the individual doesn't recognize that fact. Power is to be exercised for the individual with the individual as part of the ruling body, indirectly through the election process or directly by holding office. In a democracy, there should be no group with special qualifications to rule. Power coming from a political liberal is the same as that coming from a conservative or moderate, and there's nothing superior about conservatives or moderates. No one has a monopoly on wisdom. When power is misused by those people exercising public authority, the people who gave power to the government have the right and obligation to complain without reprisal or retaliation from the state.

Democracies can be participatory, as in ancient Greece or colonial New England; or representative as in Canada, Western Europe, Australia or the United States.

Some people claim the United States is a republic, not a democracy. But that's shallow thinking because "republic" refers only to the form, not to the substance. "Democracy" refers to the source of government power and the principles of governing. Such definitions should lead to the conclusion that the United States, under the Constitution, has a republican form of government based on democratic principles. An example of this misunderstanding of governmental terms came in a 1990 column by the assistant editorial-page editor of The Denver Post. That journalist wrote:

'I'm from the government. I'm here to help you.'

"That punchline is an old one and the joke is on us. We laugh at it because we know it is not the nature of government to help us. That's why freedom-loving people since the ancient Greeks have tried to enchain the power of government within republican constraints."

The writer didn't have a good grasp on constitutional reality because the founders created government to help the people, and power isn't enchained within "republican constraints," whatever they may be. A republic is merely a government headed by a leader selected by others, normally by election, but not necessarily an election in which the citizens participate. A small portion of the population is chosen to exercise power – heredity isn't a factor. This arrangement may look good on its surface, but Hitler's Nazi Germany and Stalin's Soviet Union were also republics, and few Americans would say their government powers were enchained. Many monarchies have had less power than those republics. No Jew "enchained" the power of the Third Reich when the leaders of that republic used the "Final Solution" to murder more than six million Jews. No Kulak could petition Stalin's republic for a redress of grievance when the state decided to collectivize society to control the economy, which meant eliminating them.

How America's Founding Fathers felt about a republican government can be found in Federalist Paper No. 39. James Madison made it clear many European republics were unacceptable, and the new nation shouldn't be compared to them. The Founding Fathers understood the proper manner in which power is given to a government. They weren't confused, or uncertain about what they were doing when creating the Constitution.

John Jay said it best in Federalist Paper No. 2. He wrote: "Nothing is more certain than the indispensable necessity of government, and it is equally undeniable ... the people must cede to it some of the natural rights, in order to vest it with requisite powers."

Some people are convinced that the United States was founded on "Judeo-Christian principles," and created as a "Christian nation." Jay's statement should tell them otherwise. He said "natural rights," a phrase some religionists think is a "secular humanist" principle. Jay made it clear, that governmental powers came from the people, not from God. The Constitution says in Article VI that "no religious Test shall ever be required as Qualification to any Office or public Trust under the United States." That clause means the United States is not a theocracy; theocratic government is an un-American form of government.

Jay's statement says "the people must cede" powers to the government. The Preamble of the Constitution says, "We the People of the United States ..." There's nothing in either statement suggesting a superior, or elite, class of people as the source of power. There's nothing suggesting power is to be exercised for the benefit of one group, or class, to the exclusion of other groups or classes.

Article I, Section 9, of the Constitution says, "No Title of Nobility shall be granted by the United States," and adds that U.S. office holders cannot accept titles of any kind from kings, princes or foreign nations without consent of Congress. Section 10 says that states cannot grant titles of nobility. These clauses mean that principles of aristocracy are not found in the Constitution. Aristocracy is, therefore, an un-American system.

Jay's statement says the people must cede some of their natural rights in order to create necessary powers for the new government. He didn't say states must cede their powers, or government has powers it automatically gets from itself just because it's government. The Tenth Amendment in the Bill of Rights echoes Jay's statement when it says, "The powers not delegated to the United States by the Constitution ..." That clause makes it clear that powers of government come from a source outside government. That source, according to Jay, is the people, which means autocracy is not a Constitutional tenet but is an un-American principle.

Jay said power was to be ceded by the people; it was not confiscated by military conquest. The Constitution says in Article I, Section 6, "... no person holding any Office under the United States, shall be a Member of either House during his continuance in office." That rule keeps military officers out of the law-making or law-enforcing functions of government.

Article I, Section 8, says in the 14th paragraph that Congress has power, "To make Rules for the Government and Regulation of the land and naval Forces;" which means the military is subordinated to Congress' will;

it isn't a source of governmental powers. Jay and the Constitution make it clear that principles of militocracy aren't constitutional, they are un-Americanism.

The only principles of the five forms of government to be found in the United States Constitution, or in the writings of the Founding Fathers, are the principles of democracy. Democratic principles, therefore, are the only forms of true American principles. All other governmental principles are unconstitutional and un-American, and people who adhere to them are un-American.

THE FOUNTAIN OF POWER

Americans have heard slogans indicating government springs from the people, but they obviously haven't fully accepted that concept. Abraham Lincoln's statement in the 1863 Gettysburg Address about "government of the people, by the people and for the people" is the most-noted such statement. "By the people" means the citizenry created the government, and because government is power, it's the people's power that government uses. Ignorance about the source of governmental power was reflected in a report on two important Supreme Court decisions in June of 1990, by USA TODAY, which wrote:

"A splintered Supreme Court Monday gave states new powers to intervene in two hotly contested areas of medical choice: limiting teens' access to an abortion and restricting comatose patients' right to die.

"In the right-to-die case:

"The court ruled 5-4 that Missouri can prohibit the removal of feeding tubes from a woman in a 'persistent vegetative state' since a 1983 crash."

That reporting was wrong. The Supreme Court didn't give the state of Missouri any powers; new, old or otherwise. The Supreme Court doesn't have powers to give, it has only judicial powers to carry out its duties to decide controversies and to order corrective remedies. In using the phrase "new powers," the newspaper sounded as if the Supreme Court could conjure up powers from a vacuum and bestow those newly created powers on any governmental body it wishes. The court cannot do that. The court doesn't create powers for others; it decides if others are making proper use of the powers they have, or are trying to create powers for themselves.

This wasn't a right-to-die case, though much of the American media reported it as such. The case involved efforts of the woman's parents to allow their daughter to "die with dignity" by having the feeding tubes that kept her alive for seven years removed. The state hadn't allowed the tubes to

Government as Power

be removed even though there was no medical hope of survival for the comatose woman.

The unstated point USA TODAY missed is that Missouri relied on legitimate and existing "police power" to protect this woman's life from the actions of others; in this case the medical practitioners who were caring for her. Missouri wasn't arguing for a new power; police power is the main power of government, and the state already had that. The need for police power was what made government necessary in the first place. Missouri – even though it didn't use the exact words – based its position on the contention that all Missourians empowered that state, through their constitutional covenant at the time of its creation, with police powers to protect and punish. Missouri didn't petition the Supreme Court for permission or power to act in a certain area; it acted in the first place on the conviction its police powers covered its actions. The Supreme Court only said Missouri was correct.

In writing the majority opinion, Chief Justice William Rehnquist made it clear that a state shouldn't suspend its power of protection to an individual without knowing that person's explicit desires. It's not necessary to mention police power to understand that it's present. Police power has been given to the state by everyone, to be used for the protection of everyone, either individually or collectively.

The condition of a person's mental or conscious state doesn't alter a state's exercise of its powers in regard to that person, and the state doesn't make value judgments about the use of its power based on statements by a third party. The state owes police-power protection to every person until that individual speaks for him/herself and waives that protection. When that protection is explicitly waived, a person's right to die is secured.

To "die with dignity" should be the fate of all humans, and such a death should be preferable to a "vegetative" existence lacking meaning or hope. The family might have taken the utmost moral position, especially in a society calling itself Christian and teaching a person's final reward is an eternity in paradise. Missouri, in denying that afterlife paradise, seems to be opposing that morality. But the state was judged to be constitutionally correct because morality isn't a constitutional principle, and calls of morality don't negate a legitimate governmental power.

By reporting this as a right-to-die case, America's media missed the point. Everyone has the right to die and, until death is conquered, everyone has the destiny to die. This was a police-power case. As a police-power case, the Missouri legislature has authority to put up "stop signs" at points where Missouri's state power ought to end, which was partly done later with legislation some thought still left the state too much leeway for interference in family matters.

The manner in which the media reported this case again shows the "engine of democracy" malfunctioning because many "drivers" lack basic knowledge of that engine's "horsepower."

If USA TODAY had been correct on the court's access-to-abortion decision, it would be saying no state ever had power to regulate abortion; the power over human reproduction came into being by this decision in 1990. States seem to be saying they have always had the power to regulate abortions because they keep enacting such laws. Chapter 10 shows the states are wrong.

The newspaper's casual reporting about government powers would suggest that the United State's federal system of government was based on the principles of autocracy, which has been shown to be un-American doctrine. The national government doesn't give powers to the state governments, just as the state governments didn't give power to the federal government when it came into existence. Under the United States' constitutional system, all governments get all powers from all people at all times.

The powers the people give to their governments have two forms – specific powers and implied powers. There are no unknown or mystery powers; all powers are found in the constitutions of the federal government or the state governments. If it's impossible to find a power, it's impossible to have a law or action based on this unfindable power. The Supreme Court has been saying that for more than 200 years, but many people have yet to understand the court's message. Specific federal powers are easy to find; most congressional powers are listed in Article I of the Constitution. Presidential powers are in Article II, while judicial powers are in Article III. There are other powers scattered about, and they are findable. But, not all people can recognize a power, even though it is listed. Several examples of powers going unrecognized by critics of Constitution and court are spread throughout these pages.

Implied powers are harder to find, but they can be uncovered with a thorough understanding of the Constitution. The last paragraph of Article I, Section 8, reflects implied powers by saying Congress has the power, "To make all Laws which shall be necessary and proper for carrying into Execution the foregoing Powers, and all the Powers vested by this Constitution in the Government of the United States, or in any Department or Office thereof." In considering the Tenth Amendment, Congress purposely altered the proposed phrase "powers not expressly delegated" to read "powers not delegated" in order to preserve implied powers.

Government as Power

Examples of implied powers: Congress has no explicit power to create, fund or operate the Internal Revenue Service, but it does have power to "collect Taxes, Duties, Imposts and Excises." The IRS is a creation of an implied power. Congress must have an implied power to conduct hearings and proscribe punishment to those who perjure themselves before such hearings, because it has power to make law. Few people would want a legislative body making law without accurate knowledge about problems addressed.

Powers need to be broad to be usable over time. What was not considered a problem in a sparsely populated nation of less than four million people in 1789, may need governmental action in 1889 or 1989, and flexible powers allow government to act. To protect the rights of many minorities in the United States, Congress had to rely on its power to regulate commerce. The grant of power reads "To regulate Commerce with foreign Nations, and among the several States, and with the Indian Tribes." Such a statement puts no limitations on use of power, and shouldn't be interpreted to mean regulatory power is limited to products, sales or contracts. The absence of restrictions, makes the power broad and nonspecific, and "regulate" isn't defined. Many social problems have been solved, and many civil rights protected, by government using its power to regulate commerce.

One example of a behavior not considered a problem in one period of history being viewed much differently at later times is settling feuds by dueling. Shortly after the United States was formed, former Vice President Aaron Burr killed Hamilton in an 1804 duel following a political life of animosity between the two. For his act, Burr received only discredit, showing the act was beginning to lose favor after a long history of being an acceptable way to preserve personal honor. Today the practice has been expunged from civilized society because it's no longer acceptable to the majority of people. Constitutions don't need to mention dueling by name, they only need to give government the power to act. And governments have acted, to the point that any modern duel more dangerous than dirty words at thirty paces could be illegal.

Another constitutional principle is power needs to be consistent. When a state needs a legitimate power to act, it has a legitimate power to act, and that power isn't diminished by outside factors. A power valid in one situation is not invalid in another situation. An example came in 1990 when the Supreme Court decided a drug-use case, Oregon vs. Smith, after Oregon punished an Indian employee of the state for smoking peyote during a religious ceremony. The ruling only meant that the law banning use of controlled substances isn't invalidated because those substances were used in the name of religion. No mature person would argue that religious practices should take precedence over a valid government power; there should be no sacrifices of virgins or children in the name of religion. The argument that smoking peyote in a religious context is such a minor incident that it should be immune from state power was also rejected. Constitutions don't give differing degrees of power. The state can act or it cannot act. If it has power to outlaw the use of hard drugs, such as cocaine and heroin, it has power to outlaw the use of soft drugs. To outlaw or not to outlaw are political questions to be handled by legislatures, which would determine if an act is a felony, a misdemeanor, or is legal.

A state legislature can outlaw or regulate growing, harvesting, refining, manufacturing, transporting and selling of any drug, hard or soft, because it has power to regulate intrastate commerce. The state can outlaw or regulate the providing to another person by any method of any drug it deems harmful because of its police power to protect individuals from actions of others. Whether smoking peyote falls under those two powers wasn't the issue; states have always assumed their powers could control drug use, and no court decision has said otherwise. If freedom of religion negated the power to regulate a minor act, it would negate power over a major act. Only legislation can make exemptions to laws. Congress did that in 1993 with the Religious Freedom Restoration Act, allowing an exemption on drug use in a religious situation. Whether such interfering with equal treatment under law or making a law concerning only religion is valid or not is still subject to court judgment.

Governments have too long been captive to the thought that separation of church and state would preclude action in religious areas. Many things that were punished if done in secular society were overlooked if done in religion; the most obvious being the obtaining of money under false pretenses. In secular society that could be called fraud. In religion that may be called "accepting a love gift." Recent convictions of religious leaders for various acts have been closing that "loophole." Applying secular criminal law to religious figures is not the persecution some people claim; it's a consistent-and-equal application of government powers. Persecution would be present if a religious act was punished while a similar act done in secular areas wasn't punished.

The argument for applying laws equally leads back to the 1989 Los Angeles Times complaint about a Supreme Court decision concerning execution of teen-agers and the mentally retarded. That complaint, voiced in an editorial cited in Chapter 1, said: "With its decision that the Constitution does not forbid execution of teen-agers and the mentally retarded, the Supreme Court has done violence not only to the Eighth Amendment, but also to the ability of Americans to stand unblushing among civilized nations of the world."

The Times argument is immaterial. The Constitution doesn't mention differing degrees of power or exemptions to legal governmental power for any particular groups or people. Like the Missouri case, that's a political question. If teen-agers and the mentally retarded are to be spared the death penalty, it would have to be through political actions of the legislatures that make the law. The court should not be attacked and belittled because it reminded lawmakers that judges cannot alter the words or meaning of the Constitution because executing the young and retarded is barbaric to some people. Many people think any execution by the state, regardless of any "justification," is barbaric. The Fourteenth Amendment only says no "State (may) deprive any person of life, liberty, or property, without due process of law ..." The Fifth Amendment says the same thing about federal power. A "Rule of Opposites" makes that mean that with due process of law a state may deprive a person of life, liberty or property. On this point, USA TODAY was wrong when it wrote in an April, 1994, editorial that the death penalty " ... can't be reconciled with the Constitution."

Like the Oregon peyote-smoking case, this capital-punishment controversy falls into the category of consistency of powers. The power to execute is consistent and can be applied as the law specifies if that law doesn't violate any other constitutional standard. The Constitution doesn't say or imply there's an IQ too low or an age too young, even though the court seemed to suggest that in 1988 with a ruling that those 15 and younger are excluded from capital punishment.

When the Times mentioned that Iran, Iraq, Bangladesh and Barbados were the only other members of the United Nations executing persons who murdered before the age of 18, it missed another important constitutional point. What other nations do has absolutely no bearing on what the United States or its 50 states are empowered to do. The Supreme Court doesn't make decisions on other nation's principles or lack of principles.

Advocates of capital punishment also miss the point in this argument. Before a notable Florida execution, columnist Don Warrensford, of the Gannett Corporation's Florida Today newspaper, railed against opponents of the death penalty by writing in 1989: "Alas, some will still sue for mercy in behalf of the rogues who kill us. Those advocates give 'obnoxious' a new meaning. So it isn't surprising that they've been pleading for mercy for (mass murderer) Ted Bundy over the past several days." This statement couldn't be more off the mark, because opponents of capital punishment aren't suing for mercy for "the rogues who kills us." People oppose capital punishment to prevent the state from being one of those rogues, and that's not advocating mercy for Bundy; it's trying to prevent Florida from doing what Bundy did – kill a human. Whether convicted murderers "deserve to die" doesn't create the power to kill them.

Another Gannett columnist, DeWayne Wickham, in opposing capital punishment, wrote: "Earlier this year, Supreme Court justices gave in to their rage – not their hearts – and said it was all right for states to put to death juveniles or retarded persons who commit capital crimes."

That statement is nonsense. Journalism may be governed by rage and heart conditions, the Supreme Court is not. The court makes decisions on what the Constitution says, and what the Constitution says is in the Fifth and Fourteenth Amendments. The judges' rage and hearts should have nothing to do with their decision. It's possible some were opposed to capital punishment, but, as with Oliver Wendell Holmes, their personal politics are buried by the words of the Constitution; that's an admirable trait expected of all judges.

To requote Justice Anthony Kennedy: "The Constitution cannot be thrown about as a panacea for every social ill." That means even if Americans think the greatest social ill is for a state to kill one of its citizens, they cannot call on the Constitution to stop it, because the Constitution doesn't do that.

Because a state gets its power from the people, the presence of capital punishment suggests each individual has an inherent right to terminate life in some circumstances. Jay's description of the formation of government would suggest the population surrendered the power to kill to the state. The state cannot create its own power to execute.

Strict adherence to constitutional principles does bring beneficial results. The right to petition government creates long delays and large legal expenses before a person is executed. Such was the case when Illinois executed mass murder John Wayne Gacy in May of 1994 for the slayings of 33 boys and young men in Chicago. He had been convicted in 1980. The long appeals process is criticized by many – especially relatives of the victims – but it has positive aspects by retarding government's innate desire to exercise capricious authority over its citizens because the constitutional principles used to delay execution are the same principles that protect law-abiding citizens from government. The cost of the appeals process often runs into millions of dollars, and that too retards the capriciousness of government. When faced with such delays and costs, governments will be exceptionally judicious before embarking on a mission to kill one of its citizens. Many authorities believe that as many as 23 innocent people have been executed in this century for crimes they didn't commit, and recent developments in extending the process for a decade or more should reduce that number in the future.

Power must also be real; it can't be created by subterfuge or inaction. An example of governmental bodies trying to use imaginary powers by refusing to act was illustrated for three decades following the *Brown v. Board of Education* decision (1954) which found that segregated public schools violated the equal-protection clause of the Fourteenth Amendment. This decision didn't say it was only unconstitutional to create segregation, it's also un-American to maintain this subversion by devious means such as building new schools in the middle of minority and white neighborhoods then drawing attendance lines to maintain that racial separation.

Conditions leading to segregation aren't at issue because the Constitution doesn't indicate "housing patterns," or any other outside influence, would legalize an illegal state action legal. It also isn't possible to create a legal power to segregate schools, or other public facilities, through "voluntarism." But states and school boards in all areas of the nation assumed that if they did nothing to integrate, they could continue segregation. Some seemed to be saying that if the population adopted a voluntary plan, but didn't voluntarily desegregate, a segregated system could continue. What the population does really doesn't matter; it's what the governmental body does that counts.

STATES' WRONGS, NOT RIGHTS

If there's one concept that should have stood out, and been recognized by now, it's that states and governments have powers, not rights. The "States Rights" movement, which reached its zenith with the awareness in the 20th century that civil rights were to be taken seriously by government at the national level, is a fraud. States have never, in the history of the world, held rights. States have power – that is all they have – for government is power. People have rights. Jay's statement that the people must cede to government some of their natural rights in order to vest it with power clearly divides the two: rights are the property of the people; power is the property of the states.

A statement by the Los Angeles Times in a review of then-proposed Supreme Court Judge Kennedy in 1987 read: "In weighing the rights and powers of individuals and jurisdictions, Kennedy holds particularly dear the protection of states' rights."

This is a situation that both Kennedy and the Times should have recognized as being impossible; judges can't protect what doesn't exist. Jay told us the rights people give up are transposed into power for government by means of the United States Constitution. If that's acceptable as a truism, then it's also true the same thing occurred with the creation of state constitutions before and after the federal Constitution was created. The Constitution nowhere mentions or implies rights as belonging to states. In every mention of rights, they are tied to individuals.

Because rights, according to Jay, are transposed into power by means of a constitution, rights and power cannot be held side by side by the state under that constitution. A state either has rights or it has power; it does not have both. Individual rights and state power exist within an uneasy truce, power being a natural enemy of rights. Government power exists much like a superior beast in the food chain, gobbling the smaller and weaker rights in order to grow bigger and stronger.

Sen. Strom Thurmond, R-S.C., who ran for president on the States' Rights Democratic ticket in 1948, served as a spokesman for states' rights in a column he wrote for USA TODAY in 1984. Senator Thurmond penned:

"To understand the doctrine of states' rights, we must first focus on three points:

"– States' rights is merely a shorthand label to indicate that states have certain responsibilities under our federal Constitution.

"– The history of our country underscores the importance of states' rights.

"– Our Constitution gives implicit and explicit support to the doctrine of states' rights."

Senator Thurmond was perfectly correct in stating that states have certain responsibilities under the federal Constitution, and those responsibilities were to be carried out through the powers given to the states. Thurmond didn't say that the states, in many instances, failed to live up to those responsibilities; too often exercising their power for only part of their citizens, not for all.

It was Thurmond's beloved South that denied its black citizens the right to vote for many years by using several devious methods to keep them disenfranchised. But no power to do this was ever given to the Southern state governments. All power given to them was given equally by both black and white citizens, and states didn't get from black citizens the power to deny blacks the right to participate in public business. Whites never had the power to deny blacks the voting right; therefore, they couldn't empower the states such authority.

On the second point, Thurmond's statement doesn't reflect reality. A study published in the 1981 book The *Supreme Court* by Prof. Lawrence Baum of Ohio State University casts an understanding light on the matter of states' devotion to constitutional principles. Professor Baum reported that through 1978 (the year his study was completed) the Supreme Court had overturned parts or all of 105 federal laws. By that year, Congress had passed more than 60,000 laws. That's not a bad ratio when one considers that knowledge of the Constitution isn't required to be in Congress and the Supreme Court was wrong in a few of those cases. It's also important to note that very few of those laws were of major importance. A third of those overturned were from the economic-regulation era of the 1920s-30s (when the Supreme Court was sometimes wrong) and the civil-rights era of the 1960s-70s (when the Supreme Court was often misunderstood). By the same year, Baum reported, the court had nullified 1,007 state laws and local ordinances. He said that's a misleading number since the court voids only one state action while the decision may invalidate laws of the other 49 states. Baum also said this number doesn't include state administrative and judicial practices that were also negated. Thurmond was wrong – the history of our country underscores the disregard the states have had for constitutional government. Justice Holmes commented on this obvious truth by saying, "The United States would not come to an end if we lost our power to declare an Act of Congress void." He added, "I do think the union would be imperiled if we could not make that declaration as to the laws of the several states."

As to the third point, the Constitution gives absolutely no support to the doctrine of states' rights. All the Constitution says on the matter is found in the Bill of Rights. The Ninth Amendment says: "The enumeration in this Constitution, of certain rights shall not be construed to deny or disparage others retained by the people." That means rights, under the Constitution, belong to the people. Nowhere in that statement does it say, imply or, in any way, suggest that rights are retained by states.

The Tenth Amendment says: "The powers not delegated to the United States by this Constitution, nor prohibited by it (the Constitution) to the states, are reserved to the States respectively, or to the people." That clearly means that government – federal and state – have powers, not rights. It also says the people have powers, such as illustrated by the man north of the river, the man south of the river, the fool on the hill and the farmer in the dell. The Constitution recognizes them – the people – as the source of its authority. Granting authority for government to regulate our lives isn't a one-time, unrepeated event. Giving such power must be an ever-existing, eternally continuous action – much like loving or living – in order to include powers of everyone entering or exiting the realm of that government.

THE UN-AMERICANS

Later in the same column, Thurmond wrote, "From the beginning of our constitutional form of government, there was an implicit understanding that individual states retain certain rights."

Thurmond was wrong; there never was such an understanding. There was an understanding that the people reallocated some government power to create the federal government and thereby left some power in the hands of the states. The states retained certain powers, not rights; that's what the Tenth Amendment says. The Constitution's wording clearly shows that a doctrine of states' rights is not included in the United States Constitution and is, therefore – under Justice Antonin Scalia's definition – un-American.

This misguided concept of states' rights was the driving force behind the violent struggles for civil rights in the 1960s. By claiming such a concept, those persons who would use government power to benefit themselves, their friends and their allies while denying equal treatment or protection for black Americans, were trying to give credibility to an un-American concept. To defend this un-Americanism, they blamed all the troubles at civil-rights demonstrations on "outside agitators." They may have been correct; they were just wrong about the identity of the "outside agitators."

When modern thoughtful Americans look back on those struggles, they can see that the civil-rights workers going into the South to combat racism were doing so to protect the constitutional covenant. The real American patriots were those people who came from hundreds of burgs in North and South, East and West, and who rallied in defense of the covenant. Those battling them in an attempt to prevent equality for all were the real "outside agitators" because they were outside the covenant and against the covenant. The "outside agitators" were governors standing in school-house doors to keep some American children out; they were mayors and police officials ordering the use of police dogs, fire hoses and electric cattle prods to keep some constitution-seeking Americans "in their place." Those wearing the uniforms of police officers and sheriff deputies who carried out those anti-constitutional orders and those prosecutors and judges who failed to put a stop to this un-Americanism were also "outside agitators." And they were cheered on by ordinary white citizens, the final group of "outside agitators."

Chapter 5

POWERS THAT BE

PRINCIPLE LOST

Everyone who has ever sat in a civics class of an American school has been taught that the United States government operates on the principle of "separation of powers." But it seems many Americans haven't properly determined what that phrase means, and its mention has been reduced into nothing more than "speaking Sloganese." It's disturbing that this separation goes unnoticed by many people who have made government their careers and may be in a position to erase the line between the three branches of government. Many of them conduct government business as if "power" is the only word they can define. People in private life, trying to survive in a money-based society, shouldn't be expected to keep constitutional principles intact; that must be handled by those who administer government's power. This obligation isn't to be restricted to elected officials; it must be protected by all people in government. "Separation of power" refers to only one power – government power – which is divided into legislative, executive and judicial powers.

A situation where the constitutional principle of separation of powers was lost to politics was the Iran-contra affair of the 1980s, during the administration of Ronald Reagan. Whether a main "culprit," retired Marine Lt. Col. Oliver North, was a heroic patriot or committed common crimes isn't an issue here; separation of government power is the only issue.

The incident concerned whether the power of the President to formulate foreign policy took precedence over law. Congress had enacted law prohibiting financial aid for the rebel contras trying to overthrow the Sandinista government of Nicaragua. The administration attempted to get around that law by selling arms to Iran to raise money to finance a Nicaraguan civil war. North was a star player in this game.

An important point is that this was a government action, carried out by government officials, drawing government salaries, working in government offices in the name of the United States government. They were dealing with government property which, when sold, generated government income. One of the most-important constitutional principles of the United States is that the government needs to have legal authority for any action of its personnel. Motives are never sufficient to allow a governmental act. A self-proclaimed sense of patriotism, or personal opposition to any other form of government, never justifies an act by a United States official. There is nothing in the Constitution to suggest other philosophies are to be abhorred; they just are not to be instituted in the United States.

An apologist for North wrote in a guest column in USA TODAY: "Forgotten in the grand hurrah from those on the left who abhor patriotism and hate what this country stands for is the plight of Nicaragua. Oliver North tried to save Nicaragua from communist dictatorship."

Of course, nonsensical words such as these also have nothing to do with the constitutional issue, nor do they legitimize questionable actions by a government official.

(An observation: the views of the former U.S. intelligence analyst who wrote this book is that disobeying law and Constitution is not "patriotism" or "what this country stands for." Wanting officials to obey laws, just as everyone else must do, isn't abhorring patriotism. The claim that North "was trying to save Nicaragua from communist dictatorship" is equally questionable because the aim seemed to be returning Nicaragua to virtually the same right-wing dictatorship that the so-called communist Sandinistas had displaced. Dictatorship on the right is just as distasteful as dictatorship of the left, and apologizing for the Iran-contra mess is the same as apologizing for dictatorship. Many dreaded American leftists also had been telling the world for decades that communism would eventually do away with itself, so it was stupid to slaughter millions of people in dictatorial crusades under the guise of anti-communism. The events of 1989-91 in Europe have proven the left correct. Democratic republics do not come into existence "snap, crackle and pop" with revolution; they evolve over long periods of time as people learn about and yearn for democratic principles.)

North's secretary testifying in congressional hearings cited the doctrine of "higher law" as justification of the Iran-contra affair. In his defense at his trial, North said he wasn't shocked with a proposal and creation of an entity that was accountable to no one but itself. He said he couldn't see where it violated any law, regulation or policy.

These two points certainly relate to the Constitution. North's secretary was partly correct in citing a higher law; there are really two higher laws; one spiritual, the other constitutional. The first, and probably the most-important higher law, is found in the Bible at Leviticus 19:18, Matthew 22:37-39, and 1 Peter 2:17. That law, in the King James version, says:

1) "... thou shalt love thy neighbor as thyself;"

2) "Jesus said unto him, 'Thou shalt love the Lord thy God with all thy heart, and with all thy soul, and with all thy mind. This is the first and great commandment. And the second is like unto it, Thou shalt love thy neighbor as thyself.' "

3) "Honour all men. Love the brotherhood. Fear God. Honour the king."

The second higher law states' "All legislative Powers herein granted shall be vested in a Congress of the United States, which shall consist of a Senate and House of Representatives." This second higher law is the first sentence of the Constitution. It's the foremost principle in the separation of powers, which is why the Founding Fathers put it first. It was put first because the founders knew the dangers of despotic government brought about by arbitrary lawmaking by kings, queens or colonels.

The higher law of the Constitution says "All legislative Powers;" it does not say "some legislative powers," "most legislative powers" or "nearly all legislative powers." There's nothing there to suggest that legislative powers are to be shared with a president or that administration policy is in any way superior to an act of Congress. It should be evident that North was wrong about creation of a government body by the executive branch. Such a creation may not have violated minor laws, regulations or policy; it violated the supreme higher law. That higher law – the Constitution – empowers Congress with authority to create because it says Congress has power, "To make all Laws which shall be necessary and proper for carrying into execution the foregoing powers, and all other powers vested by this Constitution in the Government of the United States, or in any department or Officer thereof." This statement, paragraph No. 18 of Section 8 in Article I, relates to all laws, all powers, all departments and all officers. That empowerment means if a governmental body must be created to carry out a function of government, Congress must make the law which creates that body. Article XI adds that "all Laws of the United States ... shall be the supreme Law of the Land;" which must mean that if a congressional law says "no" to the administration, it says "no." The higher law of the Constitution also says in Article I, Section 9, that spending of the nation's money must be authorized by law and any spending must be accounted for with published accounts.

There's nothing in any of these constitutional principles that would suggest that Congress can be bypassed merely because a doctrinaire administration does not agree with its law or if there's a perception Congress was wrong in its laws. Congress isn't required to be perfect.

The Constitution says the law-making branch of government is composed of a Senate and a House of Representatives, and nothing more. There's no allowance for any other entity – whether it be president, department, commission – to be part of the legislative process other by than proposing law or signing a bill once passed. Another entity may write a regulation to enforce laws Congress made, but regulation writing must be authorized by law. And if Congress is "wrong," the administration can propose "correct" law.

It's not surprising that people who can't find the first sentence of the Constitution also can't find a higher law in the Bible, even those who profess to follow its teachings. The Iran-contra affair didn't reflect love of fellow human beings; it reflected a hatred based merely on theory and application of politics. To illegally arm dictatorial forces to slaughter other dictatorial forces has absolutely nothing to do with "love thy neighbor" or "Honour all men." These commandments also aren't restricted to American neighbors or men, they pertain to all humans. The constitutional and biblical "higher laws" weren't specifically cited by North's secretary, but they are the only "higher laws" that could apply to the situation, and they were violated just as congressional law was violated.

When Alexander Hamilton wrote that "the safest course for your liberty" was through the Constitution, he was referring to a government in which Congress makes law, a president executes law, and courts settle controversies arising from law. Any other method of conducting affairs of state is counter to the Constitution and as such, using Justice Antonin Scalia's definition, is un-Americanism.

LEGISLATIVE POWERS

Between the Constitution's first sentence and Section 8, where most of Congress' powers are found, are powers which are internal to the operation of government and are mostly noncontroversial.

Section 2 deals with composition of the House of Representatives, qualifications for its members and allocation of representation among the states.

Section 3 does the same for the Senate but adds the power of impeachment.

Section 4 provides for the election of Congress.

Section 5 provides for making rules for Congress.

Section 6 provides for paying a congressional salary.

Section 7 provides guidelines for enacting law. (The complete article is in the Appendix.)

Section 8 is the depository for powers Congress can use to regulate the nation. Most of these powers are so obvious they are easily recognized. Others are not. Not recognizing constitutional powers and principles isn't restricted to journalists, colonels and secretaries; many people, including politicians wanting "government off the people's backs," also can't find certain powers.

A case of not finding a power is the statement of a less-government organization calling itself TRIM (Tax Reform IMmediately), and claiming to be a national movement. In a 1983 bulletin, TRIM said: "The Constitution authorizes the Federal Government to protect our God-given rights and to provide for the common defense. It does not authorize fedgov to provide foreign aid handouts, temporary loans for unemployed homeowners, unemployment health insurance, subsidized housing units, food stamps, agriculture price supports, or other share-the-wealth schemes."

In 1985, the same organization stated, "Congress does not have the authority to provide aid for economic development, farm programs, child nutrition programs, or health and human services."

TRIM was wrong. The Constitution provides for such programs, and many more programs some people think are unauthorized. The problem here is not that "fedgov" has exceeded its authority; it is that the TRIM leaders may not fully understand the Constitution.

When the founders designated powers for Congress in Section 8 of Article I, the first was: "The Congress shall have Power to lay and collect Taxes, Duties, Imposts and Excises, to pay the Debts and provide for the common Defence and general Welfare of the United States; but all Duties, Imposts and Excises shall be uniform throughout the United States."

TRIM couldn't see the meaning for the words. In modern language, the meaning is, "Congress has the power to tax and spend for public well-being," as well as defense. The objectives of the new nation were mentioned in the Constitution's Preamble and one of those goals was to "promote the general Welfare." There's no definition for "general Welfare," so there would be implied power for Congress to define it when considering legislation. Congress can say "general Welfare" means loans, health insurance, gifts, housing, food stamps, price supports and other share-the-wealth schemes. Social Security, Medicare and any spending program promoting civilization, culture, decency and the well-being of society can be included, and can be stated with any words or phrases defining "general Welfare."

The Founding Fathers had no way of anticipating needs of future generations, so they didn't mention specific programs that could or could not be enacted, nor did they place prohibitions on needs that would be unknown or unanticipated in 1787. The founders knew such an arrangement was unworkable. They knew the Constitution wasn't to be a list of possible legislation; it was to give power to the new government so it could use legislation to create what might be needed to "promote the general Welfare" as need arose.

THE UN-AMERICANS

In Federalist No. 3 John Jay wrote that he saw Americans "firmly united under one federal government, vested with sufficient powers for all general and national purposes."

The founders could only trust that future generations could read the Constitution and determine what governmental actions were permitted. They had no intention of binding government to such an extent that it couldn't address society's problems; and if they made any mistake, it might have been that they overestimated the abilities of late-20th-century American minds.

Having a protest organization unable to find certain powers in the Constitution isn't a major concern because many people can find such powers. It's a different matter to populate Congress with people who can find no authorization to do certain things or who are unable to understand that the Constitution's Preamble specifies objectives for the United States government. These people would hinder, not help, the promotion of the general welfare.

Recent incidents demonstrate the reluctance of some elected officials to "promote the general Welfare." In 1990 Sen. Jesse Helms, R-N.C., attempted to block a bill authorizing $600 million for research of Acquired Immune Deficiency Syndrome (AIDS) and treatment of some victims. Helms' arguments suggested the victims of AIDS created their own problems and weren't entitled to assistance because of that. The Constitution doesn't agree with Senator Helms. It says "general Welfare" is entitled to government spending, and fighting AIDS certainly qualifies as "general Welfare" because controlling or conquering that condition will benefit society. A person doesn't need to be a physician to understand that diseases thrive on immune-system problems. It follows that any research into AIDS could lead medical science to cure or prevent other diseases such as cancer, Alzheimer's, the common cold, or any of hundreds of other maladies. No one knows what is yet to be discovered, so it's foolish to close avenues to future knowledge. If AIDS research does lead to cures for several diseases, then delay in beginning research funding could be a contributing factor in the death of millions of Americans who die just prior to discovery of cures. The very people who blocked funding may be among those not cured. Spending to seek cures or preventions of fatal or incapacitating illnesses is most obviously providing for the "general Welfare."

The cost of health care – even the most-basic care – in the United States was starting to come under scrutiny at the same time. With millions of people using their entire incomes to meet the cost of living, they're unable to pay for health insurance. If they can't afford insurance, they certainly can't pay for any needed health care. What to do about this problem was debated on the television show *Critical Choices: America's Health Crises* on Seattle's KING-TV in January of 1990. A member of the House of Representatives from the Seattle area stated that he didn't want to do anything about the situation because it might jeopardize the immediate availability of health care for his daughter, even if that care wasn't much more than cosmetic. This position was much more than insensitivity on the part of a man who had all the health-care protection he needed through the generosity of American taxpayers; it lashed out against the Constitutional objective of promoting the general welfare. The individual welfare of a well-paid politician isn't a constitutional principle; the well-being of all Americans is.

A third situation concerns funding of arts in America. Ongoing arguments over what sort of arts are to be funded, whether money should go into exhibits some person might consider obscene, or if the National Endowment for the Arts plays favorites with funding. Some people argue that government should stop spending money on the arts and leave funding to the "private sector." But if Congress decides a society with symphony orchestras is preferable to a society without, it has power to spend for symphonies. That's promoting the "general Welfare." The same holds true of painting, sculpture, photography, dance or drama companies, or any other art form. Many outside interests argue that government funds artists they don't think worthy and doesn't fund others some think more worthy. But Congress has power to spend for such purposes, so it has implied power to establish a funding plan. What others think is immaterial. Government funding for the Public Broadcasting Service has long been opposed, but if Congress decides an informed public is preferable to masses only entertained by commercial broadcasters, government can spend. In all instances, the "general Welfare" is being served by taxing and spending.

Other powers specifically given Congress are:

– "To borrow money on the Credit of the United States;" (This may be the most-abused power.)

– "To regulate Commerce with foreign Nations, and among the several States, and with the Indian Tribes;" (This will become the most-used power, if it isn't already. It has been used to protect rights of minorities, to create a healthy middle class and a powerful economy, and to help prevent environmental destruction.)

– "To establish an uniform Rule of Naturalization, and uniform Laws on the subject of Bankruptcies throughout the United States;" (The first half may be the most appreciated because it's through this power that most American families became American.)

– "To coin money, regulate the value thereof, and of foreign coin, and fix the Standard of Weights and Measures;" (This is a power tax protesters don't want to admit. It gives Congress the duty to determine what is of value. It doesn't require gold or silver coins, and doesn't require gold or silver to be used to support the value of paper money. It doesn't require coins to be minted in any particular way. What tax protesters think is immaterial.)

– "To provide for the Punishment of counterfeiting the Securities and current Coin of the United States;" (Self-explanatory.)

– "To establish Post Offices and post Roads;" (This is all that was needed to establish the federal highway system, although power to regulate interstate commerce could also have been enough, as could taxing and spending for the general welfare and providing for national defense.)

– "To promote the Progress of Science and useful arts, by securing for limited Times to Authors and Inventors the exclusive Right to their respective Writings and Discoveries;" (This covers patents and copyrights.)

– "To constitute Tribunals inferior to the supreme Court;"

– "To define and punish Piracies and Felonies committed on the high Seas, and Offenses against the Law of Nations;"

– "To declare War, grant Letters of Marque and Reprisal, and make Rules concerning Captures on Land and Waters;"

– "To raise and support Armies, but no Appropriation of Money to that Use shall be for a longer Term than two Years;" (This reflects the fear the Founding Fathers had of permanent professional armies. Armies were to be raised when needed and disbanded when not needed. Such an arrangement would be unrealistic today.)

– "To makes Rules for the Government and Regulation of the land and naval Forces;"

– "To provide and maintain a Navy;" (There wasn't an equal fear of a navy, which would help delay an invader until an army could be raised.)

– "To provide for calling forth the Militia to execute the Laws of the Union, suppress Insurrections and repel Invasions;" (These state citizen armies would be the first land defenses against invaders until United States armies were raised, but the U.S. armies would be made from the militias.)

– "To provide for organizing, arming, and disciplining the Militia, and for governing such Part of them as may be employed in the Service of the United States, reserving to the States respectively, the Appointment of the Officers, and the Authority of training the Militia according to the discipline prescribed by Congress;"

– "To exercise exclusive Legislation in all Cases whatsoever, over such District (not exceeding ten Miles square) as may, by cession of particular

States, and the acceptance of Congress, became the Seat of Government of the United States, and to exercise like Authority over all Places purchased by the Consent of the Legislature of the State in which the Same shall be, for the erection of Forts, Magazines, Arsenals, dock-Yards, and other needful Buildings; – And

– "To make all Laws which shall be necessary and proper for carrying into execution the foregoing Powers, and all other Powers vested by this Constitution in the Government of the United States, or in any Department or Officer thereof." (This provision should be used more often by anyone who thinks government is too intrusive; it can be used to negate unnecessary laws or regulations.)

What's said in Section 8 of the Constitution granting powers to Congress should be obvious. What isn't obvious is what's not said, and understanding the Constitution requires knowing what isn't said.

LEGISLATIVE LIMITS

Empowering Congress wasn't the only thing on the minds of the founders. They knew a legislature will exceed its authority if not restrained. The Constitution does that following the granting of powers (Section 8) with prohibitions on Congress (Section 9) and on the states (Section 10).

Section 9 told Congress that it couldn't stop importation of slaves before the year 1808, but could impose an import tax. It's important for a future presentation to note that Congress could prohibit importing of slaves after 1808 because of this section, but wasn't given the power to prohibit slavery. This was a critical point to the infamous Dred Scott decision of 1857.

The second paragraph of Section 9 prohibits the suspension of the writ of Habeas Corpus except in dire situations. Other prohibitions were no Bill of Attainder or ex post facto Laws; no capitation, or other direct taxes (repealed by the 16th Amendment) except in proportion to the census; no export taxes; no preference in commerce of one state over others; all money taken from the Treasury must be by law; the United States can't grant titles of nobility.

The states had many powers taken from them by the Constitution, and Section 10 tells which ones they lost. This is the reallocation of powers discussed in Chapter 4 under the heading "States Wrongs, Not Rights." State functions were dramatically shifted by three Constitution paragraphs saying:

"No State shall enter into any Treaty, Alliance, or Confederation; grant Letters of Marque and Reprisal; coin Money; emit Bills of Credit; make any

THE UN-AMERICANS

Thing but gold and silver Coin a Tender in Payment of Debts; pass any Bill of Attainder, ex post facto Law, or Law impairing the Obligation of Contracts, or grant any Title of Nobility.

"No State shall, without the Consent of the Congress, lay any Imposts or Duties on Imports or Exports, except what may be absolutely necessary for executing its inspection Laws; and the net Produce of all Duties and Imposts, laid by any State on Imports or exports, shall be for the Use of the Treasury of the United States and all such Laws shall be subject to the Revision and Control of the Congress.

"No State shall, without the Consent of Congress, lay any duty of Tonnage, keeps Troops, or Ships of War in time of Peace, enter into any Agreement or Compact with another State, or with a foreign Power, or engage in War, unless actually invaded, or in such imminent Danger as will not admit of delay."

These prohibitions took from the states those powers that define a sovereign nation; forcing states into an inferior position in relationship to the newly created national government. The founders weren't interested in a system in which states would be coequals with the national government. Most limitations are beyond question. Judges, attorneys, professors and a few journalists can readily tell what powers states lost and how these limitations apply today. But many persons can't quite understand those words.

The first prohibition was all that was needed for the Union to justify its Civil War against the Confederate States of America when they banded together. It was un-American for Southern states to make "any Treaty, Alliance or Confederation" or "enter into any Agreement or Compact with another State" in their rebellion over opposition to slavery. This should suggest allegiance to such an unconstitutional act is un-American.

Tax protesters should be able to recognize the requirement of gold and silver as legal tender applied only to the states and is no longer in force, as Chapter 6 will explain. It was put into the Constitution to cure and prevent postrevolution problems that no longer exist, and it kept the states from circumventing the federal government's power to coin money for the nation.

When the Supreme Court negated New Deal regulation of interstate commerce in the 1930s, the judges cited legislative impairment of contracts as one of the reasons to void laws. The judges were wrong, as Justice Oliver Wendell Holmes often told them, because the prohibition against impairment of contracts applies only to the states. Many modern business executives hold to the idea that contractual impairment is unconstitutional. They are wrong. One of the four conditions of a contract is "legal objective," which suggests contracts have always been subject to legislative control.

PRESIDENTIAL POWERS

The first sentence of the Constitution's Article II states: "The executive Power shall be vested in a President of the United States of America." The Founding Fathers were able statesmen in colonies with executives administering laws passed by legislatures, they knew what "executive power" was and saw no need to define it. They might have served modern America better if they would have said what executive power wasn't, because it sometimes seems that presidents, governors and advisors don't understand their authority under constitutional government. Studying the constitutional powers the founders intended the president to have, and noting what powers are absent, should show how far the executive has strayed far from constitutional intentions.

The President's powers aren't numerous and shouldn't be hard to understand. They are found in Sections 2 and 3 of Article II. They are:

– "The President shall be Commander in Chief of the Army and navy of the United States, and the Militia of the several States, when called into actual Service of the United States:

– "he may require the Opinion in writing, of the Principal Officer in each of the executive Departments, upon any subject relating to the Duties of their respective Offices,

– "and he shall have Power to Grant Reprieves and Pardons for Offenses against the United States, except in Cases of Impeachment.

– "He shall have Power, by and with the Advice and Consent of the Senate, to make Treaties, provided two-thirds of the Senators present concur;

– "and he shall nominate, and by and with the Advice and Consent of the Senate, shall appoint Ambassadors, other public Ministers and Consuls, Judges of the supreme Court, and all other Officers of the United States, whose Appointments are not herein otherwise provided for, and which shall be established by Law; but the Congress may by Law vest the Appointment of such inferior Officers, as they think proper, in the President alone, in the Courts of Law, or in the Heads of Departments.

– "The President shall have Power to fill up all Vacancies that may happen during the Recess of the Senate by granting Commissions which shall expire at the End of their next Session.

– "He shall from time to time give to the Congress Information of the State of the Union, and recommend to their Consideration such Measures as he shall judge necessary and expedient;

– "he may, on extraordinary Occasions, convene both Houses, or either of them, and in Cases of Disagreement between them, with Respect to the

Time of Adjournment, he may adjourn them to such Time as he shall think proper;
 – "he shall receive Ambassadors and other public Ministers;
 – "he shall take Care that the Laws be faithfully executed,
 – "and shall Commission all the Officers of the United States."
The president's power to veto legislation is in Article I, Section 7, which deals with powers of Congress. It was put into Congress' Article I rather than the president's Article II to emphasize its purpose as a restriction on congressional power.

It's with good reason that modern presidents have been accused of exceeding their authority. The list of powers above shows there is nothing allowing the executive branch to go its own way, doing as it wishes with no restrictions on its behavior. Some powers are to be exercised in cooperation with Congress; others only apply after Congress has enacted law.

In the role as commander in chief, the president is restricted by Congress' power "To make Rules for the Government and Regulation of land and naval Forces;" because the commander is part of those land and naval forces and is to faithfully execute the laws in force, even those which might restrict presidential authority.

The powers to make treaties and appoint ambassadors aren't exclusive, as is obvious. They are to be exercised in co-operation with the Senate. This is intended to restrict the president's authority and make the exercise of foreign policy a jointly shared power. Thomas Jefferson wrote into the Declaration of Independence a condemnation of the British king for abuses in relations with the colonies – even though Parliament was more to blame – and the founders didn't want such a one-man policy-making arrangement for the new nation.

The "power to appoint" may be the most-confused presidential power. It doesn't say what most people think. After the Robert Bork nomination for a Supreme Court position, a Bork supporter got it wrong in a guest column in USA TODAY. That columnist, Bruce Fein, identified as a visiting fellow for constitutional studies at the Heritage Foundation, wrote: "The Constitution empowers the president to appoint Supreme Court justices, with the advice and consent of the Senate."

That's what the Constitution seems to say to careless readers, but it really says something entirely different. The Constitution empowers the president to "nominate" – not "appoint" – ambassadors, ministers, consuls and judges of the Supreme Court. "Nominate" only means to propose a person for approval by another body. After nominating, the president must receive approval from the Senate to make the appointment. In the political process, "nominate" means to put a person up for election to a particular office. That is what basically happens here. The president only puts names before the Senate to be "elected" ambassadors, ministers, consuls and judges. That's what the Constitution says. President Reagan couldn't appoint Bork to the Supreme Court because he didn't get approval in the Senate's "election." But the president does retain the option of not following through with the appointment, even if the candidate is approved by the Senate.

The constitutional principle here is that these important powers are shared by the president and Senate. The president isn't empowered to do as he wishes but must co-operate with the law-making branch of government. That co-operation is reflected in the presidential power to "recommend" to Congress "Measures as he shall judge necessary and expedient." This principle seems to have been rescinded in the past half century without that rescinding being recorded by words in a constitutional amendment.

Perhaps Americans deserved the savings-and-loan scandal that erupted in the late 1980s with multi-billion dollar expenditures to protect savers under the government's insured-desposit programs because voters have the obligation to know the person they are electing.

Whether such insurance programs are worthy isn't the issue; they're constitutional under the taxing-and-spending authority of Congress, under the regulation-of-commerce power and the power to regulate monetary values. It was all too easy for many to blame others for the failure of a large part of the industry without focusing on the constitutional powers that were intended to protect the nation. Congress was blamed for raising the insured limit to $100,000 from $40,000, but that didn't create the problem, only made it more expensive. Congressional easing of some regulation of the industry by law also wasn't the cause, but it may have allowed some problems to begin. Congress became the scapegoat for the mess and some members played a contributing part. But, in all fairness, Congress didn't have the major role in this drama.

The Founding Fathers envisioned a system that should have worked. If elected officials were obedient to the Constitution and not to their political backers, the crisis probably could have been contained if not averted. Several powers granted by the Constitution, including the separation of powers, were subverted in bringing on the savings-and-loan crisis. The Constitution gave legislative power to Congress and executive power to the president. That means Congress makes the laws, the president enforces the laws. To blame Congress for not supervising the savings-and-loan industry is nonsense because congressional oversight would breach the separation-of-powers doctrine of the Constitution.

THE UN-AMERICANS

Other subverted constitutional principles:

– The Constitution says the president "shall take Care that the Laws be faithfully executed," and that doesn't leave room for a president to ignore laws he doesn't like. This also applied to the Iran-contra affair. Ignoring law would be the same as repealing law, and the executive doesn't have that power. Real patriots learn to submerge personal views and obey the law, and a president must do the same thing if the republic is to continue. While the S&L crisis was building momentum, the executive branch was in charge of the regulators – that is "executive power." The president's oath of office requires him to "Faithfully execute the Office of President" and that means execute the laws faithfully, and the laws said to watch the bankers by enforcing the regulations that applied.

– The president is constitutionally mandated to "Commission (direct) all the Officers of the United States." The heads of all regulatory bodies are "Officers of the United States" and it was the responsibility of the president to direct them in their duties. If they weren't doing their duty because they didn't like the laws, the president was to see that they did their job or seek their removal. A bureaucratic official isn't authorized to reject any law; their duty is to enforce that law.

– The Constitution empowers the president to "require the Opinion in writing" of any regulatory officer. Detectable problems in the S&L industry or weaknesses in regulatory powers could have become part of the public record if this power had been used conscientiously. That could have helped halt the problem before it got out of hand.

– The president has power to "recommend to their (Congress') Consideration such measures as he shall judge necessary and expedient." If the regulations of the savings-and-loan industry were causing the crisis, the president could have proposed remedies at any time. There's no evidence that such a crusade was ever anticipated.

There is no constitutional principle allowing a president to supplant or abandon legitimate law, statutes, regulations, directives or the Constitution. Ignoring law and regulations, Constitution and oath of office contributed more to the S&L fiasco than did any act of Congress, and American voters have the obligation to elect people who obey law and Constitution. There is no constitutional principle allowing the executive branch to ignore law, so according to Justice Scalia's definition, the crisis was a monster of presidential un-Americanism, nothing else.

This desire by presidents to do as they wish with no regard to restrictions of law and Constitution has given birth to the doctrine of "executive privilege," which everybody can see, wasn't mentioned in the list of presidential powers. "Executive privilege" must, therefore, be an implied power, but implied under which explicit power? Like the implied powers of Congress, any implied power of the president must be used only in carrying out the duties of a specified power.

Two events during the Reagan administration may help explain this little known constitutional principle. In the first episode, the administration attempted to withhold legal documents from Congress concerning cleanup – or lack of cleanup – of toxic-waste dump sites.

An administrator, Anne Gorsuch of the Environmental Protection Agency, obeyed a Reagan decree and withheld the documents and was cited for contempt of Congress. Because Congress has the explicit power to legislate, it has an implied power to gather information relating to its mission. That's what it was legally trying to do in requesting the documents. The administration has power to execute the laws so it must need implied power to carry out its function. The key here is "carry out." Implied power of presidential privilege isn't valid if it's being used to thwart the creation or implementation of law. It cannot be used to prevent legal use of a constitutional power by another branch of government.

The second episode concerned the Iran-contra trial of Colonel North and involved whether President Reagan or then-Vice President George Bush should be required to testify in North's defense. Many North apologists argued for testimony that would show North "was only obeying orders." Conservative writer and lawyer Fein, who missed the point on the power to appoint, got the issue correctly in his support of executive privilege. He wrote, "As a defense witness, a president would confront a conflict of interest in undercutting a prosecution under a law he was constitutionally bound to execute." The president, as the chief of all federal prosecutors, can't be compelled to refute the very prosecution he heads. Executive privilege can be cited to prevent such conflicts.

But executive privilege also leads to problems with administrations that use it as an excuse for law making. That seemed to be the case following the 1989 massacre in China of students demonstrating for democratic reforms. Thousands of students studying in the United States feared for their lives if they were forced to return to China following graduation. Congress passed House Resolution 2712, the Emergency Chinese Immigration Relief Act, to allow them to stay in the United States legally. Rep. Nancy Pelosi, D-Calif., wrote the bill, which passed 403 to 0, only to be vetoed by President Bush, who said he could waive a legal requirement that students return home for two years before seeking immigrant status in the United States. In arguing for an override of that veto, Pelosi wrote in a guest column in USA

THE UN-AMERICANS

TODAY that, "Immigration law prohibits a waiver of the home residence visa requirement for Chinese students. A presidential directive will not change the law – only a new law will. And, since the Constitution states, 'Congress shall make all laws,' an act of Congress is required."

She could have added that the Constitution requires the president to "take Care that the Laws be faithfully executed," not changed by presidential fiat. Changing law by a president isn't a constitutional principle, executing the law is and the law called for all students to return home. In this case, Congress was the only body to offer constitutional protection to the Chinese students.

The last section of Article II says: "The President, Vice President and all civil Officers of the United States, shall be removed from Office on Impeachment for, and Conviction of, Treason, Bribery, or other high Crimes and Misdemeanors." It seems that presidents often miss the point of this statement. This section tells presidents and all officers they aren't free to commit crimes. There's no power to circumvent laws the rest of society must obey, and a president can't commission subordinates to be common criminals.

President Richard Nixon, in a 1977 television interview, said that any act approved by the president was legal. The Constitution says he was wrong. In Nixon's Watergate scandal, some burglars claimed innocence because they were serving their government. That was proven wrong; they were serving an administration that didn't understand the Constitution. An administration or a president isn't the government. Government is guided by a Constitution saying no treason, no bribery, no high crimes, no misdemeanors.

This was the same issue behind illegal break-ins by the Federal Bureau of Investigation under the guise of "national security." Under the direction of J. Edgar Hoover, the bureau used several illegal tactics, claiming it knew better than anyone else what must be done to protect the country. Civilian critics of government had no power to use to subvert the nation and intelligence agencies knew fairly well what foreign powers were up to. The FBI is a division of the executive branch of government and is subject to the "no crimes" provision of the Constitution.

Many law-enforcement agencies and individuals argue that it's too difficult to protect society and government because of numerous restraints. But restricting government was an "original intent" of the founders who knew restraints would help prevent the imposition of despotic government. One restraint was that government officials could not commit crimes. Criminal behavior by government officials is un-American.

JUDICIAL POWERS

Legislative and executive powers shouldn't be difficult to understand. Judicial power isn't as easy because the Founding Fathers didn't list specific powers one by one, all in a row, for everyone to see like they did with legislative and executive authorities.

The first sentence of Article III says, "The judicial Power of the United States shall be vested in one supreme Court, and in such inferior Courts as the Congress may from time to time ordain and establish." That's all it says. It doesn't define judicial power, and it doesn't put any limitations on that power. The Constitution doesn't say what the courts are empowered to do and it doesn't say what they cannot do. For this reason the Supreme Court is the least understood and, sometimes, the most vilified of all three branches of the government. But those knowledgeable in United States government have come to recognize the Supreme Court as being the least-dangerous branch of government – contrary to the howling of various conservative or liberal interests – and the most sympathetic to the individual. A legacy has grown throughout American history showing political conservatives hostile to regulation of commercial behavior, but endorsing massive regulation of individual actions, while political liberals would free individuals and control commerce. The Supreme Court has been called on to mediate the battle between these two political philosophies, and has done a much better job of it than critics of court and Constitution will ever admit.

All the Constitution says about judicial power is in Section 2, which states: "The judicial Power shall extend to all Cases, in Law and Equity, arising under this Constitution, the Laws of the United States and Treaties made, or which shall be made, under their Authority; – to all Cases affecting Ambassadors, other public Ministers and Consuls; – to all Cases of admiralty and maritime Jurisdiction; – to Controversies to which the United States shall be a party; – to Controversies between two or more States; – between a State and Citizens of another State (repealed by Eleventh Amendment); – Between Citizens of different States; – between Citizens of the same State claiming Lands under Grants of different States, and between a State, or the Citizens thereof, and foreign States, Citizens or Subjects." Section 2 also tells which cases begin in the Supreme Court; all others begin in lower courts to be appealed. Though the grant of judicial power seems too thin to decide what the Supreme Court can do, it is possible to determine its function.

One court critic writing for New York's Newsday newspaper couldn't determine the court's function as she complained in 1981 after a decision that said women may be excluded from registration for a military draft, if there's ever again a draft. The critic wrote: "The Constitution guarantees 'the right of the people to be secure in their persons, houses, papers, and effects, against unreasonable searches,' but still the court deems it appropriate for itself, not 'the people' to rule on the constitutionality of searches. By the same logic, while the Constitution gives Congress the power 'to raise and support armies' the court, not Congress, is the final guarantor of constitutional process in the method of raising armies.

"But mad as I might have been 10 years ago at this gobbledygook passing for judicial precision and thoughtfulness, I would have been mighty glad that those chivalrous old men had decided not to draft me."

Whether the court was indulging in judicial "gobbledygook" or was performing its function must be determined by seeing what the Constitution says about the matter. The Constitution says "The judicial Power shall extend to all Cases ... (and) Controversies ..." That means the Constitution "deems it appropriate" for the Supreme Court "to rule on the constitutionality" of all cases and controversies. The Constitution doesn't vest judicial power in the people; it vests judicial power "in one supreme Court, and in such inferior Courts as Congress may from time to time ordain and establish." John Jay told us the people cede a right (to make judicial decisions) in order to vest the court with power to decide cases and controversies. If the people have a complaint about the reasonableness of a search, they take it to court for the court to decide. The same holds true concerning Congress' duty to raise and support armies. If a person has a complaint about Congress' actions, the complaint is a case or a controversy and is to be decided by the courts. Congress can not to sit in final judgment of its legislation because it wasn't given judicial power; the court system has the judicial power. That's what the Constitution says, and what a journalist thinks about the matter isn't important.

The Constitution also says the Supreme Court must decide real cases; it isn't an advisory board. Real cases and controversies will involve real issues, and often containing real harm and real injustices. If the court has power to decide real cases and controversies, it must have power to order remedies to the harm and injustices it finds. Following the *Brown v. Board of Education* decision of 1954, hundreds of school boards across the nation did nothing to remedy the harms and injustices that their uses of illegal power were creating. They assumed that if they did nothing, they could continue business as usual. They were thus pretending that the Supreme Court was just an information board whose decisions were advisory opinions meaning nothing in the real world. The Supreme Court isn't an advisory board; it is a court, and as such, its decisions are sanctioned by the constitutional principle of judicial power. Disobeying a constitutional principle, as many school boards did for up to three decades, is an un-American act.

The prohibition on using the court for advisory opinion was first articulated by the Supreme Court in 1793 in response to President George Washington's request for the court's legal views. The principle is thus one of the oldest and most-established principles of the Constitution, but hundreds of school boards – who are in charge of educating millions of American children about the principles of America's democratic republic – and their publicly paid attorneys were unable to find it, or unable to understand it. Many critics of the Supreme Court argue against the court's history of determining a law or government action unconstitutional and declaring null and void such laws. They can't find such authority spelled out in clear-and-precise language, so they assume there must be no such power. That position doesn't make sense, because if such an implied power didn't exist, the court would be only an advisory board.

When a person suffering harm under an act of government raises the question of the legality of that government action, the court needs to be able to say "yes, the act is constitutionally legal" or "no, the act isn't constitutionally legal." If there were no power to negate an unconstitutional act, all acts would be constitutional, and to allow a legislature freedom to undo its dirty deed at its convenience would leave numerous un-American laws in force if the legislature refused to amend its sins. That wasn't what the Founding Fathers envisioned for the court or the nation.

If the court couldn't negate illegal law, a most-precious right of Americans would be negated – in effect amending the Constitution without going through the proscribed constitutional amending process. That First Amendment right – to petition government – has come under attack in Congress, and that assault will be dealt with in the next chapter.

The Founding Fathers weren't naive politicians groping for their way in a confusing world. They understood how a court system should work in relation to the other branches of government. When they created the Constitution, they had knowledge of the workings of court systems throughout the world and throughout history. They weren't surprised later by a court using an unnamed power to negate law, because the point had been argued in the Constitutional Convention, but wasn't put specifically in the Constitution partly because the founders understood it to be part of judicial power. They apparently saw no need to state the obvious. They understood judicial power and assumed that future Americans likewise would be able to understand it. They may have been mistaken there.

THE UN-AMERICANS

In discussing the concept at the convention, James Madison said, "law violating a constitution established by the people themselves would be considered by the judges as null and void." No argument disputing that statement was adopted. In the Federalist Papers seeking support for the adoption of the Constitution, Hamilton wrote it would be the duty of the Supreme Court "to declare all acts contrary to the manifest tenor of the Constitution void."

The power to negate acts of government, called judicial review, wasn't invented hastily to avoid consequences of a law some judge disliked. It began in 1610 in England, and was espoused by Sir Edward Coke in the Dr. Bonham case. Because England didn't have a written constitution, it was difficult for the English to apply constitutionalism with certainty, so in many instances, they didn't try. But the colonists had constitutions, charters, compacts and other government documents in writing, so it was easy to apply judicial review. Since the concept of review was well known before the revolution, it was only natural it would be included in the new nation.

Another principle seemingly being lost in the United States, and acerbated by modern crime rates, is the separation of the judiciary from other branches of government. Too often, in localities where judges are elected, political campaigns of judicial candidates center on the promise "to crack down on the criminals." That appeals to many voters, but it isn't a principle in the American system. The founders envisioned a court system acting as an arbiter between the government (police and prosecutors) and the individual (defendant).

They didn't envision judges as crime fighters – there are many crime-fighting opportunities in prosecutors' offices and in law-enforcement organizations. Crime fighting falls first upon the legislatures to declare what isn't acceptable and to enact conditions of punishment. Law-enforcement departments come second with prosecutors third. Keeping judges out of crime-fighting is one feature separating the United States from the rest of the world. Millions of people in other lands are going through the painful process of tearing down their old systems and rebuilding new ones with United States' principles, so it makes little sense for the United States to pick up discarded concepts of failed systems.

The founders relied heavily on the doctrine of implied powers in writing Article III. It should be obvious that most judicial power in the Constitution is implied. The grants of power to Congress and the president suggest there are limitations, and government can be challenged if some persons think authority has been exceeded. Constitutional recognition of individual rights also suggests that power has limits, and there is an implied power to hear challenges to acts that infringe on those rights. The Supreme Court is the least-biased body where challenges can be heard because it doesn't create or enforce the laws challenged.

Two types of judicial power are "original jurisdiction" and "appellate jurisdiction." A case originates in a court with original jurisdiction, and the Constitution specifies that the Supreme Court has original jurisdiction in cases "affecting Ambassadors, other public Ministers and Consuls, and those in which a State shall be Party." All of its other cases are appeals, which represent nearly all of the court's work. One of the most-important principles of appellate jurisdiction is that it doesn't involve determination of the guilt or innocence of an individual. Appellate jurisdiction involves determining proper or improper use of government power and tries to discover whether the defendant was convicted legally because legal conviction is a constitutional principle that must be protected.

Failure to understand this principle leads to attacks on the court system and the state and federal judges who do understand this tenet. A case useful for learning from arose in Colorado in 1990 with the overturning of the conviction of a murderer who killed a deputy sheriff while trying to escape custody. The Colorado Court of Appeals negated the conviction on the grounds the defendant didn't get a fair trial.

This case is ideal for examining the appellate function because the appeals court recognized that the defendant was obviously guilty; the journalist attacking the court served as foreman of the jury that convicted, and the murderer was already serving prison sentences that would keep him in custody until he is 108, so the reversal wouldn't free a dangerous felon.

The appeals court judgment said, "The record before us shows that, throughout the trial, the court demonstrates an attitude of prejudice against the defense ... This was not a fair trial. Although the evidence of defendant's guilt could well be considered overwhelming, the judgment must be reversed."

Most people may think nothing needs to be said following a finding of obvious guilt, but that isn't a constitutional principle. A fair trial is, and obvious guilt isn't proof of a fair trial.

Another constitutional principle is that a person may not be deprived of "life, liberty or property without due process of law." Due process of law requires a fair trial, it doesn't accept a "mostly fair" trial, a "nearly fair" trial or a trial "99 and 44/100% fair." Fair, under the Constitution of the United States and the constitutions of the states, must be total, absolute, complete. There's nothing in any American constitution suggesting that requirements of fairness can be repealed because a defendant is as guilty as Satan in Eden.

THE UN-AMERICANS

The attack on that reversal, published Aug. 26, 1990, in The Denver Post, missed the message the appeals court was sending. The court clearly said overwhelming evidence of guilt isn't proof the trial was fair, and unless the trial was fair the defendant couldn't be convicted. The Constitution makes that clear.

The newsman wrote, "It means that everyone in this case ... can go through their special hell all over again. It means taxpayers can waste hundreds of thousands of dollars retrying a case already thoroughly disposed of."

That was nonsense. A case isn't thoroughly disposed of until it was shown to be in accordance with the constitutional principle requiring fairness in all criminal prosecutions. Fairness isn't determined by the money the judicial system spends. Even though it might be easier and more pleasant for the relatives of victims and witnesses to put the whole affair behind them, that shouldn't determine the quality of justice. The only alternative to a fair-trial conviction is no conviction at all. That's what the Constitution says and means.

When the newsman wrote: "The reality is that the Colorado Court of Appeals's description of the evidence against (Timothy) Vialpando as 'overwhelming' is the simple truth. He was convicted by immutable evidence despite effective and at times brilliant defense ... " he was demonstrating a misunderstanding of constitutional principles. Overwhelming and immutable evidence, and effective and brilliant defense, are important to courts of original jurisdiction, but they mean little in the appeals process because appellate jurisdiction doesn't pretend to find guilt or innocence. It seeks to determine if the state was obeying its law – constitutional law. A citizen has an obligation to obey the laws or to be judged a criminal. A government is likewise to be judged criminal if it disobeys its laws.

By running a diatribe against the judicial system under the headline, "Court's Vialpando ruling insults both judge and jury," the paper may seem accurate in the eyes of journalists. But few journalists understand America's constitutional system, and the quest for fair justice should insult no one. The search for fairness in the judicial system is something much of the rest of the world seems to be seeking; America has long tried to practice fairness and should keep doing so.

The Post ran a sidebar story written by the mother of another murder victim. She said:

"The legal and judicial systems were designed to protect the innocent, the key word here being innocent.

"In recent years the 'rights of the accused' seem to be taking precedence over everything else."

Decisions to reverse convictions have little to do with "the rights of the accused." The accused have the same exact rights as everyone else: unaccused, guilty or innocent. People who criticize the "rights of the accused" have those same "rights" when they are falsely accused of some misdeed. There are no differences in rights. The argument that the "legal and judicial systems were designed to protect the innocent" is likewise inaccurate. They were designed to convict the guilty, but to convict them legally because the Constitution doesn't allow for an illegal conviction. Everyone should be thankful that appeals courts take seriously the principle of legal convictions. It's through that principle that the United States differs from the despotic governments of theocracy, aristocracy, autocracy and militocracy that have infested the earth throughout history. It's through legal convictions that the governments are allowed to "deprive" the criminal of "life, liberty or property" and to prevent governments from maintaining despotic rule by designating any opposition as "criminal."

The journalist made the statement that, "No one, not even Vialpando, will be served by another trial ... Equal justice under law is the most sacred goal of American society. But there is a difference between justice and pettifoggery." The attack on the legal system was the real pettifoggery because it trivializes the principle that government has no power to deprive anyone – including the guilty – of "life, liberty, or property" without "due process of law," which requires fair trials. So, who is being served by reversing convictions of the obviously guilty? The United States Constitution is being served.

PRINCIPLES THAT MADE A NATION

After the three branches of government were empowered, there remained the task of binding together the states to form a union. That was the failure of the Articles of Confederation which were so weak that states tended to ignore what they didn't like; specifically paying of taxes. Cementing the union was done with four additional articles, which say:

ARTICLE IV:
SECTION 1. Full Faith and Credit shall be given each State to the public acts, Records, and judicial Proceedings of every other State. And the Congress may by general Laws prescribe the Manner in which such Acts, Records and Proceedings shall be proved, and the Effect thereof."

(This is no longer a major controversy in the United States since all states have learned to exist peacefully with each other. The governmental functions of one state are known in all the states which creates a bond among the states. The absence of such a bond may be why sovereign nations must spy on each other and cannot exist without war.)

"*SECTION 2. The Citizens of each State shall be entitled to all Privileges and Immunities of Citizens in the several States.*

(This makes most laws of one state applicable in the other states, if they need to apply. The driver's license of Ohio is valid in Oklahoma because of this constitutional principle. And a man married in Minnesota is married when he's in Mississippi, whether he likes it or not.)

"*A Person charged in any State with Treason, Felony, or other Crime, who shall flee from Justice, and be found in another State, shall on demand of the executive Authority of the State from which he fled, be delivered up, to be removed to the State having Jurisdiction of the Crime.*"

(There's no sanctuary in one state from the police power of another state. But there is, likewise, no authority for the police power of one state to cross state lines. Each state is expected to co-operate with the others in administration of justice. That hasn't always happened, but technological advances are making co-operation much easier.)

"*No person held to Service or Labour in one State, under the Laws thereof, escaping into another, shall in Consequence of any Law or Regulation therein, be discharged from such Service or Labour, but shall be delivered up on Claim of the Party to whom such Service or Labor may be due.*"

(This provision was one of the main points of the infamous Dred Scott decision of 1857 – for which the Supreme Court is still criticized – and which was repealed by the 13th Amendment.)

"*SECTION 3. New States may be admitted by the Congress into this Union; but no new State shall be formed or erected within the jurisdiction of any other State; nor any State be formed by the Junction of two or more States, or parts of States, without the Consent of the Legislatures of the States concerned as well as of the Congress.*"

(There are few controversies over this stipulation, but dissatisfied politicians pretend at times their cities or counties can leave one state and join or create another because they feel slighted or abused by city hall, the county, or the state capital. They can't.)

"*The Congress shall have Power to dispose of and make all needful Rules and Regulation respecting the Territory or other property belonging to the United States; and nothing in this Constitution shall be construed as to Prejudice any Claims of the United States, or of any particular State.*"

Powers That Be

(This provides Congress with the power to enact laws for territories not yet admitted as states and to make rules for management of national parks, forests, monuments and other property that have been obtained through the power to tax and spend for the general welfare. It also gives government the authority to conduct some commerce as shall be explained in Chapter 11.)

"SECTION 4. The United States shall guarantee to every State in this Union a Republican Form of Government, and shall protect each of them against Invasion; and on Application of the Legislature or the Executive (when the Legislature cannot be convened) against domestic Violence."

(This was helpful during the civil-rights struggles and authorized the use of National Guard units to try to keep the peace in the face of mob violence.)

"ARTICLE V:

The Congress whenever two-thirds of both Houses shall deem it necessary, shall propose Amendments to this Constitution, or, on the Application of the Legislatures of two-thirds of the several States, shall call a Convention for proposing Amendments, which, in either Case, shall be valid to all Intents and Purposes, as part of this Constitution, when ratified by the Legislatures of three-fourths of the several States, or by Conventions in three-fourths thereof, as the one or the other Mode of Ratification may be proposed by the Congress; Provided that no Amendment which shall be made prior to the Year One thousand eight hundred and eight shall in any manner affect the first and fourth Clauses in the Ninth Section of the first Article; and that no State, without its Consent, shall be deprived of its equal suffrage in the Senate."

(Some people pretend that an amendment isn't part of the Constitution and, therefore, doesn't replace an original intent of the founders. Such thought is nonsense because this says amendments "shall be valid ... as part of this Constitution" after being ratified. It also says no one can call for an amendment or convention except Congress. If 50 state legislatures want a convention, but Congress doesn't want to call one, nothing can be done to circumvent Congress.)

"ARTICLE VI:

All Debts contracted and Engagements entered into, before the Adoption of this Constitution, shall be valid against the United States under this Constitution, as under the Confederation."

(Because pre-1789 debts have been paid and engagements ended, this no longer applies, but it does remind us that government must pay its debts.)

> "This Constitution, and the Laws of the United States which shall be made in Pursuance thereof; and all Treaties made, or which shall be made, under the Authority of the United States, shall be the supreme Law of the Land; and the Judges in every State shall be bound thereby, any Thing in the Constitution or Laws of the State to the Contrary notwithstanding.
>
> "The Senators and Representatives before mentioned, and the Members of the several State Legislatures, and all executive and judicial Officers, both of the United States and the several States, shall be bound by Oath or Affirmation, to support this Constitution; but no religious Test shall ever be required as a Qualification to any Office or public Trust under the United States."

(These two paragraphs seem to be the only parts of the final four articles still needing to be defined. When America was going through its civil-rights struggles, these paragraphs were subverted throughout the nation. Governors who stood in school-house doors trying to prevent equality under the law were ignoring their oaths requiring them "to support this Constitution." When members of State legislatures enact law to thwart or circumvent United States laws, they subvert the constitutional principles of Article VI because it says that "the Members of the several State Legislatures ... shall be bound by Oath or Affirmation, to support this Constitution." If state legislators don't know what the Constitution says, they have an obligation to learn. If they are incapable of learning, they shouldn't hold elective office. State judges, engage in subversion when they turn their backs on the constitutional principles of the United States. No state doctrines or principles in constitutions, law, custom, practice, institution or precept are equal or superior to national principles. That's what the Constitution means when it says, "Judges in every State shall be bound thereby, anything in the Constitution or Laws of the State to the Contrary notwithstanding.")

ARTICLE VII:

> "The Ratification of the Conventions of nine States shall be sufficient for the Establishment of this Constitution between the States so ratifying the Same."

(This became a nonissue June 21, 1788, when New Hampshire was the ninth state to ratify the Constitution, which took effect March 4, 1789.)

A MISS BY THE EXPERTS

Trying to understand the Constitution can be a difficult job, even for the most-knowledgeable and astute students of that document. In a book used to teach constitutional law at top universities, the experts missed the point on some issues. This book, *American Constitutional Law*, by Alpheus Thomas Mason and William M. Beaney, contains the following statement:

"In our fundamental law of 1789, there is no mention of the President's cabinet, no reference to Senatorial courtesy, to political parties, or to national nominating conventions for choosing candidates for election."

That is true, of course, but it is also true that such things don't need to be mentioned because – except for the cabinet – they don't have anything to do with governmental powers. Jay told us that the Constitution was the method by which the American people give power to the government to allow it to function and carry out its governmental mandate. Political parties have no legal authority over society, so government has no part in the functioning of those parties. The government's relationship with political parties is the same as its relationship with any social organization or club. It can regulate those clubs, organizations or political parties where it has power to do so, but that doesn't make them governmental. Because political parties aren't governmental entities, the Constitution wouldn't say anything about their nominating conventions, which can be held by any other persons or groups. Senatorial courtesy concerns only personal relationships; no governmental power is involved.

The cabinet was an implied creation of the Constitution through the mention in Article II, Section 2, of executive departments, the heads of those departments and officers of the United States which the president is to control through the power to "Commission all the Officers of the United States." Commission can mean to empower, direct, lead, enable, license, authorize, delegate; all of which are accomplished through the cabinet arrangement. Congress' power to make law to carry out the execution of specific powers – which cabinet members do – also would imply power to create a cabinet.

Chapter 6

PARING POWERS

BUT WHO'S BEING CUT OUT?

Power struggles – often between political and constitutional powers – seem to be persistent features in the American system of self-government. The Founding Fathers were the political leaders of the time and knew how politics functioned, which is why many warned against political divisions – factions, as they were called – dominating constitutional government. So the founders included methods in the Constitution to try to prevent politics from devouring constitutionalism. Principles of separation of powers and checks and balances were included to prevent any branch of government from dominating the other two.

In spite of complaints Americans have about the system, it seems to have worked reasonably well. The executive branch has become the most visible and influential part of the triad, but presidents can be controlled. Not easily, of course, but easy government isn't a constitutional function. Congress, which gets most of the blame for the nation's troubles – even when it isn't at fault – is controlled by its own cumbersomeness, a president's veto or a court's judgment. The judiciary is controlled by having its actions dependent upon some other branch of government acting first. A president or Congress not wanting their actions reviewed and negated needn't take offending actions. Any constitutional action will be allowed by the court. Unconstitutional actions most likely will be negated. The safest way to not lose in court is not to perform an unconstitutional act in the first place. That would require politicians understanding the Constitution, which doesn't seem to be the case now. The Supreme Court is controlled in a fashion because it doesn't activate itself; someone else has to ask it to perform its job by presenting a case to it.

When politicians have their biases and opinions continually rejected in court, they blame the courts, not themselves. They claim the court is ignoring the Constitution, making law from the bench, is going too far, is dishonest or is un-American in its decisions. To their credit, Supreme Court judges don't resort to political pontificating. They know their work doesn't require swaying a population unfamiliar with constitutionalism, so they can afford to do their jobs correctly without attacking and criticizing others.

Politicians, on the other hand, often try to exact some form of revenge because of decisions rejecting their biases. Frequently they try new laws.

Paring Powers

New laws usually don't work because they don't create the constitutional powers lacking in the first place. If the legislature doesn't have authority to make a certain law, rewording the same concept doesn't create the authorization. At times, need for a certain law is so overwhelming that the Constitution is amended to create the necessary authorization, as it was after an income tax was declared unconstitutional. The Sixteenth Amendment authorizing a specific tax on income was adopted in 1913. Congress couldn't eliminate alcoholic beverages – although it could keep them out of interstate commerce – so the Constitution was amended to create Prohibition. (Crime created by Prohibition proved the folly of using the Constitution for legislation rather than for its original function of empowering government.)

In was natural following several years of decisions by the Earl Warren Court, which some people called "liberal," that the administration of President Ronald Reagan, that called itself "conservative," and its supporters would try to prevent additional decisions of similar nature. The "liberal" administration of Franklin D. Roosevelt tried similar tactics on a "conservative" court nearly 50 years earlier.

The New York Times reported that less than three months into Reagan's first term, 22 bills had been introduced in Congress to take jurisdiction away from the Supreme Court in cases involving prayers in school, abortion, school busing, a men-only draft and state-court rulings. Times columnist Tom Wicker said, if any of those bills had been adopted the court would have been unable to enforce decisions already made, which would return all matters back to the political arena and, supposedly, make legal some powers that had been illegal. Wicker's assertion was probably incorrect, as will be explained in the following pages.

Within months, the new attorney general, William French Smith, announced the administration's campaign to prevent the federal courts from "overstepping their bounds." By November, 1981, when the campaign was outlined, 31 bills had been introduced in Congress. None of them ever succeeded. Why such a dismal failure on an issue many politicians thought was so major in importance? One reason was that there was never an overwhelming support from the American people. There was support among doctrinaire groups and individuals, but that usually doesn't succeed unless widespread support develops. There was also the question of which branch of government was "overstepping their bounds."

The anticourt movement was pinning its hopes on one Constitution power. Article III, Section 2, includes the statement "the supreme Court shall have appellate Jurisdiction, both as to Law and Fact, with such Exceptions, and under such Regulations as the Congress shall make." Court foes thought that statement would allow them to prevent decisions they wouldn't like. The court couldn't get around any prohibition by taking cases without appeal (original jurisdiction) because the Constitution specifies which cases of original jurisdiction the court has. That couldn't be altered by law or court decision. That seemed to settle the issue, but did it?

One of the most-active leaders of the court-stripping effort was Sen. Jesse Helms, R-N.C., who took the lead on the school-prayer issue, attaching an amendment to a regular bill. His amendment was designed to forbid federal court jurisdiction over state laws, "which relate to voluntary prayers in public schools and public buildings." In opposing the effort, The Denver Post editorialized saying, "State laws requiring school prayer might flout the First Amendment, but federal courts would be helpless to rule on the merits of such laws because they didn't have jurisdiction." The paper may have been wise to oppose Helms' effort, but was mistaken in assuming his proposal, if enacted, could do anything. The Senate rejected the Helms effort by the fall of 1982. The administration then attempted to amend the Constitution. Helms and his supporters may have thought their effort would change things to their liking. It would not. Under the Constitution, Helms' plan would have resulted in the exact opposite of what he was trying to accomplish.

There were major problems with Helms' proposal, among them:

– If law was involved, "voluntary prayer" was probably absent. The courts would have to decide. Logic dictates that true voluntary prayer could be possible only by the absence of laws. If a child sought divine help before a math test, the state agent (teacher) would pay no attention – that's allowing voluntary prayer. A child saying grace in the lunchroom is an example of prayer that's truly voluntary. And no laws are needed.

– There would be no voluntary prayer if there were state laws requiring prayer; therefore federal courts would still have jurisdiction.

– Government can't create voluntary prayer; therefore the only state action that could be taken in the matter would be to prevent prayer. That would be unconstitutional, but the courts wouldn't have jurisdiction to protect the child's right to free exercise of religion. That's the exact opposite of Helms' stated intentions.

– Helms' proposal would have been unconstitutional had it become law, as Chapter 9 will show.

The most-serious problem with Helms' campaign was that it was an attempt to subvert the Constitution without resorting to the amending process. It was a threat to a most-precious right, one that few other nations recognize as existing. Helms' efforts wouldn't have affected the Supreme Court or the decisions it had made or could make in the future. His proposal went after the First Amendment right of the American people to "petition the Government for a redress of grievances," clearly an un-American act, because mere law can't eliminate constitutional principles. The right to petition government isn't restricted to writing a letter to a senator or representative, and it isn't restricted to signing a petition to be mailed to a government bureau or agency. The right to petition government isn't restricted to printing a complaint on a placard and marching in protest. The right to petition the government includes the right to file legal charges against the government and to take the government to court. That right would not exist if courts couldn't hear the petition. This is a right that seems to be recognized only in a small part of the world. It's a right that may be behind much of the world seeking Americanization.

The inclusion in the First Amendment of the right to petition government created a situation that even constitutional experts seem to have missed. What occurred may not have been planned by the first Congress, which proposed the amendment, or the American public, which approved the Bill of Rights through their representatives. What the First Amendment did was to effectively repeal the very constitutional power Helms was trying to use. Congress cannot, and could not since 1791, make exceptions to the court's jurisdiction if those exceptions eliminate an individual's right to "petition the government for a redress of grievances." Since courts recognize that it's government power involved in the cases and controversies they decide, a corporation or other type of business has the same rights as an individual. Because power is consistent, that status must also extend to any organization which exists under law to own property, make contracts and function as an entity. Because all have the same rights, all possible plaintiffs have the right to petition government.

The First Amendment doesn't place any conditions or restrictions on the right to petition. All petitions must be allowed. The amendment doesn't say Congress could define or make exceptions to those petitions. Therefore, Helms – who went to battle like a mighty unarmed warrior in a war in which mental acumen was the only usable weapon – was trying to amend the Constitution illegally. His actions weren't aimed at reducing power and authority of the Supreme Court; they were trying to subvert the rights of all American citizens. The Senate rejected his measure.

A similar tactic was tried by Helms and others against busing of public-school children in the attempt to gain racial balance in education. But the effort to curtail busing didn't try to restrict court jurisdiction outright; it would have prevented the Justice Department from representing citizens seeking busing as a remedy in school-segregation cases. The idea was that if the Justice Department couldn't ask for busing to overcome illegal use of power, the courts couldn't order it. This created a second but related constitutional problem.

President Jimmy Carter vetoed one effort in late 1980. The drive was revived months after the inauguration of Reagan. In February of 1982, the Senate passed a ban on federal courts ordering busing for equality if the ride lasted more than 30 minutes or was more than 10 miles round trip. In December the House of Representatives passed legislation to prohibit the Justice Department from seeking busing.

All kinds of arguments were voiced to oppose busing. Some said busing didn't work, but didn't say in reference to what. Test scores were cited to prove the failure of busing. In some areas test scores fell over time, in some areas test scores rose, and in some areas test scores were virtually the same. But busing has nothing to do with test scores or quality of education. Busing is concerned with equality under the law through equal opportunity and the legal use of power by school boards. Quality of education depends on competence of school boards and educators – they are supposed to use the same degree of competence to educate all children. Some people argued that busing would interfere with neighborhood schools or with the children's "pecking order." People whose inclination is to protect only those rights found written in the Constitution, can't find a right to attend neighborhood schools mentioned; therefore they argue against themselves defending neighborhood schools that are used to preserve racial discrimination. Children's pecking order doesn't overrule the constitution principle of equality under the law – in this case, educational laws. Most often, the children were much less concerned about busing for equality than were the adults. Many people said busing caused whites to flee public schools. That's true, but the Constitution doesn't allow for bending its principles in order to prevent undesirable social reactions. Bending constitutional principles would allow a subversive power – power to discriminate by segregation – to continue. That would be a more serious problem than "white flight," according to constitution lovers, who would rather preserve that document than give in to fears.

Conservative newspaper columnist James Kilpatrick was one of those antibusing proponents who missed the constitutional points in saying Congress had legal authority to prohibit busing. Following the Senate vote, he cited the "exceptions and regulations" clause of the Constitution that Senator Helms tried to use to no avail. Kilpatrick said, "no child, black or white, will be denied judicial review of his constitutional rights. All that will be denied is a court order compelling the child to be bused long distances from his home." That is, of course, nonsense. If the court was stripped of its authority to order an end to illegal use of power, that child will be denied equality under the law. The child's constitutional right to petition for a redress of grievances would be made meaningless if there was no redress at the conclusion of the petition. Redress means to set right that which is wrong. If the courts were prevented by legislative action from being able to order a halt to illegal deeds or to correct the wrongs, they would be rendered into nothing more than debating panels, and that would subvert their functions to decide all cases and controversies. Congress cannot change the courts' role to decide "all" cases and controversies arising under the Constitution into "some" cases and controversies.

This antibusing effort also would have infringed on the president's constitutional duty to "preserve, protect and defend the Constitution of the United States," because the Constitution demands an equality of its citizens and a prohibition of illegal power. The president has a constitutional order to commission the head of the Justice Department to protect the rights of all Americans, and that includes representing those damaged by state subversions. None of the antibusing politicking changed anything.

Lack of knowledge about the Constitution often leads to frustration and confusion by the public. In 1978, voters in the state of Washington voted overwhelming to prohibit busing of students outside their neighborhoods for the purpose of integration. The Supreme Court voided that vote in 1982, prompting massive criticism of the justices. The critics were wrong, as usual, because there's nothing in the Constitution that indicates a simple vote of the people can negate a constitutional principle, and equal protection under state laws is a principle that cannot be eliminated by referendum. Public acceptance or popularity of any issue has nothing to do with its constitutionality. The result of all these anticourt efforts would be government abandoning people most in need of equality. The job of government is to work to insure equality – even if the majority opposes that equality.

If people frustrated by busing were truly serious about ending it, they could work toward eliminating the causes that bring busing about, not merely vote against efforts that seek equality. Housing patterns are generally cited to justify segregated schools, but they don't legalize discrimination. Those patterns can create a racial imbalance, but balance of a school's student body isn't proof of equality, nor is imbalance proof of incquality. It is the equality or inequality of the educational process at the heart of all busing decisions.

THE UN-AMERICANS

AT WAR OVER WAR

Perhaps no feature of the Constitution causes as much confusion as do its war powers. And perhaps no feature is so little understood, even among people who wield the powers and experts who study and explain the Constitution.

The Constitution's drafters must have thought they handled the war powers in a manner that would make abuse difficult. They did – but what they created hasn't been fully understood or delineated in law or custom. These war powers seem simple and easy to understand, and those who don't comprehend the Constitution read them that way – with simplicity. Of course, what the "original intent" of the founders was, is of little importance in the modern world because of changes in technology, war-making capabilities and world politics. Legal uses of the powers they created is all that matters today.

Following the 1990 Iraqi invasion of Kuwait, a national debate arose over President George Bush's role as president and commander in chief of the armed forces. The debate concerned which branch of government had authority over which part of the war powers. No one seemed capable of explaining the relative functions of Congress and the president. This argument has been going on since early in the republic's life, and has never been totally settled. That is a puzzlement, because it isn't that difficult to understand. The Constitution addresses Congress first because the founders intended it to be the first branch of government to take action. The other branches were to be powerless until Congress authorized, by law, some action for them to take legally.

Congress' role in the nation's war powers are listed in Article I, Section 8, of the Constitution, which says Congress has the power:

"To declare war, grant Letters of Marque and Reprisal, and to make Rules concerning Captures on Land and Water;

"To raise and support Armies, but no Apportion of Money to that Use shall be for a longer Term than two Years;

"To provide and maintain a Navy;

"To make Rules for the Government and Regulation of the land and naval Forces;

"To provide for calling forth the Militia to execute the Laws of the Union, suppress Insurrections and repel Invasions;

"To provide for organizing, arming, and disciplining the Militia, and for governing such Part of them as may be employed in the Service of the United States, reserving to the States respectively, the Appointment of

Officers, and the Authority of training the Militia according to the discipline prescribed by Congress;"

Section 9 adds:

"The privilege of the Writ of Habeas Corpus shall not be suspended, unless when in Cases of Rebellion or Invasion the public safety may require it."

The president's role in war powers is in Article II, Section 2. It says:

"The President shall be Commander in Chief of the Army and Navy of the United States, and the Militia of the several States, when called into the actual Service of the United States ..."

The controversy arose as Bush was deploying more than a half million American troops to Saudi Arabia and the Persian Gulf following the Iraqi invasion. Arguments about the president's action centered on whether any subsequent military conflict would be illegal under the Constitution. It soon became apparent to those arguing that deployment of troops wasn't war, so it was dropped as a point of contention. The argument then centered on whether the president needed Congress' authorization to go into battle. As the debate continued into 1991, it seemed those who believed Bush needed approval by Congress became more vocal. Many of Bush's fellow Republican politicians didn't address the question directly, giving the impression they too believed he needed Congress' permission to fight Iraq. It seemed the people arguing against the point were mainly administration officials.

The constitutional argument centered on Congress' power to declare war and the president's role as commander in chief. The position that seemed to be most accepted throughout the United States was voiced on a *Donahue* television program Dec. 10, 1990, by syndicated newspaper columnist George Will, who said he thought it was legal for Bush to deploy troops to the Mideast, but fighting definitely needed congressional approval.

Another spokesman from the conservative perspective was publisher William R. Hearst Jr., who wrote in a newspaper column Nov. 18, 1990:

"What concerns me isn't so much the constitutional provision that reserves the right to declare war to the Congress. As commander-in-chief of the armed forces, the president also has important prerogatives under the Constitution in matters of national security.

"But if our recent history has proved anything, it's that when a president takes the country into a major war solely on his own authority, no matter how morally justified he may be, the result isn't a happy one.

"Harry Truman sent American forces to Korea on the basis of a United Nations resolution approving multinational action to stop communist aggression ...

THE UN-AMERICANS

"Truman described it as a police action. For the first time in our history, a president didn't seek Congress's endorsement for going to war ...

"Vietnam has to be counted as a far worse example of the consequences of a president failing to obtain congressional approval before heading for war. The closest that Lyndon Johnson came was the so-called Gulf of Tonkin resolution, which wasn't intended as a blankcheck to launch an all-out conflict."

Will and Hearst showed they didn't understand the Constitution fully; just as many with a liberal perspective failed to grasp the full extent of this matter. After the 102nd Congress convened in January of 1991, Sens. Brock Adams, D-Wash., and Tom Harkin, D-Iowa, proposed a resolution that the Seattle Post-Intelligencer said would declare that "Congress, not the president, has the power to declare war and 'any offensive action against Iraq must be pursuant to an explicit authorization by Congress before any such action may be initiated.'

"Adams argues that only Congress has the constitutional authority to declare war, but that U.S. presidents have repeatedly flouted this principle, sending troops into combat from Korea to Panama without approval."

Echoing Adams' concern was fellow liberal, Sen. Edward Kennedy, D-Mass., who told the American Broadcasting Company television program *Good Morning America* Jan. 8, 1991, that only Congress has the power to declare war. In answer to a question if it would be illegal for the president to commit troops to combat, Kennedy said: "Well, very definitely in these circumstances because the Constitution is very clear that the president has to go to the Congress; the Congress has the power to declare war. It says so in the Constitution of the United States in Article I, Section 8. The Founding Fathers made it extremely clear that they wanted shared responsibilities between the president and the Congress that no individual ought to bring this country to war. Now we have an unprecedented situation; 400,000 troops in the (Persian) Gulf from a standing start. And clearly the American people ought to be involved in this extremely important decision. The president has a responsibility to go to Congress and the Congress – and only the Congress – has the power to declare war."

Appearing with Kennedy on the program was Sen. John Warner, R-Va., who said, "No one really knows (if the action would be illegal). This debate over who has the right to order troops and to commence a war has been going on since Thomas Jefferson sent troops – that is ships – to the Barbary pirates, then came back and apologized to Congress." Warner added that "History has shown that we've had this debate since 1801 about the President's powers and the powers of the Congress. It's clear that we can declare

Paring Powers

war, it's clear that he's commander in chief, can deploy the troops ..."

On the Adams-Harkin resolution, Kennedy said it "would have to be consistent with the Constitution that the Congress has the power to declare war. There's two issues – one, whether the president has the constitutional responsibility to go to the Congress – clearly he does – 241 of the leading constitutional professors from law schools from all over the country representing every kind of political spectrum have indicated so." The second issue mentioned was whether the United States ought to go to war, which doesn't concern an argument over constitutional powers.

When discussing the United Nations resolution authorizing all necessary means to expel Iraqi forces from U.N. member Kuwait, Kennedy said, "There's nothing in the U.N. that overrides the Constitution of the United States. The power to declare war rests with the Congress." While citing 211 incidents when the United States conducted military action without a declaration of war, Kennedy said, "The fact that the Senate of the United States has failed to meet its constitutional responsibilities in the past is no excuse for not meeting them today."

USA TODAY reported in January that some legal scholars accused Bush of "erring legally and politically in ignoring Congress." Among 127 law professors signing a letter stating Bush needed Congress' approval before ordering U.S. troops "to make war in the Persian Gulf" was a Duke University professor, who was quoted as saying, "There are many difficult and uncertain constitutional questions, but this is not one of them." The paper quoted the professor as accusing the president of "flagrant disregard" of key provisions of the Constitution.

Countering that argument was a University of Illinois professor who said that Bush "has all the authority to do whatever he wants. The (Constitution's) framers debated and changed the phrase 'make war' to 'declare war' because they did not want to tie the president's hands."

All these people had two things in common: they were correct in the obvious areas and wrong in obscure areas. Even the Bush administration had trouble identifying its proper role. In November 1990, national security advisor Brent Scowcroft told the American Broadcasting Company television show *This Week With David Brinkley'* "The Constitution is ambiguous" on war-powers roles. The Constitution isn't ambiguous; it just isn't obvious.

While it's plain Congress has power to declare war and the president/commander-in-chief has power to wage war, these provisions didn't wholly cover the Persian Gulf situation. The crisis made it clear journalists, politicians and law professors don't fully understand the Constitution because the provision covering this situation is in Article VI, paragraph 2. That provi-

provision covering this situation is in Article VI, paragraph 2. That provision says: "This Constitution, and the laws of the United States which shall be made in Pursuance thereof; and all Treaties made, or which shall be made under the authority of the United States, shall be the supreme Law of the Land ..." That provision was put into the Constitution to cement the concept that the national government was superior in every way to the state governments. But, in a quirk of constitutionalism, that also allows a president to go to war without direct approval or a congressional declaration of war. Not any war, of course, but some war.

It's clear a declaration of war by Congress would be "law(s) of the United States which shall be made in Pursuance (of the Constitution)." It's also obvious that "Treaties made ... under the authority of the United States" share the designation of "supreme Law of the Land." Treaties, according to Article VI, aren't inferior to law; therefore, there are two ways to go to war – Congress may declare it, or the Senate may concur to presidentially negotiated treaties that call for the United States to provide military assistance to its treaty partner. That authorizes the president to wage war without direct congressional approval because he would be taking "Care that the Laws be faithfully executed ..." (Article II, Section 3)

Will was correct in saying Bush could deploy troops, but he was wrong in thinking congressional approval to fight was needed. Bush was able to deploy troops to Saudi Arabia and fight there because of treaty obligations. It didn't matter that he had to beg, plead, whimper and whine to get the Saudis to ask for protection – when they asked, he was authorized to go to war. But that allowed him authority only if Saudi Arabia had been attacked because that is the only condition under which the treaty obligation had force. The president needed authorization for offensive action, and that was available in two places. He could have gotten that authorization from Congress or through the United Nations. He got authority from both. Membership in the U. N. is by treaty – that's not negated because the document is called a charter – which obligates the U.S. to support U.N. actions; including waging war. It's the treaty that the president would obey, not the United Nations.

This is why President Truman could fight a war in Korea without congressional approval – he was faithfully executing the laws. And that's why Hearst was wrong in his newspaper column. Truman didn't take "the country into a major war solely on his own authority." He sent the United States into war on the authority of the U. S. government, which funneled authorization through the United Nations by treaty. Hearst also was wrong with his statements about the Vietnam war. President Johnson (and later, President

Paring Powers

Richard Nixon) wouldn't need congressional approval to fight in South Vietnam when the Southeast Asia Treaty Organization authorized that. But the president was restricted to only South Vietnam; the Gulf of Tonkin resolution allowed fighting outside South Vietnamese borders.

(This is a point militaristic critics miss when they complain that the armed forces weren't allowed to win the Vietnam war, or had their hands tied. There was never any intent to use the Vietnam war to vanquish communism because there was never any legal authority through treaty or congressional resolution to do any more than what the treaty required – assist South Vietnam in its defense. A president can't conquer the world just because he wishes to.)

The metaphorical "engine of democracy" of journalism needs metaphorical fuel and lubrication to operate. In this case fuel and lubrication would be knowledge and understanding, which Will and Hearst lacked. They weren't alone; their views were consistent with the views of journalists across the nation. Adams and Harkin were correct that Congress declares war. But they were wrong to think that "any offensive action against Iraqi must be pursuant to an explicit authorization by Congress." Action could be taken under the authority of treaty approved by the Senate. The House Democrat Caucus had passed a resolution 177 to 37 urging Bush to obtain congressional approval before going to war. The constitutionality of that resolution may be questionable because it seemed to interfere with the treaty authority of the Senate and president. Kennedy was definitely wrong in saying "the president has a responsibility to go to the Congress." His responsibility was to faithfully execute the laws of the United States, and a treaty is a "supreme Law of the Land."

Senator after senator and representative after representative argued that only Congress could declare war; concentrating their arguments on armed hostilities, and only hostilities, during congressional debate in January 1991 about whether to give authorization to the president to engage in hostilities. Declaring war is much more encompassing than authorizing military action. Declaring war reverses the Third Amendment, removing the prohibition of housing soldiers in private homes. Declaring war could affect Article I, Section 9, paragraph 2, which says, "The privilege of the Writ of Habeas Corpus shall not be suspended, unless when in cases of Rebellion or Invasion the public Safety may require it." Suspending Habeas Corpus allows the government authority to do many things it can't do when Habeas Corpus is in effect. After the Japanese invasion of Pearl Harbor in 1941, a declaration of war enabled the government to inter Japanese-Americans in concentration camps; censor newspaper and radio journalists; restrict speech, assembly and travel; ration food and fuel; confiscate property for government use and order factories to make armaments. Declaration of war can allow for martial law and other measures that make the United States similar to the authoritative nations it may be fighting. Since the Persian Gulf crisis didn't involve rebellion or invasion of the United States, all these measures wouldn't have applied, but many could have. Declaring war would suspend the Thirteenth Amendment's prohibition against involuntary servitude. A declaration would allow the states to "lay any duty of Tonnage, keep Troops, or Ships of War ... as stated in Article I, Section 10, paragraph 3. So it may be that, in some instances, war by treaty may be preferable to war by congressional declaration.

It might be a bit much to ask journalists and politicians to understand all the nuances of the Constitution – they're not trained to do so. It's another matter that many law professors would miss the point. The Bush supporter didn't quite get it right either, even though he was closer to the truth than the other professors. Bush didn't have "all the authority to do whatever he wants;" he had authority to do what treaties allowed him to do or compelled him to do. Of those 200-plus incidents in American history in which a president waged war without Congressional approval; some were legal, most weren't. In 1983, President Reagan invaded and conquered the island nation of Grenada without congressional approval and without treaty obligations. That may have been unconstitutional. The United States miniinvasion of the newly revolted Russian nation in 1918 – a move that hampered U.S.-U.S.S.R relations until the Soviet Union fell ghastly ill with untreated maladies and self-inflicted trauma in the late 1980s – was another questionable presidential act. Bush could argue that his 1989 invasion of Panama was because its leader, Manuel Noriega, was an "indicted fugitive" and he was merely pursuing a suspect of illegal drug dealing.

Kennedy was certainly correct in saying the Senate has failed in the past to meet its constitutional responsibility because an important responsibility of the Senate is to know what it's getting the United States into when it approves a treaty. One undesirable facet of making war through treaty is that it allows the nation to go to war on the authority of the president and 67 senators, who could all be from a previous generation. This arrangement permits one body of government (the Senate) to subvert the authority of another entity (the House), something not envisioned by the founders, but something that nevertheless can occur. That isn't what the founders had in mind, but that is what can happen if the president responds to a treaty obligation and commits the United States to war before the Congress can take action to prevent it. The founders couldn't foresee 13 minor nation-states

Paring Powers

united by a document growing into the world's most-powerful nation, one that would be called on for protection by much of the world.

America has to accept war by treaty because of one important concept – law must be considered constitutional until declared otherwise. For a statute, that would involve challengers proving a law wasn't made in pursuance of the Constitution (wasn't based on a valid constitutional power and objective, or went too far and infringed on an immunity). For a treaty, the challenger would have to show it wasn't made "under the Authority of the United States" (wasn't made by the president and approved by the Senate, or wasn't a national treaty – states may not make treaties: Article I, Section 10).

Whether the Constitution allows only Congress-approved hostilities or permits war by treaty is a controversy "arising under (the) Constitution, the Laws of the United States and Treaties made ..." People who read the Constitution fundamentally to recognize only Congress' power to declare war, must also read it fundamentally and admit only the court system has authority to decide this controversy (Article III, Section 2). Since war by treaty has never been questioned in court – let alone, understood – it must be considered legal until it is challenged and negated. Legislative action will not negate the concept, only a court decision will. There has been one challenge to a treaty that rearranged governmental power, and it was decided in 1920. That case – *Missouri v. Holland* – was based on a treaty between the United States and Great Britain that sought to protect overhunted birds migrating between Canada and various sections of the United States. Congress had to pass a law in 1918 establishing closed seasons and other rules to carry out its treaty obligations. Missouri sued – correctly claiming the U.S. had no authority because the law was an infringement on power reserved to the states – but lost the case.

There is one aspect of the decision written by Oliver Wendell Holmes that applies to the war-by-treaty controversy. The decision made it clear that a treaty, if made legally, knows no limits – none are listed in the Constitution – on subject matter, which makes it legal for the national government to enact a law that it couldn't enact if there were no treaty. This rearrangement of power by treaty permits the national government to take powers from the state, and also makes it legal – until proven otherwise – for the Senate to approve a treaty that could authorize military action.

But the founders gave the Congress another method to control or prevent illegal war-making by a president. Article I, Section 8, empowers Congress the authority "To make Rules for the Government and Regulation of the land and naval Forces." Making law to regulate the military doesn't

THE UN-AMERICANS

mean Congress is restricted to those in uniform; its authority extends to all who govern the military – including the commander in chief. If Congress can make it a crime for a private to refuse to report to his/her post in a zone of hostilities, it can make it a crime for the commander to create hostilities without any form of authorization. If the commander in chief commits a crime by flaunting Congress' law, he can be impeached and removed from office upon conviction. A president/commander in chief is subject to law, just as is a private. The Constitution isn't ambiguous on the question of making war; officials must learn to use all of the Constitution, not just the most-obvious parts.

Congress made one wimpy attempt at addressing the problem when it passed the War Powers Act over President Nixon's veto in 1973. That law, brought about because of the Vietnam war, called for the president to consult with Congress "in every possible instance before introducing United States Armed Forces into hostilities or into situations where imminent involvement in hostilities is clearly indicated." The president was to report major troop deployments within 48 hours to congressional leaders if war had not been declared. Then, if Congress didn't approve his actions within 60 days, the president must withdraw the troops. Congress was also allowed to vote on troop withdrawal. This appears to have constitutional problems because it involves the House in the treaty powers of the president and the Senate, but Congress has always been allowed to alter or negate by statute a treaty's effects on domestic law because laws and treaties are equal as "the supreme Law of the Land." As just shown, declarations of war allow vast encroachments on rights, so it may be wise to allow some war by treaty.

A final point on making war through treaty is that there is no provision in the Constitution for the United States to get out of a treaty against the wishes of the treaty partner. The nation could merely breach the treaty, something the United States pretends it never does. Another alternative is to sneak around the issue as the United States did with the Apache, Pawnee and the Sioux; the Arapahoe, Seminole and Nez Perce, too. After getting tired of shunting the Indians around to evade treaty obligations, Congress used its powers in Article I, Section 8, paragraph 4, and simply granted United States citizenship through naturalization, even when it wasn't sought by the Indians. That removed the tribes' status as foreign nations – making them substates under the jurisdiction of a superior sovereignty. The United States makes treaties with foreign states, not subordinate political entities. As subordinate political groups within the United States, the Indians wouldn't be permitted under the Constitution to be part of any treaty, even a treaty with their own nation. The Founding Fathers didn't intend that abuse, either.

THE PEOPLE GIVETH

It's not surprising that various branches of government fight among themselves over the exercise of power and for authority to control society. Almost everyone likes to believe he or she has solutions to all problems – real or imagined – while thinking others have nothing to contribute. This is the mindset of those who think they are the only ones who know how to protect "voluntary prayer" in public schools when, in reality, voluntary prayer doesn't need protection because it has been never threatened. People who think they know a nonbusing method to provide equal protection under the laws in educating children should provide that solution, not try to subvert efforts of those seeking solutions. Ignoring racial discrimination and trying to prevent attempts at solving segregation-caused problems perpetuate un-American action true patriots are trying to eliminate. Arguing about war powers few seem to understand while doing nothing to define them allows presidents opportunity to abuse those powers. Fighting about the exercise of power keeps alive constant strains between the federal government and state and local governments. School boards – in the North as well as the South – which wouldn't take action to eliminate their unconstitutional activities, have fought the federal government in battles they can't win, just as cities have done over housing, police and local courts have done over fair trials and illegal evidence, and all states have done concerning regulation of commerce and numerous other concerns.

As governments try, and sometimes fail, to cope with the complexities of modern society, the failures – or perceived failures – of government give rise to antitax and "throw-the-bums-out" movements or to other forms of disdain for government. Americans have long pretended to be overtaxed and underserved by government. Elections are often won or lost on one issue – who can promise the least amount of taxes. How an advanced-and-sophisticated society is supposed to function without paying for the services that helped create, and now maintain, that advancement and sophistication seems never to enter voters' minds. Some political pundits call themselves "libertarians" and argue against government in nearly all facets of human existence. Many say military defense is the only legitimate function of a national government. The Constitution says they are wrong. Who would "establish Justice, insure domestic Tranquility ... promote the general Welfare, and secure the Blessing of Liberty to ourselves" if government didn't take action to do it? Who would protect our equality under the laws if government didn't? Often the arguments of "libertarians" call for elimination of protections afforded to all citizens by constitutional government. Elimination of these protections could possibly lead modern societies back to the medieval social conditions mankind uses civilization to escape. Antigovernment sentiments contribute nothing to the well-being of the human beast. Properly administered constitutional government has much to contribute.

When government doesn't properly administer its legal powers and duties, many ordinary people make a constitutional statement with their actions rather than with their words. They don't consider themselves to be making any statement, and their actions aren't perceived as constitutionally motivated, but they are. And the constitutional ramifications are worth noting.

One "constitutional statement" that drew brief national attention was made in the late 1980s by a Washington state woman – Delia Alaniz – but her action was considered an ordinary crime. It's a crime many women commit, and which is never perceived as having any constitutional meaning. Mrs. Alaniz was convicted for the 1987 murder of her husband, who had reportedly abused her physically and psychologically for 17 years. The beatings and threats to her and her four children had been reported to local police, but she received nothing of the police-power protection government has to give its citizens. Public outcry about her conviction led Washington Gov. Booth Gardner to grant her clemency in 1989 after she had served less than two years of a 10-year sentence. The man she hired to do the killing wasn't granted clemency. Mrs. Alaniz was prosecuted for murder, according to the prosecutor, because the killing wasn't committed while trying to defend herself, it was carried out by a hired assassin after considerable planning and there was payment made for the killing. The state said that was murder.

With domestic violence reportedly affecting up to 6 million women annually and with as many as 4,000 women being killed during that violence, it isn't surprising that many seek refuge in the same solution – and the constitutional issue is always missed. The issue is best illustrated by John Jay's contention that government is formed when citizens surrender rights in order to vest the state with the power it needs to govern. The power the state exercises must have a source, and the source is the people. In Washington state, Mrs. Alaniz was, and still is, one source of the state's power. She surrenders rights to the state in return for the state's police-power protection. This aspect of the covenant carries a tacit agreement that a citizen wouldn't exercise individual authority to function as an independent sovereign government. That right is surrendered. The state was at fault in the Alaniz case because it didn't use the powers given it to protect a person who gives it power. So the solution was clear; Mrs. Alaniz repealed her grant of governmental power and functioned, in this instance, as a state. She determined what actions against her weren't permitted (legislative power), how that decision was to be administered (executive power), who was guilty and what the punishment must be (judicial power), and how punishment was to be carried out (police power). These are functions of government. And when she hired an executioner, Mrs. Alaniz was doing the same thing the state does, albeit with less finesse and sophistication.

Many people might argue that murder isn't acting as a state. But any state having capital punishment as part of its judicial code – as Washington does – is indicating it gets authority to kill from the people. The state cannot get authority to execute from God, that happens in a theocracy. The state cannot create its power to execute, that's a feature of autocracy. In a democracy, the state gets all of its power from the people, and that includes the power to execute criminals. If the people can give power of execution to the state, they would have that power themselves if they hadn't created the state. If they had that power before establishing government, they would be reclaiming the power when leaving the constitutional covenant. Government has a tacit agreement with its citizens to function honestly and fairly in their best interest, and it must protect all, so that many don't feel the need to leave the covenant in order to secure protection on their own.

Hundreds of women annually commit this "act of governance," as Mrs. Alaniz did, in an attempt to "establish Justice" and "insure domestic Tranquility" (two constitutional objectives). Some political leaders seem to be catching on – as Governor Gardner did – and admit with pardons and clemency that failure of government is the villain and that battered women are victims of that failure.

There's nothing in the Constitution allowing citizens to take power back from government by any means other than amendment, but revoking powers seems to be done more and more as society becomes more complex and government seems to lose perspective about its objectives. Reclaiming power from government in times past was accomplished merely by leaving the area over which government had jurisdiction. That is virtually impossible now because little of earth's surface is untouched by government authority. If a person reclaims power by leaving the jurisdiction of one government, that power must be surrendered to a new jurisdiction, either given voluntarily to a democracy or taken by force by the other types of government. Stripping power from government has taken many forms in the past few decades in both legal and illegal methods.

An obvious reclamation of power came in the 1960s with the antiwar movement. Persons opposed to the war in Vietnam weren't in position to declare war, but they were in position to declare peace, and did so by refusing to cooperate with the government. Some went to Canada to escape the military draft, some refused to pay taxes they thought were going to the war effort, and others engaged in sabotage and revolt. Another antiwar attitude was present as the Persian Gulf crisis deepened. At that time, the people demanded to be part of the process of declaring war (or nonwar).

After the war with Iraq started in January 1991, opposition to the war increased, as did opposition to the "peace advocates." It seemed easy for many to claim a First Amendment "freedom of speech" right for opponents to the war to voice their opposition. That claim misses the point. When the United States wages war, it uses the powers obtained from all Americans, those who favor war and those who oppose it. Since power coming from opponents of war is used, those against war certainly have authority to question how their power is used – or misused. The same refusal to rely solely on government judgment was instrumental in the nuclear-freeze movement of the 1980s and the environmental concerns that became serious about the same time.

Frustration with government and displeasure with its failures are usually the underlying causes of stripping power from the state. Frustration and displeasure were behind creation in the late 1970s of the Guardian Angels in New York City. This citizen crime-fighting movement spread to other cities across the nation as crime reached what many people perceived to be unacceptable levels. Police – like all other persons and organizations in society – are controlled by law, which made it seem to some people that police were unable to cope with the crime problem, so citizen involvement increased. Other anticrime movements, including homosexual patrols following increases in violence against gays, have become common nationwide. Many groups attempted to do what government normally does, including regulation of television and determining educational material for the public schools. Some efforts were attempts to usurp governmental power, while others were merely attempts to retain powers not delegated to government (Tenth Amendment). Citizens conducting some government functions, such as aiding the homeless, is fine. Some citizen action isn't.

GOING TO EXTREMES

Much of the nation has pockets of individuals who have broken away from government, claiming the nation "is going to the dogs." These people claim that their rights are being destroyed, conspiracies are all around them, plots are advancing one worldwide government and insidious influences are conspiring to destroy the country. Some of these people form townships,

Paring Powers

establish courts, militias, ambassadors or whatever else they think government needs. Many claim to be experts on the Constitution and call themselves "constitutional patriots." Few states have managed to avoid such movements and have been forced to deal with these people in the criminal system. These rebels are taking total power back from government, unlike those who take power in one or two matters. Many of these movements came into being following the antiwar movement of the 1960s, as if the '60s taught many that government wasn't needed.

Some "constitutional patriots" in the western United States have gone as far as claiming to be totally free of government influence and are, themselves, the government. They apparently think themselves re-created in the images of colonial patriots of the Revolutionary War. They have issued driver's licenses and automobile plates to themselves, contending that the state has no authority to force them to be so registered or to carry automobile insurance. When arrested and fined for such infractions, many refuse to pay the fines leveled in state courts. One such man said: "I didn't pay any of the fines because the state ... hasn't adhered to the Constitution as far as what legal tender is. The Constitution is very specific. It says no state shall make anything other than gold or silver coin a payment of debts."

There are problems with many of these positions, and the Constitution covers all arguments. As earlier explained, government surely has power, both explicit and implied, to regulate the use of government property (Article I, Section 8). Highways are government property, so the government can make rules pertaining to how traffic is controlled (speed limits and driving technique), who may use the roads (licensed drivers and vehicles), how vehicles must be equipped (lights, brakes) and if there shall be punishment for disobeying its rules. And uninsured motorists or vehicles may be excluded from government property. States, counties and cities have the same power as the national government to manage their properties. Constitutional experts can find such powers with ease.

The Constitution says unequivocally that all governments must honor the laws and authority of all other legal governments – (Article IV, Section 1). It says, "Full Faith and Credit shall be given in each State to the public acts, Records, and Judicial Proceedings of every other State." That requirement isn't restricted to state governments since cities, counties and villages are "in each State." To drop out of legitimate government and claim it doesn't exist, isn't giving full faith and credit to the prevailing sovereign. Full faith and credit means recognizing the state's authority.

Any new state must be approved by Congress, and no state can be formed within the jurisdiction of an existing state without the approval of the state's legislature and Congress. Article IV, Section 3 says, "no new States shall be formed or erected within the Jurisdiction of any other State; nor any State be formed by the Junction of two or more States, or parts of States, without the Consent of the Legislatures of the States concerned as well as of the Congress." A dropout group claiming to form its own government free from authority of the existing state has to be saying that it's forming a *new state* because counties, cities, townships or villages are still subject to state jurisdiction. And, "parts of States" would include any village, township or farm. If that "new government" hasn't been formed according to constitutional principles, the creation is un-American.

Whether a state cannot make anything but gold or silver a legal tender is a special case with an interesting history and is related to the constitutional prohibition of the states from impairing an obligation of contracts (Article I, Section 10). But, its meaning isn't what the so-called "patriots" claim it to be. In colonial times, political participation was restricted to property-owning adult males (nearly always white, but it's possible a descendant of freed slaves could own property in the North). Consequently, most government at all levels came to be dominated by agriculture interests who found markets in Canada and Great Britain no longer available to them because of the revolution and break with the mother country. Being unable to turn crops into cash, lawmakers from state legislator to village alderman were unable to meet financial obligations, so they sought to serve their interests first, to the exclusion of others in society. By using creative legislation, they would forgive debts on their farms or make their crops a legal tender for payment of debt. It didn't matter to plantation owners that a Southern bank had no way of selling cotton given as legal tender, just as they couldn't sell it. The legislators' only concern is that they didn't lose their property by foreclosure.

When it came time to write the United States Constitution, the founders displayed a little more honesty – they also were property owners – and did the right thing by eliminating this opportunity of self-serving politicians. Commodities such as cotton, corn and cucumbers could no longer be legislated as currency to pay off debt, only money could be used. The granting of power to Congress "to coin Money, regulate the Value thereof ..." (Article I, Section 8, paragraph 5) only made it possible for the national government to create one legal tender for the nation. Nothing in the Constitution made gold and silver the legal currency of states; gold and silver were what served as money at that time. Nowhere in the power to coin money by the federal government is there a suggestion that gold and silver are forever to be the nation's currency.

Paring Powers

With the national government taking over authority for currency from the 13 states – they were forbidden to coin money – it determined what could serve as payment of commercial or personal debts. Whether state or local courts were restricted to gold and silver as payment for fines was determined in 1868. But, because that determination isn't specifically mentioned in the Constitution, few people can find it. What happened was the adoption of the Fourteenth Amendment, an action that had nothing to do with money or debts, but which left state and local courts free to legally demand payment in paper dollars for fines they impose. One clause of the Fourteenth Amendment says, "nor shall any State deprive any person of life, liberty, or property, without the due process of law." That clause means that with due process of law, a person may be deprived of life, liberty or property by the states. By giving Congress the power to create money and regulate its value, the Constitution established an authority to create property. Money – whether gold, silver, paper, copper or nickel – has value and is therefore property to be owned just as any other property is owned. That property can be taken as fines by state courts following any conviction.

Such ignorance of the Constitution shows numerous self-proclaimed "experts," or "constitutional patriots," are merely un-American – according to Justice Antonin Scalia's definition – and haven't the faintest idea of what the Constitution does. This problem similarly affects others who proclaim a patriotism or love of country. Waving flags and singing anthems aren't adequate substitutes for constitutional knowledge, and that's the basis of true patriotism.

Chapter 7

FREEDOM IS

AN ARGUMENT FOR NONPOWER

Chapter 5 clearly shows the United States Constitution doesn't address itself to freedoms of the individual; it deals with authority of government. The Constitution doesn't create freedom or liberty, even though Americans think it's the basis of those concepts. The Constitution doesn't guarantee protection of freedoms, although that's what it does when it's administered correctly. The Founding Fathers didn't mention individual freedom in the Constitution because they knew they weren't granting freedom to American citizens; they were reducing freedom of the individuals in order to empower a new government. They weren't under a delusion that they or the Constitution were sources of liberty. Freedom can be thought to come from a higher being, or to be natural to life. Freedom *IS*, it isn't created or granted. The Constitution isn't the source of freedom; it's an instrument of power – government power – and one of its primary functions is to specify the limitations of individual freedoms. That's what John Jay was saying when he said Americans must give up some rights in order to give certain powers to government. Americans did that, and freedom was lost where rights were eliminated or reduced.

The Constitution recognizes one form of freedom by specifying areas where governmental power has restraints, such as Article I's prohibitions in Section 9, and very few freedoms are found there. The Bill of Rights specifies more freedoms, but many are really superfluous statements, as should become obvious in the next few chapters.

True freedom, therefore, falls outside the United States Constitution and the state constitutions. Freedom exists where there is no authority to restrict it. The absence of government power is freedom, and absence of power is at the center of many contentions where courts are called on to decide cases and controversies. If everyone had an expertise in constitutional philosophy and were principled enough to allow constitutionality to reign, there would be little need for an elaborate court system. But few Americans have constitutional knowledge, so they must rely on government officials to handle the philosophies of the covenant. But sadly, government officials are no more qualified for this task than anyone else, and they fail badly in understanding and upholding the Constitution, which will be evident as notable constitutional controversies are examined. These failures are demonstrated by

Freedom Is

thoughts and actions of elected officials and in citizens' animosity toward the court system of a nation that is operating on the principles of law and constitutionality.

Oliver Wendell Holmes opined early in the 20th century that an untrained mind assumes those things it endorses are constitutional and what it opposes it perceives as unconstitutional. He was correct, as the next few pages will show.

In the 1988 presidential election campaign, George Bush gained considerable political support from the electorate by claiming he endorsed laws to allow children to recite the Pledge of Allegiance in public schools. He alluded to an assumed unpatriotism by his opponent, Michael Dukakis, for vetoing a 1977 bill that would have made a teacher-led pledge a school ritual in Massachusetts. Bush anticipated that such a charge would be politically beneficial and it was one of the issues he rode to victory, but he a showed lack of patriotism by distorting the constitutional principles and history involved.

There never has been a court decision or legally enacted law that would stop anyone from voicing allegiance to the United States or saluting the flag in a public school. Dukakis' veto of the bill in no way prevented children from pledging their allegiance to the United States or to Massachusetts. The right to do so is possessed by everyone, to be exercised as one wishes. The right to determine for oneself personal allegiance to a nation or a cause is called "freedom."

This issue had been settled by a 1943 Supreme Court decision – *West Virginia Board of Education v. Barnette* – that Dukakis used as guidance in deciding whether to sign or veto the 1977 bill. The court had to take two tries on this issue; it admitted error in deciding *Minersville School District v. Gobitis* (1940) in favor of government. Both cases have been considered freedom-of-religion cases because they involved school children from families of Jehovah's Witnesses. In both cases, names were misspelled. Witnesses report Barnett and Gobitas were the correct spellings.

Because of their Bible-based beliefs, the children in both cases didn't join in compulsory teacher-led rituals of nationalism in the public schools. They were guided by such Bible "commands" as Mark 12:17 which told them to "Render to Caesar the things that are Caesar's, and to God the things that are God's." That verse was taken to mean they were to render to (Washington in the District of) Caesar respect and submission to secular law, when it didn't violate God's laws. But allegiance was to be rendered to Jehovah God because Matthew 6:33 told the children "seek ye first the kingdom of God," not the kingdom of the Potomac. Matthew 6:24 said they could serve only one master. They chose God. They stood up to the state because Jesus Christ wouldn't swear allegiance to any one state, because three Hebrews in Babylon went to the fiery furnace rather than bow down on a king's command to participate in a nationalistic ritual, and because early Christians were neutral in all matters between states. Christianity, to the children, was a full-time commitment; therefore allegiance to Jehovah must be total, complete, whole. Sunday-morning Christians, to Jehovah's Witnesses thinking, fail to grasp the concept by pledging allegiance to God when in church, but to Caesar Monday through Saturday. Christ-like neutrality is the Witnesses' quest.

Whether Witnesses have unerring understanding of the Bible isn't the issue because there's no legal authority that can question their beliefs. That principle was decided in 1940 in *Cantwell v. Connecticut* – another Jehovah's Witnesses case – when the court said government has no power to regulate any religious thought or to decide what's valid biblical interpretation, but religious actions are subject to the same control as nonreligious actions. That second point is why the court could decide the Oregon peyote-smoking case as it did. Witnesses' neutrality may be little more than illusory because of the nature of government by covenant. It's their power the government is using and, by being peaceful and law-abiding citizens, Witnesses are tacitly agreeing to surrender that power through the covenant while trying to be "no part of this world" about how government uses that power.

In the Gobitis case, two children were expelled for remaining neutral in the daily ritual of saluting the American flag. Their father had to enroll them in private schools to comply with mandatory-attendance law of Pennsylvania, an extremely expensive proposition for a working man. He had a legitimate case because of the financial damage the state action had caused. He sued and won all trials up to the United States Supreme Court, where most of the judges missed the point. One of America's finer judicial practitioners, Felix Frankfurter, put those errors into print in the majority opinion which said the expulsions were legal.

Frankfurter was in error by the third paragraph when he wrote: "We must decide whether the requirement of participation in such a ceremony, exacted from a child who refuses upon sincere religious grounds, infringes without due process of law the liberty guaranteed by the Fourteenth Amendment." The error was that this case didn't involve the guarantee of due process of law; it involved the "privileges or immunities" clause of the Fourteenth Amendment. Frankfurter hit the "incorrect" button again with the statement that, "The mere possession of religious convictions which

Freedom Is

contradict the relevant concerns of a political society does not relieve the citizen from discharge of political responsibilities." He added, "The ultimate foundation of a free society is the binding tie of cohesive sentiment." The errors in Frankfurter's logic occurred because he was relying on a governmental power that simply doesn't exist. It didn't exist when the Constitution was written, it didn't exist when these events took place before World War II, and it doesn't exist now.

Not one word in the Constitution gives government power to compel patriotism, nationalism, or allegiance, or the authority to punish a citizen because some government official is unsatisfied with that individual's beliefs. The Constitution isn't concerned with "political responsibilities" of American citizens or the "cohesive sentiment" of society. Any "political responsibilities" a person can find by statement or implication in the Constitution would apply only to the government and the people who exercise governmental power. Political responsibilities are required of the president, and they include obeying and faithfully executing the laws. Political responsibilities apply to military officers, and they require obeying all laws created by Congress. Political responsibilities are applicable to elected legislators, and they require legally using only those powers constitutionally given. Political responsibilities are obligations of judges – from the Supreme Court down to the local justice of the peace – and they require knowing and supporting all constitutional principles.

Americans can and should be bound in a "cohesive sentiment" by the liberty they all enjoy under a covenant in which all are equal partners, not by a government that coerces rituals of allegiance or nationalism. Nazi Germany tried that.

The court admitted its error three years later in the Barnette case. Some Bush apologists claimed the Barnette case involved students being forced to salute the flag, not pledging allegiance. They lied. The court decision in 1943 said, "We think the action of the local authorities in compelling the flag salute and pledge transcends constitutional limitations on their powers and invades the sphere of intellect and spirit which it is the purpose of the First Amendment to our Constitution to reserve from all official control." In plain language, the Supreme Court said there's no power given to government to compel patriotism or allegiance. Freedom to select objects of allegiances or to determine degrees of patriotism is a "constitutional immunity" protected from the federal government because to compel statements of allegiance is a violation of free speech, a First Amendment right. The Fourteenth Amendment makes that freedom immune from state encroachment. In this respect, these were absence-of-power, rather than freedom-of-religion,

THE UN-AMERICANS

controversies because immunity would remain if religion wasn't involved.

One Bush apologist, then-Rep. Lynn Martin, R-Ill., remarked in a 1988 television debate that, "Most people think it's okay to start a classroom with the Pledge of Allegiance. Most people don't think that's unconstitutional." Starting a class with a pledge wasn't the issue; government compulsion was. "Most people" haven't studied the Constitution – just as Martin obviously hadn't – so what they think has nothing to do with constitutionality. The Constitution specifically vests in "one supreme Court" and inferior courts the judicial power to decide the controversy over whether "it's okay to start a classroom with the Pledge of Allegiance." Judicial power wasn't vested in "most people." Martin, who later served in Bush's cabinet, is one of those people who haven't come close to understanding their proper "discharge of political responsibilities."

Another Bush apologist, Tottie Ellis of the Eagle Forum, wrote a USA TODAY guest column (Aug. 31, 1988) under the headline "Make kids pledge, it's patriotic." In the column, she said:

"There is a real danger if we surrender our schools to people who have a hostility to America's values, interests and purposes."

Allowing freedom isn't surrendering to people who are hostile to our values; it *IS* one of America's most-precious values. Forcing children to recite a pledge is denying freedom, and that's a real "hostility to America's values, interests and purposes." There's simply no power for government to do as Bush and his apologists advocated; therefore it's their patriotism that's questionable. A principle of compulsive nationalism isn't in the Constitution, meaning those who advocate such force are the real un-Americans under Justice Antonin Scalia's definition.

Between the Gobitis and Barnette decisions, a situation arose that should demonstrate that advocating forced recitation of the Pledge of Allegiance in schools is a scornful and ludicrous matter. Early in World War II, the American government imprisoned about 120,000 West Coast residents of Japanese descent – about two-thirds of them United States citizens – for national security and to prevent the possibility of sabotage. There had never been an act of, or an intent to commit, sabotage by any of those Americans. But there had been years of pledging allegiance, saluting the flag, singing the national anthem, making oaths of loyalty to the United States and generally being near-perfect citizens who loved their United States. There was never a case of a Japanese-American child declining to participate in pledging, saluting and singing during public-school rituals of nationalism. None ever swore allegiance to another nation. But by placing them in concentration camps without due process of law or evidence of any crime or wrongdoing, government officials said pledges were meaningless, saluting the flag was meaningless, singing an anthem was meaningless and oaths of loyalty were meaningless.

A BURNING CONTROVERSY

Protecting freedoms isn't appreciated if much of the nation's population doesn't regard those freedoms to be important, and defending liberty can be inflammatory when it offends a majority of people who don't understand the function of the Constitution.

Perhaps no other recent issue has inflamed the nation as did the flag-burning decisions of the late 1980s. Virtually everyone had an opinion to voice after the Supreme Court voided laws that prohibited burning the United States flag in protest. In June of 1989 the court overturned the Texas conviction of a man who burned the flag in a demonstration at the 1984 Republican National Convention in Dallas. The court ruled that the law infringed on the First Amendment protection of free speech as applied by the Fourteenth Amendment to the states. Most of the population was outraged, and Congress immediately jumped into the controversy by enacting a federal law to outlaw the burning of the flag in protest. All flag burning wasn't outlawed because that's still considered the only proper method of disposing of worn-out flags. A federal judge in Seattle declared the law void law after four Seattle demonstrators were arrested for burning a Post Office flag moments after the federal law took effect. The Supreme Court upheld this reversal on the basis that burning the flag was "symbolic speech" and, therefore, protected by the First Amendment of the Constitution.

It was a balanced majority that came to that conclusion – there were two liberals, one moderate and two conservatives. Their logic may be a bit flawed on the "symbolic speech" aspect of the controversy. By carrying that thinking a bit further one would come to the conclusion that public female nudity would be a "figure of speech" deserving constitutional protection. Such a conclusion might not apply to men because they don't have figures, they have whatever it is that "hunks" have. Because the Supreme Court has the power to decide controversies, Americans have to accept its conclusion that flag burning is "speech" in a metaphorical sense.

Opposing the decision were four political conservatives – Chief Justice William Rehnquist, Judges Sandra Day O'Connor, Byron White and John Paul Stevens. In his dissent, Rehnquist wrote, "I cannot agree that the First Amendment invalidates the act of Congress, and the laws of 48 of the 50 states, which make criminal the public burning of the flag ..."

He was correct in his assessment about the First Amendment; it should not invalidate such laws. The federal law had to be invalidated because the Constitution never vested in Congress the power to make such a law. Article I, Section 8, contains most of Congress' powers, and if power to regulate such behavior is to be found there, it was Rehnquist's duty to find it and show those who can't see it. He needed to say just which power was being used – it certainly wasn't the power to coin money, to regulate commerce, to establish Post Offices, to raise and support armies. The truth is that there is no power in the Constitution to authorize such a law. The "privileges or immunities" clause in the Fourteenth Amendment makes this vacuum of power applicable to Texas and the other states, and the individual has the right to be free of governmental authority.

Rehnquist wrote, "... one of the high purposes of a democratic society is to legislate against conduct that is regarded as evil and profoundly offensive to the majority of people ..." That is true when the legislative body of that society has a valid power to use. Police power is enough in situations involving victims and victimizers; it cannot cover all conduct, regardless of offensiveness. The surprising outcome of these controversies wasn't that the laws were negated; it was where in the Constitution did four conservative judges find the power for such laws to be enacted in the first place?

The problem with looking to protect only those rights found written in black and white instead of searching for constitutional powers that must be used by government is that many political conservatives fail to recognize a valid right when it comes dressed as a metaphor.

Former federal Judge Robert Bork labeled the decisions "plainly wrong" in hearings before a House of Representatives panel considering a constitutional amendment. He didn't identify what legitimate constitutional power the court majority had missed.

A syndicated columnist, Thomas Sowell of the Scripps-Howard News Service, wrote an anti-Supreme Court diatribe based on severe misinterpretations. His attack stated that, "Those who wrote the Constitution probably would turn over in their graves if they knew what strained meanings were being given to their words. Burning the flag is not speech but action."

Sowell criticized the court because he didn't understand the founders' words, but the court majority understood the founders quite well. Those who wrote the Constitution understood that their words were dealing with government power. Their words gave power to government to do what was needed to be done. Their words said nothing about giving power to Congress to curtail protest of words or action. Their words in no way authorized a universal power for government to do anything it wished. If "those who wrote the Constitution" had a failing, it was in assuming that Americans would be able to see that if a power isn't mentioned or implied, it isn't valid. There's nothing in the Constitution suggesting that a symbol of nationalism would be superior to liberty. If those who wrote the Constitution were to "turn over in their graves," it would be from discovering their democratic creation was in danger of being turned into an autocratic hybrid by those persons who want an absolute power to persecute protesters or other unpopular people. The fact that something is action, rather than speech, doesn't empower the government to do as it wishes – it must have a legal power. The flag-burning decisions reaffirmed the principle of limited government.

Sowell accused the judges of having "gotten themselves tangled in their own cleverness" going "far beyond the Constitution," using a "dishonesty of pretending that (a decision) came from the Constitution," and of indulging in "verbal sleight of hand."

People who understand the Constitution know these vicious charges to be nonsense, and it's the journalist who's being dishonest by pretending to know what he's writing about when he knows nothing. There is nothing clever about reading the Constitution and seeing it has no power to trample dissent. Telling government to restrict its actions to its constitutional power isn't going "beyond the Constitution"; it's making Congress or the states obey the Constitution. There's nothing dishonest in seeing limitations to power, and "verbal sleight of hand" is mainly apparent to those who can't read competently.

Sowell added, "even those justices who sincerely want to uphold the Constitution, as written, are faced with the tough choice of upsetting legal precedents or continuing to add to the problem." The truth is, the Constitution is being upheld by all the justices – conservative, moderate and liberal – and there is no problem other than journalistic misrepresentations. It's journalists who have no knowledge about the "Constitution, as written."

Sowell's nonsense added,"Much bigger things are involved in all these decisions than simply the legal issues that arose in each of these cases. Constitutional democracy is about the people's right to govern themselves ..."

In the United States' constitutional democracy the people govern themselves by giving power to make law to Congress, power to execute the laws to a president and power to decide cases and controversies to a judicial system. The people can choose who exercises those powers, but it would help if they were not being constantly mislead by journalists of no knowledge.

Sowell also railed that property rights were recently being eroded, but the flag-burning decisions in a small way reaffirmed those property rights, as shall become apparent.

THE UN-AMERICANS

In a column critical of the court, conservative journalist George Will quoted Judge Harry Blackmun who had once written, "The flag is a national property and the nation may regulate those who would make, imitate, sell, possess or use it ... There would seem to be little question about the power of Congress to forbid the mutilation of the Lincoln Memorial ... The flag is itself a monument, subject to similar protection." Some of that is true, some isn't. Certainly Congress can make laws concerning those who make, sell, imitate or transport the flag or use it in advertising because it has power to regulate some commerce. Congress certainly can prohibit mutilation of the Lincoln Memorial because the Constitution gives it power in Article I, Section 8, "to exercise ... Authority over all Places (such as) needful Buildings" and in Article IV to "make all needful Rules and Regulations respecting ... Property belonging to the United States."

The issue here is whether Congress or state legislatures have authority over property that is obviously private and isn't used as an endangerment of others. The United States was the first nation in history to write into its basic law the sanctity of private property after breaking with Great Britain where property was considered to belong to the crown. America's property right was one of the most-prized principles of John Locke, the nation's patron creator. When an individual purchases a flag, that item is the personal private property of the purchaser; it isn't the property of a neighbor, city, state, nation or any other entity. The Constitution doesn't give power to the federal government to "make all needful Rules and Regulations respecting" property belonging to the individual. Private ownership of any object – including flags – isn't subject to the same legal control as government-owned property, and the decisions said that.

The Seattle flag burners weren't freed from their actions. In mid-October of 1990 they were sentenced after being convicted of a real crime. Their action was punished because they destroyed United States property – the flag they burned was stolen from the Post Office building. Their actions might also be subject to prosecution on antipollution laws, littering, obstruction of a public passageway or many other charges bright prosecutors could think of. Their protest could not be punished. These cases, similar to the Pledge of Allegiance controversies, were really "immunity" cases, not freedom of speech.

Blackmun had altered his views somewhat as he evolved into a learned and competent Supreme Court judge. As part of the majority in these cases, he came to recognize immunity of the individual from government encroachment in some matters.

The response to these flag-burning cases proves the wisdom of the late

Justice Holmes. Those unschooled in constitutionalism wasted no time attacking the court without knowing what the Constitution says. They assumed the Constitution endorsed and supported their personal ignorance. It didn't.

TO AMEND OR NOT TO AMEND

Of course, many people who couldn't recognize the principles of immunity or limited government immediately called for a constitutional amendment to outlaw flag burning on the grounds it was "desecration," and the flag needed "protection." Use of the word "protection" was puzzling. Did it mean that without government action a flag would die, suffer irreparable damage, couldn't reproduce, become ill or be impoverished? Or was seeking "protection" merely "speaking Sloganese" by those who sought to politically capitalize on the situation?

One unschooled critic calling for the amendment was Cal Thomas, a Los Angeles Times Syndicate columnist, who wrote, "more than a constitutional amendment to protect the flag, we need some 'amendments' to the Supreme Court to protect us from 'lone ranger' judges. These liberal judges have felt called to protect loonies, but not the flag." Two of those "liberal" judges were Anthony Kennedy and Antonin Scalia, called "conservatives" by many knowledgeable people. Thomas added, "Until enough justices with common sense can be named to the court, Congress ought to demonstrate some guts and protect our national symbol with a constitutional amendment."

Discerning people would call for justices with "constitutional sense," and there were five of them in the majority on decisions Thomas couldn't understand. What "amendments" Americans really need are fewer "loonies" writing newspaper editorials and columns.

USA TODAY reported that immediately after the second decision, 69 percent of Americans supported an amendment. An amendment giving Congress power "to protect the flag" would create the legal authority to make law that couldn't previously be enacted, laws which probably would be immune from judicial destruction. A few months later the newspaper reported that support for the amendment by the American people had waned, going from an overwhelming majority favoring police action against demonstrators to a majority thinking protecting the Constitution from political tampering might be a better idea.

Unfortunately, political opportunists and their allies didn't see the shift and proceeded with the amendment hyperbole. The proposed amendment

THE UN-AMERICANS

said, "The Congress and the states shall have the power to prohibit the physical desecration of the flag of the United States." That seemed mundane enough to some who thought it wouldn't be harmful. Supporting the proposed amendment was Sen. Robert Dole, R-Kan., who wrote in USA TODAY: "After the court's mistake, President Bush took the lead by calling for a constitutional amendment during a speech at Washington's Iwo Jima Memorial. The huge Stars and Stripes flying proudly above that awesome monument reminded us again of the courage and sacrifice Americans have made for their country and flag." This sort of "Sloganese" shouldn't have been taken seriously for several reasons:

– The court didn't make a mistake; it only said what the Constitution said – Congress and the states didn't have power to do what they tried to do.

– Bush, during the 1988 campaign, showed disdain for constitutional immunities.

– Dole ignored "courage and sacrifice Americans have made" for their country and Constitution. Americans who died for constitutional freedoms made just as serious a sacrifice and are just as dead as those who died for the flag. To allude that their sacrifice was somehow inferior to others' sacrifice was ludicrous and insulting. And to tamper, for political gain, with constitutional freedoms Americans died for would be desecration of their sacrifice.

Groups calling themselves patriotic joined in the effort to have the Constitution amended. Several jointly sponsored an advertisement in USA TODAY urging pressure on senators to support the amendment. Listed in the ad were: The American Legion and Auxiliary; Veterans of Foreign Wars and Auxiliary; Disabled American Veterans and Auxiliary; American Veterans of World War II, Korea, Vietnam (AMVETS) and Auxiliary; Catholic Wars Veterans, USA, Inc.; American Ex-Prisoners of War; United States JayCees; Fraternal Order of Police; American Federation of Police; National Association of Chiefs of Police; Military Order of the Purple Heart; Polish Legion of American Veterans; Paralyzed Veterans of America; and Blinded Veterans Association and Auxiliary.

Spokesmen for some of these organizations also took to the pages of newspapers with compositions calling for the amendment. American Legion National Commander Miles S. Epling, reported in a USA TODAY guest column that delegates to the Legion's 1989 national convention voted unanimously for a resolution supporting the amendment. He called the flag "the living symbol of this great nation." But "living" is a word usually associated with the Constitution.

David Pickett, an assistant district of attorney and a life member of the Veterans of Foreign Wars, wrote from Dallas, "The flag represented the very

Freedom Is

soul and spirit of America to our Founding Fathers; it will be the badge of our greatness and the emblem of our destiny to posterity." He added, "The weak and permissive reasoning of the court's opinion ... plays into the hands of those who seek to destroy our country."

It seems a shame that truth should detract from such fine poetic phrasing, but our Founding Fathers didn't say a word in the Constitution about the flag, which the Continental Congress created with one sentence a decade before the founders created a nation of liberty with what some people consider the greatest document of national unity ever written. The flag got no mention in that document, a strange "oversight" for the "soul and spirit of America." The truth is: the Constitution was the "soul and spirit of America" to the Founding Fathers. People who regard that document of freedom as inferior to a cloth symbol are more apt to destroy the country than are those who would burn that cloth. That's not "weak reasoning."

Screenwriter and novelist Jesse Hill Ford wrote in USA TODAY that "Our Supreme Court cannot ... be viewed other than as dimwitted ... they have wounded the sensibilities of that special segment consisting of our war veterans and the survivors of our war dead." Of course, that statement is nonsense. The court isn't dimwitted for reading the Constitution correctly, and it didn't wound the sensibilities of people who know what the Constitution says.

Phyllis Schlafly, president of Eagle Forum, wrote that the "court is the one out of step with the laws of 48 states, the federal government and the overwhelm majority of the American people." Schlafly added, "the purpose of the First Amendment is to promote freedom of public and private discourse ..." She was, of course, wrong. The Constitution doesn't contain any suggestion that laws are permissible if most of the states, the federal government and the majority of the American people approve; laws are valid only when based on a valid constitutional power. The First Amendment doesn't promote anything; it reminds government there are areas in which its power does not reach. Schlafly was the one out of step; out of step with the Constitution.

President Bush, in calling for the constitutional amendment, said flag burning "must carry a price."

All of these people helped prove Chief Justice John Marshall correct in his 1819 assessment that the public couldn't understand the Constitution. Those who haven't the faintest idea of what the Constitution is all about have the right to say and write what they did – that's protected by the First Amendment they don't comprehend. They also didn't understand the issue behind the protests.

THE UN-AMERICANS

Epling wrote: "Anyone who cannot deliver a message without committing mayhem does not have a message worth sending."

They weren't sending a message, and that was the issue. Protesters don't burn the flag to elicit sympathy for their causes, even when there is validity to their stances. They put flame to the flag to arouse the exact response that was aroused. Flag burners know they aren't gaining support for their point of view – they lose any possibility of support, and that's what they want. The flag is burned with the knowledge the burning will cause irrational and un-American reactions. Flag burners may believe that by trying to slay freedoms Americans will show the world they're hypocritical about principles of freedom, as happened with flag burning. People calling for a crackdown on flag burners were being used as allies by those flag burners in demonstrating hypocrisy.

The Supreme Court wouldn't be used.

But politicians apparently don't learn from their failure if trying to make a political gain. The issue of the constitutional amendment was again raised in March of 1995, shortly after Congress was taken over by the Republicans.

The proposed amendments are never what they're presented to be because they don't deal with desecration of the flag, only physical destruction. There are other desecrations the pseudo-patriots ignored – maybe on purpose, maybe by not thinking.

An example of potential desecration occurred in the summer of 1990 when the Professional Golfers' Association discovered (with help from the press) that it was holding prestigious events at country clubs practicing un-American racial discrimination. Some clubs also practiced un-Americanism in discriminating against Jewish golfers and un-Americanism in discriminating against women. For the flag to be associated with un-American discrimination could be just as much desecration as burning, and the amendment wouldn't "protect the flag from being desecrated" by its display in segregated facilities. If "patriots" were really concerned about desecration of national symbols, they could have proposed a prohibition on using any or all symbols, emblems or titles in association with un-American or racist rituals. As an example, if a group calling for the constitutional amendment practiced racial, religious or sexual discrimination, it could be punished for displaying the American flag, playing or singing the national anthem or using "American" or "USA" in association with itself. Punishment could be inflicted for using an eagle in name or depiction by any group opposing equality and civil rights for all. The proposed amendment didn't do that.

Those types of "desecration" wouldn't "carry a price."

Freedom Is

GOVERNMENT CAN BE CRIMINAL

Protection of Americans' freedom isn't the only benefit derived from a judiciary deciding all cases and controversies arising under the Constitution, the laws, treaties and government behavior. Protecting the integrity of the nation and Constitution is also an important function of the courts. And government definitely needs to be controlled by an active and competent judicial system.

Infringement on a person's rights and freedom is sometimes hard to determine because of problems with interpretation. It's often difficult to detect discrimination before a controversy is decided in a fair hearing by an impartial arbiter. What's discrimination to one, may be oversight, mistake or accident to another. An action that may seem by a "victim" to come from discrimination may be perfectly justified from the perpetrator's point of view. Some people see discrimination everywhere and every problem to them is the result of discrimination. Some see discrimination nowhere and seem not to know what the word means.

Deciding such issues is what makes the Constitution seem to be ever changing and why constitutional authorities refer to it as a "living Constitution." It's meanings can seem to modify slightly as social mores change, and keeping track of those shifts, improvements and advancements in thought and civilization is what gives joy to real patriots and constitution-lovers. And each positive outcome is seen by them as another step in the journey mankind is making toward a new Eden.

Protecting the integrity of the nation and Constitution is often one of those steps. That protection can related to crime committed by government. A crime that could send an individual to prison for several years is a "right of government" by some crime-committing officials. Government doesn't have rights; it has powers, and there is nothing in the United States Constitution giving the government power to commit common crime. There's nothing in any state constitution authorizing any criminal conduct. Crime is what law says it is, and the Constitution indicates law applies equally to pauper and to president.

Actions by individuals need to be regulated by law – no one argues that point. Actions by businesses need to be regulated by law – almost no one argues that point. Actions by governments need to be regulated by law – many people argue that point – but it was never intended by the Founding Fathers that government officials needed, or should have, the power to commit crimes. The constitutional principle covering this matter is Article II, Section 4, and it says:

THE UN-AMERICANS

"The President, Vice President and all civil Officers of the United States, shall be removed from Office on Impeachment for, and conviction of, Treason, Bribery, or other high Crimes and Misdemeanors." If there had been any intent that government have power to commit crime, this statement wouldn't have been included.

Jay's contention that citizens surrendered some rights in order to create powers for government certainly wouldn't support a principle of government crime. The individual doesn't have a right to commit crime; therefore, there is no right to be surrendered to the state. The power for government to create power for itself is found in autocratic systems, which are un-American. Therefore, crime by government is an un-American principle and, as such, subversion. And subversion is more serious than is a common crime.

President Richard Nixon, who rose to national power by "fighting subversion," tried to justify the Watergate crimes of his administration with the contention that other administrations had resorted to such escapades. Other administrations may have broken laws, but that didn't create a power for the Nixon administration to commit crimes. The courts continually told him that. Nixon's duty, according to the United States Constitution, was to seek prosecution of those previous perpetrators, not to emulate their dirty deeds, if there were any such deeds. The Constitution said the president is to execute the laws (prosecute), obey the laws (don't perpetrate) and generally be a good citizen. He wasn't authorized to use the teen-age argument that "everybody else is doing it."

While the actions of the miscreant Nixon administration seemed by some people to be petty, it was their subversiveness that made them important to American history. When the judiciary ruled Nixon couldn't withhold tape recordings relating to the crimes, the principle of the police power to obtain evidence was reaffirmed. Legal gathering of evidence is a fundamental part of police power and a president couldn't negate that power.

Other administrations had events minor in nature but major in meaning that threatened the nation's integrity. Some were out of judicial reach, such as President Ronald Reagan's 1981 pardon of two former Federal Bureau of Investigation officials who were convicted of authorizing burglaries during the Nixon administration. The President has constitutional power to grant the pardons, but he also has the obligation to honor the constitutional principle of crime-free government. The pardons endorsed crime by government.

The crime problem was part of the Iran-contra affair years later. Many apologists said the perpetrators of crime should go free because they "were just following orders." Law doesn't justify or legalize crime if ordered, or every criminal would use that defense. And a criminal is anyone who commits a crime. Others apologists said the issue was only a dispute between Congress and the president about foreign policy. They lied. The dispute was about who made laws and who obeyed the laws. Evidence was destroyed, a criminal action in itself, and an act that undermined police power to collect evidence. Reagan and his administration often called on the judiciary to obey "original intent" of the Founding Fathers. "Original intent" was put into Article II, Section 4, and it said *NO CRIMES.*

The mess of government crime became even more clouded in 1990 with the escapades of Washington, D. C., Mayor Marion Barry, and his troubles with drug usage. Barry was lured into a criminal act – smoking crack cocaine – by an FBI task force and was subsequently convicted on one minor charge of possession. This raised a constitutional question that has never been resolved. That is, how can the "no-crimes" provision of the Constitution and principles of equality and consistency of powers allow the head of one executive branch of government (Barry) to be guilty of a crime when subordinates of another executive branch (FBI agents) aren't guilty, even though they were parties to the same illegal activity? It seems that if Barry could be convicted of a crime that he obviously committed, those who provided the drugs would also be guilty of a crime because the Constitution doesn't authorize criminal actions as a duty of government.

After the Abscam scandals in which congressmen accepted bribes from FBI agents Judge William B. Bryant of the U.S. District Court in Washington, let it be known that he didn't appreciate government-sponsored crime as he overturned the conviction of one bribe-taker in 1982. It wasn't that the ex-congressman was innocent – he wasn't – it was that government was the real criminal. The principle of crimeless government may need to be more firmly established.

Police power allows use of what are called "stings" to trap criminals. If done properly, there usually is no constitutional problem. Letting others know a person is receptive to buying used property isn't criminal. When buying this "used property," police don't know positively it's stolen; therefore, they aren't knowingly receiving stolen property, they are investigating and gathering evidence. To create a crime to manufacture evidence is another matter; it ignores the no-crime principle of the Constitution, and subverts the legitimate evidence-gathering power.

This leads to a court-defined principle not mentioned in the Constitution, the "exclusionary rule." Critics of the judicial system would eliminate this rule immediately if given the chance. This rule basically says that evidence illegally seized must be excluded as evidence in a trial. It doesn't mean a trial can't be held or a defendant can't be convicted, only that evidence seized by illegal methods is contrary to law and its taking is a crime in its own right. Court critics can't find where the Constitution supports such a rule, but those who understand constitutional principles find that support easily.

The first basis for the exclusionary rule is that no officers of government may commit crime. Also supporting the rule are the Fourth Amendment, which says only reasonable seizures of evidence may be made, and the Sixth Amendment, which says the accused shall be entitled to a trial before an impartial jury. The Fourteenth Amendment applies these standards to the states. Police and prosecutors are officers of government and are required to be crime-free. While using in a trial evidence illegally seized may seem to be reasonable, it is not. It can be likened to possessing and using stolen property by a private citizen, and that's criminal. A punishment for possessing stolen — or unreasonably seized — evidence can be confiscation. The Sixth Amendment doesn't suggest an impartial jury is possible if swayed by illegality. Such a jury cannot be impartial and fair. While the exclusionary rule makes it difficult to prosecute a few cases, it also assists in prosecution by making sure all convictions are constitutionally valid. Illegal convictions free more criminals than does the exclusionary rule. If it's hard to convict the guilty, it's harder to convict the innocent.

Critics claim that criminals are allowed to go free on a "technicality." That isn't true. Competent police and prosecutors learn to live within their law just as law-abiding citizens learn to live within theirs. A few prosecutors and police will never try to obey the law, just as a few citizens will never do so, but others are still learning and are making fewer and fewer mistakes. If a guilty person should be freed, it would be because of the Constitution, the greatest "technicality" ever glued to paper by printer's ink.

EASY DOESN'T DO IT

When government, like a person, develops a habit that's difficult to shed, the habit often becomes the master, and the addicted becomes a slave. Government is not unlike people in such matters, and many in government develop an attitude that what's useful is acceptable. Some officials believe it's okay to do what they think will work or what they can get away with. There is nothing in the Constitution to suggest that's the American way. The Constitution was designed to make governing difficult. Government with ease too often turns into cruel totalitarianism. Those who seek office and power usually think themselves best equipped to deal with society's problems, and many go into government thinking they will lead the masses to a promised land. When the masses balk at the masters' guidance, it's tempting for leaders to resort to authoritative methods to "save" this insolent lot from itself.

Perhaps no movement proposing social salvation subverted itself more than communism, which offered "liberation" and a "workers' paradises." No movement – outside of religion – fancied itself to have so many "right" answers and "correct" thoughts as did Marxism of the 19th and early 20th centuries. While Marxists' thoughts were confined to paper, all the right answers and policies made perfect sense to believers. Putting their answers and policies into practice in societies that had real people, not fantasy comrades, was a bit different than anticipated.

Marxists with what they perceived were all the correct answers and solutions to social problems assumed all people would welcome their wisdom with little question, and installing a perfect social order under the directions of the political sages would not be troublesome. It doesn't work that way. Most people don't want someone else's directions in seeking perfection. They think themselves to be just as wise as (if not wiser than) those with all the answers. When it became apparent that society wouldn't surrender to the correct methods of the Marxists, the saviors resorted to the next technique – easy government.

Easy government always seems to offer a method to get the right answers accepted. Communists made government easy by outlawing the questioning or opposing of their correct answers. They imposed on government the principle that party members – who held the government positions – couldn't oppose party policy, which was formulated by a handful of high party officials. The party represented democratic principles and freedom; therefore, opposing the party was opposing democratic principles and freedom. By this reasoning, democracy and freedom became antidemocratic and had to be crushed. The failure of the Marxist movement should be evidence that easy government doesn't work.

The United States Constitution was designed to prevent easy government.

Because it was hard to get things accomplished or have one's way, many United States leaders resorted to bending the rules concerning elections, relations toward a minor Central American nation, a drug-using mayor and bribery-taking politicians. It wasn't surprising then that government would cite a national illegal-drug crisis in 1988 and resort to whatever officials claimed would control the problem. It seemed to many civil-liberty advocates that government actions were unwarranted and illegal. But government seeing a "war" will resort to war-like powers.

THE UN-AMERICANS

A portion of "the war against drugs" that irked many constitutional scholars and freedom-lovers was the "zero-tolerance" policy of the Reagan administration begun months before the administration was to leave office. The policy basically said all laws would be so strictly enforced that nothing relating to illegal drugs would be tolerated. Many people immediately claimed government abuse of authority after abuse of authority. Cars and trucks were seized at the borders because some trace of a drug was discovered. That trace may have been left months previously by a friend of a relative, and the owners may have had no knowledge that a drug was present. Commercial fishing boats were seized because a crew member may have had a marijuana cigarette. The owner may be guilty of nothing, but lost an expensive boat while the crewman lost nothing. In one instance, a commercial airliner was temporarily seized because a passenger had traces of marijuana. How the plane's owners – company stockholders – could be responsible for that is unknown.

Government used federal law that permitted authorities to confiscate assets of career criminals. The law allowed "administrative seizures," which didn't require an owner to be convicted of any crime. Civil-libertarians wondered how that could be tolerated under the Fifth Amendment to the Constitution, which says that no person can be "deprived of life, liberty and property without due process of law." Many civil-libertarians think that would require arrest, arraignment and conviction. "Life, liberty or property" could then be taken as penalty after a conviction. When the Constitution says "no person," it means just that; it doesn't differentiate about persons involved in different types of incidents, yet no such program was instituted for other crimes, such as fraud in savings-and-loan failures.

Federal authorities weren't required to return property, but sometimes did if the owners could prove they knew nothing of the offending drugs. Sometimes that involved thousands of dollars in legal expenses, not to mention thousands more lost from not being able to conduct business without a seized truck or boat. It was up to the accused to prove their innocence. This raises questions about a situation totally unrelated to the drug problem. In 1990, President Bush vetoed a civil-rights bill partly because it might require businesses to prove hiring practices weren't discriminatory even if employment figures seemed to say otherwise. Bush said people making the accusation against businesses should prove discrimination existed. Government didn't apply this concept to itself in the drug arena. Easy government isn't always consistent, either.

Perhaps it was just coincidence this concern about illegal drugs began occurring six months before the 1988 presidential elections.

Freedom Is

After much criticism, some iron-fisted rules were adjusted. Some knowledge by owners of drugs being present had to be established before vehicle seizure, and boats at sea couldn't be stopped and boarded just to search for drugs.

What some critics thought to be overreaction also was used locally throughout the nation. In Seattle, police closed an apartment building in 1988 to force a man suspected of drug dealing to move on. This forced law-abiding residents of that building to also move on with only 24 hours notice, and they were forced in one day to find new apartments, pay advance rents and fees and move all belongings. What this accomplished was unknown. If the suspect was a dealer, he just went to another location to continue business. Seattle police also posed as drug dealers, offering to sell drugs to anyone on the streets. Persons who responded to the offers were arrested and their vehicles were seized. Of course, if buying drugs is illegal, selling them is illegal, and government doesn't have power to engage in illegal activities. But, if buying drugs were illegal, police couldn't buy them to gather evidence against the sellers.

Drug testing also became controversial with many arguing it was needed to protect the public. Some employers believed they could test just because they wanted to. Many civil-rights advocates argued that testing wouldn't protect the public, had no valid purpose in most jobs, and would be an invasion of privacy. One antidrug crusader, who advocated suspending liberties to fight this "war," used a guest column in USA TODAY to compare the drug situation to piracy problems of the 1600s. He argued that piracy was finally ended after government cracked down. Strong laws and judges who ordered hanging of pirates were cited as contributing factors for the absence of pirates today. The problem with this argument is that laws that might have worked in the 17th century may not be applicable today. The 1600s are separated from the 1900s more by a Constitution than by three centuries.

Other advocates of zero tolerance said the roots of confiscation laws go back to medieval times in which property became the property of the crown because of some wrongdoing. But the Constitution should have put an end to such thinking. Law now can only go back to 1789. Ancient common law attempting to cross over into constitutional times must pass the constitutional test. Confiscation by the crown fails that test. Advocates also said confiscation of property is a civil matter, not criminal. The Constitution doesn't differentiate. It does say "private property (shall not) be taken for public use, without just compensation." That appears to be the only statement concerning taking of property in a civil matter.

THE UN-AMERICANS

Zero tolerance seems to have done little in curbing importation of drugs, trafficking in drugs or use of drugs, but it's futile to argue over the results of any government action without knowing what reality would have been had that action not been taken. But what seems to be overreaction, silliness or political campaigning may not be as unconstitutional as civil-libertarians think. The government has the power to control importation of any object because of its power to regulate commerce with foreign nations. Controlling what passes over the borders is part of that power. The Constitution doesn't specify that the power is to be used in relationship to foreign governments, foreign companies or foreign businessmen. Any person in the pipeline of commerce is subject to that regulation, even if merely a tourist. A major part of police power is the seizing of evidence. There would be little use of having police power if gathering evidence wasn't included. Seizing a vehicle used to transport illegal cargo certainly qualifies as legitimate police-power evidence gathering. But keeping that vehicle would seem improper if there was no conviction in a proper trial. Testing for drug use also qualifies as collecting of evidence, where there's a need for evidence.

Another problem with the zero-tolerance policy, and why it was widely opposed, was it was "easy government." And it may have reflected poorly on the nation's integrity because of many instances of seemingly injustice.

Missing the point about "easy government" sometimes leads to movements to "throw the rascals out" when the public becomes upset with government gridlock. What that would ever accomplish is unknown because it would rid government of competent rascals as well as inept rascals. The movement usually comes after long periods of time in which government is deadlocked over political issues. Frustrated citizens calling to "throw the rascals out" miss the point embedded in the Constitution that government ought to be difficult. The rascals need to be controlled by separation of power, checks and balances, vetoes and impeachment and by a judiciary that nullifies law. Throwing them out doesn't accomplish as much as making government as hard as possible for them to manipulate. The rascals may petition the American people for some power they want, which could be given through amending the Constitution. Americans can take power away from them and control them in the same manner.

Thomas Jefferson told us, "Even desirable goals cannot be employed that trample upon the rights of citizens." He was warning about "easy government."

Chapter 8

A PRIZED POSSESSION

THE BILL OF RIGHTS

If anything in the Constitution draws widespread approval by Americans it would be the Bill of Rights, the first 10 amendments to the Constitution. It doesn't matter that few people can tell what issues the Bill of Rights covers; they just know "the Bill of Rights gives us" fundamental rights, and that's perceived as making the United States superior to all other nations.

Many Americans seem to venerate the Bill of Rights with religious-like reverence, as if it were written in a heavenly kingdom by a divine being who crossed every "t" with a comet tail and dotted each "i" with a star.

With adoration and proclamation, Americans marked the 200-year anniversary of the Bill of Rights in 1991 just as they had earlier observed the adoption of the Constitution. Such observations would indicate Americans have a high regard for the Bill of Rights and have accepted it as their guiding principles and savior of freedoms. But when the Supreme Court makes a decision reaffirming the principles of the Bill of Rights, many opportunists attack the decision with ferocity if it goes against their political prejudices and opinions. They deride the court as if it were a subversive organization out to destroy the union. But the truth is – as has been shown several times already – it's the critics whose patriotism should be questioned, for it is they who know little or nothing about the Constitution.

Many people think the absence of the Bill of Rights from the original Constitution was a mistake or oversight by the Founding Fathers. Many of the founders also thought it was a mistake not to have a Bill of Rights. The majority didn't think so. In some areas, the majority was correct. In some areas, the minority was correct. It was a conscious effort, led in part by Alexander Hamilton, that prevailed at the Constitutional Convention not to include a bill of rights in the original Constitution. It wasn't that Hamilton and his supporters didn't appreciate the importance of individual rights; they argued that such a collection of statements of rights, as listed in the state constitutions, would be unneeded and confusing, even to the point of posing a threat. They had three major points. The first point was that it didn't make sense to mention a specific right being immune from government encroachment when there was no government power in that area in the first place. That is, there's no reason to specify a free-press right when a mere reading of Article I, Section 8, reveals no power for Congress to regulate the press. To Hamilton, citing a free-press right would be an unnecessary redundancy. This argument reflects the original intent of the founders that all government action must be based on a valid grant of constitutional power. A second argument was that a list of rights couldn't be complete because no one could perceive all the rights that exist. To overlook a right would leave that right subject to elimination by the government. The right of privacy is just such a right – it isn't mentioned in the Constitution, so many people think it doesn't exist. The third argument – and maybe the most valid – was that there would come a time when government would look upon listed rights as the only rights an individual has and, therefore, the only rights deserving government respect. That would be dangerous because a listed right would limit government power, but if there were no right in writing, government would see no limitation. That prophecy by Hamilton has come to pass, as he thought it would, and with enough accuracy to make Nostradamus jealous because it's far more specific than any prediction by the 16th-century French physician and astrologer, who gained considerable renown for his prognostications.

Hamilton's fears became most obvious during the Senate hearings over the nomination of Robert Bork for the Supreme Court. Bork was quoted by several publications as saying the only rights a judge could protect were those found written in the Constitution or in the founders' intentions. He vocalized that view again in criticism of the Supreme Court after its flag-burning decisions. There is nothing in the Bill of Rights allowing the right to burn the flag in protest; therefore, government had authority to punish the protesters, the argument goes, even though there is no power to do so mentioned in the Constitution. That would be an obvious example of government creating power for itself because a specific right wasn't written into the Bill of Rights. Such practice was precisely what Hamilton and his supporters were warning against when they opposed a bill of rights. But the prevailing attitude among many who have a vested interest in political life seems to be government can ignore any right not mentioned in the Bill of Rights.

That attitude is found among those exercising governmental power in all three branches of government and at all levels of government. It is found among editorial writers and columnists who don't understand the Constitution or court decisions and who don't respect the rights of others. It is found

A Prized Possession

in education from junior-high civic classes to law schools and Ph.D. programs that don't emphasize the Bill of Rights as establishing prohibitions, not rights. That attitude is why Supreme Court Judge Antonin Scalia said the concept of a limited federal government doesn't seem to be present today; too many people want limited rights, not limited government.

Arguing against Hamilton in the Constitutional Convention was a minority wanting to pattern a bill of rights after the one in the Virginia Constitution. After much concern during the ratification process about the lack of a Bill of Rights, Virginia's James Madison was called on to head an 11-man committee to write the proposed bill during the first Congress in 1789. What was written wasn't intended to give rights to the citizens, it was to remind government that there were limitations and prohibitions to its power. And the correct way to read the Bill of Rights is as a reaffirmation of liberties based on an absence of power, not as a source of rights.

In presenting 12 proposals – 10 of which were approved as the Bill of Rights – to the states for ratification, Congress included a preamble not usually published because it has no legal authority. It said, in part, "The Conventions of a number of States having, at the time of their adopting the Constitution, expressed a desire, in order to prevent misconstruction or abuse of its power, that further declaratory and restrictive clauses should be added." The gist of the statement is "misconstruction or abuse" of power, which conveys the founders' fears that later generations would subvert the Constitution by allowing government to exercise powers not specifically listed or implied.

Madison and his colleagues, in the nine proposals they wrote, emphasized concepts that went beyond merely reminding government of a lack of power where a lack of power was obvious. Specifics that may not have been deduced from the body of the Constitution, such as prohibitions against excessive bail or fines, double jeopardy, self-incrimination, and the rights to face accusers and have the assistance of legal counsel in criminal prosecutions were included. Those provisions justified the demand for the Bill of Rights. The Ninth and Tenth Amendments were included to reflect concerns of Hamilton, specifically that rights aren't limited to those listed in the Bill of Rights and government operates within the powers given to it by the people.

Ignorance about the Bill of Rights was obvious in a "test" prepared by the St. Louis Post Dispatch and circulated by the Knight-Ridder News Service. The test was published Dec. 15, 1991 – the 200th anniversary of the Bill of Rights – in the Seattle Times, which stated that material from the Los Angeles Times was included in the report. The presentation merely

157

showed the editors of the various news organizations know little about the Bill of Rights.

One true-and-false question said: "The Establishment Clause is violated by a teacher who begins each day at a public school with a voluntary prayer." The answer given was: "True. The Supreme Court has held that even voluntary prayers can have the effect of coercing students to pray even though they do not want to do so." That is not what the Supreme Court ruled. The true ruling is explained in Chapter 9. A second true-false question was: "The Bill of Rights is concerned solely with individual rights, not states' rights." The answer: "False. The Tenth Amendment is the states' rights amendment, which prevents the United States from infringing on state sovereignty." That answer is nonsense, as will be shown in the last section of this chapter. In a breakdown of the Bill of Rights more misstatements were made. The listing said:

"First: Freedom of religion, press, speech and assembly.

"Second: Right to keep and bear arms.

"Third: Right to refuse to house soldiers in private homes.

"Fourth: Protection against unreasonable searches and seizures.

"Fifth: Right to refuse to testify against oneself.

"Sixth: Right to a speedy, public trial before an impartial jury, to be told the nature and cause of accusation, to have legal counsel.

"Seventh: Right to a jury trial in civil suits. (Article III of the original Constitution guarantees right of jury trial in all crimes except impeachment.)

"Eighth: Protection against cruel and unusual punishment.

"Ninth: Individual rights not limited to those listed in amendments.

"Tenth: Powers not given to federal government or prohibited to states are retained by states or people."

This breakdown was incomplete or wrong on six of the 10 amendments. It was incomplete on the First Amendment, misleading on the Second, incomplete on the Third, seriously incomplete on the Fifth, incomplete on the Sixth and wrong on the Eighth. The description of the Tenth contradicts the answer in the preceding test.

Americans may tend to overvalue the Bill of Rights, but are lucky to have it. Learning to read the Constitution correctly and restricting government to those powers the people intended government to have would make much of the Bill of Rights seem superfluous; but government doesn't read the Constitution correctly, so Americans are fortunate to have reminders to show when government exceeds its authority. These reminders will be considered one by one.

A Prized Possession

THE FIRST AMENDMENT

Congress shall make no law respecting an establishment of religion, or prohibiting the free exercise thereof; or abridging the freedom of speech, or of the press; or of the right of the people peaceably to assemble, and to petition the Government for a redress of grievances.

This amendment seems to get more recognition than all the others combined. For that reason, the portion concerning religion has been given an entire chapter for itself. The rest of the First Amendment is in this chapter.

"Congress shall make no law ... abridging the freedom of speech" appears to have a clear meaning, but Americans seem more confused now over this matter than they were 200 years ago. This lack of modern understanding may be attributed more to advancement in areas in which speech applies, such as mass communications and technology, rather than a decrease in cognitive abilities. Changing social mores also play a part in misunderstanding the concept of free speech.

Some past Supreme Court judges had a clear-cut view of the matter. Hugo Black thought free speech was an "absolute." In a 1982 newspaper column citing that view, columnist George Will added his opinion which said, "That (the First) amendment is an instrument of government. It concerns the democratic disposition of public power. Hence, its protections extend only to political speech."

There is nothing in the Constitution or writings of the Founding Fathers that should lead anyone to that conclusion. If Madison and his colleagues were concerned with protecting only "political speech," they would have said something to that effect. They were afraid government would go too far in all areas, so they wrote the First Amendment as an instrument of the people to restrain government and, as such, it extends to all forms of speech because people engage in all forms of speech.

The First Amendment is not an "instrument of government"; it's an anti-government instrument and carries no implication that power prohibiting or punishing political speech is forbidden while all other speech – supposedly that would include gossip and idle chatter – could be regulated by government. To restrict freedom of speech to only political matters might allow punishment by the city of Buffalo of those who vocally criticize the dismal Super Bowl performances of its Bills. The First Amendment's "disposition of public power" is concerned with definite limitations to public power, not the isolation of only one type of speech for protection.

Will, in discussing a court decision concerning pornography, added,

THE UN-AMERICANS

"The First Amendment, properly understood, protects not 'expression;' but speech. As part of a political instrument, the amendment protects political speech – language addressed to other persons with a view to persuading them about political matters."

The idea that only political speech is to be free has recent origins and is held by numerous political activists. It seems to be a reaction to the behavior of Sen. Joseph McCarthy in the 1950s and to the anticommunism crusades throughout most of the 20th century, which were predicated on denial of freedom for political speech or thought. If political speech was to be the only free speech, a reasonable person would conclude that McCarthy and other anticommunism crusaders were the nation's most-flagrant un-American subversives in history because their efforts were aimed at punishing Marxists for political speech.

There is no evidence that anyone has been able to properly understand the First Amendment; Americans are still trying to establish a specific definition to its words. Until such a definite meaning is found, we will have to accept a constitutional concept that has evolved since the first freedom-of-speech decision of the Supreme Court in 1919. That concept, known as "balancing," involves weighing a government power granted by the people with a right retained by the people. Balancing is best understood through knowledge of history and of the creation of the Constitution and the Bill of Rights. Madison, often called "the Father of the Constitution" because he advocated writing a new document rather than edit the old Articles of Confederation, holds the key to understanding freedom of speech. He subscribed to the concept that Americans surrendered rights through the Constitution to empower government with the authority it needed to carry out its functions. When Madison lead the writing of the First Amendment about two years after the Constitution was written, he in no way gave the impression the amendment was to reduce those powers or reclaim rights ceded to government. Perhaps Americans would be better served if Madison would have left instructions to balance the many constitutional principles, but he did not. He may have thought that educated and intelligent descendants would see a need to balance power and rights. So far, few Americans have recognized the principle.

Oliver Wendell Holmes expressed the balancing concept in a 1919 Supreme Court decision *(Schenck v. United States)*. He wrote, "The question in every case is whether the words used are used in such circumstances and are of such nature as to create a clear and present danger that they will bring about the substantive evils that Congress has a right to prevent." It may have been better if Holmes had used "authority" or "power" of Congress rather than "right," because that would have alluded to the rights-versus-power concept of balancing.

This case involved antiwar activists trying to persuade Americans not to comply with the World War I draft. Their specific offense was printing and distributing antidraft leaflets. Holmes' statement did contain some key words on which balancing must rest, for he specified that a restriction on speech must be in "such circumstances" that limitations are needed – conducting of a war in this situation – restrictions couldn't apply at any time. He said restrictions on speech must be applied to situations in which specific and "substantive evils" are to be prevented, if government has power to combat those evils. The key words are "substantive evils." Offensive speech, embarrassing words or degrading statements may not meet the test of evilness Holmes had in mind; they don't appear to create substantial evils.

William O. Douglas, dissenting in a 1951 anticommunism case, explained Holmes' position when he wrote, "There comes a time when even speech loses its constitutional immunity ... When conditions are so critical that there will be no time to avoid the evil that the speech threatens, it is time to call a halt ... The restraint to be constitutional must be based on more than fear, on more than passionate opposition against the speech, on more than a revolted dislike for its contents. There must be some immediate injury to society that is likely if speech is allowed." In this case, American communists were convicted of organizing study groups to teach their beliefs with the aid of four books: *Foundations of Leninism* by Stalin (1924), *The Communist Manifesto* by Marx and Engels (1848), *State and Revolution* by Lenin (1917) and *History of the Communist Party of the Soviet Union* (1939). There was no question about legality of the books; they weren't, and couldn't be, restricted. Only the communists' speech was involved because a foe of Marxism could have used the same books to teach opposition to communism without fear of arrest.

Douglas wrote, "If they (the books) are understood, the ugliness of Communism is revealed, its deceit and cunning are exposed, the nature of its activities becomes apparent, and the chances of its success less likely." That observation indicates Douglas was one of the first to see that most anticommunism crusades weren't needed because communism was its own worst enemy and there was no valid reason to weaken the Constitution with crusades against a movement that was sure to fail.

Balancing requires there be a valid government power in addition to an overwhelming need. The power for Congress to regulate interstate commerce is one such authority on which a restriction of speech is authorized to combat fraud, false advertising or misrepresentation . Others authorizations would include Congress' power to make rules for the military and to raise armed forces, to provide for copyrights and to conduct government functions. Government certainly may restrict criminal speech, such as conspiracy and speech in the conduct of trials; both criminal and civil. Political speech isn't to go unregulated during trials, just as it may not interfere with the government's efforts to protect the nation during wartime.

Because of the Fourteenth Amendment state and local governments are under the constitutional mandate to respect the rights of their citizens, just as the federal government must do, because of the Fourteenth Amendment. As with the federal government, state governments have the obligation to balance rights and powers against each other, but the use of power rests on the absolute need for such an exercise of state authority.

Areas in which the freedom-of-speech controversy has become prominently featured involve schools, entertainment and the arts. Disturbing to some civil-libertarians is a recent tendency of college administrators – and in some cases, lower schools – to censor obnoxious speech on the grounds that it isn't considered "politically correct." There should be no question that the legal role of schools is to educate, therefore speech can be regulated during the educating function. That is, a mathematics teacher certainly has authority to suppress in the classroom all speech that doesn't deal with math. And, when a student enrolls in that class, there's a tacit agreement the right of free speech is ceded to the educational authorities in order that they have power to educate. The problem arises when educators assume that surrendering of rights extends beyond the scope of the educators' legal authority to educate.

One liberal advocate of politically correct speech restrictions wrote in USA TODAY in November 1993 that, "Free speech isn't 'free' when it's used to bludgeon and oppress, to perpetuate ugly stereotypes, to push minorities to the periphery by ignoring them. If university administrators support hate speech in the name of the First Amendment, they abdicate the responsibility to create a civil environment on campus." That's not true. University administrators have authority to educate; they do not have authority to punish those who are immune from the civilizing aspects of education, such as those who use stereotypical slurs or other undesirable language. The First Amendment is to prevent government from exceeding its authority, and keeping government power within its legal boundaries isn't supporting hate speech.

The First Amendment's protection of free speech is often misinterpreted in other areas as well. After Columbia Broadcasting System television personality Andy Rooney was suspended in 1990 following allegations he made bigoted remarks, a fellow TV journalist from the American Broadcasting Company told USA TODAY, "I have wondered since the suspension why few have raised Andy Rooney's First Amendment rights." This statement shows that electronic journalists can be as confused about the Constitution as are print journalists.

The same situation arose when Cincinnati Reds owner Marge Schott was punished by organized baseball for her remarks. One critic wrote in USA TODAY in February of 1993 a column addressed to "holier-than-thou busybodies:"

"Have you forgotten that in the USA, people have a constitutionally guaranteed right to freedom of speech?"

Not true. The Constitution applies to government, not to private corporations or organizations. The First Amendment says "Congress shall make no law"; it doesn't say "businesses shall make no law." The Fourteenth Amendment extends First Amendment immunities to the states and other local governments, not to private entities or individuals.

After numerous court cases and laws aimed at limiting or protecting speech, nothing better than "balancing" has emerged. It's easy to label some speech "political" and proclaim only it immune from control, but it's not that simple. Each controversy must be handled on its own merits until wiser future mortals define true free speech. Perhaps they'll adopt Douglas' view, from a dissent of *Beauharnais v. Illinois* (1952), that "... the peril of speech must be clear and present, leaving no room for argument, raising no doubts as to the necessity of curbing speech in order to prevent disaster."

"Congress shall make no law ... abridging the freedom ... of the press" says more than most Americans think. It doesn't say what many journalists think it says and it appears to have some politicians completely baffled. As with freedom of speech, this liberty isn't isolated. The national government's authority to make law regulating individual or group conduct is in Article I, with most of the powers that can be used listed in Section 8. An examination of that section reveals there's no power to regulate the press or control it in any way. But this doesn't mean the right of a free press is an all-exclusive absolute, just as speech isn't an absolute, because the First Amendment must be read in conjunction with the entire Constitution and history before its real meaning becomes clear.

Journalists have been subjected to considerable criticism by many Americans who perceive an arrogance of an elite group. Many journalists agree with some criticism and consider some colleagues to be basking in self-determined importance and unfounded self-praise. American journalists, perhaps enjoying the greatest freedom of any journalists in the world, often refer to a "sacred trust" or "First Amendment obligations" as badges to be worn proudly. It's as though many think the First Amendment confers upon journalists a special status or privilege to be protected from outside criticism. This self-administered grandiosity is why many journalists refer to their profession as the fourth estate, a fourth branch of government, the watchdog of government or the engine of democracy. There's a reluctance of the press – both print and broadcast – to admit its performance is subject to outside criticism because many journalists think outsiders don't understand the profession. Much of that is valid, but some of it isn't. All that self-promotion has nothing to do with the First Amendment's freedom-of-the-press clause. And it's the press' failure to fully understand the Constitution and First Amendment that is at the heart of journalistic arrogance.

When the First Amendment's freedom-of-the-press clause is interpreted correctly, a person sees that it isn't what many journalists think it is. It doesn't convey status, grant a right, or impose an obligation on a particular industry. It doesn't create a special niche in society for the press. The First Amendment only reaffirms that the Constitution is devoid of a power to regulate the press. The freedom-of-the-press clause is a prohibition to governmental action; it has nothing to do with privileges of a special group. The clause isn't concerned with protecting privileges or prerogatives of a few publishers; it only does for the written word what the freedom-of-speech clause does for the spoken word, it admits a vacuum of governmental power. Misunderstanding about a vacuum of regulatory power is at the heart of many press-government battles of recent years.

By reading the First Amendment incorrectly, the press has been able to pretend it has been granted a special status or privilege. That stance has been routinely rejected by the Supreme Court, which reads the Constitution correctly. Since there was never granted to Congress a power to regulate what or how the press reports, the founders perceived the press to be free. When Madison's committee wrote the First Amendment, it didn't change a government power, it only reaffirmed an absence of power. The founders understood that later government officials might not restrict themselves to the powers enumerated, so an immunity from regulation had to be stated. They also understood that future governments would try to keep errors secret by controlling the press. That's what they wanted to prevent.

The First Amendment, therefore, is a prohibition on government, not a protection for the press. It tells government not to use a power it doesn't have, and in no way is to be taken as an endorsement of the press or of the press' function, behavior or position. The press, also, didn't gain any authority or power through the Constitution. The press was looked upon by

A Prized Possession

the founders as an outsider, with no authority greater than that of any other group or individual. The Constitution and First Amendment created a separation of press and state, just like the separation of church and state, except journalists haven't seen the partition because no one has told them it's there. The wall between press and state would be a glass wall, allowing the press to look in but not to have any privilege or authority as a coequal (or co-conspirator) with government.

Many politicians are as baffled as journalists about the freedom of the press and that became evident during the 1991 Persian Gulf War when the American-led coalition drove the Iraqi army from Kuwait. Many politicians – the most noticeable being Sen. Alan Simpson, R-Wyo. – moaned that the press wasn't "on our side." Complaints by critical politicians included charges that some journalists managed to finagle themselves into Iraq to be used as dupes by the enemy, and some questions in United States military briefings were belittling to American military leaders or would help Iraq.

Opinions of these politicians seemed to be shared by a considerable portion of the American public. Many voiced the opinion the press wasn't enthusiastic enough in support of the allied effort or seemed to lack patriotism. They seemed to want the press to act as a cheerleader for the American troops or serve as a propaganda organ for the government. Such desires by the public and politicians reflect a lack of understanding of the Constitution, the First Amendment and neutrality of a free press. (Press neutrality should never be mistaken to mean neutrality by people employed by the press. Most reporters can separate their personal views from their professional duties.) If the press were to serve as its critics wished, it would breach the separation of press and state; it would have to break down the glass wall erected by the founders.

Any action to erase that separation or to make the press a partner in governing would be refuting freedom of the press and, therefore, would be un-Americanism. Journalists may not realize that their reluctance to become publicity agents for government or its officials is an act of true patriotism, but it is. Those who try to coerce the press into surrendering freedom in order to serve government are not patriots.

By not understanding the concepts of the First Amendment, the press has generated many problems for itself. It had a long history of noncontroversy (the first freedom-of-the-press Supreme Court decision came in 1931), but created image-damaging controversies by trying to define the First Amendment to its liking, not according to what the amendment really means.

A controversy in the late 1970s and early 1980s would help explain the real First Amendment. In that confrontation, The New York Times and one of its reporters, Myron A. Farber, went to battle with the judicial system of New Jersey. Farber, while investigating 13 mysterious deaths in a New Jersey hospital in the mid-1960s compiled thousands of pages of notes and documents that resulted in 1976 stories linking the deaths to a specific physician. Because of Farber's efforts, authorities reopened investigation of five deaths, which lead to the indictment of Dr. Mario E. Jascalevich. A judge dropped two charges and Dr. Jascalevich was subsequently acquitted of the others.

What was thought to be a battle of free-press rights of Farber and the Times and fair-trial rights of Dr. Jascalevich erupted after Farber refused to surrender his files to a New Jersey court. The files were sought by the defense, which said it needed them to assist in defending the accused. The court was to review the files to see if there was anything in them that would assist the defense. Farber and the Times argued that the defense had access to the same sources as the reporter – it just had to work at finding them – and to disclose confidential sources could eliminate future confidential sources. That, many journalists argue, would undermine "First Amendment obligations" by scaring away persons who wanted their identities kept secret after exposing crimes or other misdeeds.

Such arguments weren't accepted by the court, and Farber was jailed and fined. The Times was fined. An appeal to the Supreme Court was turned down with Justice Byron White saying a journalist has no special right to resist a legal subpoena in a criminal case. The Supreme Court had ruled in 1972 that journalists had no right to refuse to testify when subpoenaed, just as any other citizen had no right to resist that legal obligation.

Most journalists supported Farber and the Times, but a few began to leave the cause when the real issues became clear. This case didn't involve the free-press right because the Times was free to publish what it wished or not to publish what it didn't want to publish. The right of a fair trial was only a collateral issue because the true issue rested on the power of government to gather evidence. Defense attorneys, under the U.S. judicial system, are "officers of the court" and, as such, enjoy powers of the state. Among those powers is the power to gather evidence. That was the issue in this case, gathering of evidence, and that involves the Fourth Amendment, not the First Amendment. The Fourth Amendment says government is powerless to make unreasonable searches and seizures, which means government may make any reasonable search or seizure, and that includes searching through a reporter's files. Having a judge screen such files in confidentiality would determine the reasonableness of the search and would protect sources who wish to remain unknown if their involvement in the case wasn't great enough to make them witnesses against the defendant.

The Sixth Amendment pertains to this situation because it says, "the accused shall enjoy the right ... to have the compulsory process for obtaining witnesses in his favor ..." That clause means more than summoning persons to testify in court; it means the accused has the power to discover who might be a potential witness, and that involves "reasonable searches."

These specified Fourth and Sixth Amendment powers take precedence over a claim that a reporter is free from powers affecting all other persons because those powers were written into the Constitution at the same time as the free-press clause, and there's no indication they don't apply to journalists. No journalist has authority to determine what evidence, or search for evidence, is valid. Only courts have that power, according to Article III, Section 2, which gives the courts power to decide all cases and controversies arising under the Constitution. When the press claims a First Amendment right, it brings the Constitution into the argument, and that gives all authority to decide to the courts, which includes state courts under the Sixth Amendment, which says, "In all criminal prosecutions ..." and adds "... jury of the State ..." Article VI says the Constitution is "the supreme Law of the Land; and the Judges in every State shall be bound thereby ..." Courts decide, and all journalists must obey.

This situation didn't involve two conflicting rights; it involved a peripheral right of confidentiality of news sources against valid governmental powers, and powers usually rule when applied legally. When the First Amendment was adopted, there was never any indication it should be used to negate the police power to gather evidence. The courts wouldn't allow the amendment to be used that way.

Some knowledge about the history of a free press would help explain where the press went wrong. The 13 original states developed their political and legal systems as part of the British Empire, which introduced the concept of a free press in 1693 by abolishing press censorship and license requirements. The colonies had nearly a century to get used to a free press before the revolution. After independence, the colonies were governed by constitutions containing principles developed under British rule, including press freedom. The federal Constitution emulated the state documents in that it didn't contain a press-regulation power. Therefore, the First Amendment changed nothing. It didn't alter or remove any power of state or national governments because there were no powers to regulate the press in the first place. The First Amendment didn't create free-press rights because they already existed, nor did it create obligations and duties. And the press certainly isn't defending an amendment most journalists don't understand.

Farber was quoted by United Press International as saying, "What I'm trying to do is uphold the Constitution of the United States." Farber's actions belittled his statement because the Constitution is upheld by placing rights and powers in proper perspective, and specific legal powers are superior to peripheral rights. The right of a news source to remain anonymous is certainly outside the argument of press freedom versus constitutional power. Denver's Rocky Mountain News editorialized that, "The public's right to know what its government officials are doing (as opposed to what those officials say they're doing) is at stake in a New Jersey courtroom, along with other free-press issues."

Its rival stated, "In The Denver Post's view, the confrontation between the press and the court need not have taken place if the judge had considered the constitutional ramifications instead of only the procedural matters that led to contempt of court citations.

"Farber and the Times have contended – and rightly so in our view – that the First Amendment's protection for the press extends to the gathering as well as publishing of the news."

The real "constitutional ramifications," had the courts ruled to the newspapers' desires, would have been to partly negate constitutional powers of "reasonable search" and "compulsory process" in favor of tertiary rights, such as the public's "right to know" and the "gathering of news." These silly know-nothing arguments were made nationwide by the press a short time after the Supreme Court had ruled ex-President Richard Nixon couldn't shield Watergate tapes from government power to gather evidence. Most of the press loved that decision, but didn't want to apply the same rule of law to itself.

After failing to find constitutional endorsement of its arguments, the press turned to legislative means to try to secure privileges with "shield laws." Many such laws have been declared unconstitutional. It should be obvious that any law used to deny exercise of the power to legally collect evidence would be unconstitutional; constitutional powers can only be altered by constitutional amendments. Some arguments contended the press was a third party and shouldn't be subject to the same powers as someone suspected of wrong doing. The fallacy of that argument will become apparent with study of the Fourth Amendment.

Another press inconsistency was demonstrated in 1988 when the comic strip *Cathy* ridiculed the Republican Party record on women's issues. Several newspapers refused to publish the episodes that offended the GOP and some, according to USA TODAY, canceled the strip. A similar incident

A Prized Possession

involved the strip *Doonesbury* when the cartoonist attacked Vice President Dan Quayle in 1991, over allegations of past drug use. About two dozen newspapers refused to publish the strip and cited "unproven charges" to defend their decisions. This is the same industry whose leaders, who may have never studied the Constitution, continually attack the Supreme Court without understanding a decision. Apparently, some newspapers were saying freedom of the press applies only to publishers.

While it may appear many journalists are only half qualified to fight the battle of wits, the press must be defended. There have been situations when reporters invented "news," which damaged the press' credibility. But, those few instances have been reported and criticized by the press. What Americans know about the press usually is based on what the public sees in movies, television shows or televised press briefings. The press was heavily criticized during the Persian Gulf war for some questions reporters posed to the nation's military "heroes." Critics seemed unable to understand that questions aren't news, the answers are the news, and sometimes it takes an inane question to pry loose an intelligent answer. The desire of many to see the press used as a propaganda or public-relations agency for government is also unwise. The press as an instrument of government is at the heart of the ability of totalitarian nations to control the thoughts of their populations. The Founding Fathers and authors of the First Amendment didn't want the United States press to serve that function. That was the role of the press in Nazi Germany and in all communist nations.

A free press, able to roam the world free of government regulation, also serves the nation in a manner unseen by public and politicians. Government officials read news reports from all over the world, and those reports may provide information which adds to understanding of a particular problem or situation. The press, in that way, benefits the nation more by being free than by being a propagandist. Many foreign sources of information would be inaccessible if the American press was perceived as an arm of government, and that loss would harm the nation's intelligence-gathering efforts.

Publishers, editors, columnists and editorial writers don't adopt anti-Constitution attitudes purposely. Neither do politicians or any other person. Bias against the Constitution is easy; it's easy to rely on one's opinion rather than on constitutional principles. It takes time and effort to understand the Constitution, and it takes a mind trained in constitutionalism to battle through verbose decisions penned in obscure meaning to determine just what point of law a judge is making. Many journalists, like politicians, often don't try; they assume their opinion is superior. Uninformed opinion is easy.

THE UN-AMERICANS

Rejecting the principle of press freedom is metaphorically killing the messenger that often tells us what we don't want to know in a manner we don't understand. Slaying the messenger is a human penchant, and it puts the press in good company. After all, the Gospel of Jesus Christ is a story ending with the killing of the messenger, even one bringing "the good news."

"Congress shall make no law ... abridging ... the right of the people peaceably to assemble ..." seems to be easy to understand. But legislators, law officials and the general public appear to have trouble understanding and applying this constitutional principle to real life. Too often, they put qualifications on this right in an attempt to create authority of government to control peaceful gathering and activities of people or groups disliked and despised by the majority of the population.

This prohibition has been overlooked by those who want to quell civil-rights demonstrations, antiwar protesters and peace proponents, labor-rights workers and any group espousing political thought not liked by those controlling government. Abused can be heaped on persons demonstrating or protesting for constitutional government when the rulers govern according to their desires and interests without being restrained by the nation's supreme law.

Part of the problem comes from the tendency to read the Constitution incorrectly. If it's thought government bestows rights upon the citizens, it's a simple hop of logic to conclude that government may repeal those rights if it doesn't like how those rights are being used. It was popular during the Vietnam war to try to justify administration denial of free speech and assembly to war opponents on the grounds those rights were being "abused." With such logic, any statement government officials didn't like – even the truth – was considered an "abuse." Peaceful demonstrations were attacked and broken up by government authorities on the basis of that "abuse."

A correct reading of the Constitution clearly shows that rights – which are facets of human existence others are powerless to deny – aren't the property of only the "responsible." Nothing in the document suggests government power is created if a right is "abused." Absence of power is consistent – power doesn't come after "abuse" and disappear with "responsibility – so there can never be a power to deny peaceful assembly. That, of course, means there is power to deny or halt nonpeaceful assembly. That's within the state's power to regulate use of public property, and police power can be used to halt illegal acts. Peaceful assembly isn't an illegal act.

Because the peaceful-assembly clause affirms an absence of power, rather than a granting of a right, it applies equally to everyone. The most-

A Prized Possession

admired individuals or groups in society have the same standing as the most-despised. The only qualifying condition is the peacefulness of the gathering; pleasantness of the gatherers is immaterial.

A well-publicized battle over the "right of the people peaceably to assemble" was fought in the late 1970s in Illinois. The fight concerned a despised group, the National Socialist Party of America, which sought to stage a march in Skokie, a suburb of Chicago. The group named Skokie, in part, because it was the home of thousands of Jewish survivors of the World War II Holocaust. Of Skokie's 70,000 citizens, 40,500 were Jews, a situation that allowed Jewish control or influence in making the rules and exercising power over local society. Some people hoped that controlling local authority would end 1,900 years of persecution, at least in one small spot of the world. But, in America, it isn't that easy; the Constitution must be considered.

The controversy began in 1977 when Francis Joseph Collin, leader of the National Socialists, petitioned Skokie officials for permission to march in the city. Because city government has power to regulate street use, requiring a petition was within its prerogative. City officials were agreeable to the request, at first, to avoid confrontation and not to draw undue attention to a march by two dozen Nazis. Survivors of the Holocaust denounced the plan, which touched off a controversy that had to be settled in court. Four days before the May 1 march, Skokie went to court trying to halt the march it had approved.

On April 28, an elected Circuit Court judge, Joseph Wosik, ordered the Nazis barred from marching. He said: "I think these pamphlets (Nazi literature to be handed out) in this situation on these facts are completely repulsive. I think they're intended to cause trouble. I think they are intended to incite riot, to cause bodily harm, and to do all these things that the Constitution does not give a defendant a right to do." The judge's conclusion didn't hold up on appeal because the Constitution doesn't "give rights" to people, it gives power to government. The absence of power to deny peaceful assembly applies to Skokie because of the Fourteenth Amendment. What anyone thinks about the repulsiveness of Nazi pamphlets also didn't create the power Skokie that officials were trying to use.

In early May, Skokie officials adopted three ordinances to prevent the Nazi march. One ordinance required marchers to obtain a permit 30 days in advance and to post public-liability insurance of $300,000 and property-damage insurance of $50,000.

The permit would be approved "if the conduct of the parade, public assembly, or similar activity will not portray criminality, depravity or lack of virtue in, or incite violence, hatred, abuse or hostility toward a person or group of persons by reason of reference to religions, racial, ethnic, national or regional affiliation." The city could waive any provision, which it surely would for favored groups. With such an ordinance, a parade by American veterans of World War II could theoretically be denied because it could "portray" former enemies in Japan and Germany as less than virtuous or bring to mind the "depravity" of the Third Reich and would incite hostility toward persons because of their national affiliation to Japan or Germany. But no one would expect the city to apply the ordinance in such a way, and that would allow favored people to exercise a right the fascists couldn't exercise. Another ordinance was to outlaw dissemination of material "which promotes and incites hatred against persons by reason of their race, national origin or religion." That prohibition could be applied to Jews disseminating photographs of victims in Third Reich extermination camps because those photos incite "hatred" in some people towards Germans. The third ordinance said, "No person shall engage in any march, walk or public demonstration as a member or on behalf of any political party while wearing a military-style uniform." That would be criminal. Expecting to see that ordinance applied to mainstream veterans' groups parading on Memorial Day, Fourth of July or Veterans' Day would be unrealistic.

These ordinances were ruled unconstitutional by federal Judge Bernard M. Decker, because they were subject to arbitrary use against unpopular people. The ordinances would make it a crime for a handful of people to do what would be legal – even patriotic – for virtually everyone else. No constitutionalist would ever accept that.

On June 22, 1977, Collin petitioned Skokie for a July 4 march, but was refused because he couldn't raise the $350,000 insurance requirement, and the city wouldn't grant the waiver. The Jewish Anti-Defamation League joined the controversy and asked a permanent injunction against the Nazi march. On June 29, a circuit court judge denied an American Civil Liberties Union motion to set aside the ADL suit. The Nazis didn't march July 4.

On July 12, the Illinois Appellate Court approved the march with the provision that no swastikas be displayed. On January 27, 1978, the Illinois Supreme Court ruled Nazis couldn't be prohibited from marching or wearing swastikas. Following that ruling, the case went to federal court in the Northern District of Illinois where Judge Decker voided the ordinances. The Nazis then set their march for April 20, the birthday of Adolf Hitler. They then changed the date to April 22. They kept postponing the march while appeals on the three unconstitutional ordinances went through federal courts. After the U.S. Supreme Court ruled 7 to 2 upholding the lower courts, the

A Prized Possession

Nazis scheduled the march for June 25, but abandoned Skokie to march in Chicago's Marquette Park after getting a court order to do so. They wanted the park all along and used Skokie for publicity.

While the march of the Nazis didn't amount to anything of importance, the situation demonstrates the right to assemble. As usual, when there's a controversy, journalists are quick to air opinions about a Constitution that they don't quite comprehend. Such it was with William F. Buckley Jr., who penned a May 1978 column in which he wrote:

"And the argument over the right of Nazis to march in Skokie, Ill., brings up the controversy yet again, with the ideologues, represented by the American Civil Liberties Union, doing their abstractionist can-can in behalf of the rights of Nazis, flaunting the paraphernalia of genocide, to parade down a city suburb substantially inhabited by survivors of the Holocaust."

Errors of constitutional logic included thinking this case concerned rights of Nazis. It concerned rights of everyone since everyone has the same rights. There's no difference between the rights of the Nazis and the rights of Buckley. The ACLU wasn't working "in behalf of the rights of Nazis"; it was working – with a Jewish attorney handling the case – to restrict government power within legal boundaries. The Nazis were only incidental to the principles involved. This case was about power; rights were secondary issues. There's no constitutional principle that would suggest powers of government are different in any city because it's inhabited by a specific class, such as survivors of the Holocaust. Powers in that city are the same as powers in all other cities.

To his credit, Buckley agreed that the Nazis should be allowed to march, but his reasoning was wrong. He ended his column thusly:

"It is one thing to say: let the Nazis march in Skokie as an act of contemptuous permissiveness. Another to say that they have the right to march through Skokie. (Thomas) Jefferson is frequently summoned implausibly. He said, 'Those who wish to dissolve the union or to change its republican form should stand undisturbed as monuments of the safety with which error of opinion may be tolerated where reason is left free to combat it.'

"That, please note, is a prudential statement. Jefferson feels free to speak of error – without suggesting that the majority are in a position to baptize error and make it truth. He speaks merely of his confidence that the majority will reject error. Jeffersonian protection for the Nazis is an act of indulgence of perversion, not a constitutional recognition of a protected idea."

Jefferson was correct. The founders allowed "error of opinion" to remain as free from regulation as does truth, but they did it by not including powers that could be used to outlaw "error" or "abuse." What's recognized by the Constitution is a lack of power, protecting an erroneous idea is immaterial.

Buckley was wrong in thinking government ought to "let the Nazis march ... as an act of contemptuous permissiveness." To assume government has powers that can be turned off to permit only government-allowed conduct is out of touch with constitutional principles. Constitutional government wasn't created to be a paternalistic entity that would "permit" or "indulge" some "perversion" by erroneous – or less-intelligent – subjects. Buckley was reading the Constitution backwards because the people "permit" or "indulge" government actions. Nazis certainly had the right to march, and that right existed because the city lacked the power to prevent the march. If legal power existed, there would be no right. Permission by government had little to do with it.

Those who would preserve the union's republican form would do that best by learning the principles of the Constitution and governing themselves by those principles. Denying rights to others – even despised groups like Nazis – will not preserve the union. Even though the Nazis would deny rights to others if they had power, that doesn't create the power for government to deny the rights of Nazis. Learning the Constitution is the best protection against fascism or similar evils.

Trying for protection by denying rights to others often backfires. Aryeh Neier, national executive director of the ACLU at the time of the Skokie-Nazi confrontation, explained in his book, *Defending My Enemy*, how good intentions can go astray if not properly based on principles of liberty. Neier, born into a Jewish family in Berlin after Hitler came to power, said he lost most of his relatives in the Holocaust, but that wasn't reason to allow subverting of America's constitutional principles. The book, based on the Skokie controversy, related the effort by Great Britain to control right-wing and fascist activities that created violence in London's East End after the rise of nazism. The Public Order Act (1936) made it a crime to use "in any public place or at any meeting, threatening, abusive or insulting words with the intent to provoke a breach of peace or whereby a breach of the peace is likely to be occasioned." Police could limit the time, place and routes of marches if they thought trouble was possible, and could seek a ban from the town or borough council if they thought the other powers weren't enough. The act also banned wearing in meetings and public any uniform intended to express a political point of view.

After the act was approved, all marches were banned in the East End. When World War II began, all marches were denied in Britain. One right-wing leader, Sir Oswald Mosely, was imprisoned in 1940 under the act and

A Prized Possession

freed in 1943. Marches in London were again banned from 1948 to 1950 during the height of the Cold War. But this time the law was aimed at Communists, not Nazis. In 1959, the Campaign for Nuclear Disarmament group marched in what was to become an annual event (from Aldermaston to Trafalger Square in central London). A leader, Bertram Russell, was prosecuted and sentenced to a two-month confinement. In 1965, Parliament adopted the Race Relations Act making it a crime to incite racial hatred. In 1974, the National Union of Students adopted a resolution saying representatives of "openly racist and fascist organizations" were to be prevented from speaking on campuses, "by whatever means necessary." In 1975, the United Nations General Assembly approved a resolution branding Zionism as racism. The Race Relations Act was amended in 1976 and 1977 so that intent to incite didn't have to be proved. The British students used that provision of the act to prevent the Israeli ambassador to England from speaking at one college. A student Jewish society was denied funds from the Student Union because it had supported Israeli speakers. The student actions were praised by the Nazi-like National Front.

The result was that a provision created to control the fascists by denying them basic rights was used to deny the rights of Jews. Jews became the victims and the Nazis became supporters of a law, that in two decades, was turned around and used for fascist gains.

The ACLU helped prevent that from beginning in Skokie.

"Congress shall make no law ... abridging ... the right of the people ... to petition the Government for a redress of grievances" is overlooked by most Americans and gets virtually no respect by government officials. Few people know it's in the First Amendment and fewer still could tell what it means. The rights of freedom of religion, speech, press and assembly are certainly important, but they pale in comparison of the right to petition government.

To practice religion freely assists in maintaining individual liberty. No government, regardless of how restrictive, can eliminate an individual's freedom to hold beliefs or divine hope. No state can take from its people their reliance on a higher authority or spiritual devotion, which the communist movement discovered after failing to establish atheist states in Eastern Europe. Freedom of religion is important for what it does to government as well as what it does for individuals because the separation of church and state allows a person to obey laws of God while resisting laws of men. The importance of that is that man is able to legally resist the government.

Resistance to government – illegal in much of the world – is honored mainly in democratic republics. It began in the West in a small way with the Magna Charta in 1215, but then it applied only to nobles in a few areas. Resisting government had been taught to first-century Christians, but wasn't honored by the state. Resistance is not rebelling against the state, and it complies with the biblical commandment to render unto God what is God's and unto Caesar what is Caesar's. It doesn't matter that Caesar's laws are largely the same as God's laws because the commandment involves devotion, not legal behavior. Faithfulness to God sometimes requires resisting the state in its demand for allegiance.

The Founding Fathers recognized that devotion to government can't always be absolute, so they made it legal – imperative in some instances – to resist government. That principle was demonstrated in the Jehovah's Witnesses cases (Chapter 7) where government was stymied in its attempts to demand exclusive allegiance to secular authority because government was never given power to extract such compliance. That principle was solidified by the First Amendment that indicates government can't prevent resistance that is encased in a petition for a redress of grievances. It's imperative that citizens resist illegal acts by the state in order to restrict government to proper constitutional powers.

In the Islamic world, when the laws of Allah have been historically administered by the authorities of Baghdad, Teheran or Cairo, resistance to secular authority is considered revolt against Allah. To petition for a redress of grievances against Allah is unthinkable, which is the main reason democratic principles are difficult to establish and why the Mideast trails the world in development of democracy. The prevailing attitude among the masses is that democratically challenging authority would be rebellion against Allah.

To speak freely and openly is important and valuable in gaining and protecting freedom. But, its companion – freedom of thought – is what's important, and no government may seize an individual's thoughts. That the communist world also discovered. While citizens of the Soviet Union were punished for three-quarters of a century for speaking of freedom, thoughts of freedom were never controlled, they remained free. Freedom of speech helps hamper the desire of government to become authoritative. It helps, but speaking freely isn't the same as being free.

A free press is certainly important, but a fair and knowledgeable press would be preferable. The benefits of press freedom benefits apply to a few thousand newspaper and magazine publishers, but they don't necessarily extend to the journalists who work for the publishers. Freedom of the press benefits a few thousand people who have the time and inclination to write books, if their freedom is acceptable to publishing firms. Freedom of the

A Prized Possession

press applies to a handful of basement pamphleteers who wish to vent frustrations. It applies to the public only by allowing individuals to read what they wish. But it doesn't assure that what one wishes to read would be available. Press freedom is important because it prevents government from controlling what is written and disseminated, what is read and thought. Press freedom slightly retards the tendency of government to become autocratic.

A person can enjoy most freedoms in private without a right to assemble. Because the right to peaceably assemble doesn't include rising up in rebellion to secure freedoms, it isn't the most-important First Amendment principle. It's usually a companion right to more-substantial issues of freedom of religion, freedom of speech, freedom of the press or the right to petition government.

The most-important right could be the right to petition government for a redress of grievances. It puts an individual or a group on equal footing with government. When petitioned, government must justify its actions; it must defend itself. Forcing government to defend itself and justify its actions has never been recognized in most of the world. Christendom's theocracies of the Middle Ages would never have stood for being forced to defend themselves, just as aristocrats would never have submitted to demands by commoners that aristocracies justify their actions. No one ever took the Third Reich or Stalin's Soviet Union into court. The concept just wasn't allowed. The militocracies of Argentina's past just made people "disappear" when government didn't want to be petitioned.

The right to petition for a redress of grievance is the cornerstone of a democratic republic. It's important as a means to resist government, and resisting government without fearing retaliation is freedom. The right can be appreciated more by realizing it is something that isn't readily available in a church or corporation – appealing their decisions is often perceived as disloyalty. That isn't the case with constitutional government.

When the Supreme Court voided six civil-rights bills in 1989, it was criticized by civil-rights advocates because the rulings made it more difficult to sue employers for bias in employment. One of those decisions – *Martin v. Wilks* – involved the right to petition government. The case was based on a consent decree requiring Birmingham, Ala., to begin "affirmative action" in hiring and promoting police and firefighters. The decree, made between the city and black employees, was attacked by white firefighters claiming that implementing some provisions of the agreement violated their civil rights. The court agreed. When Congress wrote a new civil-rights bill in 1990 to overcome court objections, it included a measure to forbid parties from attacking consent decrees with legal action unless they were involved in the original suit. That prohibition against challenging consent decrees should have been enough to negate the measure because it was law abridging the right to petition for a grievance.

Whether or not whites suffer reverse racial discrimination because of affirmative action isn't the issue. And it isn't important that whites weren't involved in the creation of affirmative-action policies, decrees or laws. When persons have a grievance with any governmental act, they have the right to petition the government which created that grievance. Such complaint is a constitutional controversy, which only the court system can handle. Congress can't prevent that.

President George Bush vetoed the bill, but for the wrong reason. He based the veto on the argument that employers would be forced to hire by "quotas." But that wasn't governmentally mandated, so quotas would be business decisions. The drive to overturn those six decisions resulted in a civil-rights law of 1991 which was essentially the same as the act vetoed in 1990. Of course, arguments on this new bill also focused on so-called employment quotas while ignoring that the one court decision protecting the right to petition should not be overturned.

The bills were curiosities, considering Congress' record of trying to protect minority rights. The acts also were dangerous to the people they were trying to assist, for minorities have always had to rely on the right to petition government for protection. That is the clause of the Constitution used to begin the court battles that ended with the 1954 *Brown v. Board of Education* decisions. In that situation an 8-year-old black Wichita, Kan., girl had a big grievance in 1951 concerning racial segregation of public schools. Her father petitioned government for her to have her grievance redressed. It was.

This clause is vital to the continued freedom of all, especially those who must rely on civil-rights laws just to try to lead a normal life, and it must not be tampered with. It must not be weakened, ignored or unused. It must be recognized in all that government does, and it must not be slighted as President Bush did in his anticrime bill of 1991. That proposal, reflecting a nation's increasing frustration with long and costly appeals of criminal convictions, sought to limit appeals to one. Such a law could have constitutional problems if the appeal was used before a major grievance – such as manufactured evidence or perjury – became known and a wrongly convicted person was denied the right to petition government. President Bill Clinton's 1994 crime bill tried similar restrictions for persons on death row. Republicans, who gained control of Congress in the 1994 midterm elections, promised to toughen that crime bill further by limiting death-row appeals even more. But, it appears that the Constitution probably requires an appeal for each grievance regardless of how major the complaint or when the reason for grievance was discovered.

This provision for the right to petition government is the only one in the Bill of Rights that disturbs a power given in the body of the Constitution. It didn't repeal outright the power to withdraw jurisdiction from the courts, but made it extremely difficult for Congress to use that power. If Bambi and Thumper continually sued the Forest Service for its woodland management, perhaps Congress could withdraw authority to hear cases brought by baby bucks and brainy bunnies, but in the real world the right to petition must be preserved.

The right to petition may be the most-important of all rights, and it represents the heart of real freedom. But, in the newspaper test at the beginning of this chapter, it was ignored by the news organizations as if they had never heard of it or completely missed its significance.

THE SECOND AMENDMENT

A well regulated Militia, being necessary to the security of a free State, the right of the people to keep and bear Arms, shall not be infringed.

This amendment went uncontested for most of the nation's history only to become a point of contention when crime seemed to some people to be out of control in the second half of the 20th century. Prior to that, owning weapons of any kind wasn't much of a controversy. For decades every farmboy and most farmgirls owned, and learned to use, firearms. With most of the nation populated by farmboys and farmgirls, there was little to argue about. And, in the yet-unindustrialized society, guns were important for providing meat for many dinner tables, so gun ownership was virtually a requirement, in addition to being a "right." But as society developed and population increased, the necessity of gun ownership became less important. Few Americans now need firearms for food gathering. Few need firearms to protect farm animals from wild predators.

As anticrime concern grew and pressure mounted to do something, USA TODAY said in December, 1993, "Nobody knows quite what it means. But the Second Amendment, ungrammatical and ambiguous, still looms large in the national debate over guns."

The amendment's meaning isn't difficult to find. The problem is that many parties to the argument don't want to read the entire Second Amendment, as creators of the test at the beginning of the chapter didn't read it all.

THE UN-AMERICANS

Many groups, such as the National Rifle Association, the Gun Owners of America, the Citizens Committee for the Right to Keep and Bear Arms, and the Second Amendment Foundation have taken the lead to oppose infringement on the Second Amendment right. Many groups, including law-enforcement organizations, have opposed the opposers and argued for stricter gun control. With an estimated 20,000 gun-control laws in effect at all levels of government nationwide, it seems that gun-control legislation may be one of the greatest failures of all time. Many areas with the worst crime problems also have the most-stringent gun legislation. But, there's no way of knowing what the crime statistics would be if there were no gun-control laws. It's possible that crime could be much worse. The number and strictness of gun legislation may be a reflection of the severity of crime, not a sign of failure to combat crime. Therefore, such statistical arguments by those opposing gun control are meaningless.

Larry Pratt, executive director of Gun Owners of America, distorted the amendment in December of 1993 by writing in USA TODAY, "the Second Amendment uses such absolute language '... the right of the people to keep and bear Arms, shall not be infringed'." That's a familiar tactic; reading only half of the amendment, the half that supports a particular bias or opinion. Just like freedom of speech and of the press, this right must be considered in relationship to the whole Constitution to discover true meaning. To isolate one clause and pretend it stands superior to the rest of the document is dishonest.

Another gun-control opponent, Stephen Halbrook, was quoted in a 1990 USA TODAY interview as saying, "The Second Amendment guarantees the right of the people to keep and bear arms. We're talking about law-abiding citizens, not violent felons. Traditionally in a republic or a democracy, law-abiding citizens are allowed to have weapons for personal defense and as an ultimate safeguard against tyranny." The Second Amendment makes no such guarantee and makes no mention of a difference between law-abiding citizens and felons. Tradition means nothing, only the Constitution has meaning in this matter. The confusion about a right to keep and bear arms stems from dismissing the first portion because it's "ambiguous." It says: "A well regulated Militia, being necessary for the security of a free State ..." That statement is totally without meaning; it's a collection of words saying nothing. But, no part of the Constitution is meaningless; nothing can be dismissed as empty, vacant or pointless. The reason this clause appears to lack meaning is because it must be coupled with the second half of the amendment; they can't be separated. That's the "original intent" of the creators of the Bill of Rights.

A Prized Possession

After the revolution, hard economic times lead to uprisings, such as Shay's Rebellion of 1786 and 1787. Pressure to disarm the population had to be eased to assure future military forces, so the Bill of Rights committee secured the right to keep and bear arms by tying it to an obligation to serve a state militia. Madison and his committee knew how to use the English language, and they used it so the right to have weapons couldn't be separated from a militia obligation and was related to Article I, Section 8, paragraph 16, which says Congress has the power to "provide for organizing, arming, and disciplining the Militia ..."

Pratt claimed in a 1990 USA TODAY "opposing view" column that, "Gun control can only be enacted by changing the Constitution." That is absolute nonsense. Madison and his colleagues did everything necessary to make gun control within the legitimate scope of congressional power. The only thing needing change is Congress.

The Second Amendment actually lessened the right to gun ownership and increased the authority for gun control. The amendment extended Congress' authority from power over the organizations to power to regulate individuals who may be called on to serve in the militia. Before the Second Amendment, there was no power in the Constitution to regulate private gun ownership; after the Second Amendment, there was that power. Article I gives Congress the power to make laws regulating the militia – National Guard, in modern terminology – through organizing, disciplining and arming. If Congress wished, it could enact one law negating the estimated 20,000 laws nationwide and require that possession or ownership of any firearm must be accompanied by participation in the National Guard. Congress may have power to mandate that all firearms be stored in local National Guard armories, to be removed only upon the authorization of the commanding officers and that all members of the Guard receive permission to obtain any future weapons. Congress could probably make ownership or possession a crime if not accompanied by militia participation. These possibilities would suggest states or cities couldn't outlaw ownership of guns because that would interfere with congressional power, but they might prohibit guns for anyone not eligible for participation in the National Guard. Cities and states can regulate possession of weapons on public property such as streets and highways.

When resolving one gun controversy, the Supreme Court ruled that the Second Amendment guarantees no absolute right to keep and bear arms (*United States v. Miller,* 1939). Any right must have "some reasonable relationship to the preservation or efficiency of a well-regulated militia," the court said.

Pratt presented further distortion with his statement that, "President Bush's ban on some imported semiautomatics, so called 'assault weapons,' is unconstitutional. A law banning all such firearms, both imported and domestic, would be equally unconstitutional." Those statements are nonsense because of Article I giving Congress power to regulate foreign trade and Article II giving the president power to execute the laws of the United States. Power to regulate commerce allowed Congress to outlaw manufacture of certain guns in the 1994 crime bill.

When a special interest loses out to government regulatory power, it assails the media among others. Alan M. Gottlieb, chairman of the Citizens Committee for the Right to Keep and Bear Arms and founder of the Second Amendment Foundation, did that in a 1994 USA TODAY "opposing view" column. He wrote: "... anti-gun politicians and media elite don't play fair. And politicians who don't play fair can't trust you with the facts or a gun. Any kind of gun.

"That's exactly why the Founding Fathers wrote the Second Amendment and why it must be defended."

Gottlieb had written months earlier that gun control makes streets safe for criminals because, "It disarms their victims – you and me."

But, Gottlieb was as guilty of not playing fair as anyone in the media. The Second Amendment was written for the reasons just explained, not because politicians "don't play fair" and "can't trust you with the facts or a gun." Gottlieb didn't play fair by ignoring that portion of the Second Amendment that couples gun possession to an obligation for militia duty, and that obligation doesn't threaten to disarm anyone except those who shirk their duty, who would be criminals.

Another tactic is to claim that gun-control legislation doesn't work because criminals don't obey law. Jim Baker, an official for the National Rifle Association, wrote in USA TODAY in 1990, "only law-abiding people bother to comply with the law. Criminals do not register their firearms." His colleague at the NRA, Wayne LaPierre, also wrote that same year in USA TODAY that, "Justice Department statistics show that five out of six criminals don't buy guns in stores anyway. They don't obey laws." But that statistic would indicate one out of six criminals do buy guns in stores, or did until 1994's Brady Law prevented thousands nationwide from buying guns in stores.

These simple observations by gun-control opponents do nothing to support gun freedoms or the right to keep and bear arms. There's no such freedom or absolute right, and what criminals do or don't do has nothing to do with the debate. Gun ownership isn't an immunity because the Second

Amendment clearly ties it to governmental power to regulate. Five out of six criminals don't have to buy weapons in gun stores because of more than 200 years of Congress' failure to properly regulate the arming of the militia. That failure was led, in part, by groups intent on distorting the Constitution to serve themselves.

Intelligent people don't expect law to transform felons into law-abiding citizens. Law doesn't change human nature or the behavior of those who have developed personality and behavior patterns. Law only gives government one more charge to level at those who don't obey – the criminals – and any change in behavior comes when new generations grow up under new principles.

The last, and silliest, argument is that gun owners need weapons to protect liberty from government tyranny. The founders feared professional armies – not government, as gun advocates claim – so they preserved the right to keep and bear arms in order to maintain amateur armies then known as state militias. The best, and most-proven, method of protecting liberty from government tyranny is the right to petition government for a redress of grievances. That can be accomplished best by learning the Constitution, not by distorting it or selfish gains.

THE THIRD AMENDMENT

No Soldier shall, in time of peace, be quartered in any house, without the consent of the owner, nor in time of war, but in a manner to be prescribed by law.

This appears to be only one of two amendments in the Bill of Rights without controversy or constantly under attack from some special interest. But, being without controversy or free of attack doesn't mean it's understood. It was included as a protection after the British army used colonists' homes to house soldiers stationed here to combat the 18th-century independence movement. That doesn't mean the problem disappeared with the end of the Revolutionary War.

Madison and his committee recognized that there might come a time when an American leader might try the same tactics as did the British leaders, so this amendment was included. This amendment doesn't mean there's an absolute right to refuse to house soldiers, as the Knight-Ridder newspaper test suggested. The right only applies during peacetime; after a declaration of war, law can be enacted to require citizens to house soldiers. With a declaration of war, the national government could take or use private property legally under any law Congress might make, and the Founding Fathers didn't want to preclude such governmental authority because they had no idea what threats the nation might come under in the future. They had to leave power flexible enough to provide for all possibilities. Should any nation ever be foolish enough to attack the United States, seizure or use of private property might be necessary for a variety of reasons. It's only logical that housing nearby would be needed. This is one reason it might not always be wise for Congress to declare war when other options to wage armed conflicts are available – lack of a war declaration protects individual rights from the massive power of government.

THE FOURTH AMENDMENT

The right of the people to be secure in their persons, houses, papers, and effects, against unreasonable searches and seizures, shall not be violated, and no Warrants shall issue, but upon probable cause, supported by Oath or affirmation, and particularly describing the place to be searched, and the persons or things to be seized.

Many people say the unenumerated right of privacy is ensconced in the Fourth Amendment, and they are partly correct. It should be easy to see that a person and his or her possessions are protected from public scrutiny – that's what being "secure in their persons, houses, papers, and effects" means. These words clearly imply that the privacy of any citizen is protected from government activity. The privacy right is also recognized to be protected from state power by the Fourteenth Amendment. The privacy right is also implied in other portions of the Constitution, and, like any other right – named or unnamed – it must be balanced against legitimate governmental powers.

The power to conduct reasonable searches and seizures is implied by the clause prohibiting "unreasonable searches and seizures," and that inference establishes a limitation to the right of privacy. Like other controversies about constitutional meaning, whether a search is reasonable or unreasonable is decided by judicial power in a fairly contested court test. Article III, Section 2, requires that federal controversies be decided in federal courts. The Fourteenth Amendment applies that principle to state governments.

Rules for determining proper searches or seizures are included in the amendment; a person only has to read it to understand what "reasonable" is. Reasonableness requires "probable cause." Police or prosecutors aren't allowed to conduct any investigation without showing that an investigation

A Prized Possession

is necessary. That's the first rule in obtaining "warrants." Those who want a warrant must swear an "Oath or affirmation" that there's a need to obtain such authorization and they must make known what place they wish to search and what person or things they want to seize.

A California incident, and the subsequent reaction by the courts and press, demonstrates the meaning of this amendment and how it's applied. In 1971, police obtained a warrant to search the offices of the Stanford University newspaper for photographic evidence to identify assailants who had injured nine officers during a sit-in at the university's hospital. The newspaper had published a photograph of the protest, and police thought there may have been some unpublished photographs showing the incident. There were none, and nothing came of the search other than the controversy.

When the Supreme Court made a final decision in 1978, the police's power to search the offices under authority of the warrant was upheld 5 to 3. Media groups blasted the decision, as expected. One group – the Reporters Committee for Freedom of the Press – labeled the decision a "constitutional outrage to the First Amendment rights of every news organization in this nation and to the citizens they serve," according to United Press International. Media groups based their opinions on the free-press clause of the First Amendment, assuming it made news organizations immune from a power few others may elude.

Media groups based their argument on a distant right – the Stanford newspaper wasn't prevented from publishing any report or commentary it wished, so its freedom wasn't threatened – while police based their position on a specific power of government. The issue was how the Fourth Amendment affected that power, not how it affected any right, real or imagined. Much of the media didn't argue police couldn't get evidence from the university newspaper; they argued police should have obtained a subpoena instead of a search warrant. Lower courts ruled for the subpoena, saying non-suspects – especially newspapers – must be given greater protection from unreasonable searches and seizures than that given others.

The Supreme Court, in *Zurcher v. Stanford Daily,* rejected that argument correctly – because a search under a warrant is just as reasonable as a search by subpoena. The point of constitutionality is the reasonableness of the search, and the rules for determining reasonableness are listed in the Fourth Amendment. The Fourth Amendment refers to "The right of the people." As earlier shown, corporations and other organizations have the same constitutional standing as individuals; therefore, under the Constitution the newspaper was a "person."

What the amendment doesn't say is almost as important as what it does say. The amendment says nothing about a university, a student newspaper or a commercial newspaper being a different type of person or having rights unlike rights of others. As previously stated, the free-press clause of the First Amendment applies to government – it prevents a specific power – it doesn't authorize an escape from a legitimate power for any commercial venture. The Fourth Amendment doesn't say or imply anything about a third-party nonsuspect being different from a suspect, and it doesn't suggest that it doesn't apply if a nonsuspect third party is involved in the controversy.

A popular Denver Post columnist, writing the media line, attacked the decision thusly:

"The Supreme Court of the United States, led in this instance by Colorado's own Justice Byron White, has said confidentiality of sources be damned, policemen are free to rummage around in newspaper files whenever they can fast-talk a pliable judge into signing a search warrant."

That charge is not true because "describing the place to be searched, and the person or things to be seized" has to be made known. Police aren't immune from legality, and deviating from a warrant would expose the police to action by the newspaper – either legal or printed denunciations. The press has a history of complaining when the court system invokes the "exclusionary rule" to keep police within their legal boundaries in gathering evidence against criminals, arguing the exclusionary rule allows criminals to go free on "technicalities" because it restricts honest policemen in their obtaining and using evidence – usually with search warrants. The exclusionary rule puts too much restraint on police, much of the media say. When the press is subject to a search warrant, the media argument is that a manipulated judicial system can be "fast-talked" by glib constables into issuing warrants allowing police to "rummage." These arguments are contradictory and nonsensical.

The columnist added, "You share Justice White's view that police will be restrained in such searches? I salute your tender innocence. You must know a different set of policemen than I have met.

"You doubt, as Justice White doubts, that there are pliable judges who will freely sign police rummaging warrants? I kiss on both cheeks your dewy-eyed view of the world. You must know a different set of magistrates than I have met."

Beautiful writing doesn't disguise ugly reasoning. The Supreme Court wasn't passing judgment on the integrity or personalities of police or judges. The power of government is consistent; it is the same for ideal police and perfect magistrates as it is for monster cops and flawed judges. The court was saying that valid constitutional power is valid constitutional power; it

A Prized Possession

doesn't change with the differing qualities of the people exercising power. It's like journalism where there's no difference in press freedom for a columnist who might know what he or she is writing about and one presenting eloquently stated ignorance.

The editorial page attacked the decision, proclaiming, "The student newspaper subsequently sued on the presumption that First Amendment protections for a free people's free press forbade storm trooper access to newsrooms, except under careful control and only under conditions where public interests clearly outweighed the need to protect an independent press."

This wasn't a First Amendment case; it was a Fourth Amendment issue, and it concerned state power to conduct an investigative search for evidence. That was the only issue considered and the only issue involved in the decision.

The editorial added, "The press is often considered arrogant in seeking special legislative protection for its news-gathering function. Usually the perceivers of arrogance ignore the fact that the news is being gathered on behalf of the public and to make the democratic system work better."

That is self-serving pap. The press is gathering news on behalf of itself – that's how it continues as a profitable commercial venture – and the democratic system might work better if the press learned something about the Constitution and represented it accurately. Having editorial writers and columnists attack the Supreme Court for making a valid constitutional decision isn't making the system work better. The media occupy a unique position, having easy access to public records and government deeds and the means of disseminating what is learned. When policemen and magistrates misuse their authority and offices, the media can publish or broadcast details of that misuse. Having power to influence public opinion is an envious position few institutions share with the media, even the Supreme Court lacks that capacity because it must rely on the media to accurately report its decisions so those rulings would be understood and accepted by the public.

A most-bizarre argument by the press was that the Constitution required the police to obtained a subpoena, not a search warrant. A newspaper would surrender the subpoenaed evidence, the argument went. But this was the same American press – under the leadership of The New York Times – that said in the Farber controversy a few weeks later that journalists aren't obligated to respect the "compulsory process," which supports the subpoena power.

The lower courts were wrong in their decisions because they didn't regard the newspaper as one of "the people" having the same rights as all other persons. If their decisions were allowed to stand, "equal protection under the laws" would have been denied. In this case, the protection under the laws everyone shares equally would be freedom from "unreasonable searches and seizures."

THE FIFTH AMENDMENT

No person shall be held to answer for a capital, or otherwise infamous crime, unless on a presentment or indictment of a grand jury, except in cases arising in the land or Naval forces, or in the Militia, when in actual service in time of War or public danger; nor shall any person be subject for the same offence to be twice put in jeopardy of life or limb; nor shall be compelled in any criminal case to be a witness against himself, nor be deprived of life, liberty, or property, without due process of law; nor shall private property be taken for public use, without just compensation.

Once the most-despised part of the Bill of Rights, the Fifth Amendment gained respectability after it conveniently protected government officials from embarrassing revelations of political or criminal behavior. When private citizens cited the Fifth Amendment while politicians questioned their loyalty during the hysteria of the Cold War, many called for the amendment's elimination because it "shielded traitors." It was common during frenzied anticommunism crusades to argue that the ban on self-incrimination threatened national security and was an outdated artifact from a bygone era. As crime increased, the argument became the need for "law and order" must supersede any right, and "criminals" should be required to confess their sins in order to make the "streets safe again."

But when the ban on self-incrimination was used by government officials during the Watergate affair of the 1970s and the Iran-contra scandal of the 1980s, the Fifth Amendment became a valuable tool for politicians and their supporters who once wanted it scuttled.

Seemingly, unknown by the Fifth Amendment's critics is that the ban on self-incrimination is a small – although important and logical – part of the amendment, and its elimination would undermine the supposedly accepted democratic principle that a person is presumed innocent until proven guilty. This amendment is much more important to Americans' liberties than many think, and to discard it because critics don't understand it could be hazardous to the very people calling for its demise. For many, it's easy to denounce the Fifth Amendment because it applies to "criminals" or "traitors," and the critics seldom think it useful to themselves. They assume

A Prized Possession

they would be better protected if "rights of criminals" were eliminated and they could live in peace and quiet. That's shortsighted because all tyrannical governments maintain power by calling any opposition "criminal." That tack was tried in the United States during the Vietnam War but the Fifth Amendment prevented it from going beyond the propaganda stage. Those persons having government power tried to use criminal law to prevent civil-rights work in which the goal of the "criminals" was to secure constitutional freedoms and protections for every American.

Questioning the loyalty of others was behind efforts to prevent labor rights for the working class after World War I and was a tactic used during the McCarthy rampage of the 1950s. Declaring others to be "subversive" or "criminal" without any effort to prove the claim was the method used to imprison 120,000 Americans of Japanese descent during World War II. The Fifth Amendment wasn't written to protect real criminals, it was written to protect the innocent who are accused, but not convicted, by putting definite limitations on government.

The amendment has five parts, each to be considered in order.

The section that states, "No person shall be held to answer for a capital, or otherwise infamous crime, unless on a presentment or indictment of a Grand Jury, except in cases arising in the land or naval forces, or in the Militia, when in actual service in time of War or public danger" isn't subject of much controversy. Most people understand the principle that government can't constitutionally jail or punish anyone without charges being legally made. Some advanced modern nations – such as Great Britain, Israel and South Africa – allow such jailings and punishments under certain circumstances. All dictatorial nations do that as a matter of everyday "justice."

The Fifth Amendment applies to the serious act of "capital, or otherwise infamous crime," to restrain government power and prevent tyranny by addressing situations usually resulting in the death or confinement of the accused, if convicted. It was also the intention of the Bill of Rights committee that this amendment wouldn't interfere with Congress' power (Article I, Section 8) to make rules and regulations for the armed forces and the militia.

The section stating, "No person shall ... be subject for the same offence to be twice put in Jeopardy of life and limb" isn't as easy to understand as is the necessity of an indictment. The clause doesn't mean a person can't be charged with several crimes in the commission of one illegal act, nor does it exclude charges from several jurisdictions for the same criminal deed. When the federal government filed charges against four Los Angeles police officers after they were acquitted on state charges in the celebrated Rodney King beating incident, some apologists for police crime complained, claiming double jeopardy was used against the officers. They were wrong because double jeopardy pertains to the "same offence," not the same deed, and one act can violate many laws of many jurisdictions resulting in several offenses. Double jeopardy doesn't allow criminals to escape lightly for illegal acts; it only prevents abuses prevalent in other nations. Before communism failed in the Soviet Union, it was possible a that person, acquitted in a trial important to the state's image, could be tried again on presentation of charges by the procurator general. Charges didn't have to differ from those that failed; the same charges could be brought over and over until the state found a jury that would convict.

Prohibiting double jeopardy wasn't embraced as a "criminal right;" it was to restrict governmental power, for tyranny rests on the ability of government to do as it wishes, when it wishes, to whomever it wishes. The founders had witnessed such abuses in the theocracies, aristocracies and militocracies around the world, as well as in the autocratic republics of Europe. They didn't want the same for the American republic.

"No person shall ... be compelled in any criminal case to be a witness against himself," is the part of the Fifth Amendment most despised by people who don't appreciate the value of the Constitution. It was included because tyrants can control their people as they wish by charging any crime, based on any opinion. Many despots pride themselves on their "ability" to recognize treason, disloyalty or criminal intent in others with no visible evidence of such intent. Even dictators have a need to rule "according to law," if for no other reason that to persuade a population it's being protected. That perception of protection would lessen the urge to dissent or resist government because people complain about government when they don't feel protected. Ruling by law requires some form of trial needing evidence, so a dictator with no evidence merely made it a crime to refuse to confess what the "infallible" regime says is true. The Fifth Amendment prevents that.

The principle against self-incrimination forces the government bringing the criminal charges against an individual or group to prove that the accusations are true. The prosecution, not the accused, is forced to furnish proof of guilt. The principle does nothing more than make a person innocent until government proves guilt.

The section saying that, "No person shall ... be deprived of life, liberty, or property, without due process of law" isn't always respected by government because of the difficulty in defining what's meant by "due process of law." Many people think a law prohibiting any act is all that's needed to have due process. That would suggest that government could do anything it wished to obtain social peace or law and order, but evidence of police and

A Prized Possession

judicial misconduct should have scrapped that thinking. The United States justified imprisonment of 120,000 Japanese-Americans on the claim a declaration of war suspended this provision for due process.

Even the courts have a poor history of trying to define "due process." In its earliest effort (1856) at a definition, the Supreme Court said in *Murray's Lessee v. Hoboken Land & Improvement Co.*, "The words 'due process of law,' were undoubtedly intended to convey the same meaning as the words 'by the law of the land,' in Magna Charta ... The constitution contains no description of those processes which it was intended to allow or forbid. It does not even declare what principles are to be applied to ascertain whether it be due process." The court said the entire Constitution must be considered in trying to define "due process." Subsequent efforts included delving into English history to emulate the British tradition because the men who wrote the Constitution were products of English culture, government and education.

But that might be making the quest a bit more muddled than it needs to be. A person only had to go back to drafting of the Constitution in 1787 to find a description of what the Founding Fathers may have wanted to be "due process." In Article I, Sections 2 and 3, the founders created power of Congress to impeach, and included the provision that anyone convicted in an impeachment case would be "liable and subject to Indictment, Trial, Judgment and Punishment, according to Law." That is, an official removed from office would stand before the law in the same manner as a lowly citizen charged with a common crime. The body of the Constitution was inscribed by Gouverneur Morris of Pennsylvania. The Bill of Rights wasn't. Madison's "due process of law" may be more poetic than Morris' "according to Law," but that's no indication they don't have the same meaning.

It appears Madison's committee may have been referring to that phrase when writing the Bill of Rights because of the structure of the amendment. In comparing Article I, Section 3, with the Fifth Amendment, there's a similarity that indicates "according to law" and "due process of law" are the same. The Fifth Amendment's first portion concerns indictment, while the second – double jeopardy – addresses the trial. In the third portion – self-incrimination – judgment is the concern, and the fourth section which covers depriving one of life, liberty or property concerns punishment; the same provisions and same order as Article I, Section 3.

"Process" designates a system of steps, starting with a beginning and leading to an end. "Due" means rightful, fitting, proper or fair treatment as in "giving a person his due." So due process of the law needn't mean anything more than a proper or rightful procedure. Madison and the Bill of Rights committee didn't copy the wording exactly from Article I because "nor be deprived of life, liberty, or property according to law" didn't make sense. A new phrase was coined, but it was encased in a structure that should have depicted its meaning. Those four parts of due process of law don't free government from other constitutional limitations on its power or immunities retained by the citizens. There was no confusion on the issue of due process until constitutional apostasy began arising after all the original creators had died.

It's not surprising the legal profession hasn't found a clear constitutional definition for due process because its members are trained to follow the letter of the law. That may be a weakness in the profession because it prevents clear and understandable communication. It's also strength because it says "close enough" isn't good enough for law. That has to be specific.

If the two clauses do have the same meaning – the courts have never said they do or don't – government has been making the administration of law much too confusing, and possibly a little bit illegal. The most-noticeable indication of that is the much-ballyhooed "zero-tolerance" anti-drug policy begun under the Ronald Reagan administration, in which property could be taken without criminal convictions. When presenting an anti-crime bill to Congress in 1990, the Bush administration included provisions that allowed government to seize the assets of people suspected of drug dealing. Such authority appears to blatantly violate the provision that no person shall be deprived of property in a criminal case "without due process of law" for that requires indictment, trial, conviction and punishment. That requirement is also why gun-control opponents are most silly in their fears gun-control laws would lead to confiscation; guns are property that can't be taken without a conviction for a crime. Some politicians or law-enforcement officials might argue the Fourth Amendment's allowance of reasonable seizure would authorize taking of property. But that amendment pertains to evidence and arrests. The Fifth Amendment applies to government in the prosecution process and the Sixth Amendment relates to a citizen's prosecution status.

The Fifth Amendment is the Constitution's strongest requirement that the federal government obey laws when dealing with its citizens. Government obedience of law is as important to limiting the state as the right to petition is to resisting government, and liberty can't exist without both principles. To dismiss the Fifth Amendment as only a "right to refuse to testify against oneself," as the Knight-Ridder testers did, is a major shortcoming in constitutional understanding.

The phrase "... nor shall private property be taken for public use, without just compensation" is the only mention in the Constitution of the

A Prized Possession

"private property right," and property is mentioned again in the Fourteenth Amendment. The power to regulate interstate commerce (Article I, Section 8) implies that commercial property would be owned by private citizens, and the Third Amendment mentions ownership of houses. Private ownership of property was the arrangement before the Constitution was adopted, and the document gave the government no power to change that.

This clause doesn't prevent private property from being taken by the government; it only says fair payment must be made when property is taken. And there's the implication the property taken must be for public use, it can't be taken just to deprive someone of possessing it. Nor does this clause imply that private property is free to be used in any manner the owner may wish. Property – like people, government, commercial ventures or other organizations – is subject to regulation when government has power to do so. If a persons owns an acre of swampland, he only has claim to that swampland. He can't claim, under the Fifth Amendment, that he's deprived of property if government prevents changes to that land. Nor is this provision restricted to land and buildings, it embodies any object that is owned, including money, animals, vehicles, tools or anything else on which a person can claim ownership and government may need.

Attacks against the Fifth Amendment often come from people strongly endorsing "property rights." Should they be allowed to eliminate the Fifth Amendment and its ban on self-incrimination, they also would be subverting their property rights, at least those rights of property applying to a federal government power. People who successfully protect the Fifth Amendment also protect property rights of many others who oppose their battle.

THE SIXTH AMENDMENT

In all criminal prosecutions, the accused shall enjoy the right to a speedy and public trial, by an impartial jury of the State and district wherein the crime shall have been committed, which district shall have been previously ascertained by law, and to be informed of the nature and cause of the accusation; to be confronted with the witnesses against him; to have the compulsory process for obtaining witnesses in his favor, and to have the assistance of counsel for his defence.

While obeying the letter of the law can prevent abuses through misapplication by government, there are times when such strict obedience would be foolish. Such it is in regards the Fifth and Sixth Amendments when rights are screened from government with the words "himself," "him" and "his." No one but the most-rigid perfectionist or thoughtless "strict constructionist" would imply that these Bill of Rights principles don't apply to women. It's apparent by reading the Bill of Rights correctly that those amendments place prohibitions on power, and since government is prevented from exercising some specified powers in regards to "him," it can't exercise against "her" powers the Constitution says it doesn't have. Government gets its authority from the people, who included no capacity in their Constitution to treat women under a power that doesn't exist regarding men; therefore, women have the same Fifth and Sixth Amendment rights men have. That arrangement creates an implied principle of equality of the sexes some people can't find.

There was no stated principle in the Constitution of "equal protection of the laws" until the 1868 adoption of the Fourteenth Amendment, which affects powers of the states, not the federal government. Because there's no explicitly stated declaration of equality under federal law, the question is whether there can be a difference where government does have power. The founders must have thought so because they had no qualms about excluding women from participation in the governing process – it took a 1920 amendment to allow women to vote, after an 1870 amendment outlawed denying the vote to nonwhites. In 18th-century America, women and other minorities were regularly excluded from other social areas including education, commerce and the professions.

Many judges protect equality under federal law by including that implied principle in due process because all people are equally included in the Preamble phrase, "We the People." The inclusion of all people forces questions about equality into the court system under Article 3 because those questions are constitutional controversies. With judicial involvement, battles over equal rights may be debated fairly so that minorities aren't victims of misused government power. Society can then escape such silliness as speaking with inane words like salesperson, spokesperson and waitpersons. Asinine words contribute nothing to equal rights; equality is established through law, education, commerce and government. The lack of a provision for equal protection under federal law may not be the negative civil-libertarians might think. The positive aspects of such a vacuum will be shown with study of the Fourteenth Amendment.

The fair-trial principle is attributed to the Sixth Amendment, even though it's nowhere mentioned. What the amendment does mention is "a speedy and public trial," and then provides a description of a fair trial in much the same manner the Fifth Amendment describes due process. The Sixth Amendment requires an impartial jury, but says nothing about an

A Prized Possession

impartial judge. But judges must also be fair to have an impartial jury and because they are bound by the provisions of the entire Constitution.

When the Supreme Court makes a decision relating to the real Sixth Amendment, critics immediately emerge to place their self-interests ahead of constitutional principles. The Denver Post did that in attacking the court after a 1979 decision *(Gannett v. DePasquale)*. In an editorial headlined "The high court confuses itself" (Chapter 3) the newspaper opined, "... there are two rights of public trial – that specified in the Sixth Amendment as the right of the defendant, and the implied right of the public to watch its justice processes at work."

The newspaper may have been partly correct if this decision involved a trial. It involved a pretrial hearing, and the Sixth Amendment isn't concerned with making public any aspect of the legal process other than the trial. The amendment doesn't require investigations, arrests, indictments, arraignments, hearings or other procedures to be public – it requires only the trial be public.

The newspaper claimed the press to be a "public watchdog in criminal cases" and its attendance somehow "keeps the powers of government in some sort of balance." But that, even if it were true, has nothing to do with the Constitution. The Constitution indicates that the press is free to print what it wishes without government interference and is free to refuse what it doesn't want to print. Exclusion from a pretrial hearing doesn't infringe on freedoms to print or to remain silent.

The newspaper cried that an implied right of the public to watch the entire judicial process was infringed by the decision, but that wasn't true, either. The only thing implied by the Sixth Amendment is the right to watch a trial – if the accused doesn't waive the right to a public trial and opt for a closed session. To talk about watching the "justice processes at work" would imply witnessing every step. The Fifth Amendment indicated the four due-process steps of criminal prosecution are indictment, trial, judgment and punishment. Indictment involves secret grand-jury meetings, which the newspaper didn't condemn, and the Fifth Amendment doesn't say grand-jury work must be done in public. Nor is there any right of the press or the public to be included in deliberations when a jury's trying to determine guilt or innocence, the judgment aspect of due process. Nor is punishment to be visible to all; prisons aren't required to conduct open houses for the public. The Sixth Amendment requires only one part of criminal prosecutions – the trial – to be public, and it makes a point of treating "public trial" as a subordinate part of "criminal prosecutions." Since court proceedings are a matter of public records, they're open to review by the press and the public. The

Constitution allows the media to function without government restrictions, it does not require government to be the source of the press' information.

When the court decided a trial case in 1980, the newspaper praised the ruling, saying the decision "... may reduce the confusion the high court triggered ... when it decided there was no comparable right of public access to a criminal pretrial hearing." People who could recognize the difference between a trial and a pretrial hearing weren't confused by the 1979 ruling, and the 1980 ruling changed nothing about the earlier decision. Editors and editorial writers were confused, not the "high court."

The second principle of the Sixth Amendment is trial before an impartial jury. Determining what an impartial jury may, or may not, be isn't as simple as it might seem. Prosecutors and defense attorneys have been trained in jury selection, and it would seem that their efforts would balance each other resulting in an impartial jury. What a jury hears also determines its fairness. When a prosecutor hides evidence that shows possible innocence of the accused person, it's apparent the jury couldn't be impartial even though all members do their best to be fair. A misled jury isn't impartial. The defense can avoid using damaging information because the Constitution places the burden of fairness only on the government and the accused can't be compelled to furnish incriminating evidence.

Prosecutors and defense attorneys often seek a change of location for a trial because it appears publicity might prevent the required impartiality and work against the defendant. But a request for a change of venue should also be made when it appears the accused might get preferential treatment from a jury. An example would be when a black defendant can claim to an all-black jury that charges against him were the results of racism on the part of a white government. Such a situation could arise in Washington, D.C., with its mostly black population providing the jury in a prosecution instituted by a mostly white federal government.

A situation during the civil-rights struggles in the South in the 1960s illustrates the point. A white Mississippi man was tried twice in 1964 on charges of assassinating black civil-rights leader Medgar Evers. Both trials ended when all-white juries failed to reach verdicts. The defendant went free until reports of irregularities were printed by a Mississippi newspaper in 1989. The accused, Byron De La Beckwith, was convicted in a fair trial early in 1994. What started as a murder case, falling under jurisdiction of a local district in Mississippi, evolved into much more – it became a Sixth Amendment issue when the Clarion-Ledger of Jackson, Miss., reported state manipulation of justice. The paper said the Sovereignty Commission – created by Mississippi officials to protect racial segregation – had screened

A Prized Possession

potential jurors in the second trial and provided that information to the defense attorneys. That involvement in the case created state subversion of the United States Constitution because it was conducted to empanel a sympathetic jury for the defense. That was a denial of an "impartial jury," and that denial is un-Americanism. The Sixth Amendment doesn't restrict fairness only to defendants who lose, fairness can be denied even to the winners.

The quest for total impartiality led the Supreme Court to formulate the much-criticized 1966 Miranda Decision *(Miranda v. Arizona)* that said the accused could refuse to talk to police until after conferring with an attorney because government doesn't have power to extract information from the accused. The attorney's knowledge would put the accused on an even footing with the police, and that is fairness. The decision has little to do with "protecting the rights of criminals," as critics claim, instead it preserves the principle of an impartial jury by preventing self-incrimination by people who know little of the due-process procedure. Impartiality would be imperiled if defendants were forced to defend themselves against their own statements, which may have been extracted by compulsion, trickery or terrorism. Such statements may not be true – there are numerous instances in which innocent people are forced by terror to proclaim guilt. Tyrannies survive on such tactics. Without impartiality, the principle that the accuser must prove the accusations would be lost. The Miranda decision, therefore, was a method of preserving the state's legal authority to deprive the convicted of "life, liberty, or property" under due process of law.

Such noble principles often escape the awareness of many people, even those entrusted with protecting the constitutional covenant. Edwin Meese, attorney general in the Reagan administration, was quoted by USA TODAY as criticizing the Miranda Decision in saying, "it only protects guilty defendants." That's not true, as just shown, it protects everyone because it forces government to act legally. Some police leaders credit the decision with forcing them to develop better investigative techniques, and improved investigation protects both innocent people and constitutional principles.

The third principle is that the accused must be informed of charges, which isn't controversial any longer, but it's helpful to protect against government encroachment. Under the Constitution, everyone must know the specific accusation in order to present a defense – vague charges aren't allowed. Under tyrannies, the accused often are unable to defend themselves because they aren't always sure what crime they've been charged with. Soviet citizens were subjected to defending themselves against charges of "counterrevolutionary" or "antigovernment" activities without knowing just what actions were under attack or how to defend against such charges. Such vague charges also made it difficult to avoid accusations because few could know what actions of the individual were forbidden.

One aspect of the fourth principle – witnesses for and against the accused – hasn't been completely defined. It appeared to be beyond question until child-abuse cases became numerous nationwide. Many states enacted laws allowing children to be excluded from courtroom appearances while presenting testimony, and that brought the argument that the defendant wasn't properly confronted because the witness gave testimony by closed-circuit television or other devices that left the child in a protected and non-traumatic environment. When the defense has ample opportunity to conduct cross-examination in the presence of a judge and prosecutor, the counterargument said, the constitutional requirement is met. The Constitution says nothing about the confrontation being in court or that the defendant isn't confronting the witness through the defense attorney. The Sixth Amendment can also be used to protect the privacy of victims because it pertains to public trials, not public records. As such, the identity of child-abuse or rape victims can be kept from the public or press because only the accused is entitled to know who the accuser is, and nothing says an alias for a victim can't be included in either a trial or public records. The Sixth Amendment's main thrust is to outlaw the tyrannical practices of charging people with crime when no crime exists and claiming witnesses when no witnesses exist.

The final principle – the right to have legal representation – is under attack by many people who don't understand the completeness of the provision. One critic, Thomas Sowell, a Scripps Howard News Service columnist and senior fellow at the Hoover Institution, attacked the Supreme Court over this issue in a 1989 newspaper column. He wrote:

"For years the Supreme Court has been on another binge, regarding the constitutional right to be represented by a lawyer. The Constitution never said that the government has to pay a criminal's lawyer, but the Supreme Court could not resist stretching the principle into a fetish. The net result has been that murderers have used the taxpayers' money to have lawyers think up one flimsy excuse after another to appeal their cases and thereby delay execution.

"This Supreme Court finally has cut that back to only one appeal paid for by the taxpayers. That is still one more than the Constitution required."

Those who understand the Constitution know that's pure bunk and is an ignorant misrepresentation of constitutional principles. The Sixth Amendment says "the accused shall enjoy the right ... to have the Assistance of Counsel for his defence." That doesn't mean the accused has only the opportunity or possibility of legal help. It doesn't say the right to be represented by an attorney dies if the accused can't obtain legal assistance. It doesn't say the accused can have legal representation only if he (or she) can find an attorney who will take the case or only if the accused can afford an attorney. The amendment says government can not try, convict or punish persons not assisted by legal representation. Those who represent themselves are that counsel. When a defense attorney defends an obviously guilty defendant, it isn't because that criminal "is entitled" to a defense. It isn't to preserve "criminal rights" because there are no differences between the rights of the criminal and rights of the noncriminal. By defending the heinous criminal, a defense attorney is serving a vital function in due process because due process is the only constitutional way government may legally deprive anyone – even the most vicious – of life, liberty or property. Criminals are lawbreakers for economic reasons – that's how they obtain money. Without crime, they would have no money and, therefore, couldn't afford legal representation. And if they couldn't have legal representation, they couldn't be tried. That's why public defenders are paid by government – it's the only constitutional method to bring action against criminals, even though columnists can't understand that principle. The argument that defense attorneys delay executions by thinking "up one flimsy excuse after another to appeal" is likewise trash. Appeals – petitioning government for redress of grievances – don't go far if lacking merit. That's the first thing determined on appeal; competent judges don't grant stays automatically – there must be some validity to an appellant's claim. Judges aren't fooled by "flimsy excuses."

To claim the Constitution doesn't require public defenders to appeal convictions is also foolish. The Constitution pertains to government power, not actions by individuals in resisting that power. What the Constitution requires is that every "petition of government" be decided regardless of how the petitioner's agent is paid or how many petitions are made.

Attacking the Supreme Court simply because the critic can't understand the Constitution is something American journalism has stretched into a fetish as complexities of modern life make it imperative that judges look beyond a few words and seek the total meaning of any constitutional issue. It's apparent most journalists are incapable of doing that.

THE SEVENTH AMENDMENT

> *In suits at common law, where the value in controversy shall exceed twenty dollars, the right of trial by jury shall be reserved, and no fact tried by a jury, shall be otherwise re-examined in any Court of the United States, than according to the rules of the common law.*

THE UN-AMERICANS

The Seventh Amendment is understood to refer to civil law that evolved throughout history and came to be law without need of legislation. But, such law must be incorporated into a system that requires constitutional authority for any act of government. That was accomplished by creating by legislation institutions to administer this law created by custom and usage. These institutions include a court system and other dispute-settling entities to make administration of common law a government function even though government didn't create the law. While it might be less cumbersome for disputes to be settled in a nongovernment setting, a court decision or arbitration finding puts the authority of the state behind a settlement, which provides for punishment for those who refuse to obey the decision.

The Seventh Amendment might best be regarded as a paragon for the Bill of Rights. It's so noncontroversial that it isn't claimed by any group or special interest as providing a unique protection. It's easy for a columnist to claim a special protection or right in an area directly related to being a journalist. It's easy for another journalist to claim that unpopular people don't have the same rights as highly regarded people. No one feels compelled to test government resolve or adherence to the amendment by public displays of outrageousness, as did the Nazis in Skokie. That's a legacy of the First Amendment that has eluded the Seventh Amendment.

Nobody forms special-interest groups to campaign to preserve rights that don't exist. No one creates full-time jobs to lobby legislature to put selfish interests above the welfare of the society. And, nobody ignores half the amendment in order to distort the remaining half into becoming something it wasn't written to be, as happened with the Second Amendment.

Nobody claims a right, supposedly secured by some other amendment, creates an automatic immunity from any power that might be implied by the Seventh Amendment. Nobody claims their rights from other constitutional provisions are superior to the Seventh Amendment rights of other people. That's what has happened in regard to the Fourth Amendment.

Nobody calls for repeal of this amendment because it restricts power of government in an area that displeases them. Nobody claims the nation is being subverted by other people who cling to rights mentioned in the Seventh Amendment. There are no descriptions of procedure that have escaped the attention of a nation for two centuries, as has happened with the Fifth Amendment.

Nobody claims immunity from a specific aspect of the amendment, as often happens with the "compulsory process" power of the Sixth Amendment. No one accuses the Supreme Court of disregarding the Constitution when it makes a decision based on a provision that isn't obvious to those

A Prized Possession

who have never studied the Constitution, as happens when some can't find a requirement for public defenders in the Sixth Amendment. Nobody misreads the amendment's words or misconstrues its meanings. No one forgets high-school English lessons in distorting powers and immunities in an attempt to justify their actions or political biases as they do with the Eighth Amendment. And nobody ignores the Seventh Amendment because they can't figure out what meanings are included. That has happened to both the Ninth and Tenth Amendments

Nobody claims government is denying Seventh Amendment rights. No one calls for the repeal of this amendment and seldom is the Supreme Court attacked over a Seventh Amendment decision. The Seventh Amendment has ordinary citizens, not bureaucrats or out-of-touch administrative judicial officers, determine facts and responsibility in civil cases of negligence or wrongful injury through the jury system. And the jury's findings can't be set aside to please some vested interests. But special interests do try to lessen the amendment's impact by seeking legislation to restrict compensation victims of wrongful injury or death may seek.

THE EIGHTH AMENDMENT

Excessive bail shall not be required, nor excessive fines imposed, nor cruel and unusual punishments inflicted.

Perhaps no other part of the Constitution includes such a wide range of illustrations that demonstrate wisdom of the founders, but allow as much confusion, as these 16 words. It was wise of the founders not to define "excessive," for each succeeding generation is free to redefine the word to fit the social circumstances of the period. There will always be, of course, a few people who will claim to know beyond doubt what "original intent" was to be for bail and fines.

Also wise was an absence of anything to empower any specific person or group the singular task of defining "excessive." What wouldn't be excessive to a president who wished to administer programs based on personal perspective might be excessive to everyone else. The opinion of a president would be a part of the defining process the founders apparently envisioned. That process allows Congress to authorize suitable guidelines for bails and fines for each offense. A president has the option of accepting the legislators' opinions and signing the bill or rejecting their opinions with a veto. Once a bill became law, the courts may agree to its provisions or reject them based on the arguments of two opposing viewpoints. It was this three-pronged approach that would determine the meaning of "excessive." No one would be subject to tyranny by the opinion of one governmental body or person, as happens in nondemocratic nations.

Like many other restrictions on power, the Fourteenth Amendment made state governments subject to these principles.

The same principle applies to the word "cruel." It, too, is subject to changing social standards and practices. The same might apply to "unusual," but that may be the most-misunderstood word in the Constitution and will be analyzed later. Though accepted definitions of excessive and cruel may be written into legislation, that doesn't protect the meanings from future rejection or alteration.

In a 1910 court decision, Justice Joseph McKenna wrote that, "Time works changes, brings into existence new conditions and purposes. Therefore a principle to be vital, must be capable of wider application than the mischief which gave it birth. This is peculiarly true of constitutions." That's why in applying the Constitution to society, a person must not be trapped in pretending to know the founders' "original intent." One must understand their creation and how it relates to the accepted standards of any particular time.

In 1958, Chief Justice Earl Warren wrote that the Eighth Amendment "must draw its meaning from the evolving standards of decency that mark the progress of a maturing society." That seems to be how the founders expected the entire Constitution to be read because they purposely refused to define their adjectives. They left such definitions up to future generations.

So the question becomes, "What is meant by cruel and unusual?" In its editorial (Chapters 1 and 4), The Los Angeles Times missed the point in trying to imply that the Constitution should forbid states from executing teen-agers and mentally retarded persons because that would be "cruel and unusual punishment." Such a conclusion would have to be drawn from a personal opinion that might not be agreeable to society. Chapter 4 clearly showed that both the Fifth and Fourteenth Amendments allow taking of "life, liberty or property" under due process of law, so those amendments exempt capital punishment from the ban on cruelty. And, if capital punishment is cruel if applied to some, it would be cruel when applied to everybody, even the most-vicious murderer. As seen earlier, the Constitution must be consistent; it doesn't change to fit different people affected by its government powers.

The Supreme Court received harsh criticism 1989 after it ruled that states had power to execute juveniles and the retarded. An American Civil Liberties Union attorney said, "It's a barbaric place, that Supreme Court." A

A Prized Possession

Chicago religious leader added that capital punishment "undermines our respect for human life." In 1985, two Supreme Court judges, Thurgood Marshall and William Brennan, said use of the electric chair was "cruel and unusual punishment."

While the death penalty may be considered "barbaric" and though Americans like to claim a highly developed respect for human life, those attitudes have nothing to do with constitutionality. Evolving social mores could allow elimination of capital punishment by the courts on grounds of cruelty if it wasn't specifically authorized by two amendments. But eliminating the electric chair could be done under the constitution's prohibition of cruelty – as a federal judge ruled in 1994 regarding California's use of the gas chamber – if other forms of execution are more "humane"; the Constitution does allow that flexibility.

It was thought by many people and reported by the press that the Supreme Court ruled the death penalty to be unconstitutional in 1972 only to reverse itself by reinstating the penalty in 1976. That's a misreading of the real rulings. In the 1972 decision *(Furman v. Georgia)*, the court voided the laws and procedures by which the death penalty was prescribed as punishment. The first decision was based on "equal protection" because it was found that minorities were more likely to be sentenced to death than were whites for the same crimes. The decision pertained to court actions, not capital punishment. When the death penalty was "reinstated" in *Gregg v. Georgia* in 1976, it was because laws authorizing death had been rewritten, and supposedly sentencing would be applied without discrimination.

When the chief justice of the Utah State Supreme Court retired in 1979, he took potshots at foes of capital punishment by saying, "Any damn fool ought to know it's not unusual. It's been common since before Christ." That thinking has nothing to do with the Constitution, either, because what happened before Christ has no bearing on modern America, whose principles of government came into existence in 1789 when the Constitution took effect. Whether capital punishment is legal or not is specified by the words of the Constitution, not by historical precedent. Capital punishment's long existence only shows it was common, not usual; the words don't mean the same thing. The Constitution doesn't permit something just because it is common or acceptable to many persons.

The problem America has with the Eighth Amendment has little to do with changing standards of behavior or the inability for law to keep pace with those changes. America has a reading problem. The inability to read and understand has created a rash of questionable court actions in recent years. Some questionable actions are known as "humiliation sentences."

THE UN-AMERICANS

Many people applaud judges who invent such sentences; others decry the practice. Missing is the acknowledgement by many that such sentences may have constitutional problems.

A University of Oregon law professor did question such practices in 1988, saying one specific sentence "raises constitutional questions about cruel and unusual punishment," while conceding such sentences might prove to be effective deterrents. In the case, a Seattle woman, after pleading guilty to immoral conduct, was ordered to wear for 60 days a sign declaring that she was a convicted sex offender. The sign read, "I've been convicted of communicating with a minor for immoral purposes." The ACLU called the penalty "vindictive."

An Oregon man convicted of sexually abusing a child was ordered to display on his car and on his front door of his home signs reading: "Dangerous Sex Offender. No Children Allowed." Drunken-driving convictions nationwide have created sentences ordering bumper stickers to be pasted on automobiles in an attempt to maintain sobriety by humiliation. A Florida judge sentenced several people – convicted of soliciting for immoral purposes, shoplifting, drunken driving – to buy newspaper ads to tell of their various convictions and to publish their photos. A 17-year old Florida girl was ordered to prison for two years and to use birth control for 10 years following that sentence after admitting smothering her newborn child in a hospital lavatory. A Brooklyn slumlord was ordered to live 15 days in his run-down building. In 1994, a judge in suburban Seattle turned two teen-age Indians over to their Alaskan tribe to be exiled on uninhabited islands after being convicted of beating and robbing a pizza deliveryman.

Such sentences are readily accepted by society because they don't appear to violate the prohibition against "cruel and unusual punishment." Most people in society wouldn't regard humiliation or embarrassment as cruel or unusual; they put up with those daily, even on their jobs. Those who question such sentences on the basis of being vindictive, innovative, imaginative or malicious may be correct, but for the wrong reasons.

These sentences demonstrate a lack of reading ability because the Eighth Amendment doesn't outlaw "cruel and unusual punishment," it outlaws "cruel and unusual punishments." Those phrases don't mean the same thing, and inability to recognize the true meaning allows many constitutional abuses. True meaning is dependent on accurately understanding the relationship of adjectives and nouns in the English language. That relationship should have been understood by the time a person leaves high school.

The noun "punishments" is plural, indicating it refers to more than one type of punishment. It doesn't indicate the inflicted punishment must

A Prized Possession

include both cruelty and unusualness in order to be banned; it says only one of those aspects is needed. In the English language, adjectives modify only nouns, which means "cruel" and "punishments" are coupled as are "unusual" and "punishments." As the Eighth Amendment is written, it says cruel punishment is unconstitutional and unusual punishment is unconstitutional; it addresses two different types of punishment, not one.

When adjectives must be grouped into a single modifier, they are called "compound adjectives." How meanings can change because of modification by adjectives is illustrated by the sentences, "California has the most dangerous coeds," and, "California has the most-dangerous coeds." The first sentence concerns quantity; the second quality. The second must be compounded because the adjective "most" cannot modify the adjective "dangerous," it can only modify the noun "coeds." To further understand this principle, one must compare the compounded phrase "black-and-white puppies" with the multiple-adjective form of "black and white puppies." The first refers to a singular coloration pattern, such as on a Dalmatian; the second refers to two dissimilar colors, such as on single-hued poodles.

"Cruel and unusual punishment" is not literate – newspaper editors should know that – because there are two separate modifiers serving where one is demanded, an aberration of structure that simply can't exist in proper English. Correct usage of English would require "cruel-and-unusual punishment" if one type of punishment, including both cruelty and unusualness, was the concern. The absence of hyphenated compounding means two types of punishment are specified. As such, "cruel and unusual punishment" is "speaking Sloganese" because there's no tangible meaning.

By not knowing proper use of adjectives and hyphens, Americans – including the Supreme Court – misread the Eighth Amendment and misapply its provisions, sometimes with a cruel-and-unusual result. Justice Scalia did that in 1991 when he wrote the court's opinion upholding Michigan's tough drug laws mandating harsh sentences. He said they "may be cruel, but they aren't unusual." But proper usage of English indicates both conditions need not be present to negate a bad law. The designers of the St. Louis Post-Dispatch/Knight-Ridder News Service Bill of Rights test missed the point by not knowing how to properly use the English language in a manner that should be second nature to any copy reader.

Innovations, such as humiliation sentencing previously mentioned, could be misapplications because the Eighth Amendment specifies that acceptable punishments are to be the "usual" punishments. Judges inventing punishment to fit one situation or conviction aren't administering the "usual" punishment. It seems that for punishment to be classified as "usual," it must be that normally given in such circumstances, and which would be authorized by law. That authorization needn't be so confining that judges are unable to make the punishment fit the crime, but the "usual" punishments must come from the legislative process. Judges simply aren't allowed to create their own law, power or authority. They are bound by the Constitution, which requires that law support any government action.

Many jurisdictions rely on sentencing guidelines to govern such situations. The guidelines are usually flexible enough to be applied to unique situations but restrictive enough that judges don't stray into legislative territory. Some judges don't appreciate having their independence infringed on by legislatures. One Northwest judge said in 1984 that he planned to continue his imaginative sentencing, which he said fit the crimes, in spite of sentencing guidelines. He said his parents, immigrants from Europe, had only third- or fourth-grade educations. As such, they didn't have knowledge, only wisdom, and that's what the judge prided himself in inheriting and being capable of applying.

Wisdom requires understanding the relationship of adjectives to nouns and what meanings that relationship creates. Adjectives and nouns of the Eighth Amendment mean judges must obey law and refrain from inventing.

THE NINTH AMENDMENT

The enumeration in the Constitution, of certain rights shall not be construed to deny or disparage others retained by the people.

A great constitutional mystery of 20th-century America is how this amendment seems to have been misplaced by many people, including some who wish to occupy Supreme Court positions. Judges who say they could protect only those rights found written in the text of the Constitution or discovered in the intentions of the founders, have to base that position on totally eliminating or ignoring the Ninth Amendment because it tells them to do just the opposite.

The Ninth Amendment says there are additional valid rights beyond the handful written in the text of the Constitution or found in the intentions of the founders. The amendment tells government to respect other rights "retained by the people" even though those rights aren't named. This amendment should help dispel the notion of many people that the Constitution and its Bill of Rights, court decisions or government legislation are the sources of rights, civil, human or any other kind. This amendment solidifies John Jay's contention that rights are voluntarily surrendered to government.

A Prized Possession

When he said Americans cede rights to government in order to vest it with needed powers, Jay didn't mean that all rights are surrendered and the Constitution returned some enumerated rights. Unnamed rights were never surrendered to the government; they are the "others retained by the people."

Protecting only rights listed in the Constitution is to deny the existence of the "others retained by the people," and pretending the enumerated rights are superior to the "others" is to disparage those unnamed rights. Doing either is specifically contrary to Ninth Amendment instructions that say do not deny or disparage Americans' anonymous rights. This is another way of telling government and courts to concentrate on powers properly used, not rights to be protected. Rights are best protected by restricting government action only to constitutionally authorized powers.

This amendment validates Hamilton's that a bill of rights couldn't include the entire scope of rights possessed by the citizens nor could all rights be named. None of the founders ever tried to do that, and none of them ever said citizen rights were to be limited to any list. After including several obvious rights in the first eight amendments, Madison and his committee knew better than to try to encompass every right that might possibly exist free of government intrusion, so they simply referred to the unenumerated rights as "others." Among unnamed rights would be the right of privacy and the right to know; the right to dissent or complain, to roam and to be left alone; the right of choice, or to work and to acquire property or a fortune, and the right of free thought. All of those are unenumerated, so it's possible all could be destroyed by people in power who wish to ignore the message of this amendment.

Hamilton's most-important argument was that government officials would tend to recognize only enumerated rights. It should be evident that's precisely what's happened with a major portion of government officials in the United States. The phrase "constitutional right" indicates to some people a subversion of the Ninth Amendment because it excludes all the other rights, unnamed but alluded to by this amendment, which says without a doubt that rights aren't restricted to a few mentioned in the Constitution, they exist far beyond what is written. Rights are so numerous and so unspecified that the Founding Fathers didn't try to identify them. There was no attempt to list each and every right because they go beyond naming and beyond comprehension, and no human is so wise to know the unknowable. Rights are as numerous as the purrs in a kitten's contentment; they are the molecules that comprise the great body of liberty Americans claim to have. One right isn't liberty, nor are two, or a few more. It takes a mass of rights to form freedom, just as it takes a mass of molecules to form a body. No one feels the need to name all the molecules in the physical body; therefore, no one should try to name all the molecules forming the body of freedom.

By misreading the Constitution for decades, even experts tend to lose sight of rights just because they weren't enumerated in the Bill of Rights. That happened to Justice Black in a 1965 dissent to a birth-control decision that was decided on the right of privacy. Black, considering that unlisted right, wrote: "I like my privacy as well as the next one, but I am nevertheless compelled to admit that government has a right to invade it unless prohibited by some specific constitutional provision."

That's a backward look at the Constitution for the unenumerated right of privacy can be invaded only if government action is authorized by some constitutional grant of authority. Government needs a power, not a right, to invade privacy. In the case, in which Connecticut had outlawed use of birth-control devices for everyone, including married couples, the state argued it could do so under its police power. That was a strange argument when there was no perpetrator or victim involved. Police power generally isn't considered to be so all-encompassing that it would include protecting individuals from themselves. The state and Black argued that the right of privacy couldn't be protected because it wasn't specifically mentioned in the Constitution, but they relied on a power (called a "right" by Black) that likewise isn't listed in the Constitution. No one would negate police power because it isn't specifically mentioned, but many often try to do that to rights.

Rights – those enumerated and the unnamed others retained by the people – exist where governmental power doesn't exist or is restricted. Those rights are secured as "immunities" from government because government has no power, but those immunities end where government power begins. There are vestiges of freedom within areas controlled by government power; they're called "privileges." The importance of making such distinctions will become apparent in considering the Fourteenth Amendment in Chapter 10.

THE TENTH AMENDMENT

The powers not delegated to the United States by the Constitution, nor prohibited by it to the States, are reserved to the States respectively, or to the people.

While the Ninth Amendment appears to have been misplaced or not understood, the Tenth Amendment seems to have been obliterated. There has never been a court decision clarifying the complete meaning of the Tenth Amendment, and many people simply ignore it because they admit not

A Prized Possession

knowing its meaning. Its meaning has been suggested several times in the previous pages.

The most-obvious manifestation of the amendment's meaning is Jay's contention that Americans cede some of their rights to empower government with its needed authority. That meaning is contained in the first clause of the Tenth Amendment; powers are delegated to government, assigned by the people surrendering some of their rights. But they don't yield all rights or give all power to one government. While furnishing power to the federal government, the people took some power back from the states; that's the second clause ("The powers ... prohibited by [the Constitution] to the States ...") of the Tenth Amendment. The Constitution prohibits states (Article I, Section 10) from trying to exercise powers the people retrieved when they created the national government. But the people didn't leave the states powerless; they left considerable authority in their state and local governments. That's the meaning contained in the third clause ("The powers not delegated to the United States ... are reserved to the States ...") of the amendment.

American individuals haven't given all their power to government; much of it has been retained for personal use, and that may be the most-important section of the amendment. Individuals keeping government power is the meaning of the phrase "powers not delegated ... are reserved ... to the people." This phrase reflects the contention in Chapter 2 that all individuals would be sovereign governments if they hadn't created governments. By keeping some power, Americans exist – within limits – as a fourth branch of government beside the legislative, executive and judicial branches. And by retaining some powers to be exercised by the individual, the citizen functions as the fourth level below the federal, state and local governments. The American press has long claimed itself to be a fourth branch of government, but that's nonsense. The press isn't the fourth level of government, either; the people fill that role, just as they are the true "engine of democracy."

This amendment should dispel any thought that state governments created the federal government. To reject the states-as-creator concept a person needs an ability to read and to understand that Madison was telling everyone through this amendment that government is a creation of the people.

The significance of the Tenth Amendment is that it addresses powers retained by the people: recognizing the people as a branch of government. The first three clauses of the amendment were adequately dealt with in the body of the Constitution: powers delegated to the national government are mostly in the first three articles. Article I, Section 10, pertains to powers the states are prohibited from using, and powers not mentioned there are implied to be retained by the states, and are listed in the state constitutions.

THE UN-AMERICANS

Therefore, the Tenth Amendment has virtually nothing to do with government power; it concerns people power. And that could be the next great area of constitutionalism defined by court decisions. The Tenth Amendment is definitely not a "states' rights" amendment, it's the Peoples' Power Amendment.

Exercising people power in conjunction with constitutional government power can, at times, be confusing. Examples in Chapter 6 of individuals taking power back from government, to be exercised as one sees fit, aren't accepted methods of exercising people power. While such power-taking incidents seem to be necessary for protection, they don't blend with the Constitution, which doesn't allow power paring, except by amending. Exercising people power occurs mainly with regulatory and police powers. Gun owners like to think they would be retaining some war powers if left free to possess any firearm they wish. But that's a fantasy created as the musket faded into history and the citizen army became supplanted by sophisticated weaponry that may have grown "smarter" than its users.

Many people have resorted to pressure groups to attack television programming that presents exaggerated pictures of American life, including overly violent crime-oriented police shows, parodies ridiculing many unrealistic perfect-family programs of the 1950s or shows with sexual overtones appearing to taunt Americans for an uneasiness with human sexuality. Such groups, often pretending a superior morality or puritanical bent, try to force changes by pressuring sponsors to stop advertising. When Americans united, power to regulate commerce fell under the authority of governments – national, state or local – but the people retained some powers for their use.

Forming pressure groups doesn't seem to be a retained power because the regulatory organization Americans formed was constitutional government. Americans retain power to enforce their precepts on themselves or their group, but not to impose those canons on others who aren't part of the pressure group and who haven't agreed to its principles. All Americans are part of the constitutional group – whether they recognize that reality or not – and tacitly accept its principles, so the constitutional group regulates for society. The only way not to accept constitutional principles is to leave the nation. While complainers don't retain power to regulate television, they do possess the right to petition government for redress of grievances, and can use that right to try to alter programming. Individuals or groups can boycott offending programs, but cannot interfere with sponsors' business practices; that's an authority given to government in the form of regulatory power. Special-interest groups trying to regulate business come close to being un-American. Pressure groups trying to regulate television into accepting a

A Prized Possession

minority view isn't too dissimilar from the anticonstitutionalists who think they are free to create their own townships, administer their own law and disregard the constitutional covenant as they wish. The people retained power to regulate themselves or their property, not to regulate others.

When a controversial novel approached publication in late 1990, many people were appalled because they felt the book was too disgusting in its portrayal of violence against women. One publishing house dropped plans to issue the book, but another agreed to publish. The National Organization for Women took the lead in calling for a boycott of the book and for a year-long boycott of the publisher's entire line of work during 1991. Such is the authority of retained power; it can be used to govern individual action as long as it falls short of regulating commerce.

Objecting to books and trying to negate their influence leads to another problem much more serious than regulation of commerce. Citizen objections to textbooks and other reading material used in public education gained widespread notoriety in the 1970s and continued into the '80s and '90s. Many boards of education submitted to pressures to ban such books as *Huckleberry Finn*, *Mary Poppins,* Studs Terkel's *Working, The Diary of Anne Frank and The American Heritage Dictionary.* Also under fire were such literary masterpieces as *1984, Uncle Tom's Cabin, The Grapes of Wrath, Of Mice and Men, Death of a Salesman* and Kurt Vonnegut's *Slaughterhouse Five.* Attacked were the classics *The Color Purple, Gone With the Wind, To Kill a Mockingbird,* Desmond Morris' *The Naked Ape*, Jerzy Kisinski's *Being There* and J. D. Salinger's *Catcher in the Rye. Mother Goose Rhymes* and *Little Red Riding Hood* were also subject to fairy-tale charges.

Many groups, labeled "censors" by opponents, said the involvement was to guide their childrens' education – noneducation, as some foes saw it – and to protect youths from inappropriate books. Those "censors" were against material they considered to be antifamily, anticountry or anti-God. Many felt Mark Twain's *Huckleberry Finn* is inappropriate because it contains words that might offend some persons. The fact that such words were not offensive to most of society at the time written may be the lesson many missed. Twain's portrayal of racism and slavery as most-despicable facets of America's past might be lost on later generations that haven't experienced the degradation and debasement depicted by "naughty" words.

The same could be said for all questionable books; education requires knowledge about the world and its characteristics – good and evil – in order that individuals be able to function properly. Americans don't need to lie about their history by eliminating books that tell the truth about the nation's past. Slavery happened – and racism still does – and Mark Twain showed how ugly it was. Truth of the nation's past isn't anticountry, but to hide that history is.

One person openly calling for censorship was Terry Todd of the Eagle Forum, who wrote in a 1984 USA TODAY "opposing view" column:

"School boards acting as the representatives of the parents and reflecting the values and standards of the community have tried to remove inappropriate materials. Court cases have followed, and school districts have been forced to fund more expensive legal actions or to return the objectionable material to school use.

"Either parents are legal and rightful guardians of their children, having the right to guide their children's education, or the state has those rights. If parents have the rights, it is manifested in school board decisions that should not be subject to court review. If the state has the rights, the court will become, in the words of Chief Justice Warren Burger, 'super censors'.

"The very existence of the public schools may depend on whether they are accountable to the taxpayers who fund them, or to the courts."

That effort has many spurious arguments that must be refuted. The first being that states have rights. States have power; people have rights. The second is that school boards act as representatives of parents, and in the case of those calling for censorship, a minority of parents.

The basis for public education under the constitutional system is government's power to tax and spend for the general welfare. That's an obvious principle in the United States Constitution and in all state constitutions, even though sometimes not in clear-and-specific language. Government doesn't have power to tax and spend for a special interest or a minority viewpoint; it can tax and spend for the general good of society. It's not a constitutional principle that school boards reflect values and standards of the community. Many school boards, reflecting community standards, closed their schools rather than obey the constitutional law of the land on desegregation. Many school boards used their authority to benefit only a small percentage of their constituents – the white upper and middle classes – and that was certainly anticountry for it taught disrespect for the Constitution. What's considered inappropriate material to a small group doesn't necessarily qualify as inappropriate to all of society. A school board reflecting anticonstitutional community standards should never be allowed to continue in its erroneous ways; it must reflect constitutional values and standards. If some parents wish to bend school boards to reflect views too narrowly drawn, they should be forced to pay for costly court battles – that's the American way.

A Prized Possession

The legal guardianship of children has nothing to do with this issue – this issue concerns whether the general welfare of society is served by an educated population. Most people agree an educated society is better than an ignorant mass, so the question remains about the degree and scope of that edification. And is it possible a few parents possess truths so infallible they can dictate to a school board what's necessary for all? Or should school boards rely on the entirety of knowledge in the educating process?

Education's costs and benefits aren't the exclusive obligation or property of parents with school-age children. Many taxpayers don't have children in public schools and the educating of all is to benefit even those nonparents who, nevertheless, pay most of the costs. The commercial community pays a hefty portion of the taxes. Some business ventures may want educated newcomers to join erudite staffs. Authors, who want future readers capable of understanding their offerings, pay for education, just as parents do, so their views and standards must be honored and served by school boards. The military, which doesn't directly pay local school costs, wants people lettered enough to handle its modern sophisticated weaponry. It's a subversion, therefore, to have a school board reflect views of only a few parents, or community standards out of touch with constitutional principles.

Whether the challenged books corrupt gullible American youths or are necessary for the young to start understanding the world around them isn't the constitutional issue, either. The truth is that Americans ceded to government authority to educate for the "general welfare," and the power to determine what education entails is part of that authority. Pressuring a school board to ban some books because they're "inappropriate" to a minority is to infringe on the rights of a majority who may not find any such inappropriateness. When educated people don't find the challenged books "objectionable," professional educators would have the legal power to use those books in the education of the young.

The division of power in the Tenth Amendment indicates that authority to educate children is "reserved to the states," but powers "reserved ... to the people" don't include jurisdiction over others who aren't party to concepts of a special-interest group. Powers reserved to the people could include seeking approval to use alternative reading material, but never to remove educational matter others may not want removed. School boards and public schools, as government entities, must be accountable to all taxpayers and to the principles of the Constitution, not to a few taxpayers who may not understand the Constitution.

Suggesting that school-board decisions shouldn't be subject to legal challenges is a most outrageously anticonstitutional position. All citizens

THE UN-AMERICANS

have the right "to petition government for a redress of grievances," and special-interest gains or positions should never be immune from that process. While many censors claim they're trying to rid the schools of books they claim are anticountry, it's the censors who appear anticountry.

Romantic notions of the American heritage bring to mind pictures of heroic crusaders or possemen out to capture bad guys in the name of justice. The Old West wasn't tamed, nor the frontier modernized, by itinerant cowboys on intrepid steeds, but that image lingers on. And, there's a constitutional lesson to be had by viewing such good guys as Tom Mix, Hopalong Cassidy and Red Ryder battling for truth, justice and the American way. There are many people in all areas of the nation acting like Tenth Amendment Cowboys to actively pursue desperados under the reserved-power authority of citizen involvement.

The most-obvious citizens' group, the Guardian Angels, was founded in New York City's South Bronx area in the late 1970s. Founder Curtis Sliwa, a former manager of a fast-food restaurant, expanded the organization nationwide and into Canada and England during the 1980s, but met stern resistance by police in some cities. In other cities, the group was welcomed and embraced. The Angels, an unarmed group that volunteered itself to patrol crime-infested areas during hours of high-crime activity and to make citizen arrests occasionally, help illustrate the meaning of the Tenth Amendment.

It's clear to many people that Americans surrender to government their vigilante rights – an individual doesn't exercise police power anymore, that power belongs to the state. But, does it? Or, how much police power belongs to the state and how much police power has been retained by the individual? If individuals delegate all police power to the state, they would be rendered helpless in defending selves or property. Since no one would argue that a person wasn't entitled to self-defense, the only conclusion possible is that police power is to be shared with the state, and that sharing of power is at the heart of the Tenth Amendment. The Angels seemed better able to understand that concept than did police forces in such places as Newark, N. J., and Seattle where resistance to their activities was raised.

But, it's important to acknowledge limitations on the individual's police power. Citizens don't conduct raids on suspects, or run evidence-gathering operations, those are reserved to the police. Citizens don't obtain search warrants, that's specified in the Fourth Amendment as a function of government. Citizens don't involve themselves in police matters needing legal authorization.

Citizens retain power to act beyond the obligations of a police department. The state's powers pertain mostly to after-crime activity; government

A Prized Possession

has no responsibility to prevent crime because such obligation would make police negligent in any crime and that would be unrealistic. Prevention of crime because of police presence is a bonus. That's where Guardian Angels and other vigilant groups are valuable. Their patrols or organized alertness can help prevent crimes, and that's a power retained by the people.

The Angels' success gave rise to other groups, including homosexual activists reacting to an increase in antigay hate crimes. Gays created Angel-like squads to patrol "gay-bashing" areas in San Francisco, New York City, Dallas and other major cities. These groups were welcomed by overburdened police and illustrate an important constitutional principle. Gays provide government power proportionate to their representation in society – some people say 10 percent, others only one percent. But their power is the same provided by the straight population making homosexuals deserving of the same protections heterosexuals receive. Anything less is un-Americanism.

When people give protective authority to government in a constitution or a charter, they surrender to the state the power to take action against others, not a power for the state to act against self-abuse. Some people try to extend the retained-power principle to compulsory automobile seat-belt use, arguing it's the individual's right to use or not use a seat belt. But that's carrying the argument to areas it doesn't apply. Government has the legal authority to make rules requiring use of safety equipment on state property.

Many people think government has intruded into too many areas of human activity, using such things as building codes that grow more cumbersome and restrictive with the passing of time. Codes, operating under the principle of protection, have their places. They are certainly needed to protect the homebuyers from shoddy construction because the strength and quality of a building aren't seen through finished walls. Nor would it be possible to detect faulty and dangerous electrical wiring or plumbing; those must be prevented through a system of inspections and codes.

Regulation-of-commerce protection must extend to apartment renters and those who frequent public structures, but it doesn't necessarily mean that the system must apply to the industrious individual building for self, nor does it necessarily apply to additions or alterations made outside commerce. Codes, in such instances, seem to skeptics to be infringements on individualism and a method government uses to keep track of values for future tax increases. The Tenth Amendment says specifically that some powers are delegated to government and some powers are retained by the individual. The continuing argument over building codes leaves unanswered just which powers were surrendered and which powers were retained.

Such concepts lead back to the Missouri right-to-die case (Chapter 4).

THE UN-AMERICANS

That situation ended when its main personality, Nancy Cruzan, died in December of 1990 at age 33 after almost eight years in a persistent vegetative state. Her death was permitted when court testimony by associates showed she had no wish to remain on life-support systems when there was no chance of recovery. Many self-proclaimed right-to-life advocates opposed the court decision, but they may have been demonstrating hostility toward Tenth Amendment principles.

In the original case, the Supreme Court ruled that Missouri had the police power to protect the injured woman from harmful actions of others, but that there were routes around an all-intrusive government. Chief Justice William Rehnquist wrote, "We assume that the United States Constitution would grant a competent person a constitutionally protected right to refuse lifesaving hydration and nutrition." Rehnquist assumed wrongly that the Constitution grants rights, but correctly that there is authority to refuse treatment, and it's possessed by the individual. This case is what the Tenth Amendment is all about.

The Cruzan family, by being conscientious citizens of the state and nation, tacitly surrender some powers to government, including the protective police power. They don't surrender all their governmental power; they keep some to be exercised as needed. The power retained under the Tenth Amendment could have been exercised, if allowed, before the family's despair was forced to linger much too long. The state certainly has the power to keep alive, as protection, a severely injured woman. But, that power must have an end, at which time the individuals' retained powers take over. In such a case as this, the switch of power could come when medical professionals determine that further treatment was futile. The Tenth Amendment would allow power of government to give way to power of the citizen at that time. What's needed would be competently drafted legislation by elected officials who could recognize and specify an end of state power and responsibility and the beginning of individual power.

The woman's father was quoted as saying, "the decision of life and death belongs to the family and not the courts." With that, an ordinary man showed more constitutional understanding than those who prevented family decisions for nearly eight years, for such family decisions are protected by "powers ... reserved to the ... people."

It must be remembered, a state with capital punishment in its penal code is saying it gets authority to terminate life from its citizens. If citizens have such a power, is it not applicable as a power reserved to the people in this situation? The Missouri legislature did enact a right-to-die law in 1991.

The Cruzan case helped fuel controversies about rights of individuals to

A Prized Possession

commit suicide or of physicians to assist in suicides. The argument came to the fore after an Oregon woman with Alzheimer's disease committed suicide in 1990 with the aid of Michigan physician Jack Kevorkian's "suicide machine," and a Rochester, N. Y., physician helped a terminal leukemia patient end her life. From a constitutional standpoint, there's absolutely nothing written to indicate the national government has any authority concerning dying or an individual's choice of how to die. Whether this absence of power constitutes an immunity of United States citizens that state government can't abridge is an issue addressed by the Fourteenth Amendment. The power to regulate commerce would give states authority to control acts of a physician, but would not extend that control to an individual's actions.

The Bill of Rights may be misnamed. It's really a Bill of Prohibitions or a Bill of Interdictions because it establishes prohibitions on government, not on citizens. It grants no rights and doesn't claim to be the source of rights. In fact, the Ninth Amendment indicates just that principle. That amendment says rights go beyond the Constitution, and it advises against restricting thoughts only to a few rights mentioned in the Bill of Rights.

The Bill of Rights grants no right of free speech, of assembly, or of a free press, or freedom of religion. Those rights existed long before the Bill of Rights was adopted. The First Amendment keeps government in restraints, so it can't keep its actions secret or won't intrude too far into personal beliefs. The Second Amendment doesn't create a right to keep and bear arms, that too was a well-established right. The amendment preserved the right to keep and bear arms so Congress could use its power to arm the militia. Being free of quartering solders isn't absolute either; it can be eliminated by simple law in time of war, according to the Third Amendment. The people are only protected from unreasonable searches and seizures; they are fair game for reasonable searches and seizures under the Fourth Amendment. The Fifth Amendment paints a picture of due process of law; it doesn't establish anything that wasn't in practice at the time written. The same is true of the Sixth, Seventh and Eighth Amendments; they reflect principles already accepted. And the Eighth Amendment doesn't say what most people think it says. The Ninth Amendment says rights belong to the people, not states, a concept the founders never questioned. The Tenth Amendment tells of the source of government power. It alludes to the man north of the river, the man south of the river, a fool on the hill and a farmer in the dell creating a covenant to form government.

The Bill of Rights was written because the Founding Fathers simply didn't trust future generations to be as astute about constitutional government as they were. They were rather smart about that.

Chapter 9

SOME GOSPEL TRUTHS

UNDERSTANDING NEEDED

"Congress shall make no law respecting an establishment of religion, or prohibiting the free exercise thereof" is the wording behind numerous arguments Americans have about the Constitution. Some people find a "wall between church and state" hidden in those words. Others contend there's a total immunity from government power even for people who commit crimes in the practice of religion. Still others find room for government to promote religious tenets, and some will find antireligion positions. Some persons go so far as to pretend they can read the minds of all men involved in adopting the Constitution and the Bill of Rights to know what the creators' intentions were. Hundreds of people were involved in the adoption of the Bill of Rights, so to contend there was one intention about how the religion clauses would apply is childish thinking. Every person involved – James Madison's committee, members of Congress who approved the amendments and men who ratified the Bill of Rights at the state level – could have had intentions that differed from all other intentions.

Therefore, the only important things are what is written and what it means, and discerning accurate meaning requires sound understanding of the English language. As with the Eighth Amendment, failure to understand language properly leads to misunderstanding the Constitution, even Supreme Court judges aren't immune from misinterpretations stemming from faulty reading habits.

Reading ability hampered Chief Justice William Rehnquist in a 1985 decision involving church-states issues. His views reflected those expressed by Justice Potter Stewart in the famous 1962 decision about prayers in public schools. Rehnquist said the intent of the framers of the First Amendment was only to prevent government from establishing one religion as a favorite over the others. He rejected the contention that state neutrality between religions and between religion and what he called "irreligion" were issues. Stewart had said of the prayer issue: "I cannot see how an 'official religion' is established by letting those who want to say a prayer say it."

Echoing them was Dan C. Alexander Jr., former chairman of the Mobile, Ala., County School Board, who wrote in a USA TODAY "opposing view" column: "It was never the intent of our Founding Fathers to remove prayer from schools. They only wanted to keep our government from promoting or establishing a religion."

Some Gospel Truths

The last statement was most silly because there was no intent of the Founding Fathers about prayers in school because there were no public educational systems at the time the Constitution or the Bill of Rights were written, and those documents didn't reach into private schools. The only true intent of the founders is that government not have power applicable in any way to religion. That's what the Constitution is all about: power of government. And the First Amendment is concerned with blocking use of nonexistent power. The amendment tells government not to try to use a power over religion because such power simply doesn't exist. When a person tries to go beyond this prohibition of power in search of "original intent" that person is demonstrating a lack of constitutional understanding and may be trying to hide personal biases in the minds of dead men. Local politicians can be forgiven for knowing little about the Constitution; Supreme Court judges should never be forgiven. The Supreme Court has never adequately defined the meaning of the establishment clause, but it has provided numerous examples of its meaning.

Knowledge must come from an ability to read and to understand the meanings that combinations of words create. To argue that the first portion of the religion clause only prevents government from favoring Religion A over Religion B, C, D and others or from creating a state religion doesn't reflect a decent high-school reading level. If the framers of the amendment were concerned with such a narrow meaning they would have used the words to indicate narrowness. They didn't do so. The First Amendment says "no law respecting an establishment of religion," and it's important to define all principal words in that phrase. Many people ignore "respecting," which distorts meaning of the establishment clause. "Respecting" can mean "regarding," "concerning," "involving," "relating to," or "about." The founders used "respecting" in Article IV to mean "concerning," and Madison and his Bill of Rights committee used it the same way. That meaning must be used to read the establishment-of-religion clause correctly.

Rehnquist and Stewart read "establishment" as a verb, which it is not; it's a noun, and it cannot be the verb in this phrase because "respecting" is the verb, "establishment" is its object. As a noun, establishment means something that's been established – in this context, established by religion – as well as the act of establishing. Under that definition establishment would be something created and embraced as an integral part of the creator's existence. Prayers were established and embraced by religion as were hymns, masses, communions, rituals, holidays, symbols, idols or icons. "Establishment" can also mean "institution," or "fixture."

If the First Amendment only prohibited creating a state religion, it would have had to use a verb or gerund, such as "establishing." It would read "no law respecting the establishing (gerund) of religion," or "no law establishing (verb) religion." The word "respecting" would not have been used. The establishment clause says "an establishment of religion." If the clause were to apply to only one legislative act of Congress, such as creating a state religion, it would have to read "the establishment (or establishing) of religion." The article "the" would limit meaning of the phrase to a singular specific establishment. The phrase "an establishment" broadens the meaning so it applies to "this establishment," or "that establishment," or "any other establishment" a reasonable person would conclude was created and embraced by religion. The word "of" in "establishment of religion" carries many connotations. It means "which is," but also indicates possession, as in "that dog of mine." The founders also never mentioned the First Amendment concerned only "official religion," that's a phrase and concept nowhere found in the Constitution.

The proper meaning of the establishment clause, therefore, is that Congress doesn't have power to make laws referring to, about, relating to, involving or concerning religion or those things established, created or held by religion, such as rituals, symbols, icons, masses, communions, prayers or any other fixture. The Fourteenth Amendment passes such prohibitions onto state lawmakers. By misreading "establishment" as a verb, judges would allow some unfindable universal power to be used by government to institutionalize some religious establishments within the state. A universal power is not a constitutional principle; therefore, it's un-Americanism.

This inability to distinguish verbs from nouns, to use all meanings of prepositions or to acknowledge all words in a sentence, seems endemic to the political right and results in inevitable misunderstanding of the Constitution, In his book, *The Way Things Ought to Be*, hard-core conservative Rush Limbaugh wrote, "Those clauses are 'Congress shall make no law respecting the establishment of religion, or prohibiting the free exercise thereof.' Only a lawyer could claim not to understand the plain meaning of those words. The government is prohibited from setting up a state religion ..." As just shown, that is not what the establishment clause says. Not only does he not understand the meaning of those words, Limbaugh couldn't even copy the clauses correctly – it says "an establishment," not "the establishment" – but he attacked the U. S. Supreme Court for ruling correctly on every church-state case it has heard with the exception of Gobitis (Chapter 7), which it corrected. And the First Amendment says or implies nothing about "setting up a state religion."

A Catholic priest, The Rev. H. Vernon Sattler, calling for religion's involvement in politics, wrote in a USA TODAY "opposing view" column in 1984: "Religion has a right and duty to affect politics. The Declaration of Independence proclaims a self-evident religious truth: Men are endowed by the Creator with unalienable rights."

But, John Jay, one of the Founding Fathers who was familiar with the concepts advanced by the Declaration and the Constitution, said some of those unalienable rights are then ceded to government in order to vest it with necessary powers. Jesus Christ indicated the same thing. The First Amendment indicates no unalienable religious rights were ceded – or rendered – to government, therefore government doesn't have power to make laws concerning religious issues; the state is restricted to secular issues detectable in the Constitution. Government cannot incorporate any religious creed into its secular law, even though the majority of its citizens may belong to one dominate sect.

The "wall between church and state" Americans repeatedly cite, as if understanding the concept, is but a metaphor. It has no constitutional standing or meaning. It was used by Thomas Jefferson to describe an absence of power for people who might not fully understand constitutional principles. People who do understand those principles don't resort to trite metaphors to explain what's explainable in more-concise terminology – specifically government is religiously powerless. The "wall" metaphor has been used in the past to overlook many problems, indiscretions or crimes. Evils perpetrated in the name of religion were ignored by government officials who feared breaching the "wall between church and state." That wasn't the intentions of the Founding Fathers . The framers of the Constitution and the Bill of Rights were concerned with legal use of government power, they never excused religion from a requirement of lawful behavior. As with press freedoms, in which there's nothing in the Constitution suggesting immunity from legitimate governmental power for a special class, there's nothing indicating the institution of religion may be treated differently from other institutions.

An intent of the founders could have been to avoid what's been obvious in all parts of the world throughout history. It's particularly evident in Latin America, even today, but its roots go back to 325 A.D. when Constantine established Christianity – tainted with pagan practices – as the official religion of Rome. As Rome declined and fell, giving way to the Holy Roman Empire, a marriage of church and state evolved. The Catholic Church then served as government throughout most of the civilizing years of Europe. While governing popes, cardinals, bishops and priests didn't see anything wrong in their holding political power, people who broke free in the Protestant Reformation did. But that break didn't affect Spain and Portugal, who colonized Central and South America with dictatorships incorporating theocratic powers similar to the conditions of the Spanish and Portuguese Inquisitions, when any resistance to government/church was forbidden and was punished by torture and death for thousands of people. No spirit of independence was allowed to develop and no concept of freedom was born on the Iberian Peninsula. The idea of church and state being one was exported to the Western Hemisphere and imposed on the indigenous Indian cultures. That prevented the concept of democracy from being accepted by the Latin American ruling classes who have used governmental power to serve only themselves. While there may be millions of people in Latin America yearning for freedom, the heritage under which they live has prevented freedom from developing.

The Founding Fathers, seeing church-state conditions to the south and in other parts of the world, decided there would by no mixture of religion and government. That's evident in the body of the Constitution. If all power governing the practice or observance of religion found in the United States Constitution were added to those powers in the state constitutions and county and city charters, the grand total would be zero, aught, nothing. Had the founders wanted government to have pietistic powers, they would have said so in Article I, Section 8. The fact they did not illustrates the only intent of importance – there is no power relating to religion. All arguments over church-state issues stem from misunderstanding or ignoring this absence of power.

WITHOUT A PRAYER

Failure to understand the Constitution or to respect its principles resulted in one of the most-insidious attacks on Supreme Court integrity in more than a century. Not since the infamous Dred Scott decision of 1857 had the court and the Constitution been assailed as following the 1962 decision in *Engel v. Vitale*, the school-prayer decision. The court came under immediate attack by many politicians, journalists, religious leaders and ordinary people who accused it of saying things it simply didn't say. The attack continues, albeit with less ferocity now, and reached its zenith during the administration of Ronald Reagan when used by many seeking political gain. During debate on a 1981 bill purporting to endorse "voluntary" prayer in public schools, Sen. Ernest F. Hollings, D-S.C., railed against the Supreme Court saying, "Rather than allow freedom of religion they've forbid any religion whatsoever." Sen. Jesse Helms, R-N. C., in arguing against a countermeasure said if that effort passed, the federal courts could "keep doing what they are doing – meddling in something that was never their business in the first place."

These politicians failed to gain approval for their positions from noted fellow-conservative, political columnist James Kilpatrick, who wrote, "The trouble is, as I see it, that the Supreme Court was exactly right in prohibiting the official prayer prescribed by the New York Regents in the Engel case ... The state simply has no business in the religion business." In another matter, a few years later, the mayor of Logan, Utah, ordered the city logo depicting the Mormon Temple removed from city vehicles and stationary because it might alienate non-Mormons. While such positions and actions may be consistent with constitutional government, offensiveness to other religions and alienation that might occur aren't the issue. The issue is whether government has power to do what it had done – usurp a religious practice to be included in a government function.

When politicians don't understand a constitutional principle or a court decision, they legislate. That happened in Alabama when Gov. Fob James signed into law a bill to "allow" prayer in public schools in 1982. The Associated Press quoted James as saying the law will "challenge the fundamental essence of that '62 decision that I think is totally ridiculous." Added by James was the silly argument of what the founders "intended." The AP reported the law "allows public school teachers and professors to lead 'willing students' in prayer. It includes a suggested prayer written by the governor's oldest son ... a Mobile lawyer."

The prayer read: "Almighty God, You are our God. We acknowledge You as the Creator and Supreme Judge of the world. May Your justice, Your truth and Your peace abound this day in the hearts of our countrymen, in the counsels of our government, in the sanctity of our homes, and in the classrooms of our schools. In the name of our Lord, amen." The Civil Liberties Union of Alabama challenged the act and the Alabama Education Association executive secretary said teachers should ignore the law and continue conducting devotionals as they had been doing. He estimated that 60 to 65 percent of the classrooms in the state had some form of religious rite each school day. Of course, the Supreme Court struck down the law just as it did in 1985 with another Alabama law designed to circumvent the Engel decision with a moment of silent prayer. The court had refused in 1983 to hear an appeal of a New Mexico state court decision voiding that state's silent-prayer law.

How all this relates to the real Engel decision is now considered. What the court said in that decision has been immensely distorted since 1962 and that distortion is reflected in statements and actions by critics of court and Constitution. Excerpts from that much-hated decision state:

"... in this country it is no part of government to compose official prayers for any group of the American people to recite as a part of a religious program carried on by government."

"... establishing governmentally composed prayer ..."

"... government in this country, be it state or federal, is without power to proscribe by law any particular form of prayer ... of governmentally sponsored religious activity."

"... government encroachment upon religious freedom ..."

"... government in this country should stay out of the business of writing or sanctioning official prayers ..."

On writing and sanctioning prayers the decision said, "... leave that purely religious function to the people themselves and to those the people choose to look to for religious guidance."

As people capable of reading can easily see, there's nothing in those statements to indicate that children were denied the right to voluntarily pray in school or that "God was evicted from school." There's nothing suggesting religion be excluded or denied, and nothing to suggest that the court "forbid any religion whatsoever," as Senator Hollings falsely claimed. Because the decision involved governmental power in a case "arising under this Constitution" (Article III, Section 2), it was certainly the business of the courts. Senator Helms was wrong about that. Every restriction mentioned by the court involved governmental power; the only thing that involved individual rights was the last statement, and it protected a child's religious freedoms from governmental actions because it left all decisions of whether to pray or not to pray to the individual. The statement alluded to the Ninth Amendment's provision that some rights are "retained by the people." In this case it was the right to practice religion free of government encroachment. Kilpatrick was correct for the court was "exactly right" in ruling that government has no power relating to religion and its establishments. New York's claim that the prayer was "voluntary" because children didn't have to participate did absolutely nothing to create power for the state to make a religious law. And nothing in that decision said organized prayer – a phrase the press uses often – is forbidden; only government-organized prayer is banned. Students were left free to do their own organizing, but not to organize through class or student-body votes on the matter because that would be a student referendum, and students can't enact religious laws when regular governments can't.

Alabama's governor was out of touch with constitutional reality when

Some Gospel Truths

he said the Supreme Court decision was "totally ridiculous." There was never any mention by Alabama politicians of what power they used to create and administer prayer or any other religious ritual. If the governor knew of any constitution where Americans ceded religious rights to government to vest it with theocratic power, he was obligated to identify that authorization. He did not.

Misconceptions and distortions of court decisions continue as politicians try to capitalize on constitutional ignorance. In March of 1994, Mississippi's Senate passed a bill to allow student-initiated prayer in schools with one politician saying, "You should never be afraid to stand up for what's right." Never mind that student-initiated prayer was never forbidden, and what's right is for governments – all governments – to obey the Constitution and abstain from legislating religion. Three months later religious broadcaster and political leader Pat Robertson wrote in USA TODAY, "Students who want to pray should be permitted to do so. Those who do not, should not." The problem with that statement is that it distorts reality. No one can be prohibited from praying, as court decisions now stand.

Many notable people rushed to condemn the Supreme Court for keeping religion free from government trespass. Highly respected Rev. Billy Graham wrote in his syndicated newspaper column in 1983, "I deeply regret that our nation, built on Judeo-Christian principles, has banished prayer from the classroom ... It remains to be seen whether or not the nation's courts will reverse this trend in any measure, although we should pray that God will give wisdom to our judges as they deal with difficult church-state issues."

It's unfortunate such a respected man should distort the court's decisions so, because prayer has never been banished from the classroom. Government was banished from religion. The most-noticeable biblical principle anyone can find to claim the nation was built on Judeo-Christian principles is the command to render unto Caesar all secular authority and unto God all spiritual authority; that's what the religion clauses mean. The Supreme Court only set straight the proper rendering arrangement. The only reversal of court decisions possible would be to allow governmental incursion into religion and that would end freedom of religion. And it's the critics of the court – including Graham – who need wisdom from God, for the court knows exactly what it's saying in church-state issues.

Those claiming that God was removed from school included the Rev. Jerry Falwell, who wrote in a USA TODAY guest column, "For 170 years after the First Amendment was framed, America's school children prayed aloud in their classrooms. In 1962, the Supreme Court decided the framers did not know what they intended and, in essence, expelled God from public schools." Falwell quoted President Reagan as saying, "I have never met a child who was injured by exposure to a voluntary prayer." Injury had nothing to do with the decision; government power was the only issue. There's nothing in the Constitution that suggests government has power to act as a church if nobody is injured, offended or alienated. And the court was correct in interpreting the framers' intentions for the framers intended that government have no pietistic power – that's exactly what the Supreme Court ruled in the Engel case. It's Falwell who knows nothing of the framers' intentions.

Another notable guest columnist in USA TODAY was entertainer Pat Boone, who penned in 1984, "But school children and their teachers are forbidden by the local authorities, and by recent Supreme Court decisions, to have voluntary group prayer or to quote a Bible verse at the beginning of their school day." That's nonsense about the court, as is evident in its quoted statements, which say nothing about what a child can do other than make religious decisions for his or herself. Teachers can also make personal religious decisions, but they can't use authority given them by government to try to serve as ministerial servants or religious leaders because government in America doesn't have pietistic authority to give. He's almost correct about some local authorities who have misused court decisions.

Boone added: "In the early '60s, atheist Madalyn Murray O'Hair badgered some Supreme Court justices into 'protecting' the rights of a tiny splinter group, while depriving the vast majority of Americans of their rights. Nobody was forcing her atheist children and friends to pray, but she was determined that no one would pray publicly, and she had her way.

"Since then, the ACLU, many liberal congressmen and some misguided senators have sided with her, claiming 'separation of church and state.' These people don't know or care about the Constitution, which clearly provides only that 'the state shall establish no religion'." That last statement indicates it's Boone who doesn't "know or care about the Constitution" because the quote he used is nowhere to be found, suggesting he has never read the document, but he attacked "liberals" who know what the Constitution says. No one was deprived of rights because the last court quote previously cited protects the rights of all to make their own decisions on prayer. The issue was government practice of religion, which the Constitution clearly forbids. Supreme Court judges are never "badgered" into making decisions.

Boone made the same foolish mistake as USA TODAY concerning participants in the Engel prayer case. The newspaper reported in 1984, "Atheist Madalyn Murray O'Hair, who convinced the court to ban school prayer in

Some Gospel Truths

1962 ..." In 1989, USA TODAY's "From the Heart" columnist Barbara Reynolds wrote, "At a recent Moscow book fair, atheist Madalyn O'Hair – of prayer-out-of-schools fame – was ignored ..." A Virginia organization calling itself "The National Legal Foundation" carried on the distortion in a 1988 advertisement in USA TODAY that said, "Twenty-five years ago, Mrs. O'Hair persuaded the United States Supreme Court to ban prayer from our public schools ... Since that day, prayer has been banned from our public schools."

Those statements were untrue. Prayer was never banned from public schools; government involvement in that prayer was banned. The Engel decision clearly protects true voluntary prayer of the individual because it says decisions about praying are left to the people and the religious leaders of their choice, not to the state. When the individual makes a decision to pray, the prayer is voluntary. When the government makes that decision, prayer is not voluntary.

Madalyn Murray O'Hair had nothing to do with the *Engel v. Vitale* prayer decision. The suit was brought by parents of New York school children who were just as devoutly religious as the court attackers quoted here, the difference being that the parents understood the state lacked the power to become religiously involved. By falsely claiming the Engel decision came from atheist concerns, the critics were trying to discredit the court as if it were "serving Satan." But the truth is, the Engel decision resulted from concerns of people who lived by the Judeo-Christian principle of proper rendering of secular and spiritual authority. People espousing a conviction that government should exercise authority in religion were taking un-American positions because the Constitution contains no principle or power to do that.

When politicians are thwarted in attempts to legislate, they try to amend the Constitution, which happened under Reagan's leadership and again immediately upon the Republicans gaining control of Congress in the 1994 midterm elections. On May 4, 1982, Reagan endorsed a proposed amendment to "allow voluntary prayer" in public schools. Never mind that the court decision to be overturned allowed the exact same thing. Reagan claimed the "amendment we will propose will restore the right to pray." That right had never been removed.

The proposed amendment read: "Nothing in this Constitution shall be construed to prohibit individual or group prayer in public schools or other public institutions. No person shall be required by the United States or by any state to participate in prayer." That statement was similar to what Justice Hugo Black wrote in the Engel opinion that this amendment purportedly was to reverse. There was nothing in the court decision to prohibit praying, which ought to mean the amendment was foolishness. The state-conducted religious rite was voided on only one premise: government has *no power* to make a law putting prayer into schools. The proposed amendment did nothing to "return prayers" to the classroom because it wouldn't give the required power to government, which means it would change nothing, except encourage governments to make laws the Constitution says they can't make. The proposed amendment was nothing but a charade by self-serving politicians to pollute the Constitution with meaningless clutter. In March of 1984, the amendment was dead when it couldn't pass the Senate with the required two-thirds vote only to be periodically resurrected by religious groups and politicians who don't understand the original decision.

When Republicans won control of Congress in the 1994 midterm elections, GOP leaders unburied the issue. Less than a week after the elections, Rep. Newt Gingrich, R-Ga., announced he would introduce an amendment to allow voluntary school prayer in all U. S. schools. In the 1994 version, Republicans added, "Neither the United States nor any State shall compose the words of any prayer to be said in public schools." That, too, is the same as Justice Black had said in the Engel decision. It is puzzling why political leaders on the right don't know, or pretend not to know, that voluntary prayer has never been removed from schools. USA TODAY didn't clarify the situation by writing in a classic case of inept reporting, "Conservatives have been trying to bring back school prayer since the Supreme Court outlawed it in 1962 as a violation of church and state." The paper then reported in a sidebar that, "The Supreme Court outlawed prayer in public schools in 1962 as a violation of the separation of church and state."

The decision on school prayer has been in existence more than three decades, but the American press, politicians or people have yet to discover what was said. Voluntary school prayer has never been outlawed; making religious law by government was outlawed. It's mystifying that so many people can't read the Engel decision and find out what it says because it contains only 11 paragraphs. It is explained in detail in the Supreme Court Reporter and was shortened to eight paragraphs for textbooks on constitutional law. Those same people who don't understand the decision claim to know exactly the purposes of God, even though His statement takes up thousands of paragraphs in several books, many letters and – in the case of Philemon and two of the little Johns – three memos.

Many narrow-interest spokesmen use the prayer confusion to project personal opinions on the condition of the nation. Many celebrities were called to testify in favor of the Reagan amendment. The refrain was that when God was removed from public schools moral decay of the country occurred. The school superintendent of Florida's Nassau County was quoted by USA TODAY at that time as saying, "Many of the problems in this country's schools came in when they took prayer out." An official of the political Eagle Forum, Tottie Ellis, wrote, "This (religious services when she was in school) did not cause religious bigotry, because each school district and individual schools accommodated all faiths and were sensitive to everyone's feelings. When this stopped, the USA began its slide into moral and spiritual bankruptcy." USA TODAY's Reynolds wrote in February of 1995, "When prayer and respect for God were pushed out of public schools, drugs, guns, AIDS and murder swept in. So I want voluntary prayer in the schools."

There's no evidence to suggest those statements are true. Someone else might trace an acceleration of "moral decay" or the "slide into moral and spiritual bankruptcy" to evangelists taking to television to plead for money while distorting the true messages in the Bible and portraying spirituality as a circus sideshow run by cartoon characters. Problems in schools might be traced by other researchers to the elimination of the arts. i. e. painters and members of the choir seldom commit crimes. If removing government from religion caused any decay and slide, there should have been lower crime statistics in areas mandating prayer (such as New York and the South) and higher rates in areas with little government activity in religion, such as the Pacific Northwest. When government prayer was in New York City schools, the metropolitan area had the reputation of being crime-infested; the Northwest was an isle of relative tranquility.

School prayer did nothing to prevent or stop racial hatred in the South or in any other area. If crime or other problems were caused because state prayers were removed from public schools, there would be no statistical changes in crime beyond population growth in areas where prayers had never been administered by government. That hasn't been the case. Even the Northwest has experienced increases of crime and problems in public schools similar to that in areas where government prayer was voided. Many instances of abuse – physical as well as mental – have been reported when children didn't join the majority in state-imposed religious rituals in public schools. That very concern was evident in 1995 in a new case from Mississippi involving government in religion in which the Baptist dogma prevailed.

Mrs. O'Hair was involved in defining the First Amendment's religion clauses, but her involvement came in 1963 when the court voided laws "requiring the selection and reading at the opening of the school day verses from the Holy Bible and the recitation of the Lord's Prayer by the students in unison." The decision concerned laws in Pennsylvania and Maryland, both of which allowed children to be excused from the rituals if parents or guardians wished. That act of excusing children did nothing to create power the states needed to enact such religious laws. The Pennsylvania law was challenged by a devout Christian family that could recognize state invasion of personal rights of religion. The Maryland law was challenged by Mrs. O'Hair. In this ruling, the court stated that states cannot teach religion, but could teach about religion and the Bible, thereby refuting totally the nonsensical notion that "God was evicted from school." Reading the Bible as a daily devotional wasn't teaching about religion; it was practicing religion. It's strange that an atheist, such as Mrs. O'Hair, has done more to protect religion from government encroachment than have those anticourt complainers who continually call for government involvement in the practice and observance of religion, even though constitutional authority to do so doesn't exist.

Principles of separation of church and state aren't restricted to the Constitution and Supreme Court decisions; the Bible has lessons to contribute. Real Christians know that when Jesus was on earth he refused all efforts and desires of his followers to serve as their worldly ruler. That refusal is a rejection of the theocratic form of earthly government that has been a painful affliction on mankind throughout history. Christ told Pontius Pilate at John 18:36: "My kingdom is not of this world ..." That statement incorporates the meaning that earthly governments were no part of Christ's spiritual sovereignty. Self-proclaimed Christians who would mix mankind's government with Christ's kingdom would violate this biblical principle of separation. The Bible also says Christ is to be the only mediator between God and mankind (1 Tim. 2:5). For government to breach that command and try to make public-school teachers such mediators would violate this principle. It should be evident prayers ordained by man's laws and composed and administered by secular government or Bible-reading rituals administered by "Caesar's" state are condemned by both the United States Constitution and the Holy Bible and are, therefore, un-American and anti-Christ.

TACKLING A TOUGH ISSUE

Illegal law on a statewide basis isn't the only government action that courts rebuked as state functionaries try to enter the forbidden territory of government in religion. The situation crops up in many localities and often is carried out by many state officials or employees who appoint themselves directors of students' moral development and use government positions to impose religious practices without benefit of authority.

One such issue in the 1980s was a practice of athletic coaches at public schools imposing religious observances on members of their teams. That practice in Tennessee was widely reported in 1980 when several high-school football coaches conducted prayer sessions before Friday night games. After the state attorney general issued a nonbinding opinion that such rituals were unconstitutional, several coaches said they would ignore the opinion. They did. Said one, "We'll break the law Friday night." Another said, "It seems someone is always trying to tear down the American traditions and ideas we believe in. I hesitate to sound radical, but it makes one wonder if there isn't a communist influence, which leads to some of the challenges against the things Americans hold dear to them." A third said, "The majority of people don't want to change. So we'll keep doing it unless there's a bunch of federal marshals with guns around."

All of those coaches totally missed the point and used their positions to teach the wrong lessons. Players praying before football game wasn't the issue. The issue concerned high-school coaches using their positions as agents of government to establish practices or enact edicts in areas they had no authority to act. A public-school teacher or coach is given specific legal authority by the state over free-and-independent children. Without the power of government, those adults would have no such authority. That power is given to the state by all citizens through a constitution; the state in turn bestows authority, by law, to the coaches.

That authority to dominate constitutes a governmental restriction on the freedom of the students, so it must be sustainable by constitutional powers, either state or federal. Authority over students cannot exceed what's legally given, and the state cannot give authority to coaches in religious matters because it has no such authority to give. A coach cannot make his own authority because government agents creating power for themselves is a feature of autocratic governments, such as the petty little despotic regimes that the Founding Fathers abhorred. Government creating power for itself is not an American tradition and, as such, is un-Americanism. The coach who complained someone else is tying to "tear down American traditions" was the one tearing down the things Americans should hold dear. He had no authority over free children except that given him by law, and he was given no pietistic jurisdiction. He tried to exercise authority not given, which was teaching disrespect for the Constitution. That is subversion. It's unfortunate that some of these state employees need the threat of armed marshals before submitting to the principles of the United States Constitution which require that government and its agents throughout the nation stay out of other people's religion.

The same situation arose in Georgia later in the 1980s and was spearheaded by people who should be teaching constitutionalism, but who would rather teach subversion. A U. S. district judge in 1987 struck down government-sponsored pregame prayers at Douglas County High School as unconstitutional because the practice violated the separation of church and state. In May of 1989, the United States Supreme Court let stand the decision. USA TODAY quoted the school's attorney as saying the prayers were meant "to add solemnity and dignity. Advancing religion was the furthest thing from our minds."

Advancing religion wasn't the constitutional issue; government using a power it clearly doesn't possess was the issue. What school officials "meant" also is meaningless because good intentions don't create constitutional powers. Lawyers added that pregame prayers are "as much a part of the tradition of high-school football as the national anthem, marching bands, cheerleaders and baton twirlers." The problem with that statement is the national anthem, bands, cheerleaders and baton twirlers don't require a government power that's nonexistent. Tradition has nothing to do with constitutionalism. Some old traditions had to end with the adoption of the Constitution and many more disappeared with the adoption of the Fourteenth Amendment. Others are still being negated. What a population is accustomed to doing also has nothing to do with what is constitutionally permitted. Lawyers should know that.

In the fall of 1989, Douglas County officials said they would honor the Constitution and end state religious practices, but several superintendents announced government-ordained prayer would be part of pregame ceremonies; thereby, demonstrating to students that subversion was a Southern tradition. Several localities in Florida and Alabama joined many Georgia jurisdictions to protest the ban on government religion. In Montgomery, Ala., city and county officials led the prayers. One said, "Telling me I can't pray at a high-school game or any other gathering is an infringement on my rights."

No Supreme Court decision told anyone what they could, or couldn't, do concerning praying at a high-school football game, other gatherings or any other place. This political opportunist distorted the constitutional principle and lied about court decision in order to serve himself. The only thing ever decided concerned what governments – not individuals – could, or couldn't, do under their constitutional powers. Rulings say government cannot impose religion or any religious practice on a society of free-and-

Some Gospel Truths

independent citizens, even if most of those citizens wanted such imposition. Government doesn't have such power.

Praying by football players was never questioned. Of course, when a shy-and-sensitive linebacker detects a fat fullback snorting and stomping towards him, a prayer is obviously in order. But, it must be the player who decides if there is to be a prayer, what's said and when and how to say the prayer. No coach, teacher, principal or superintendent has authority to do that, and they can't create such authority for themselves; that's un-Americanism.

Like laws enacted by state legislatures, religious practices created by local authorities may have problems beyond the Constitution. The third of the Judeo-Christian Ten Commandments, forbids taking the name of the Lord in vain. Calling on the divine creator to intervene in war and football games may be what King Solomon termed "vanity," getting no response to pleas for advantages in contests of violence. Locally unenacted government prayer, therefore, appears to be subversively un-American, un-biblical and anti-Christian.

GOD IN SCHOOL

Ever since the Supreme Court decisions voiding government-sponsored prayer and state-conducted Bible-reading religious rituals in public schools, Americans have been subjected to the "Devilish Lie" that "God was kicked out of school." There's never been a Supreme Court decision doing that, but the statement lives on as a sloganistic cliche. The American public's link to the Supreme Court is the news media, which have never accurately reported court decisions. This misrepresentation has been accidental because reporters and editors may not understand the decisions, or stories may be tainted by personal beliefs and interpretations. There rarely are attempts to mislead readers or listeners.

One in the media who totally missed the point on school-church decisions was retired publisher of the Portland (Ore.) Oregonian, Robert C. Notson, who penned a 1981 anticourt article headlined, "Appeals to divine deity/part of national ritual;/why ban in schools?" Notson wrote, "The Supreme Court rendered its opinion in the school prayer case June 26, 1962, but the fallout is still dropping around us. It is not just the narrow question involved in the New York litigation. It is the sweeping implications that are being felt. There has been a growing effort to drive any expression of religious or spiritual and moral value from public life." That statement could have been uttered by a fangy-mouthed varmint in Eden, for there is no truth to it. There's never been any court effort to drive religion or spiritual and moral values from public life. There has been an effort in the courts to drive government from religion so citizens can practice religion and spirituality in absolute freedom.

Notson added, "Decisions of the court in these cases (prayer and Bible reading) lacked perspective and logic. The prohibition is contrary to our heritage, tradition, to established practices of government and contrary to the wishes of the great majority of American people." This, too, was nonsense. Court decisions only cited a lack of constitutional power for states to enter into the practice or observance of religion. They, in addition to being totally in compliance with the Constitution, were logical and used perfect perspective. Heritage – whether true heritage or just the imagination of those knowing little of American history – tradition, established governmental practices and wishes of the majority of people do not provide pietistic power to government. If the majority of Americans want government to have regulatory power over their religions, they would have to say so in a constitutional amendment. People who cherish religious freedom hope Americans never do that.

The former newspaper publisher continued, "But now, says the court, it is unconstitutional for a school to give any official sanction to children saying grace at lunch or to a senior class having a nondenominational benediction at graduation ceremonies." The true meaning of any court action is that it's up to the child whether to say grace, and if the child does, the school has no power to interfere with that religious practice. It's also up to senior-class members about what they do individually. A public school, as part of the state, must have legal authority for what it or its employees do. It doesn't have religious authority.

The First Amendment's religion clauses were quoted by Notson who interpreted them thusly, "Down through the years this was regarded as meaning precisely what it says – an establishment of religion, a state church ... It has been well argued that the court not only misread the first part of the amendment and gave it an application beyond its intent but also overlooked completely the second part of the sentence – 'or prohibiting the free exercise thereof.'"

The problem with that statement is the writer made the familiar reading blunder no high-school graduate should make: he read "establishment" as a verb, not the noun it is, and he totally ignored the true verb, "respecting." It's obvious, it is he who hasn't the faintest idea of what the establishment clause means. The court didn't misread that clause; it read the words correctly to mean Congress has no power concerning religion. As shown, the

Some Gospel Truths

First Amendment doesn't mention a "state church." And the Fourteenth Amendment extended that absence of power to the states. The controversial court decisions prohibited no one from practicing religion freely. All prohibitions apply to government.

The school-religion decisions also had nothing to do with the free-exercise clause; such decisions came later. The establishment clause refers to government and its powers to create; the free-exercise clause refers to individuals and their rights to be free of government creations. Journalists should learn that. Too often journalists and politicians distort Supreme Court decisions in order to present their opinions as constitutionality, and that's what happened here. A man who wanted government participation in religion, distorted court opinions – opinions he likely never read – to lend an air of constitutional credibility to his biases.

Notson also said Congress would soon consider the prayer amendment that "would, in effect, permit prayers in school." It's unfortunate that a man, once publisher of a major metropolitan newspaper, could be deceived into thinking the prayer-amendment fraud would do anything of the sort. There's no way that "amendment" would have given power to governments to become religiously active; newspapers should have been reporting that, but most of them were deceived. It's tiresome and unfortunate that Americans are bombarded with such newspaper nonsense when they should be given accurate explanations of court decisions. In fairness, it should be noted that newspaper publishers often aren't journalists; often they're accountants, and accountants are experts on numbers, not words. Journalists should be experts on words, not numbers.

What the Supreme Court decided about God in school came in the 1963 Bible-reading opinion that said: "Nothing we have said here indicates that ... study of the Bible or of religion, when presented objectively as part of a secular program of education, may not be effected consistent with the First Amendment." In nonlawyer clarity, that means objective teaching about the Bible and religion wouldn't violate the First Amendment.

In a concurring opinion, William Brennan said, "The holding of the Court today plainly does not foreclose teaching about the Holy Scriptures or about the differences between religious sects in classes in literature or history." People who claim the Supreme Court kicked God out of school are participating in the "Devilish Lie" while "speaking Sloganese."

By the 1990s, some schools had begun teaching about religion as part of their history curriculum, and that seemed to be agreeable with what the Supreme Court said in 1963. Problems occur when schools try to teach religion, as in the creationism fights. Some denominations demanded their version of creation be taught alongside the theory of evolution. Scientists labeled creationism nonscientific, and the court in 1987 voided a Louisiana law requiring teaching creationism as science. Critics attacked the court as "antireligion" in its decision, but the truth is, the court was protecting religion.

If schools were to teach creationism as science, whose version should they teach? Denomination A would argue that each "day" of creation was 24 literal hours. There is no error in the Bible, its leaders say, and a day is a day. Denomination B would tell them, "get real," and would point out that Adam was warned at Genesis 2:17 about rebellion and "thou shalt surely die" in "the day that thou eatest" of a certain tree. After the feast, Adam and Eve were evicted from Eden, Eve conceived and gave birth to Cain, then to a second son, Abel, who grew into an adult only to be murdered by Cain, who then went off to the land of Nod to marry and raise a family. After all this, a third son, Seth, was fathered by Adam, who lived to the age of 930 years after fathering many other sons and daughters. That's a lot of living for a 24-hour period, Faith B would say, so Denomination A must be in error.

Persuasion B would point to Psalms 90:4, II Peter 3:8 and Adam's age at death to show a day is a 1,000-year metaphor. Creed C would argue that Hebrews 3 and 4 indicate the seventh day of rest was still in effect at the time of Christ and still exists today. That, says C, indicates each creative day was several thousands of years in length. Ideology D would say there's no need to fight science; each creative day is a symbolic reference to a length of time that could be billions of years long. Sect E might say mankind was created on the sixth day, God rested on the seventh, then went back to work on the eighth to create the literal Adam and Eve. F Group would say all are wrong; the Bible is metaphorical, symbolic and allegorical, and it relates man's development of belief, not a literal history of existence. F Group could argue that biblical stories were how some ancient humans without libraries or computer memory banks stored their knowledge and understanding, just as others kept their lore in paintings on cave walls. Hundreds of variations of the same belief would have to be considered, including those of Islam, Buddhism, Shintoism, Native American beliefs or other faiths whose followers are in the constitutional covenant. Then, there's the agnostic who says, "I don't know," and the atheist who says, "I know everyone but me is wrong."

If schools were to teach creationism, they would face a number of problems. Which of these versions would public schools teach? Is there any way government could determine correct biblical interpretation? And, if government attempted to find "truth," would it not be elevating one religion or denomination over the others? Teachers, of course, have their beliefs, which might be difficult to suppress in order to teach objectively. It's precisely this type of entanglement the Founding Fathers sought to avoid when they decided the new government have no power in matters of religion.

But that doesn't stop some people who are determined to circumvent both the Constitution and the Bible on separation of church and state. A three-member majority of the Vista (Calif.) School District near San Diego made a policy at the beginning of the 1993-94 school year to teach creationism in English, history and social studies. In such situations, the version taught would most likely be the version embraced by the majority making the rules while the 1963 Supreme Court decision would indicate that all versions must be taught, if any were. But teaching any might require a law concerning religion.

Critics of the court seem to think establishing an official state religion would be accomplished in one act of legislation. That's a childish thought. By teaching or practicing religion, one denomination would evolve, even unintentionally, into a favorite. In an American society based on science and technology, it could well be Denomination D or F. A great mystery is why is Denomination A the one criticizing the Supreme Court the most and arguing for government involvement in religion when it could be the first damaged by such involvement? By nullifying government involvement in religion, Denomination A is protected most by the Supreme Court, and all are protected from the others.

If schools were to teach or practice religion, there would certainly be many special-interest religionists confronting school boards nationwide to favor their belief. As seen in the Tenth Amendment portion of Chapter 8, these interests have demanded books they disliked be removed from schools. It has happened with history books, social-studies books, geography books, reading books, reference books, all types of books. It most definitely would happen with religion books. There should be no one foolish enough to not know that Denomination A would complain that textbooks favored Sect C, B or F. Creed E would complain that favoritism was given Faith B, C, or D. Each sect would claim it, and only it, had biblical truth, and only its truth should be taught. If schools were to teach religion, there would be nothing but the fighting and arguing the Founding Fathers hoped to avoid.

HOLY WARS

Even though religion isn't taught in public schools, many special-interest religionists have hounded school boards for years about reading material they claim is biased against their faith. Their arguments are usually based on a contention that anything not favorable to them, must be unfavorable. They see no middle ground of neutrality.

Many special-interest religionists claim neutrality is actually a religion. They call it "secular humanism," a faith of unknown origin with no gods, rituals, beliefs or congregation. (A form of "secular humanism" is considered again at the end of this chapter.) In Tennessee, a federal judge issued a decision in 1986 to let some students skip classes they claim would offend their fundamentalist religious beliefs. In the spring of 1987, another federal judge in Alabama prohibited using 45 textbooks in public schools. He said these books promoted secular humanism as a religion. The people who brought the suits claimed the books failed to mention the historical role of Christianity and other faiths while promoting a counterfaith. Some of them alleged *The Wizard of Oz* was anti-Christian, as was science-fiction works by Isaac Asimov. Other concerns cited were that Jesus Christ was portrayed as "illiterate" and that children were shown praying to idols. Both decisions were reversed on appeal in 1987, and in 1988 the Supreme Court let stand the appellate rulings.

A critic of the appellate rulings was Robert K. Skolrood, executive director and general counsel of the National Legal Foundation in Virginia, who complained in a 1987 newspaper column, "What a tragedy that, in this year of our Constitution's bicentennial, a federal court has twisted the First Amendment, turning public schools into temples to Self (the humanist god), censoring those who share the faith of the Framers in 'Our Lord' as they stated in the Constitution." His complaint had no merit because the fact "our Lord" was used in reference to the date ("Seventeenth Day of September in the Year of our Lord one thousand seven hundred and Eighty seven") in no way creates pietistic powers. It only listed the date the convention completed writing the Constitution. If appellate courts were to allow the original rulings to stand, they would have had to find constitutional principles to do so, and a date is no more a constitutional principle than is a page number.

The other concerns reflect the problems the real framers were trying to avoid under the Constitution. Not all Christians would consider *The Wizard of Oz* or Asimov's literature to be "anti-Christian." That they are fiction is readily understandable to most, and absence of promotion for Christianity isn't considered by millions of believers to be anti-Christian. If such differences over interpretation had to be decided in the school system through book selections or course offerings, the state would be forced to be referee among factions of the world's most-splintered religion. Freedom of religion

Some Gospel Truths

can only be preserved by keeping all levels of government out of the arguing. The Founding Fathers knew that, so they wrote the Constitution in a way to prevent government from deciding religious controversies. As for Jesus being portrayed as "illiterate," the fundamentalists also have the Bible to contend with. The King James says at John 7:15, "And the Jews marvelled, saying, how knoweth this man letters, having never learned." A newer version says: "How is it this man has learning, when he has never studied?" There's no biblical reference to make one think universal education was an institution of the Roman-occupied Jewish homeland in Christ's lifetime, so being uneducated is certainly probable. If some people twist that into "illiterate," it's they who do so. Many people think the figurines, artifacts and paintings widely used in most Christian denominations are idols followers pray to. Having government in the midst of such disagreements and asking it to settle these centuries-long disputes is precisely what the Founding Fathers feared and hoped to avoid. When courts relieve government from refereeing differing interpretations of the Bible, they aren't "censoring those who share the faith," they are protecting all faiths. Intelligent people can recognize what portion of their lives has been rendered to Caesar and what has been rendered to God. Education is Caesar's; religion is God's.

Many arguments keep forcing the state into resolving differing concepts of religion, as happens with the contention that the lack of pietistic power in the Constitution prevents government from declaring Christmas a holiday. It does; but there's nothing to prevent December 25 from being made a holiday. That should settle the issue between Christians and non-Christians, but there are differing opinions concerning the event. Most Christians celebrate the date as the birth of Christ. Other Christians say, "no way"; at that time of year shepherds in the hills outside Bethlehem would freeze their flocks while standing in the snow. Some people claim December 25 was the day of conception, and the birth occurred the following September. A third Christian position dismisses the holiday altogether, saying it's from the paganism Constantine incorporated into his state religion of Rome in the fourth century. The New Catholic Encyclopedia says "The date of December 25 does not correspond to Christ's birth but to the feast of the Natalis Solis Invicti, the Roman sun festival at the solstice." People who opt for the third argument point out the Bible says Christians must observe the death of Christ, for that is the foundation of the faith. There's no mention in the Bible of celebrating his birth and first-century Christians didn't do so. It's not the function of government to use its school system to indicate one position is correct.

THE UN-AMERICANS

Even the Ten Commandments pose problems in church-state issues. Kentucky law required posting the Ten Commandments in every classroom in the state, but that law was voided in 1980 for the same reason as all the other religious laws – lack of pietistic power. Critical religionists argued the commandments were the cornerstone of American secular law, so should have been allowed to remain. But, that's not true because all civilized nations have nearly the same code of laws. The communist Soviet Union had, and Cuba and China still have, much the same laws, with some variations. The Ten Commandments were only part of more than 600 laws brought to the Jews by Moses, and many of those 600 laws concerned religious rituals.

Governments in the United States are constitutionally prohibited from having religious law, but many politicians refuse to submit to this prohibition on government interference in religion. In June of 1994, the court had to act again on the same issue. It left intact lower court rulings telling officials of Cobb County, Ga., to remove from the courthouse a panel with the Ten Commandments and teachings of Jesus because making law to put them there is government intrusion into religion.

Some Christians – such as the Church of Christ and Jehovah's Witnesses – point to many biblical passages to show that Christ created a "new covenant" with Christians to replace the Mosaic Law that had ruled the ancient Jewish nation. They can cite Deuteronomy 5:1-3 and Psalms 147:19-20 to show the commandments were for Israel only, and were to be in effect until Christ arrived (Galatians 3:19-24). Then Galatians 3:10-14, Romans 6:14 and 10:4, Ephesians 2:11-15 and Colossians 2:13-14 are cited as evidence that Christ is the end of the Jewish Law. Other denominations reject such a interpretation.

By requiring the Ten Commandments be displayed by the state, the Kentucky legislators were saying they decided biblical truth, and thoughts of a few people – who could be the only ones biblically correct – were erroneous. Deciding religious doctrine is not the function of legislators. When people try to force the state into the midst of these many differing religious concepts – even if only by imposing church holidays, pageants, decorations or other trappings on children – they are coming dangerously close to doing what the Founding Fathers dreaded, and the court must be very cognizant of that when considering church-state issues. Court critics seldom consider anything except their personal biases, and their attempts to force government involvement in religion seem to be fishing expeditions designed to extract a state blessing for one sect over all the others. Most Supreme Court judges aren't biting.

OVERCOMING OVERREACTION

While the great "Devilish Lie" hasn't impeded the Supreme Court in its work of defining the First Amendment's religion clauses, it has been fought over in many sectors of society, most obviously in the public schools. The falsehood began in the classrooms, which still serve as the major battlegrounds in the ongoing war between those who want government involvement in religion and those who want no involvement. When presidents, governors and other politicians; attorneys and judges; ministers; journalists, and parents clamor that the Supreme Court "kicked God out of school," its only logical to expect that very thing would occur, even though there's no court requirement to do so.

There's never been a Supreme Court decision ordering God removed from public schools, or even to grade Him, but there have been expulsions of Him by state officials, school boards, superintendents, principals and teachers all over the nation. Some parents, worried about mixing government and religion, also have sought the total elimination. It follows that if politicians, school officials or parents don't read court decisions – or can't understand the attorney-inflicted verbosity of them – they would seek elimination of all religion, just to be safe. The court has never said or implied elimination of spirituality needs to be done.

People who never read court opinions rely on other sources to find out what was said, and the news media, which have never accurately reported decisions, are those sources. Religious leaders pick up on sloganeering by the media to sermonize against decisions never made. Politicians, always on the lookout for votes in a society that is overwhelmingly religious, join in to exploit the issue with their nonknowledgeable criticism. There, of course, will be some holy terrors who call upon God to smite the Supreme Court with sulfur, brimstone and destructive fire from heaven. Apparently He ignores them. It's as if their entreaties are answered in a manner they don't want to hear. Rather than inflict holy punishment on the court or respond to prayers to give wisdom to the judges, as the Reverend Graham asked, God's divine silence and inaction should be taken as the heavenly command: "Read the decision."

Reading decisions might give astute preachers the very wisdom they think Supreme Court judges need. Understanding the Constitution would also help those who appointed themselves critics of Supreme Court decisions. Since few critics ever do read court decisions, most proceed as if the slogans were valid. If told often enough that "God was expelled from school," educational administrators who haven't read the actual decisions will react to that lie and "expel." The expulsion has never been approved by any Supreme Court decision.

Graham, in a 1983 Associated Press interview, claimed teachers in America are afraid to talk about God. He was quoted as saying, "Teachers have been frightened against any reference to God. They're frightened of their superintendents; the superintendents are frightened of the school boards, and the boards are frightened of the courts." Some judges have misunderstood Supreme Court decisions; one wouldn't allow students to hold prayer meetings at school on their own in 1980 because such would give "an improper appearance of official support for religion." No Supreme Court decision ever told lower courts to think like that. Decisions usually are concentrated on a power government doesn't have, not on rights students do have. Appearance is immaterial; state involvement is the important ingredient.

Graham said, "They (teachers) can talk about Islam and what it believes, but they can't do it about Christianity. They're now afraid to talk about Jesus even as a historical figure." That observation was correct. He added that, "the writers of the Constitution meant freedom of religion, not freedom from religion." That observation was wrong and is an oft-repeated distortion of the First Amendment. The truth is, the founders meant both, and they created both by leaving government without power in pietistic matters. That absence of power was reaffirmed with the First Amendment, designed to prohibit attempts to ignore the lack of power. To say Americans lack "freedom *from* religion" would indicate government could trample on the convictions of nonreligious Americans and punish them for their nonbelief. Graham added, "The First Amendment was never meant to outlaw religion and moral values from the school system or the country." No Supreme Court decision ever outlawed religion and moral values from the school systems or the country.

Graham cited incidents in which a North Carolina student was reprimanded for carrying a Bible, and a superintendent ordered a teacher not to mention Jesus. Graham complained that the courts have "gone too far." The Supreme Court hadn't gone too far; critics of the court, including Graham, are the ones who have gone too far because they were basing complaints on decisions that were never made. Overreaction in schools follow those faulty complaints. In one incident, a high-school student in Georgia was suspended from school for possession of Christian material. His suspension slip gave the reason for punishment as "refusal to follow instructions to keep Christian material off school property." No Supreme Court decision ever concerned students possessing religious material or authorized a government official to legally forbid such possession.

Some Gospel Truths

Every spring news reports tell of prayers in graduation ceremonies being banned in many areas of the nation. Courts forbid the practice in Iowa and California. Courts allowed prayers in Kentucky, Michigan, Ohio, Pennsylvania, Tennessee and Virginia. One minister, invited to be graduation speaker, was asked not to mention God. A principal in Denver removed all Bibles from the library shelves in order not to give the impression the school was promoting Christianity. In Florida, a teen-age girl was prevented from handing out religious literature on school property to students getting off a school bus. After the threat of legal action, the school board changed its policy. Other Florida students were threatened with expulsion for "evangelizing" at school.

These incidents were all overreactions to Supreme Court opinions and were never authorized by any decision. After a federal judge ruled in June of 1994 that school officials in Polk County, Fla., violated the rights of a 13-year-old girl when they confiscated religious tracts she wanted to hand out, a school board official said, "most of us were under the impression that you can't allow religious materials on school grounds. Now the courts feel that we're able to."

It's sad that people who wish to control the education of the young don't read well enough to see what was truly decided. All the Supreme Court ever felt is that governments must keep their laws – or actions that must be authorized by laws – off of religion.

The old argument that the Supreme Court and Congress begin their sessions with a reference to God in opening ceremonies is most nonsensical – such references don't involve making laws to be imposed on people. And a slogan that didn't originate with religion isn't an establishment belonging to religion.

In the 1963 Bible-reading decision, the court said "... study of the Bible or of religion ..." is perfectly legal. How school officials could prohibit Christian or other religious material or the Bible on school grounds in light of that decision is a major mystery because such items would have to be present in order to be studied. If adult social organizations can provide information to students, evangelizing teens can hand out religious matter. Bibles on library shelves are no different from any other reference book. If a student offers a graduation prayer, the student is using individual initiative; government power is absent.

Preventing these individual actions would involve government power, and that usage would violate the Constitution because it would breach the free-exercise portion of the freedom-of-religion principle and would require a law concerning religion, and both are unconstitutional. In a 1992 decision about government-sponsored prayers at high-school graduations, the court again negated state attempts to become involved in religion. The decision applied only to government; it didn't concern individual action, which the court has refused to block.

The problem of overreaction was enhanced by the Senate, which adopted legislation in 1984 calling for "equal access" of students to meet in school buildings outside school hours for religious purposes ranging from Bible study to prayer. The trouble with such law – other than being a law respecting religion – was that it was so unnecessary. Had senators spent as much time reading court decisions as they did complaining, they might have picked up on that. Students have always had the right for such groups and gatherings, because no court decision ever reduced those rights. Students calling themselves Christians have always been able to meet legally in groups just as those calling themselves Junior Rotarians, or Teen-age Democrats, or Future Farmers of America, or Young Republicans, or the Chess Club or any other group on the periphery of the educational process. Court decisions aren't the problem; overreaction by school officials is. When Bible-club meetings were upheld in 1990, it didn't reduce, or in any way alter, the establishment-of-religion decisions; the 1990 opinion came in a free-exercise-of-religion case. The Supreme Court only started minting the other side of the coin; it didn't dull the previously engraved establishment image from the school-prayer or Bible-reading decisions.

The 1990 case involved school officials in Omaha, Neb., who prevented students from forming a Bible-study club in the school, citing the First Amendment's ban against "establishment of religion." The educators' problems stemmed from misreading the First Amendment. It says "no law," which applies to government. Students aren't covered by the no-law ban. The amendment also says, "no law ... prohibiting the free exercise thereof ..." School officials didn't have authority to prevent perfectly lawful student behavior because there can be no prevention of religious practices that correspond to secular actions, such as speech and assembly. The court fight was won on the basis that school authorities prevented the club by using a nonexistent governmental power; student rights were secondary. To deny a Bible club not created under authority of government would require that school authorities use a power government doesn't have – power to prevent lawful religious behavior. That's un-Americanism.

Relying on newspaper stories or television and radio reports about Supreme Court actions usually leads many to argue a mistaken point. The court is too often reported to have voided a government action or law that "violated the separation of church and state." Reacting to cliches (separation

Some Gospel Truths

of church and state) or metaphors (wall between church and state) is the wrong way to go. Worse still is to react to false impressions, as a headline writer did at The Denver Post with a 1978 headline saying, "Anti-Christ Wave/In Schools Draws/Flood of Protests." The story by the Associated Press concerned challenges to some schools incorporating religious themes in school programs and pageants. Wanting government out of religion isn't "anti-Christ," it appears to be what Jesus himself wanted.

Overreacting to lies, slogans, cliches, metaphors and inept reporting and headline writing leads some people to strange conclusions. Some people think Supreme Court decisions prohibit teaching morals in public schools. No court decision should be interpreted to do that. What could be prohibited is to teach that moral behavior is rooted only in Christianity and is, therefore, the invention and exclusive property of that religion, or of religion in general. Some atheists live by high morals that would shame many Bible quoters.

An organization that has successfully defended free-exercise rights and was instrumental in the Bible-club victory, Atlanta's Christian Advocates Serving Evangelism – which became the American Center for Law and Justice-Atlanta in 1994 – also misses the point occasionally. In 1991, while writing about its objectives in a controversy, the group's newsletter said, "Even the United States Congress in 1782 passed the following resolution: 'The Congress of the United States approves and recommends to the people The Holy Bible ... for the use of Schools.' " Unfortunately, 1782 was nine years before the Constitution's First Amendment became the supreme law of the land and 86 years before the Fourteenth Amendment made it the supreme law of the states, also. Schools mentioned by Congress were virtually all private schools, because the states hadn't created public schools at that time; that occurred several decades later. The Congress that passed that resolution isn't the same Congress prohibited from making religious law today. And it passed a resolution, not a law.

Some states had official churches after the Revolutionary War. The Constitution didn't give power for the nation to create a national church, and the First Amendment then prohibited such action – whether a church created in a single act or brought into being one establishment at a time over a prolonged period – and the Fourteenth Amendment of 1868, in essence, repealed power for states to continue state religions. Pre-Constitution laws setting aside property for religiously based schools could not be made after constitutional government was begun. The Constitution changed the rules, just as it created a new Congress.

Prior to adoption of the Fourteenth Amendment in 1868, there were no restrictions on the states' powers in religious matters because the First Amendment applied only to the national government. In 1845, the Supreme Court had to refuse to consider a case *(Permoli v. First Municipality)* from Louisiana in which a priest was appealing his conviction and fine administered in a state court for officiating at funeral services in a church in violation of a New Orleans ordinance. The Supreme Court had to decline the case saying, "The Constitution makes no provision for protecting citizens of the respective states in their religious liberties; this is left to the state constitutions and laws." In that case, New Orleans had outlawed religious freedoms; it can't do so today. While many people argue and fight for state involvement in religion, they could be undermining their personal religious liberty because they have no assurance their beliefs would be the ones state governments would honor. The Fourteenth Amendment changed the rules so that all persons' beliefs would now be honored. It did that by applying to the states the constitutional requirement that there shall be no laws relating to religion or impinging on the individual's right to exercise personal religion freely. That's a safeguard for everyone's spiritual freedoms.

CHRISTMAS SPITE

Lessons about church-state entanglement can also be learned from a second holy war that erupted in the late 1970s and has been fought into the 1990s outside the public schools. That war concerns religious displays and symbols on state property. Many religionists seemed determined each December to have Nativity scenes in, or on, public property such as city halls, capitols or public parks. There's always someone or some group ready to challenge each display.

Battles have raged over Nativity scenes – as part of Denver's Christmas-light display at city hall, in the rotunda of South Dakota's Capitol building and on the South London, Conn., Town Hall lawn – and Arkansas' Christmas decorations at the Little Rock Capitol. The issue was decided by the Supreme Court in the spring of 1984, but the controversy continues to rage among people who don't understand court rulings. Unfortunately, that includes nearly everybody.

In Denver, the Rocky Mountain News editorialized in 1978 that the Nativity scene shouldn't be part of the Christmas display because it would suggest the city was lending its prestige to Christianity. A News columnist took issue with the papers' policy writing, "While a small amount of tax dollars is involved in presenting the annual display, no one is required to see it. Christianity is not being forced on anyone. The Nativity scene does not

Some Gospel Truths

indoctrinate." Both arguments were wrong. Suggesting or seeming to lend governmental prestige to a religion has nothing to do with the constitutional issue. The columnist was silly to suggest government could enact religious laws or customs if no one is required to observe what was created, or that laws and practices are constitutional if not used to force religion on anyone. It was also irrational to say spending public money was okay if only a small amount was spent. Public money can be spent only under authority of law, and government doesn't have power to make law to spend on religion. The physical object in the dispute had nothing to do with the constitutional question; the issue involved power of government.

A year later, in another argument over the display, The Denver Post editorialized a most-asinine position. It said, "The very act of giving public employees a holiday on the date designated as the anniversary of the birth of Christ inherently confers governmental recognition upon the religious observance. The very word 'Christmas' is derived from 'Christ's Mass'." The reality is that public employees aren't given a holiday on Christmas. While government lacks power to prefer one religion's holiday – such as Christmas – it doesn't lack power to designate, as a state holiday, a date that "accidentally" corresponds with the religious holiday. Public employees legally get off December 25 as a holiday, they do not get Christmas off, so there is no "government recognition (of) the religious observance."

When confronted with constitutional issues, many people claim to know the founders' "original intentions." Perhaps understanding some of their intentions may be of value here. The first time federal employees were given a holiday on Christmas – or December 25 – was in 1894 when President Grover Cleveland initiated the practice. "In God We Trust" first appeared on U. S. currency in 1864, possibly seeking divine forgiveness for the Civil War carnage. These incidents show involvement in religious matters came from later generations; the founders intended the new nation not involve itself in religious matters, they wanted total neutrality by the state, even though newspaper officials can't recognize that fact.

The Post also argued, "What both constitutional language and common sense dictate is that our public posture toward religion should be inclusive, not exclusive. Instead if trying to outlaw Christmas, the proper course would be to expand our official recognition of other religious faiths." The Constitution uses no such language. Its language says government is religiously powerless, and to include other religions under the umbrella of "public posture" would require making law government may not make. Common sense dictates that "no law" means "no law." These court decisions were never to "outlaw Christmas," they were to leave Christmas as

247

the sole property of Christianity. People competent in Constitution reading know that.

In arguing to display the Nativity scene in the South Dakota Capitol, Gov. Bill Janklow was quoted by the Associated Press as saying it was more a seasonal decoration than a religious symbol. "I think the Nativity scene is part of the American scene. To some people it's like Barbie dolls." That's offensive to many devout Christians because it says their celebration of the birth of Christ has little spiritual value. It says Christmas is of little worth to Christians in other lands. It certainly doesn't allow a state to elude constitutional prohibitions.

The issue was decided by a Pawtucket, R. I., controversy that began in the early 1980s. For 40 years Pawtucket had set up the city-owned Nativity scene in a park. City employees erected it. That, said a federal judge in Boston, was unconstitutional. The city then sold the display to private interests, who put it in a downtown park in 1982. When the Supreme Court allowed the display on government property in its 1984 decision, it didn't necessarily overrule the federal judge's original decision, which applied to government-owned displays. The Supreme Court ruled on privately owned religious displays. The point made was anyone may use government property on an equal basis with everyone else. If the Boy Scouts can use a public park to display merit badges and demonstrate knot-tying skills, the religious community can use the public park for its displays and demonstrations. Parks are used – as are other government properties – for displays and functions of professional organizations, veterans' groups, social clubs and private individuals. If the Westside Quilting, Baking and Manwatching Sorority can use a park to display its wares and an oil-painting club can put on art shows, the religious community can use the park for its displays and shows. One type of organization – in this situation, religious – cannot be designated for exclusion when all are engaged in lawful behavior.

Prior to the decision, Scarsdale, N. Y., had banned Nativity scenes on city property. Such a ban, if used to exclude only religious groups from property legally used by others, would violate the Constitution's principles on religion and equality. When the Fourteenth Amendment stripped state and local governments of power to be involved in religion, it also imposed on them the requirement of equality under the law. To exclude religious groups from lawful use of public property would violate two constitutional principles: free exercise of religion and equal protection of the laws. The underlying reasoning of the Christmas-display decision is that government action in creating law and custom, or by spending money in support or opposition to religion is unconstitutional. Any legal action or spectacle brought about by individual initiative and carried out without government assistance is constitutional. In that way, Christmas remains the exclusive property of Christianity; it isn't shared with government.

Too many people just can't grasp the concept that government involvement is forbidden, individual initiative is acceptable. Critics of court and Constitution cloud the issue by flocking into print to promote nonsensical arguments having nothing to do with constitutionality. Los Angeles Times Syndicate columnist Cal Thomas wrote in 1984, "Are some offended by the displays of a nativity scene? I am offended by pornographic magazines in convenience stores and by X-rated movie houses, but the First Amendment purists tell me I must tolerate them. Why can't others put up with something that might offend them (i.e. a nativity scene once a year) for the sake of my free expression and the 'pluralism' I am always hearing about." Offensiveness has nothing to do with the constitutional issue; the true concern involves only government power. First Amendment purists are also offended by pornography, but being offended doesn't create the power to make laws that the First Amendment forbids. People who oppose any encroachment by government into religious fields aren't offended by Nativity scenes. Often they are ardent supporters of such devotion, and many are religious leaders who understand that the issue is about government's use of power. They're often "offended" by many governments' continued attempts at subversion of the Constitution by becoming involved in religion. Equally "offensive" are apologists who endorse un-American positions and columnists who don't know what they're writing about.

The Eagle Forum's Ellis, wrote in 1988, "In some localities, school authorities claim the sight of Santa Clause, the elves, Rudolph or Frosty conjures up Christmas thoughts. These are excluded because a child might think of religion and this would be wrong." Such statements are absolute fiction and serve no useful purpose to understanding the controversy. But they do conjure up false notions that opposing government involvement in religion is to oppose religion. Thinking people don't accept that nonsense.

TAXING PROBLEM

Another area where Americans struggle to understand church-state issues concerns taxes. Many persons believe churches or other religious organizations shouldn't be allowed a tax exemption because that amounts to government subsidy of religion.

That argument seems to have merit, but the exemptions from taxation given by the national government and state and local governments have much more subtle existences than that. When there are exemptions, there will always be problems of interpretation and application.

One such concern ran throughout the 1970s and was settled by the Supreme Court in 1983. At issue was whether tax exemptions could be claimed by schools practicing what's perceived by government as racial discrimination. The school in the controversy was Bob Jones University of Greenville, S.C.

The controversy began in 1970 when the school was told by the Internal Revenue Service that its exclusion of minority students could cost it exemption from paying federal employment and Social Security taxes and its supporters could lose deductions for their donations. The school responded by admitting some black students, but prevented them from dating or marrying whites. That, too, was unacceptable to the IRS.

School officials maintained they had biblical scriptures on which to base their rules for separation of the races. Other denominations could find no such commandments. The school's president said it didn't matter what other Bible scholars said, his interpretation was that there was such a principle. What the government thought about the issue was totally immaterial, he indicated. He was correct on the last point because one of the principles expounded in the *Cantwell v. Connecticut* decision of 1940 was that government has no authority to determine the accuracy or validity of any religious belief. If government had such power, it would soon determine validity for only its favorites. Only when government is totally removed from determination and judgment of doctrine is freedom of religion protected.

Unfortunately, that freedom was the undoing of Bob Jones University and other schools included in the controversy. Since a religious school is free from state intrusion into its biblical interpretation, it must be judged by government on the same principles as are other institutions. Religious groups' status and actions are subject to equality-of-law considerations governing social clubs, veterans groups, foundations, or any other assemblage. They cannot use a freedom-of-religion argument to excuse themselves from the law.

Equality of law is how religious institutions initially receive tax exemptions without violating the Constitution. Government has power and obligation to tax and spend to provide for the general welfare of society (Article I, Section 8). Institutions whose functions assist in promoting general welfare are allowed tax exemptions, as are their supporters, without violating the Constitution because their efforts assist in implementing constitutional objectives. Their existence benefits government because it allows the level of taxing and spending to be kept down. General welfare includes such things as education, culture, moral instruction, humanity, charity, brotherhood or any other facet of decorous behavior, and maybe some day it will include health and justice. General welfare is civilization. Religious organizations, including schools, that share in promoting the general welfare, share in the tax benefits that go along with that promotion. To exclude religious institutions from the benefits others get legally, would be to deny them equal protection of the laws. Organizations that will help promote general welfare receive exemptions; those that won't, don't.

The Bob Jones case was settled 8 to 1 against the school in 1983, with Chief Justice Warren Burger citing "public policy" as reason to deny the exemptions. Public policy had, for years, included antidiscrimination laws and protection of rights for minorities. These laws are part of the general welfare of all of society. A private policy that contravenes general welfare contradicts constitutional principles of the nation. For that reason, the tax exemption was denied.

The chief justice wrote that, "racial discrimination in education violates a most fundamental national policy, as well as rights of individuals ... Given the stress and anguish of the history of efforts to escape from the shackles of the 'separate but equal' doctrine, it cannot be said that educational institutions that, for whatever reasons, practice racial discrimination are institutions exercising 'beneficial and stabilizing influences in community life' by having all taxpayers share in their support." "Beneficial and stabilizing influences" would be the general welfare racial discrimination doesn't promote.

Burger's decision meant that if Bob Jones University and other segregated schools weren't assisting in providing for the general welfare, they shouldn't be allowed to share benefits received by groups which were promoting general welfare. Religion didn't enter into the court's conclusion. Critics of court and Constitution turned the controversy into a religious argument rather than the general-welfare approach on which the case really was based.

Conservative newspaper columnist Kilpatrick criticized the IRS by writing, "Is such a religious institution, holding such beliefs (racial separation), a religious institution under the Tax Code? The IRS says it is not. The government's position is that unless Bob Jones University formally renounces these 'genuine religious beliefs' (words of appellate court) and abolishes its doctrinal position on interracial marriage, the university cannot qualify for tax exemption."

The IRS has no power to determine the religiosity of any institution or the validity of its beliefs, and did not in this case. It made no attempt to determine if the school was a "religious institution." The IRS could make its decision on only secular principles involving how the school participated in promotion of the general welfare, or the "public policy" Burger cited.

Kilpatrick added, "This is incredible. The government is contending, in effect, that the First Amendment's guarantee of freedom of religion must yield to a bureaucratic determination of 'public policies.' Churches and religious schools must conform to IRS decrees or face the public consequences."

This case had nothing to do with freedom of religion; the school was not pressured or intimidated to change doctrines or beliefs. The issue was that the school decided it didn't wish to promote the general welfare of the United States, so the nation had no obligation to provide the school with tax exemptions.

Another columnist from the right, Patrick Buchanan, wrote, "The lesson of this public policy, now established in our latest judge-made law, is clear: All religions in America are entitled to official neutrality and equal treatment, except those fundamentalist Christian faiths that preach and practice separation of the races. All Christian interpretations of Scripture are entitled to official respect – except interpretations that do not conform with the integrationist ideology and edicts of the national government."

That's nonsensical buffoonery. This decision didn't concern interpretation of scripture because government and courts don't interpret the Bible, or any other religious writing. For that reason, the school was judged under the same principles and laws as the rest of the nation. There are no laws allowing religious groups or institutions to operate under different rules from everybody else.

The school's president reportedly told his school's congregation, "We're in a bad fix in America when eight evil old men and one vain and foolish woman can speak a verdict on American liberties. Our nation from this day forward is no better than Russia insofar as expecting the blessings of God is concerned. You no longer live in a nation that is religiously free."

That, too, was nonsense because no religious freedoms were lost. Bob Jones University and its human rulers were allowed to continue their segregationist ways. Their biblical interpretations were never challenged or attacked. The only thing lost was the privilege of escaping taxation without joining other tax-exempt organizations in promoting the general welfare of the very nation that allows them freedom to discriminate.

There is no evidence God took notice of the critics. It's possible He understood that the decision endorsed the general welfare of all His "children," not just the welfare of a tiny special interest. If critics of the court were as interested in religion as their complaints would indicate, they should take to heart the admonition of Proverbs 18:13, which indicates a person should understand an issue before emitting a condemnation. Government can't get into religious arguments so its decisions are reached totally on secular constitutional grounds. In this case, that was the general welfare; critics should know religion had nothing to do with the outcome.

Government's prohibition against involvement in interpretation of religious doctrine is also important in nonreligious areas. Many groups having nothing to do with spirituality try to clothe themselves in righteous robes to escape the scrutiny of legitimate government interests. The South is aware of the Ku Klux Klan's attempt to mask itself with religious rhetoric in the mistaken belief that would free it from accountability. The KKK hides behind a cross in its rituals, thinking that would provide religious respectability and immunity from law enforcement. In the Northwest, the citizenry is aware of the Church of Jesus Christ, Christian operating as part of the Aryan Nations of northern Idaho. Its members attempt to use the cloak of religiosity to hide the group's obvious racist nature, but Northwesterners aren't fooled by that, and the police power of Idaho isn't stymied by such subterfuge.

Religion has long been used by scoundrels to try to evade consequences for their miscreant deeds. If governments were required to ignore impropriety in the name of "freedom of religion," there would be more illegal use of the faith. But governments must relate to religion in the same manner it relates to all of society, thereby removing many criminals from behind their curtains of religion. That has also been beneficial to the truly faithful because it helps keep their congregations relatively criminal free.

This approach to law is why the IRS and the Supreme Court had to handle the Bob Jones University tax case on secular issues, not on religious doctrine. The general welfare of the nation would be better served if columnists could understand the concept and comment fairly on the true issues of all cases.

REVELATIONS

By leaving government religiously powerless, the Founding Fathers created a separation of church and state that's virtually a one-way detachment. Their concern was that the national government should have no power relating to religious belief so it wouldn't dominate the population through control of religion which has happened since Noah's grandson, Nimrod, founded the burg of Babel in antiquity. That first settlement combining government and religion in dual rulership was the model humans used for almost all nations throughout history. The founders knew that, so they empowered the Constitution in a way not to combine the two. That's why there are no pietistic powers in the Constitution.

The founders did not, however, write the Constitution so religion would have no influence or involvement in the new nation. The population was considered devout even though formal church membership at the time wasn't significant; some historians report it was as low as seven percent. Many 18th-century Americans were of the faith of Thomas Jefferson – nondenominational deists – who practiced their religion privately. Sparsely populated areas of the nation had much to do with the low church membership; it was unwise to leave crops and homestead unprotected during the time-consuming travel of many miles with primitive transportation to attend services. Ease of transportation and heavily populated areas make religion seem more prevalent today. That may be misleading.

Madison and his cowriters drafted the First Amendment so it would leave the dissociation intact. They were obviously concerned about the institution of religion – not instituting religion – in the establishment clause. That clause has been shown to mean the church (institution) isn't to be assisted or abetted by government, but says nothing about what influence religion (a code of beliefs) may have on government. Religious beliefs or morality certainly have a place in society and they are to be permitted to be reflected in public life.

But the founders also feared that leaders of religion, if in power, might get out of control in their zeal to incorporate their beliefs in law as did Crusaders, Inquisitionists and Salem's witchhunters. Too much zeal would lead government to use powers it clearly doesn't have, so that's why the founders wrote in Article VI, paragraph 3, that, "no religious Test shall ever be required as a Qualification to any Office or public Trust under the United States," and why the First Amendment says "no law respecting an establishment of religion." Nonreligionists seldom get elected to public office in the United States, so all concerns would center on which religion has the most officeholders to control laws and actions. To avoid this, the founders intended that government be restricted to the powers granted or implied by the Constitution. No fanatics in power would be allowed to do as they wish; the Constitution was to restrain them. In the Federalist Papers, Hamilton, Madison and Jay devoted the 85 articles to the need for government and the powers it required. They devoted no article to religion.

It should be totally clear that the constitutional absence and ban of power to assist religion is why government laws decreeing prayers in public schools are un-American. It should also be clear that when school children take the initiative and exercise rights to organize prayer groups for themselves government is powerless to stop them.

That absence/ban on power is the separation depicted in the Constitution, but the division isn't total. An example of constitutional government encompassing some religion is demonstrated by chaplains in the military services. In order to authorize chaplains, Congress would have to make law to include religion in government and, on the surface, that seems to violate the ban on laws "respecting" religion and religion's establishments. But, not to have chaplains would violate the free-exercise clause. The rationale is that government power would be used to remove a person from the locale where he/she freely practices religion to put that person in a strange-and-alien location where that faith isn't observed or is scarce. With that move, government would be denying an individual the opportunity to practice religion. Therefore, by providing chapels and chaplains, government is providing the opportunity for free exercise of religion, so separation of church and state isn't breached, just as it isn't by including "In God We Trust" on coins or chipping slogans into stone on government buildings. The slogan, "In God We Trust," is not an establishment, or fixture, belonging to religion. Neither is a motto carved on the front of a building. They are allowed because they have no significant religious meaning.

The Supreme Court said in its Bible-reading decision of 1963 and the Sunday Closing Law Cases of 1961 that the ban on government aid to religion isn't violated simply because some law or conduct happens to coincide or harmonize with a tenet or practice of a religion, some religions or all religions. No one would argue that the secular state should be powerless to outlaw theft because religious law says "thou shalt not steal." The same law can serve both secular and spiritual concerns and not be in conflict, which is why the state can declare December 25 a holiday or provide Sunday as a day of commercial rest and not incorporate religious observances of Christmas or a Sabbath into the state. The court has also stated that government may observe those things begun in a religious context but which have ceased to have religious meaning – that would include Halloween, thought to have been established by the long-extinct Druids of England, but religiously insignificant now. The Druid religion couldn't have an establishment when it no longer exists.

Because the Constitution applies to government, not to religion, the state seems to respect religion more than religion respects the state. Such it is when religious figures attempt to usurp purely governmental functions, such as the regulation of commerce. That was the case in the early 1980s when a religionist in Mississippi took it upon himself to regulate the

THE UN-AMERICANS

National Broadcasting Company (NBC) by organizing boycotts of its parent company's products unless NBC repented in its television programming. While individual action to select one company's products over another is a Ninth Amendment right retained by the people, an attempt by an organization to compel commercial actions by a corporation isn't a Tenth Amendment power reserved to the people. The effort failed, and there's no evidence NBC repented.

Some religionists tried to control corporate decision-making in filming of "The Last Temptation of Christ," a wholly forgettable movie of the late 1980s. Other believers opposed the critics, demonstrating again why government is forbidden to get involved in such matters: Whose cause would it champion?

Religionists have been involved in politics from the very beginning of the government; there is no effort to exclude them, for that would be denying them equal rights, and that is unconstitutional. It also wouldn't leave many people to participate in government. Religious concerns joined nonreligious interests to move government to eliminate of slavery; pass labor-rights laws; protect civil rights; aid education, health, social work, and other national gains, and remove government from the practice of religion. Individual religious concerns will always be involved in government, but government is not to be involved in religion, as has been said repeatedly in the Supreme Court decisions on the matter.

Problems occur when religion gets politically involved in an organized fashion. Political work often can't be considered as providing for the general welfare, because such efforts usually have been in search of special interest or individual welfare. Because there's often no general-welfare benefits to be had by political work, those churches, or other organizations, active in politics run the risk of losing any tax exemption they might have under law. Such was the case in New York in 1981 when the Unification Church headed by the Rev. Sun Myung Moon was found to be primarily concerned with political and economic interests. While government is powerless to interpret religious doctrine, it isn't without power to interpret political or economic doctrines. An appellate court denied the Unification Church property-tax exemptions on three New York City buildings because the commercial aspects of the buildings demonstrated the political nature of the church, which wasn't assisting in the promotion of the general welfare.

Religion came to the fore of political involvement with the 1980 presidential election when what's been labeled the "religious right" became an important part of the Republican Party. The organized move into politics came because of what some people saw as disturbing legislation nationwide.

Some Gospel Truths

Major concerns included a stronger military, opposition to abortion and the Equal Rights Amendment. The right claims to be anticommunist while supporting the family and school prayers and against rights for homosexuals.

There are conflicting opinions about what influence the religionists' forays into politics had or continue to have. It seems many of the religious right were naive in some areas and were used by politicians for the welfare of the politicians. Rhetoric calling for the return of voluntary prayer to public schools is a case in point because voluntary prayer was never removed from schools. The religionists threw their influence behind the proposed constitutional amendments on prayer that would do little except deliver votes to pandering politicians. Robertson, who ran for president in 1988, claimed in an interview with USA TODAY in 1986 that, "Children should be allowed voluntarily to worship God if they want to in school. At the present moment, they are not permitted to do that." His statement was totally untrue, for the right of children to voluntarily worship God was never forbidden. Presidential hopefuls should know that.

Naivete was abundant in other areas also. There's little the federal government can do about family matters, which would likely fall under the Ninth Amendment's preservation of "other rights" and the Tenth Amendment's "powers reserved to the people." The pulpit, not the presidency, is where family matters are best handled.

To oppose rights for homosexuals comes dangerously close to denying them "equal protection of the laws." Homosexuals cede to government the same rights as the religionists so they also retain rights identical to those kept by the doctrinaire. There's no way religionist involvement in national politics could eliminate abortion for there's no powers in Article I, Section 8, or any other part of the Constitution giving the national government authority to legislate reproduction. Some nonpolitical religionists claim that if the politically active were truly faithful and competent in reading the Bible, they would see there's no need for a more-powerful military because the United States wasn't prophesied to lose world dominance until "Christ's kingdom" does become part of this world.

The religious right also wasn't the most-honest player in the political arena. The Reverend Falwell, was told unequivocally in 1981 on the national television program *Firing Line* that voluntary prayer in public schools was not banned. The religionists wouldn't accept that truth and continued to tell the American public voluntary prayer was illegal. In 1987, Falwell told USA TODAY that "... prayer isn't allowed in schools." Should religionists obtain government power, the nation would be better served if they practiced the morality they claim to have.

THE UN-AMERICANS

A case of religionists being manipulated for political gain came in 1983 which President Reagan proclaimed as the "Year of the Bible." The proclamation was challenged in court as "respecting" religion and its establishments, and the fight dragged on throughout the year only to be dismissed Christmas Eve – it was merely a proclamation, not a law. Nothing was accomplished by opponents of the proclamation, and the fiat by Reagan did absolutely nothing to improve the morality of society. All the political pontificating for votes would be what King Solomon called "vanity." It was worthlessness that only threatened to categorize the Bible as one of those things ceasing to have religious meaning.

Organized political activism was criticized by two prominent Americans: the Reverend Graham and conservative ex-Sen. Barry Goldwater of Arizona. Graham said in the early 1980s that he had warned Falwell and others that their mission was to preach the Gospel, and the Gospel applied to all people, not just those considered conservatives in religion and politics. Graham also said the political "right has no interest in religion except to manipulate it." On that point, Graham qualifies as a minor prophet.

Goldwater's criticism was that issues pushed by the religionists didn't reflect true-and-honest American conservatism. An important cornerstone of true belief, real conservatives say, is that government should be restricted in use of power. The Supreme Court had restricted government by reminding it that it couldn't make religious law. Goldwater, who voted against the fraudulent prayer amendment in 1984, understood that. Members of the religious right did not.

Many religionists identified their enemy as "secular humanism," calling it a religion promoted by government. The arguments reached the courts, as shown earlier in this chapter, in the mid-1980s and gained brief acceptance before being rejected by higher courts. Foes of secular humanism claimed it's a godless religion worshiping man and refusing to accept any standard of right and wrong while denying God. Phyllis Schlafly, president of the Eagle Forum, wrote in a 1986 USA TODAY "opposing view" guest column that, "Humanism denies and rejects God, faith, prayer, all divine purpose or providence, all religions that 'place God above human needs,' the existence of life after death, a super-natural, heaven and hell, 'traditional religious morality,' religious attitudes about sex, 'national sovereignty,' and a profit-motivated society.' "

Some devout Christians will say the Bible rejects some of those concepts. They will say mankind isn't guided by providence but has free will; that there is no angelic life in heaven after death because humans go without awareness to the grave (Ecclesiastes 9:5) until resurrected (John 5:28 and 29)

Some Gospel Truths

on earth, there's no hell, true Christianity knows no national boundaries and sovereignty, and Christ chased the profit-motivated society of money changers from the temple.

The real issues of such fears are found in exact definitions of the words "secular" and "humanism." Secular means worldly or nonspiritual, not sacred or overtly religious. Secular pertains to the state and to civil existence. Humanism is devotion to the humanities and culture. It means human welfare and concern for mankind, reflecting human interests and values. It asserts basic dignity and worth of mankind and the human ability to gain self-achievement through reason, science and personal efforts. It doesn't reject God.

There is a modern testimony to secularity of mankind and the nonspiritual portion of existence. That testimony includes concern for human welfare and reflects the interests and values of mankind. It asserts basic human dignity and mankind's ability to obtain self-achievement. It has no deist authority or bearing, and it doesn't incorporate supernaturalism in any form.

That testimony is the United States Constitution, which says in its Preamble that "We the People" will "establish Justice, insure domestic Tranquility, provide for the common Defence, promote the general Welfare and secure the blessings of Liberty to ourselves and our Posterity." It says nothing about relying on a supernatural being protecting us from ourselves or from our enemies, or to take care of our every need. Humans are responsible for their own destiny under the Constitution.The Constitution does reflect room for "religious humanism" in which individual self-fulfillment is obtained through the framework of religious principles, and Christian humanism, which calls for fulfillment under Christian principles.

The battle against "secular humanism" seems to go against the theology, philosophy, or a combined theosophy, of "religious humanism" and "Christian humanism," because they are creeds celebrating the individual human and lauding mankind's ability to guide human destiny. People attacking "secular humanism" have one enemy, and only one enemy. They constantly assail the Supreme Court to attack their real enemy – the United States Constitution.

Chapter 10

FINISHING TOUCHES

CREATIVITY LOST

It seems that after the Bill of Rights was added to the Constitution, Americans misplaced their constitutional creativity. Seventeen amendments follow the Bill of Rights, but except for those inspired by the Civil War, none have much bearing on everyday life of ordinary citizens. Most of the amendments could be considered housekeeping because they have little to do with defining government's power over Americans' rights and freedoms or with restraining overzealous politicians who would use powers to create personal fiefdoms for themselves. The amendments mainly affect government procedure and selection of officials who exercise government authority. They do keep government up to date, but some are recognized as mistakes. The political philosophy that worked in the 1940s for a 1951 amendment criticized that very same amendment in the 1980s. Most of the amendments exist without much notice of their presence.

Five of the seventeen amendments concern the voting privilege, but that franchise possibly could have been obtained through other articles and/or the Fourteenth Amendment, in addition to modern understanding and application of the Constitution. These voting amendments do insure that there's no ambiguity about constitutional meaning, and they prevent many of the arguments that usually follow Supreme Court decisions.

Two amendments – the Eighteenth and the Twenty-First – amounted to nothing more than throwaway clutter. The Eighteenth created Prohibition and should have taught Americans the folly of using the Constitution for legislation. The Constitution was designed to create a national government and invest it with certain powers on which legislative acts would be based. It was never meant to contain laws or rules applicable to individual behavior, but the Eighteenth Amendment was nothing more than an ordinary statute that failed. The Twenty First Amendment was required to remove that nonsense.

Five of the amendments were purely housekeeping, pertaining to the method of selecting government officials and the authority and relationship some officials have to each other.

One amendment refers to the powers of the federal courts, and has little meaning to the average American.

The most-hated amendment could be the Sixteenth, which authorized a federal income tax, but the amendment probably doesn't have much effect on the amount of taxes the government collects.

Only two of the 17 amendments have had a significant impact on Americans, and those – the Thirteenth and Fourteenth – were products of the Civil War. They may be our most-important protections of individual freedoms because they put restrictions on state and local governments, which definitely need to be restrained. Of the 1,000-plus laws, regulations and actions by state and local governments negated by the Supreme Court (Chapter 4's "States' Wrongs, Not Rights"), most were voided because of the Fourteenth Amendment, which makes it the Guardian Amendment for average Americans.

The Thirteenth Amendment has yet to be fully explored and defined. It may have far wider implications than have been determined to date

THE ELEVENTH AMENDMENT (1798)

The Judicial power of the United States shall not be construed to extend to any suit in law or equity, commenced or prosecuted against one of the United States by Citizens of another State or by Citizens or Subjects of any Foreign State.

This amendment repeals part of Article III, Section 2, which said: "The judicial Power shall extend to all Cases ... between a State and Citizens of another State." The amendment didn't significantly alter the rights of anyone; it merely says the controversy would be handled in state courts, not the federal courts. State courts are required to protect the rights of all citizens, even those from other states or nations having complaints against the state government of which the court is a part. If the state court shows bias against an out-of-state claimant, privileges and immunities (the Fourteenth Amendment and Article IV, Section 2) and equal protection of the law (Fourteenth Amendment) would possibly be violated, and that might require the federal court system to settle the issue.

This amendment prevents suits against a state without its consent because it removes the third-party neutral national courts and makes the entire procedure subject to state legislation. Suing an official of another state who is trying to enforce an unconstitutional statute is still permissible, the amendment only covers government of the state.

The Supreme Court ruled in 1890 that the principle of state immunity from lawsuits would apply also to citizens of the same state, even though they aren't mentioned in the amendment, because of equality-of-law and privilege-and-immunity concerns. If a New Yorker could sue the state of New York but a Pennsylvanian couldn't, the out-of-stater wouldn't have the same privileges as the in-stater. That's unconstitutional under Article IV, Section 2. The right to petition government is limited by this amendment, and that's one certain way that First Amendment right can be limited. The amendment would pertain mainly to commercial interests, and would be beneficial in having laws of a particular state applied to out-of-state concerns by courts of that state without requiring the third-party national courts to apply laws to which they have no interest. The amendment helps reduce the federal caseload. The impact this amendment has on society is best illustrated by the fact it was adopted on Feb. 7, 1795, but not announced publicly until Jan. 8, 1798.

THE TWELFTH AMENDMENT (1804)

The Electors shall meet in their respective states and vote by ballot for President and Vice-President, one of whom, at least, shall not be an inhabitant of the same state with themselves; they shall name in their ballots the person voted for as President and in distinct ballots the person voted for as Vice-President ...
(Complete amendment in Appendix.)

This amendment repeals paragraph 3 of Article II, Section 1, which provided that the candidate in the presidential race receiving the most votes in the Electoral College would become president, and the vice president would be the candidate receiving the second-most votes. That system of choosing presidents was shown to be flawed by the 1800 election in which Thomas Jefferson and Aaron Burr received the same number of votes, so the election was decided by the House of Representatives, as specified by Article II, Section 1.

In the original system, presidents and vice presidents would usually come from differing political parties; an arrangement not promoting unity in the Executive branch. That method could have created situations in which an incumbent president would be relegated to the vice presidency by losing a re-election bid. As such, President Jimmy Carter would have become vice president to Ronald Reagan in the 1980 election or George Bush to Bill Clinton in 1992, except that Bush may not have been president in the first place; Carter received the second-most votes in 1980, so he would have been Reagan's vice president. Bush may have been out of politics at the time of the 1988 elections that he won.

Finishing Touches

Many people think the Twelfth Amendment created the modern political structure and animosity, but political divisions were well-established before the amendment was created. In the 1800 election, all electoral votes for president were cast along party lines. Politics were prevalent in the House effort to select a president; thirty-six ballots were needed before party politics were overcome and Jefferson was chosen.

This is a classical example of why the "original intent" of the founders shouldn't be the deciding factor in determining validity of law or governmental activity. The Founding Fathers weren't legislating, and they knew that some things they put into the Constitution might not be perfect or lasting, so they attached the amending process so subsequent Americans could alter or add to their effort.

THE THIRTEENTH AMENDMENT (1865)

SECTION 1. Neither slavery nor involuntary servitude, except as a punishment for a crime whereof the party shall have been duly convicted, shall exist within the United States, or any place subject to their jurisdiction.
SECTION 2. Congress shall have power to enforce this article by appropriate legislation.

To most people, this amendment only abolished slavery in the United States after nearly 250 years of existence. But, eliminating slavery was just one function; the amendment goes far beyond that singular concern.

The true extent of the amendment's significance is indicated by the first word, "neither." By containing that word, the amendment makes the distinction that slavery and involuntary servitude aren't the same things. By linking involuntary servitude with requirements for "punishment for a crime" and for a person to be "duly convicted," that portion of the amendment applies to government powers and actions; it doesn't apply to nongovernment entities – the ban of slavery applies to those. No commercial interest, be it plantation owner or corporation, ever had authority to convict a person or exact involuntary service as punishment for a crime, so this part of the amendment doesn't refer to them; it refers to government. An attempt to "convict" or "punish" someone with involuntary servitude by any entity other than government would be dealt with through ordinary law. And this amendment would make it possible for such actions to be federal crimes.

An example of how this amendment applies to the national government would be the draft for the military. Some people think this amendment outlaws conscription, but there's never been a court decision endorsing that reading, so Americans assume the draft is always constitutionally permitted. There have been several decisions affirming Congress' authority to use the draft under its war powers to raise and support armed forces.

An example of that assumption of legality was presented in a 1980 Denver Post editorial about concerns of male-only registration for selective service should it be reinstituted. The paper said:

"When the issue of renewing registration was raised initially, this newspaper editorially supported the idea and urged that women be included in the program. Congress demurred from including women ... While that was perhaps wrongheaded on its part, it wasn't necessarily unconstitutional. After all, male-only drafts were keystones of our military effort during the Civil War, World Wars I and II, Korea and Vietnam, without violating a Constitution identical in every pertinent respect to the one we have today."

The Constitution isn't "identical in every pertinent respect to the one we have today" as it pertains to the Civil War. When the South began the draft in 1862, it wasn't operating under the Constitution, so what it did doesn't matter. The Union began a draft in 1863 under two constitutional principles. Because the South engaged in rebellion and invaded the Union's Fort Sumter, privileges under the Writ of Habeas Corpus were suspended (Article I, Section 9) allowing conscription under provisions in Article I, Section 8, saying Congress had power to "raise and support Armies" and to "provide and maintain a Navy." That Union draft was instituted before the adoption of the Thirteenth Amendment's prohibition against involuntary servitude.

The editors of the paper were only assuming that subsequent drafts weren't "violating a Constitution identical in every pertinent respect," and if the draft is ever to be found unconstitutional, it wouldn't matter whether it applied only to men. Americans seem not to want to entertain the possibility the Thirteenth Amendment would preclude involuntary selective service, but should any court ever muster up enough constitutional fortitude to say so, it might make the United States more secure, not less.

The first draft case was decided in 1918 and upheld the Selective Draft Law of World War I. The Selective Service Act of World War II was upheld in 1944. But those decisions referred to powers under a declaration of war. When the Supreme Court made its 1919 freedom-of-speech decision about balancing rights and powers (Chapter 8) it was in a case in which the appellants were convicted for advocating obstruction of the draft, claiming it was unconstitutional under the Thirteenth Amendment. Justice Oliver Wendell Holmes said government had power when at war to do things it couldn't do

Finishing Touches

constitutionally during peacetime; in this case, limit free speech. He said nothing about the legality of the draft, so it possibly could be subject to the same consideration by being a prohibited involuntary servitude during peace, but a necessary exercise of war powers following a formal declaration of war by Congress. That distinction might help assure responsible exercise of government power by preventing adventurous presidents from unnecessary war-making. It would be foolish for a commander in chief to illegally commit the United States to a major conflict if there were no authority to conscript military forces to fight the war. By restricting the draft to declared wars, the Constitution would impose barriers to war by foolhardiness.

If such arrangement ever becomes solidified by court decision, the drafts during World Wars I and II would be constitutional, but drafts during the Korean and Vietnam conflicts – and especially a peacetime draft – would be unconstitutional. Such an arrangement might have prevented or lessened the United States' debacle in the Vietnam war and its frustration in the Korean conflict. This is an area of the Constitution in which meaning is yet to be fully ascertained, which indicates the Denver Post was foolish in making an unqualified pronouncement of constitutional acceptability of the draft.

It's easy for some people to point to such nations as Norway, Sweden and Switzerland as paragons of domestic tranquility and world leaders in the quest for peace while having universal compulsive military service, then to assume the same peaceful attitude would encompass the United States if it had a universal draft. But those nations don't operate under the United States Constitution that outlaws involuntary servitude.

Often, well-meaning persons call for some form of community service for all young people, but the Thirteenth Amendment would certainly preclude any compulsion to perform public duties. Any such public service – regardless of how beneficial – would have to be based on a voluntary acceptance by those who would be affected. It couldn't be forced.

THE FOURTEENTH AMENDMENT (1868)

> *SECTION 1. All persons born or naturalized in the United States and subject to the jurisdiction thereof, are citizens of the United States and of the State wherein they reside. No State shall make or enforce any law which shall abridge the privileges and immunities of citizens of the United States; nor shall any State deprive any person of life, liberty, or property, without due process of law; nor deny to any person within its jurisdiction the equal protection of the laws.*
> (Complete amendment in Appendix.)

THE UN-AMERICANS

Perhaps the greatest confusion Americans have about the Fourteenth Amendment is how it restricts state and local governments with prohibitions that once only applied to the national government, and many people continue to act as if states were free of any constitutional restraints. The amendment's creators, as related in Chapter 3, produced it to specifically apply to states by reducing their powers. And those people who helped adopt the amendment as the supreme law of the land had an obligation to understand just how it would affect state governments. Persons who today hold government power, from the lowest village position to the highest state or national station, should also understand that effect.

Ohio Rep. John A. Bingham, who headed the Joint Congressional Committee that wrote the amendment, said the "original intent" for proposing it was to give Congress "power to protect rights of citizens against the states ..." But, original intent isn't enough – as has been said many times throughout this book – words in the amendment must do exactly what they were written to do.

So, putting "original intent" aside, analysis of the Fourteenth must seek to determine just how the specific words make it illegal for states to interfere with the rights of United States citizens and how the national government can combat any infringement.

The amendment first describes who citizens of the United States are: they are everyone born or naturalized in the United States. No other consideration is relevant. The Fourteenth makes a major change in the relative powers of the states and the national government. Article I, Section 8, gave power to Congress to "establish an uniform Rule of naturalization," but said nothing about rules for those native-born. After the Revolutionary War, each state existed briefly as an independent sovereign nation and, as such, had total authority concerning citizenship. Half the states refused to relinquish citizenship authority at creation of the Constitution because they had refused citizenship to their black "resident" slaves. Had total citizenship authority been given to the national government, slavery could have been eliminated with a simple rule of citizenship to everyone born in the United States. As it was, the new nation got authority concerning immigrants who actively sought naturalized citizenship. Congress hadn't yet learned to sneakily grant unsought citizenship as it did in 1924 for Indians, whose treaties could be evaded.

The Fourteenth Amendment created a change in American attitudes, even though that might not be readily attributed to the Constitution. Before the amendment, a person was first and foremost a citizen of the state of residency, and that state citizenship caused a secondary citizenship – that as a

Finishing Touches

United States citizen – to be bestowed. For that reason Gen. Robert E. Lee – a believer in the federal union and the Constitution – could lead the Confederate army during the Civil War. Lee was a Virginian first and forever; he was American secondarily. Slaves, by not holding citizenship in the state of residence, weren't authorized United States citizenship, which is why there was little the federal government could do about slavery except by constitutional amendment. After the Fourteenth Amendment became supreme law of the land, Americans came to view themselves as Americans first, but Virginians, New Yorkers or Californians secondarily. While it may not seem obvious, that unified the nation into a single entity.

The second aspect of the amendment is that, *"No State shall make or enforce any law which shall abridge the privileges and immunities of citizens of the United States ..."* As just seen, all persons born or naturalized in the United States are citizens of the United States, so this clause frees all Americans from state infringement of their privileges and immunities. Privileges were defined in Chapter 3 as rights falling within the prerogatives of the government's control. Congress has power to regulate interstate commerce, so engaging in business is a privilege, just as it's a privilege to hold a copyright or patent under the authority of Congress to provide for such. Use of government property, such as highways or parks, likewise is a privilege. An immunity right of citizenship exists in areas where government is powerless. Immunities would be rights such as speech, press, association, religious beliefs. The Ninth Amendment specifies there are other rights retained by the people even though it didn't name any. They, too, would be immunities when they fall in areas in which government is powerless to act.

This second aspect of the Fourteenth is confusing to some people who should know better. When Nebraska was trying in 1989 to define a "right to keep and bear arms" that confusion came to the fore. Voters had passed an amendment to the state constitution guaranteeing the right to bear arms "for all persons." Because of that state constitutional provision, a county district court judge was compelled to release a convicted felon who had been jailed for possessing a pistol following the completion of his prison term. The New York Times quoted the judge as saying "the voters of Nebraska were entitled to 'enact what they will' into the state constitution, 'even to the shock and dismay of constitutional theoreticians'."

At one time, that statement would have been mostly correct. No longer. Voters of Nebraska, or any other state, may not "enact what they will" if what they will abridges privileges and immunities of United States citizens, who are also Nebraskans. Article VI says United States laws, treaties and

Constitution are supreme, "any Thing in the Constitution ... of any State to the contrary notwithstanding." That means no state constitution may contain a provision infringing on rights existing under the United States Constitution, treaty or law.

The words of the Fourteenth Amendment make it apply to the states and to restrict their powers in a manner not envisioned in 1789 by the founders. The "original intent" of the committee writing the Fourteenth Amendment wouldn't have mattered if the panel had written the amendment in a way that it didn't do as intended. That didn't happen; the panel wrote the amendment so the words do exactly what they are supposed to do, and it's the responsibility of those reading the words to understand what they say. The amendment doesn't need to say the Bill of Rights applies to the states, it makes the Bill of Rights applicable by its wording.

Many heated arguments in recent years have arisen because some people advocating government power over individual rights can't find the "right to privacy" in the Constitution, while others who would curtail government activities claim it's there, even though not specifically named. To some, it's included in the Ninth Amendment's "others" retained by the people or is found in the Fourth Amendment's statement the people are free from unreasonable searches and seizures. The unnamed right of privacy is supposed to apply to contraceptives, to protect a woman's right to an abortion, a person's right to die with dignity, homosexual rights or any number of unspecified rights. While privacy isn't specifically mentioned in the United States Constitution, it is mentioned in a few state constitutions.

But relying on an unmentioned right of privacy to protect some activities is making the Constitution work much harder than it needs to. Logic should lead to the conclusion that constitutional protection of privileges and immunities from state abridgment makes privacy and immunity the same thing.

In June of 1986, the Supreme Court decided 5 to 4 that homosexual relations between consenting adults weren't protected by the Constitution. The Seattle Post-Intelligencer editorialized against the decision by printing, "The most stunning element of ... declaring there is no constitutional protection for homosexual relations between consenting adults, is not its condemnation of homosexuality so much as the dramatic departure from what have become generally accepted as rights of privacy."

Justice Harry Blackmun dissented from the majority on similar grounds saying, "The right of an individual to conduct intimate relationships in the intimacy of his or her own home seems to me to be at the heart of the Constitution's protection of privacy." He cited "the most comprehensive of rights and the most valued by civilized men, namely the right to be left alone."

Justice Byron White, who wrote the majority opinion, cited "ancient roots" as authority for Georgia to outlaw homosexual relationships. The majority said neither the Constitution nor court rulings "extend a fundamental right to homosexuals to engage in consensual sodomy."

They all missed the point. White and the court majority were definitely wrong in citing "ancient roots" for any law. The most ancient one may go regarding a federal law would be 1789; anything a ruler did prior to that is immaterial. The United States isn't governed by the same powers used by 17th-century Russian tsars, 15th-century British monarchs, 10th-century Japanese shoguns or first-century Roman caesars. The United States operates only under powers given it by its people in their 1789 Constitution. Chief Justice John Marshall said that in *McCulloch v. Maryland* (1819). "Ancient roots" were severed with the Constitution. States, likewise, can't call on ancient roots for their authority. They're restricted to powers given them in their post-Revolutionary constitutions, as modified by the Fourteenth Amendment of 1868. The Constitution and court rulings aren't sources of rights and don't "extend a fundamental right" to citizens. It's unforgivable that Supreme Court judges don't know that.

The Seattle newspaper and Justice Blackmun needn't have tried to find the right of privacy or a right to be left alone. They could easily conclude that if government hasn't been given a constitutional power to regulate in a certain area, any occurrence in that vacuum is an "immunity," which is protected from state encroachment by the Fourteenth Amendment. There's nothing in Article I, Section 8, or anywhere else in the Constitution, giving government regulatory authority over intimate relationships. Governments may not regulate the consented relationship a man may have with a woman, a white with a black, a Jew with a Christian. Likewise, there's no power in the Constitution for government to interfere with the relationship a man may have with another man or a woman with another woman, whether those relationships are platonic or sexual. There's nothing in the Constitution suggesting a power to regulate the love lives of American citizens or to outlaw some acts because the majority of the population is repulsed by those acts. If there is no power, there is immunity. And no state may abridge that immunity.

A state may use its police power when there's a victim and victimizers. But a state cannot create power for itself; that's a feature of an autocracy, and autocratic government is un-Americanism. If there were a power for states to regulate love lives of homosexuals, the Fourteenth Amendment's demand for equal protection of the laws would require regulations of love lives of all persons, including heterosexuals and Supreme Court judges

In 1990, retired Supreme Court Judge Lewis Powell said he "probably made a mistake" by being one of the five allowing Georgia to outlaw some homosexual activities. He said, "When I had the opportunity to reread the opinions a few months later, I thought the dissent had the better of the arguments" in the *Bowers v. Hardwick* decision. About the same time, several states were attempting to enforce pre-Constitution ethical concepts pertaining to sexual behavior.

Wisconsin filed felony charges of adultery against a woman. The law carried sentences of two years in prison and a $10,000 fine. A Virginia man faced 10 years in prison for consensual oral sex, and a Maryland man had been convicted of consensual oral sex. His five-year prison sentence was suspended.

The questionable aspect of such actions isn't whether state legislators – always on the lookout for votes – would outlaw such actions or prosecuting attorneys would prosecute; it's where do they think they get the power to do so. Under John Jay's concept that Americans cede some of their rights to empower government leads to a logical conclusion that they can't cede rights they don't have. They have no right to interfere in others' sexual preferences or orientation, therefore, government can have no such power. Freelance writer John Lofton, a supporter of restrictive sex laws, wrote in USA TODAY in 1990, "Adultery should be illegal because it violates God's Law ... The purpose of civil government is to administer God's Law. The Bible, whether one likes it or not, is the basis for Western law."

The United States Constitution refers several times to law. Nowhere does it ever mention "God's Law" or that the Bible is the basis of Western law. If the Founding Fathers wanted government to administer God's Law, they could have said so. If they thought the Bible was the basis of Western law, they could have said that, but said nothing in the Constitution on the subject. Attitudes of the pre-Revolution colonies also have no bearings on a post-Fourteenth Amendment America. Western law could easily be traced to the laws of King Hammurabi of prebiblical Babylonia, whose codes contained no religious laws – like the Constitution – rather than the Bible, which has numerous religious laws.

By separating its secular authority from its religious beliefs, the United States became the first Western nation to excuse Jesus Christ from partial responsibility for a warring nation's killings, destructions and other derogatory acts of modern civilization. Unfortunately, too many Americans, including religious leaders, want to get Him reinvolved in such unholy

Finishing Touches

political dealings as the Crusades, Inquisition, witch hunts and coronation of Adolf Hitler as the vestigial caesar of the Holy Roman Empire.

Another privacy-right case that had little to do with privacy was the notorious abortion decision of *Roe v. Wade* in 1973. That decision prevented state encroachment on the unspecified privacy right and showed the difficulty in reaching constitutional decisions because of many conflicting variables.

In *Roe v. Wade*, the court said a woman was free to have an abortion in the first three months of the pregnancy, the only requirement government could impose was that licensed health providers carry out the procedure. That condition is present in most health-care procedures, so the requirement had nothing to do with an abortion right. In the second trimester, the state had some power to regulate, the court said, to protect a woman's health. That, too, is present in other health-care areas, so it had little to do with the abortion right. In the third trimester, the court said, the state has a vested interest to protect the life of the fetus. That would make third-trimester abortion a political question, not a constitutional issue, and political questions are subject to legislative actions. The court's reasoning may have contributed to the ongoing arguments over abortions because it doesn't provide specific answers to all questions about the subject, but it may be the best humans can do. To understand constitutional issues raised by the Roe decision, a person needs to consider history. It's immaterial what supporters or critics of abortion think.

The first question any Constitution supporter should ask is, "where would governments get the power to regulate reproduction?" In the formation of constitutional government, everyone surrenders some rights in order that government might have power. They also surrender some personal sovereignty. Chief Justice William Rehnquist may have defused some arguments of many antiabortionists with his statements in the Missouri right-to-die case of Nancy Cruzan. He argued that the comatose woman couldn't make known her personal decisions regarding how state power would apply to her and no one else could speak for her; therefore, the state had no obligation to alter its use of power because the state couldn't make a unilateral decision for her. The only way she was allowed to die was after court testimony demonstrated that removing life-sustaining apparatuses was her conscious desire. The same would be true regarding reproduction in that the unborn couldn't reveal their decisions and no one else may speak for them. The state, therefore, needs some other source of power.

Logic would also indicate that the man north of the river and the man south of the river couldn't agree with the fool on the hill and the farmer in the dell to surrender to government rights belonging only to the goddess on the pedestal. Surrendering rights to the state in areas where one has no rights is an encroachment on freedom on those who do have rights. A male population pretending to give power to the state to regulate reproduction by women is stating that men think women exist in submission to them, and that bondage is being surrendered to the state.

The Founding Fathers didn't empower government with authority to regulate reproductive functions of women because they didn't know how that could be done. At that time, only men were involved in politics, and the founders knew men had no rights over a woman's reproduction that could be ceded to government. There's no way an "original intent" doctrine can be used to authorize antiabortion laws because men have no reproductive rights; they haven't had such rights since Eve first wore a fig leaf. And up-to-date damsels don't need shiny-suited heroes clanking to the fore to rescue them from the distresses of modern dragons. Most can fend for themselves.

The Preamble of the Constitution says "We the People" and the Fourteenth Amendment refers to "persons born." Neither statement applies to embryos, fetuses, zygotes or gametes. Many male legislators attempt to evade the Constitution's limitations to their power by enacting laws stating that human life begins at conception. That may be true, but it's also true that all human tissue is technically life, so an unfertilized egg also contains life. But such laws don't change the Fourteenth Amendment's words that refer to "persons born" and the Preamble's reference to "We the People."

An antiabortionist, Joseph M. Scheidler, executive director of Pro-Life Action League, wrote in USA TODAY in 1990, "Anyone who reads the Constitution objectively discovers that there is no mention of abortion. It is patently absurd to argue that the framers intended for women ever to have such a 'right.' The proper function of the Supreme Court is to apply the Constitution to cases it hears, not to invent law ... any judge who truly seeks to follow the original intent of the framers of the Constitution in applying law will be hard-pressed to find anything in that Constitution to support a right to abortion."

Scheidler was confused. That the Constitution doesn't mention abortion, reproduction, sex or relationships means but one thing – there is no power to regulate those activities. He was as wrong as a Michigan judge who denied an abortion to a 13-year-old temporary ward of the court. The judge said "the true law of the land, contained in the Constitution as written and intended by the framers of it, would not grant to a woman the right to abortion on demand."

Persons who want to cite the Constitution and pretend it supports their

Finishing Touches

personal biases should learn what it really says and how it should be applied. It's absurd for abortion foes to argue that the framers intended to give rights to women. Government and Constitution don't grant rights; they abridge rights. The framers knew that, so they were concerned with one issue: giving power to government. That's why the only meaningful design of the founders is that there be no power to regulate women's reproductive functions. Judges applying the real Constitution to cases they hear will be hard pressed to find any power to prevent abortion. That makes reproduction an immunity, and no state may make any law abridging that immunity. That's the meaning of the *Roe v. Wade* decision even though the argument in the case was that reproduction was a liberty that couldn't be abridged without due process of law.

History also gives a slight clue as to the intentions of the framers. According to USA TODAY, "There were virtually no laws on abortion when this nation was born." The paper, in citing historians earlier, said, "... it appears abortion was fairly common and not legally barred during the Colonial period and through the early 1800s. New York City's population of 1 million supported 200 full-time abortionists in 1871, a contemporary news report indicates. In the 1850s and 1860s, the newly formed American Medical Association pressed for restrictions, and by 1868 a number of states and territories limited abortions." The year 1868 is important in that it was the year the Fourteenth Amendment was adopted to protect privileges and immunities from state action. A woman's control of her body is just such an immunity

Historian and author Thomas V. DiBacco agrees with the newspaper about abortion being legal in Colonial times "if conducted prior to 'quickening,' or fetal movement." Widespread legality of abortion at the birth of the nation demonstrates the "original intent" of the founders; if they wanted the situation to change, they would have given government the power to make such changes.

This proves The Baltimore Sun's reporter Lyle Denniston wrong for reporting in April 1994 about the Roe "decision creating a right to abortion." The Supreme Court created nothing; the right to an abortion was widespread at the beginning of the nation and original intent of the founders was that it not be subject to regulation. The court decision only reclaimed that original right which was illegally abridged. And the court didn't "legalize" abortion, as the press likes to claim, it "relegalized" it; no government had power to outlaw abortion.

Critics of the Supreme Court don't seem bothered by not understanding the issue. Then-Sen. Jake Garn, R-Utah, was quoted in a national magazine in 1981 as saying, "A country that prides itself on its progress in securing human rights ought to be shamed by a Supreme Court decision which strips unborn children of their protection under the law." Words of the Fourteenth Amendment govern the issue, not Garn's opinion. That amendment says no state may "deny to any person within its jurisdiction the equal protection of the laws." The key word is "person." The amendment begins: "All persons born ..." It's clear, protection of law applies to persons born and rights to "protection under the law" weren't stripped from the unborn by the Supreme Court. Garn would have been correct if the amendment referred to persons born and fetuses and embryos conceived. It doesn't, and the Constitution's words can't be adulterated to fit politicians' opinions.

Syndicated columnist Joseph Sobran wrote in 1981, "On Jan. 22, 1973, the court struck down the abortion laws of all 50 states ...

"To this day it's not clear how seven justices managed to discover what had eluded the authors of the Constitution, not to mention generations of Americans, including 100 or so previous Supreme Court justices: Namely, that laws protecting the lives of the unborn violate the Constitution."

Another confused man. Not all states had outlawed abortion with laws "protecting the lives of the unborn." And such laws were unconstitutional because there was no constitutional power to enact such laws. That's easy to deduce. If there was a constitutional power to enact antiabortion laws, they wouldn't have been declared unconstitutional. The Supreme Court didn't say anything eluded the framers of the Constitution; it said the absence-of-power concept eluded state legislators. That absence of regulatory power was imposed on the states by the Fourteenth Amendment because of its provisions that no state may abridge Americans' privileges and immunities. That, also, is easy to figure out. A third of those "100 or so" justices served prior to 1868, so they wouldn't have any reason to consider a state power that differed from federal power. That was permissible before the Fourteenth Amendment. Many of those justices served at the onset of the nation, when abortion was legal everywhere. That eluded critics of the court.

When Sandra Day O'Connor was nominated for a court position in 1981, many antiabortionist males opposed her selection. Dr. J. C. Wilkie, president of the National Right-to-Life Committee, and columnist Cal Thomas, vice president of the Moral Majority, both were quoted as saying they would try to find enough senators to force President Reagan to find another selection, one with a strong antiabortion record.

Another critic, Richard Viguerie, author of the *The New Right*, wrote in a newspaper column: "... she voted against a resolution urging Congress to protect the unborn by extending constitutional rights to them.

Finishing Touches

"So Mrs. O'Connor's record on abortion is unequivocal: She has actively favored it."

A seventh confused man. The only way to extend constitutional rights to the unborn would be by amendment because the Constitution, as written, pertains to "persons born." Perhaps some critics can't understand the words "persons" or "born" or a combination of them both. Those words need not be defined, the meanings should be obvious, and it's simple-minded to think that observing the Constitution as written is to favor abortion. A few people opposed to abortion are honest enough to admit the Constitution contains no power to regulate procreation at the national level and the absence of power is imposed on the states by the Fourteenth Amendment. Finding judge candidates with strong antiabortion stands would only subvert the Constitution should their opinions supplant the Constitution's words.

Two cases appearing to interfere with a "right to an abortion" really weren't as they seemed. In both cases *(Webster v. Reproductive Health Services* of 1989, and *Rust v. Sullivan,* 1991) the issue was whether government used a legitimate power properly. The Webster case grew out of Missouri restricting funding for abortions. Rust arose after the Reagan administration imposed limitations on discussion of abortion at clinics receiving federal money. The cases really concerned government's power to tax and spend for the general welfare, and the controversies were whether government could withhold funds from abortion-related situations without violating rights or restricting speech of those who served as surrogate state employees by accepting government funds. The decisions for governments didn't abridge basic immunity of reproduction rights, although they made it difficult for women in poverty to exercise their rights. The decisions didn't directly relate to the right of abortion because the issue could have pertained to other aims, such as cosmetic surgery or hair transplants.

In the 1992 Pennsylvania abortion-law case, the basic premise of immunity from government regulation for reproduction was reaffirmed. Restrictions that were allowed fell under a state's power to regulate healthcare providers, the premise suggested in *Roe v. Wade.* The state requirement that a woman must tell her husband about a planned abortion was an attack on free speech, so it was negated by the court. Restrictions requiring a 24-hour waiting period before an abortion and for a minor to have parental consent were also controls on the health-care provider because the woman seeking an abortion could go to another state without such limitations and obtain the abortion without penalty.

Most foes of abortion take their position on religious grounds, claiming abortion violates God's laws. But religions seem unable to agree on just how God's laws apply. The Southern Baptist Convention opposes abortion except to save the mother's life, while Presbyterians favor individual choice – favoring choice doesn't mean favoring abortion. Other Protestant denominations are split. The Catholic Church is staunchly antiabortion, saying life begins at conception. The three branches of Judaism are likewise split with Reform Judaism tending toward choice, Orthodox against and Conservative in the middle. All base their beliefs on the Biblical laws to the Jews that Moses brought from the holy mountain during the Exodus.

The Rev. Jerry Falwell wrote in USA TODAY in 1989, "As a Christian, I believe strongly that life begins at conception. This is not a Protestant or a Roman Catholic position. This is a biblical and medical position ... As a Christian who believes in the Bible, I believe it has always been, when any contradiction exists, a matter of waiting until science catches up with God's word ... I believe it is only a matter of time until medical science exposes abortion as the hideous crime it really is."

Of the more than 600 laws given by God to Moses not one specifically addressed abortion or a woman's right to terminate a pregnancy. The Bible doesn't say abortion is a "hideous crime." It does say at Deuteronomy 4:2: "Ye shall not add unto the word which I command you, neither shall ye diminish aught from it ..." That command is echoed at Deuteronomy 12:32, and some Christians and Jews say it means that if one accepts the Ten Commandments, all 600 plus laws must be accepted. It also means adding one's personal rules and claiming they came from God is forbidden.

Some antiabortionists, after failing to have courts outlaw abortion, resort to crime to try to reach their goal. Hundreds of family-planning clinics have been bombed and more have been burned by arsonists. Mail bombs have been intercepted by postal authorities. Other clinics have been scenes of violence, including murders of two physicians and a physician's escort in Pensacola, Fla., the murders of two clinic receptionists in Brookline, Mass., and the attempted murder of a physician in Wichita, Kan. Such acts can't be justified as means of upholding God's laws because His word says in I Peter 2:16, "... and not using liberty for a cloak of maliciousness ..." In other words, religious faith isn't to be used as justification for crime.

Falwell added, "And as with the abolition of slavery and discrimination against minorities, it (abortion) will be abolished." Discrimination and slavery could only be abolished by constitutional amendment; simple law, protesting, crime and moralistic pontificating didn't do it.

There is a chance a future conservative court might find a constitutional power to abolish abortion when the moderate Burger court could find no such power. After all, the Supreme Court has found nonexistent powers to

Finishing Touches

authorize separation of the races by state government (in 1896 and reversed in 1954), compulsion of nationalism by the states (1940; reversed in 1943), power to incarcerate thousands because of race (1944; repudiated by congressional apology), the power to punish for membership in a despised organization or thinking its thoughts (1951; reversed in 1957) and the power for states to outlaw homosexual love (1986). That's five major mistakes – not a bad record in 200 years – and a sixth mistake is always possible.

Much confusion could be avoided by concentrating less on the right of privacy and more on privileges and immunities. When the court received an Indiana controversy involving nude nightclub dancing, the claim was made that such dancing was expression and thus freedom of speech. The court decided in the spring of 1991 that it was subject to some regulation. They used the logic that entertainment is commerce, and states have power to regulate intrastate commerce, so some state control was permitted. Nightclub dancing was a privilege – it wasn't an immunity – and regulation was done in pursuit of goals of "general Welfare" and "domestic Tranquility" listed in the Constitution's Preamble.

The portion of the Fourteenth Amendment that passes along to the states the requirement to be extremely careful when prosecuting anyone, even the vilest and most-despised person says, *"No State shall ... deprive any person of life, liberty, or property, without due process of law ..."* is. It doesn't reserve this protection only to citizens, as the privileges-and-immunities clause does, it applies to everyone. This clause requires state and local governments to honor the Fourth, Fifth, Sixth, Seventh and Eighth Amendments just as the section dealing with citizens' privileges and immunities requires the states to respect the First Amendment and absence of power in many other areas. Local governments exist under the authority of the states, so they must respect limitations to their powers, also.

The due-process clause also ties the states to the provisions in Article I, Section 3, that stipulate the accused are "liable and subject to Indictment, Trial, Judgment and Punishment, according to law" because the Fifth Amendment suggests "due process of law" entails those four steps.

Due process then involves:

Indictment (or presentment) – The Fifth Amendment specifies that indictment must come from a grand jury for a "capital, or otherwise infamous crime." Presidents can't indict; neither can governors or mayors. Government must go to the source of its power – the people – for authority for legal action against an individual, and that authorization is given through the Constitution which requires due process. Grand-jury indictments developed before the American Revolution with closed sessions, and there's nothing in the Constitution to indicate that was to change with the formation for the new nation. Any rule used before creation of the nation was allowed to continue under the new order if nothing was said or implied in the Constitution to change such a rule. The Supreme Court has allowed an arraignment by a prosecuting attorney at the state level (*Hurtado v. California*, 1884) because the procedure was essentially the same as a grand-jury indictment and the state constitution called for that procedure.

Trial – The Fifth Amendment's contribution to this portion of due process includes freedom from double jeopardy; that is, there can be no retrial following a judgment of innocence. The Sixth Amendment adds speedy and public trials, impartial juries, a trial in the district of the crime, the accused is to be informed of charges and is to be confronted by accusers, the power of the defense to compel favorable witnesses and the right to have legal representation. The Seventh Amendment protects trial-by-jury rights in civil cases and facts established by that jury can't be rejected by another court except by the rules of common law. Findings of common law can't be changed to protect special interests but awards are often lowered in cases of excess judgments.

Judgment – The Fifth Amendment says the accused cannot be required to convict him/herself with self-incriminating testimony – self-incrimination voluntarily given isn't forbidden if it's truly voluntary. Judgment – as with indictment – isn't to be based on evidence obtained by unreasonable searches and seizures, as the Fourth Amendment specifies. The rules for gathering evidence that states must follow are included in the Fourth Amendment, and they're the same ones the federal government must obey.

Punishment – The Fifth Amendment specifies that punishment is the fourth step of due process and the implication is that it can follow the previous three only if they're done properly. The Eighth Amendment indicates punishments are to be in harmony with prevailing moral attitudes of society by specifying no cruel punishment. And punishment is to be what is specified by law, which is indicated by the prohibition of unusual punishment. The convicted must not be subject to "excessive fines"; everything must be reasonable.

The Fifth and Eighth amendments also allude to a related aspect, that of detention at the onset of due process' four steps. The Fifth Amendment says, "No person shall be held" except under specific conditions of "presentment or indictment" of a grand jury, which is why judges must often release an accused person from custody until there is more than an accusation by police. The Eighth Amendment adds that the accused can't be arbitrarily detained; bail must be reasonable.

Finishing Touches

The due process that the states must follow also includes concepts from the body of the Constitution. Article I, Section 9, says the Writ of Habeas Corpus can't be suspended except under specific conditions. That applies to states because of the Fourteenth Amendment, as does prohibitions of Bills of Attainder or ex post facto laws. That means authorities must have "probable cause" for any official action against any person.

Article II, Section 4, says government officials may not utilize crime as part of their official duties. The ban on crime applies to state officials when viewed as an immunity of United States citizens that can't be abridged by the states.

Article IV says citizens retain their state privileges and immunities from another state's authority just as they keep their national privileges and immunities from any state's action. And a person may not escape due process by fleeing to another state.

Article VI says, "Judges in every State shall be bound" by the supremacy of the Constitution and the laws and treaties of the federal government. That means state and local judges must obey every aspect of due process. Due process also includes the First Amendment's right to petition government; therefore, anyone convicted can claim a grievance and may petition with an appeal. All these provisions – plus other rights retained by the people (Ninth Amendment) and powers reserved to the people (Tenth Amendment) – apply to the due process of law the Fourteenth Amendment imposes on state governments.

The judicial system has been Americans' favorite scapegoat for the rising tide of crime during the late 20th century, but much of this criticism is nonsense. The judicial system has all these constitutional restrictions on its power and behavior and is unable to arbitrarily change them to appease a fearful population. These restrictions aren't "technicalities" that many non-knowledgeable people claim; they're important parts of the supreme law of the land. The United States was the first nation to write down methods by which the people restrict government in the same manner government restricts people – by law. Government, at any level, cannot remove or alter those restrictions just to make it easier to convict accused people; that's un-Americanism. The judicial system isn't failing society; society is failing by not understanding constitutional restrictions.

Due-process restrictions create the principle that the accuser – government – has the obligation to prove its charges. That translates into the tenet that the defendant is innocent until proven guilty, even though that principle isn't mentioned in the Constitution.

These constitutional restrictions also justify vigorous defense of any criminal; regardless of how vile, vicious or despicable that person may be. When an attorney defends such a criminal, what's at stake is the state's power to deprive that individual of "life, liberty, or property." Critics of the system degrade defense attorneys by claiming they're trying to get criminals off, or are protecting rights of criminals. That's nonsense. Most defense attorneys don't advocate returning criminals to the streets. The concept is to see that due process is obeyed because when due process is followed, the state has constitutional powers to deprive a criminal of life, liberty or property. Without due process, the state would have no such power, and criminals would have to be freed because of constitutional provisions. Attorneys can't put up a nominal defense, either, because that wouldn't be fair, and fairness is important to due process. Politicians, journalists, police, prosecutors or citizens who can't understand all of due process and criticize spending taxpayer money for public defenders are arguing for freedom for criminals. They should be ignored.

"*No State shall ... deny to any person within its jurisdiction the equal protection of the laws*" forces states to observe equality for all persons – not just citizens – under state laws, even though such requirement isn't specifically imposed by the Constitution on national government. Examples of how the federal government legally eluded equality in the past were the military services excluding women from combat roles or trying to exclude homosexuals entirely. Such exclusions were denials of equality under the laws, and would certainly be unconstitutional if done by a state. Since there's no equality provision imposed on the national government, those exclusions weren't considered unconstitutional. That is becoming a tenuous position because equality could be constitutionally required by Ninth and Tenth Amendments' principles. The Ninth Amendment says rights not listed in the Constitution cannot be denied or slighted. Equality exists under that principle because all people cede the same rights to government in order to form the state. Since everyone begins with the exact same rights – except for female rights of reproduction – all persons retain the same rights. That's equality. The Tenth Amendment is reflected in much the same manner. Without government, everyone would exist as an individual sovereign "nation," so when delegating powers to the federal, state, and local governments, each person delegates the exact same powers. They reserve for themselves identical powers. That's the equality the national government is expected to honor, even though it isn't specifically mentioned in the Constitution.

Cities and states are having a hard time dealing with the words "any person" even though the words are clear and mean what they say: *any person*.

Finishing Touches

Most governments have made progress in protecting persons under law according to race, sex or religion – and can make more progress – but seem to have trouble including homosexuals because a large portion of the population would be offended. But homosexuals cede rights and delegate power to governments in the exact same proportion as everyone else, so they should have the exact same status under those governments' laws. Public pressure and referendums in various areas of the nation have resulted in the repeal of statutes that sought to protect rights of homosexuals. Many politicians play on public concerns by claiming homosexuals receive special rights under statutes designed to equalize rights. That isn't true because the statutes of legislatures don't give rights to the individual.

In Washington state, one politician tried to get the legislature to enact a law that would have forbidden governments and schools from hiring lesbians or gay men. The 1986 bill would also have:

– Prohibited homosexuals from working as physicians, nurses, counselors, therapists or treating disabled people, minors or the elderly.

– Reversed all antidiscrimination laws extending equal protection to homosexuals.

– Prevented homosexual parents from obtaining custody of their children following a divorce.

– Ordered all public agencies, including schools, dealing with children to fire all homosexual employees discovered on their payrolls.

The bill soon died, but the intent points out a strong anticonstitution bent of many politicians. Homosexuals are included in the phrase "any person" and "We the People." This bill was aimed at denying to persons within the jurisdiction of Washington, the state's equal protection of the laws. That was un-Americanism.

But similar efforts patterned after Colorado's infamous Amendment 2 continue in Washington and neighboring Oregon and Idaho – where voters turn them down statewide but adopt them locally – and many other states on the mistaken belief that a simple vote can eliminate rights of others. If homosexuals obtained any special status under law, that preference could be negated in court under the equal-protection clause of the Fourteenth Amendment, but opponents have never tried to negate what they call "special rights" using this acceptable method of resolving conflicts. The courts will usually void state laws that treat people differently, as the Colorado Supreme Court voided Amendment 2 in October 1994.

Race has been the area to receive the most attention as Americans try to deal with equal protection of the laws because that is where the greatest inequality has existed, and race is the area where problems probably will continue to exist, for there's no reason to think racism can be eliminated. Most unacceptable activities have existed from the beginning of civilization, and laws against homicide, theft, assault, fraud or any other crime haven't ended them. Laws likely won't eliminate racial conflict. However, there's no reason to surrender to that probability, just as societies haven't surrendered to all the other undesirable activities that defy conquest.

The Fourteenth Amendment shouldn't be expected to eliminate inequality from society; it's designed to remove inequality from government. Laws can challenge racism, but racism will continue to exist; it just won't be government-sponsored racism. The Fourteenth Amendment has been successful in that area because it hasn't been long since racial inequality was mandated by people in power, even though they had no constitutional authority to make or enforce such decrees. The requirement that state governments may not deny equal protection of the laws has been the supreme law of the land since 1868, but that requirement wasn't taken seriously for a century. Inequality was openly practiced.

From just after World War II, when equality has been sought a little at a time, state power has been wrested from control of blatantly racist politicians to be passed to moderate persons. Old-time racists didn't change their nature because of the Fourteenth Amendment, so they wouldn't change because of civil-rights laws. Racists had to be replaced. Racist politicians didn't care about the Constitution's quest for equality; they felt that people in power could make any law they wished. And they did. That isn't the American way; governments can make laws only within the perimeters of powers given them in their constitutions, and no constitution gave power to discriminate against any minority; therefore, bigotry is un-American and using government as a vehicle for bigotry is subversion.

Taking power from obvious racists has been the first movement toward equality under law. Trying to eliminate subtle racism is the second step. Civil-rights proponents decried an apparent rise in racial intolerance in the 1980s and '90s, which should have been expected as a reaction to equality gains made in the 1960s and '70s. A reaction to the reaction is to be expected as America resumes its quest for equality in the 21st century. It's important to note that increased racial incidents weren't government sponsored; many were acts made criminal by government. Other incidents were acts of insensitivity outside government's powers.

Two specific powers of the Constitution are used in the quest for equality – the power to tax and spend for the general welfare and the power to regulate commerce. The tax-spend power overwhelmingly involves public-school systems, which take about half of state spending. Efforts to desegregate the schools since the *Brown v. Board of Education* decision of 1954 have created considerable animosity and confusion. It's important to know what the Brown decision was all about, and it's also important to try to avoid being caught up in extraneous arguments that have nothing to do with constitutionalism.

Sometime court critic James Kilpatrick wrote in his syndicated newspaper column in 1982, "But the Supreme Court in 1954 ... looked at school segregation and said it was immoral; therefore it was unconstitutional. Proceeding with the nonsequitur, the court found humane reasons ... to justify judicial intrusion into political decisions that until that moment had been regarded as the responsibility of the states."

But, even though Kilpatrick favors equality, he's guilty of misreading the true decision. The court said, "Separate educational facilities are inherently unequal." The Fourteenth Amendment says states may not deny equal protection, and the finding of unequal facilities proved states were doing what was specifically forbidden. That means state-imposed segregation of public schools could not be considered "political decisions ... regarded as the responsibility of the states." Unconstitutional law cannot exist and neither can any political responsibility falling under such illegality. Morality or immorality had nothing to do with the decision. The reason for "judicial intrusion" was that the issue was a controversy "arising under this Constitution (Article III, Section 2)."

Other critics aimed equally spurious arguments against the court. In 1971, the court said school authorities could legally use busing (*Swann v. Charlotte-Mecklenburg Board of Education*) as a method to eliminate segregation under a court requirement for equal protection. Busing hasn't been the only method school boards have had to end illegal segregation; they have always been free to use other means to provide equal protection of the law, but have few other methods within their authority.

A Chicago Tribune writer in 1982 wrote, "But mandatory busing doesn't improve racial tolerance and understanding, nor does it increase academic achievement, extensive research shows."

Another writer said, "In ordering mandatory busing, courts have subverted the intent of the 1960s civil rights legislation, which was that the federal government should enforce the right of minorities to make their own decisions." A black law professor said, "No one has substantial proof of either academic gains (for black students) or gains in people getting along well." Another professor wrote, that efforts seeking racial balance carried an "idea that non-white children cannot learn unless they are exposed to whites."

Countering these arguments was a 1980 study from Hartford, Conn., indicating that inner-city minority students bused to suburban schools got better jobs after graduation than did those who stayed in city schools. The New York Times reported the same year that Boston claimed "increased achievement and better quality schooling" despite racial turmoil during its court-imposed desegregation plan. Charlotte, N. C, also reported improved scholastic testings of both blacks and whites under desegregation efforts.

But such arguments and counterarguments have nothing to do with the constitutional issue. The Constitution says no denial of equal protection; it doesn't say anything that would indicate the equality provision can be evaded if improvements in racial tolerance and understanding or other social conditions don't accompany parity.

Americans claim individual responsibility is an important aspect of the nation. School-desegregation efforts don't interfere with that; government's responsibility is to provide equal opportunity, the individual must use personal initiative to take advantage of that opportunity. Academic gains are up to the individual, and busing children to achieve equal access doesn't take from minorities their rights to decide how much initiative to exert. Whether personal relationships between white and black students were markedly improved by busing didn't have anything to do with the constitutional issue, the intent of all civil-rights efforts is to influence government power by making that power apply equally to all.

Critics may be totally wrong about the value of busing, considering results in some elections. Seattle, with about a 10 percent black population, elected a black mayor in 1990, then overwhelmingly re-elected him indicating many persons of different races may be "getting along well." The tolerant demeanor of Seattle, an overly damp yuppie village suffering peninsula envy (it would rather have been San Francisco), may have been enhanced by having many of the younger voters attend schools integrated by busing. Whether minorities can or cannot learn except in the presence of white children is also immaterial to the principle of "equal protection of the laws."

The second area of government trying to create equality is through the power to regulated commerce. By regulating commercial ventures into accepting equality, the theory goes, society benefits. Society will be more peaceful if all persons enjoy its economic benefits because people purposely excluded from the nation's general welfare must resort to unacceptable actions, such as crime, to survive; employment and patronage are contractual so they must be based on only commercial concerns by all parties to the contract; government must represent the interests of all Americans and those people who enjoy the nation's benefits contribute to its improvement.

Finishing Touches

And people who aren't excluded from participation in the nation's general welfare don't have to rely on financial welfare for their survival.

Business leaders are no more apt to alter their nature than are politicians, so commercial acceptance of equality had to rely on "affirmative action." The concept had an innocent beginning in the administration of Lyndon Johnson, who acknowledged that discrimination wouldn't disappear because a few civil-rights bills were passed. Johnson promoted the idea that employers should act "affirmatively" to base hiring practices on only commercial concerns, which would mean eliminating race, sex or religion as conditions for employment or to exclude applicants from employment. Many critics complained that such a positive concept soon developed into reverse-discrimination quotas favoring minorities. During the 1980s, the Supreme Court allowed some actions in which race or sex could be the deciding factor in hiring to overcome past discrimination. The key was "deciding factor" when qualifications were similar. The decisions wouldn't allow preference of an unqualified minority applicant over qualified nonminority applicants.

The court could allow such slight edge for minorities because the Constitution doesn't place a strict "equality of law" principle on the national government as it does state governments. The court did reject arbitrary percentages favoring minorities; it voided a Richmond, Va., requirement that minorities get 30% of the dollar amount on all city construction contracts, but the court didn't say that the city couldn't take "affirmative action" to see that minorities were treated fairly in areas where actual past discrimination had been shown. Richmond couldn't arbitrarily reserve a predetermined quota to benefit one race because the city is governed by the absolute "equal protection of the laws" principle.

Political arguments also didn't have anything to do with the issue. Critics said affirmative action amounted to social engineering or meddling in business ventures. Civil-rights bills were constantly argued over because of "quotas," even though the bills might have outlawed quotas. The only issue of importance is whether government could use its power to regulate commerce to promote racial or sexual equality, as part of promoting general welfare. Another undecided issue is whether "discriminating for" is the same as "discriminating against." Reagan administration officials argued that compensation for past discrimination must go only to individuals who were direct victims, not any member of victimized groups. That seems a reasonable position, except it doesn't fully address the equality concept. If a black received "discrimination for" in order to obtain a benefit, that action wouldn't "discriminate against" specific whites who were never considered, but it would discriminate against whites as a group. With the Reagan argument, whites could have no complaint about reverse discrimination.

Arguing against affirmative action creates problems for the concept that politicians or government institutions can undertake any action except what's expressly forbidden by the Constitution. The Constitution doesn't expressly prohibit federal compensatory legislation that might favor minorities burdened by the legacy of past illegalities. The Constitution doesn't prohibit quotas imposed by federal law, only quotas imposed by state law. The concept that government may only use power or undertake act detectable in the Constitution doesn't have such problems.

In a 1991 Reader's Digest article, Justice Antonin Scalia was presented as opposed to compensatory legislation. The articles said, "... Scalia disputed the idea that governments are allowed to discriminate to overcome the effects of past discrimination. 'Where injustice is the game, turnabout is not fair play,' he wrote (in dissent to a Supreme Court decision)." Scalia's dissent added, "Even 'benign' racial quotas have individual victims, whose very real injustice we ignore whenever we deny them enforcement of their right not to be disadvantaged on the basis of race."

A judge who would rely heavily on "original intent," who would protect only rights found in the Constitution, and who would defer to the political process on federal affirmative action would have to compromise Scalia's principles because the right of equal protection under federal laws is not stated anywhere in the Constitution, which means a "turnabout" law would have to stand. Nor is there any evidence in the Constitution or the writings of the Founding Fathers that their "original intent" was to exclude compensatory benevolence.

One area in which turnabout law wasn't allowed to stand was at the state level. It was decided in the landmark *University of California Regents v. Bakke* decision of 1978. In that incident, a white applicant had twice been denied entrance to the University of California-Davis Medical School. The relatively new school decided it had an obligation to increase the number of "disadvantaged" students and to promote a more-rounded racial mixture. Of its 100 yearly openings, it set aside 16 with the express intention that they be filled by minorities.

The court said that couldn't be done because minorities could, theoretically, fill all 100 positions if they comprised the 100 most-qualified applicants while whites could compete only for 84 positions not reserved for minorities. That wasn't equal protection of the law. The court added that equality was denied when an innocent person was forced to bear the burden of "turnabout" in trying to cure evils of past discrimination. The court did

Finishing Touches

say that race could be a factor. In totaling all attributes of applicants, minority status might be a plus. Race just couldn't be the entire consideration for admission.

Another school case decided in 1982 helped explain equal protection of all persons under the laws and involved Texas' obligation to provide the same free public-school education to children of illegal immigrants as it does for citizens. In 1975, Texas enacted a law allowing school districts to charge tuition to children not "legally admitted" to the United States. If the aliens couldn't afford the tuition, their children – who amounted to about one percent of school enrollment – were to be banned from school.

Texas argued that the United States excluded illegal immigrants from social programs such as food stamps and aid to the blind. Why should different rules apply to the states, it asked? The Supreme Court said the state couldn't charge tuition or exclude children because the Fourteenth Amendment says, "No state shall ... deny to any person within its jurisdiction the equal protection of the laws." That clause doesn't restrict protection to citizens or legal residents, it applies to all persons.

The Fourteenth Amendment doesn't recognize differences; it says "any person," and that would include citizens, both native-born and naturalized; aliens, both legal and illegal; any person without regard to age, sex, race, nationality or social and legal status. (Should a spacecraft from a distant galaxy ever set down deep in the heart of Texas, any occupant of that vehicle would be entitled to state treatment equal to that given any oil baron or cowboy if he, she or it can be shown to be a "person") Everyone is the same under the Fourteenth Amendment, and no state can make any law contradicting the amendment. States don't excuse illegal immigrants from criminal law or tax law. Illegals are arrested, convicted and incarcerated for crimes; they have taxes taken from their paychecks, just as do legal residents; money they earn and spend contributes to the economy that supports public schools, especially money spent on rent.

Illegal immigrants pay federal taxes – including Social Security – if their employers are honest, but they can be legally excluded from national benefits. The reason they cannot be excluded from state benefits as they are from national programs is that equal protection of the laws for "all persons" is imposed on states, but not on the national government where the requirement for equality can be restricted to "We the people of the United States." Texas state attorneys should have known that.

The decision didn't settle the argument. In 1994 – an election year – it was back in full force, most notably in Florida and California. In a Reader's Digest article entitled *"Welfare for Illegal Aliens?"* author Randy Fitzgerald wrote, "Asserting that federally mandated benefits for illegals are draining the state treasury, Florida Governor Lawton Chiles filed suit against the federal government in April to recover up to $1 billion a year his state spends on their health and education. Additional complaints are made by the governors of Arizona, Illinois and other states experiencing budget-busting waves of illegal immigration." A California suit asked for $10 billion. Both were quickly dismissed by judges.

California Gov. Pete Wilson was quoted as saying, "We're forced to cut aid for the needy, elderly, blind and disabled who legally reside in California because Washington mandates we spend billions on illegals." California voters then overwhelmingly adopted Proposition 187 that purportedly would deny state social services to illegal immigrants. But it was blocked in court the day after being passed and for good reason. The Fourteenth Amendment's equal-protection clause ought to be understood by all to mean no law can exist if it treats any person or group of persons differently from the treatment afforded other persons.

But many people don't read it correctly. Conservative newspaper columnist George Will claimed only days before the election that the vote was about Californians "trying to reclaim a right of self-determination" that had been usurped by the court. He tossed in the discredited argument of the court legislating – when it only read the clause correctly – and claimed the 1982 Texas decision hinged on, "Whatever the judges deem unfair or unwise must be unconstitutional." Will's arguments were nonsense. State laws are unconstitutional when they treat people differently. Washington, D. C., isn't mandating spending for illegal aliens, the Constitution is. Will demonstrated more shortage of constitutional knowledge by writing:

"By 1982 Congress had made its thinking clear through laws barring illegals from Supplemental Security Income and Aid to Families with Dependent Children. In 1986, Congress did the same regarding nonemergency Medicaid services.

"In 1990 Congress created 'Temporary Protected Status' for legal or illegal aliens unable to return home because of circumstances such as civil disorder. Congress, doing something like what Proposition 187 would do, said people with this status are ineligible for most federal benefits. And this year, in providing disaster relief for California, Congress excluded illegal aliens from almost all benefits."

As shown in the Texas case, the Constitution does not contain a requirement that the national government extend provisions of its laws to all "persons"; federal law can exclude illegal aliens. State laws can't.

During the time Wilson was campaigning for Proposition 187 because of the high cost of providing social services to illegal aliens, Republican Senate candidate Michael Huffington was proposing to end all federal welfare programs and send that money to state and local governments. After the 1994 midterm elections, in which Republicans gained control of Congress, the same kind of proposals popped up from GOP functionaries at all levels of government. But sending all welfare programs to the states would make them available to illegals because the Fourteenth Amendment requires equal treatment for all persons, which would be even more costly. (It's important to note that under the Reagan administration Republicans and conservatives sent many social programs to the states, which must provide equal benefits to all persons within state jurisdiction, instead of keeping them at the federal level, where equal benefits need only go to citizens and those noncitizens Congress decides are eligible. Because they are responsible, Republicans and conservatives should stop whining about costs of those programs.)

This difference in constitutional power is the reason states must comply with the "one-man, one-vote" principle: legislatures must be structured under the requirement of equality under laws not germane to the United States Congress. That's why California has two senators in the United States Senate as does Wyoming even though their population ratio is about 50 to 1. States are barred from allotting their state senatorial seats along county lines as a facsimile of the federal model because of the equality principle imposed on them by the Fourteenth Amendment.

The 1987 case that caused Scalia's statement repudiating "turnabout" actions for civil rights involved a woman receiving a promotion over a man who scored slightly higher on an oral test in California's Santa Clara County Transportation Agency. Both were capable and equally qualified except for a two-point difference on the test. Because of past hiring and promoting practices, only men held the job to which the woman was promoted, and the agency decided to gradually eliminate the imbalance through affirmative-action efforts. The court said the county had the authority to promote the woman – with gender being the deciding factor – without violating civil-rights laws ordaining equality. Apparently gender was worth three points in totaling qualifications of the two promotion candidates.

Political conservatives, who claimed remedy for past discrimination could only be offered to a specific victim of that discrimination, criticized the decision. But because there is no constitutional requirement that federal civil-rights laws reflect absolute equality, they – like Scalia – lost their arguments. It's ironic that this very act of miniature inequality would probably have been prohibited by the Equal Rights Amendments to the Constitution conservatives prevented from being ratified in 1982.

THE UN-AMERICANS

The argument that compensatory action for past discrimination should go only to the individuals discriminated against, also confuses the issue. The constitutional concern is government power – not individual rights – and power can be directed towards groups as well as individuals, because groups, not individuals, were targeted by un-American segregationist laws. Blacks were discriminated against as a group by laws segregating schools, so blacks can be compensated as a group by antisegregation laws. Government can protect both individuals and groups. If government couldn't protect group rights, it couldn't protect corporations. But, as documented earlier in this book, corporations are due the same consideration as individuals.

In early 1995, a movement began in California to end all state affirmative-action laws by referendum. But, as shown, any state affirmative action using inequality could be negated in court for denying the "equal protection of the law" the Fourteenth Amendment requires. Using the courts would be less costly and less acrimonious than lengthy arguments and free of the rancor caused by political battles. White firefighters hurt by Birmingham's affirmative-action decree cited on page 177 used the courts for a peaceful win. The Supreme Court in April of 1995 let stand a lower-court ruling to compensate those damaged by reverse discrimination in the program that ended in 1989. Any reverse discrimination can be negated the same way.

Politicians arguing against affirmative-action usually don't cite evidence that the laws work both ways. In 1983, predominately black Howard University in Washington, D. C., was forced to rehire and compensate a white faculty member who was dismissed so less-experienced blacks could be promoted. Antidiscrimination laws, properly used, work both ways.

Section 5 ("The Congress shall have power to enforce, by appropriate legislation, the provisions of this article.") should make it clear that the Fourteenth Amendment removed several powers from the state governments and gave them to the national government. Section 1 of the amendment contains that shift in four distinct facets: 1) citizenship was made a national concern; 2) states can't abridge citizens' national privileges and immunities assured under the Constitution; 3) states can't circumvent due process, and 4) state laws must assure equal protection for everyone. Section 5 empowers Congress with the authority to make law to protect everyone from state governments or to force states into obeying those four basic constitutional principles of fairness. What politicians or the majority of the people in any state or city want is immaterial because there is no provision allowing the Constitution's principles to be ignored or altered by popular demand.

Many supporters of intrusive Big Brother Government don't accept limitations to the powers of the states. Conservative newspaper columnist

Finishing Touches

Patrick Buchanan celebrated the change in the Supreme Court makeup from Earl Warren liberal to Warren Burger moderate to William Rehnquist conservative with a July 4, 1991, diatribe. He wrote, "From the death of court activism can come a rebirth of the politics of accountability. If liberals want birth control clinics to do abortion counseling, they can vote for it. If they want racial set-asides and busing for racial balance, they can vote for it. If they want prayer out of the public schools, they can vote to remove it, after the court has again let communities decide."

What Buchanan apparently didn't understand, is the Warren court only reminded politicians that they lacked certain powers. The Constitution makes it clear, to those who know how to read it, that there are some things not subject to political action. Equality of all races under state laws isn't subject to politics. The religious practices of Americans aren't subject to a vote, as Buchanan suggested. States can't enact prejudicial laws, so Americans don't vote for racial equality in the schools. No government can make religious law, so Americans can't vote for state-imposed prayers in school, and the Supreme Court can't "again let communities decide" if they want government to make religious law – that is un-Americanism.

Another supporter of governmental intrusiveness, Sen. Slade Gorton, R-Wash., criticized the Warren court for its "activism." His complains were reported in a Seattle newspaper in 1991 thusly:

"Gorton, a former three-term state attorney general, was critical of the legal legacy left by the activist Supreme Court led by Chief Justice Earl Warren from 1953 to 1969. The Warren Court issued landmark rulings on school prayer, racial segregation, legislative reapportionment, the rights of the accused, and the right of privacy.

" 'I think its great weakness was substituting the political and philosophical judgments of court members for decisions made by elected legislative bodies,' Gorton said."

The great weakness of that argument was substituting political and philosophical judgments for the truth. The Warren court only said New York didn't have the power to make a law creating school prayer – the First and Fourteenth Amendments say that. The court said forced racial segregation by government was "inherently unequal" – segregation by law contravenes the Fourteenth Amendment. Warren's court ruled legislatures must be apportioned to afford equality of the law – the Fourteenth Amendment indicates that. The Warren court held that rights of the accused are listed throughout the Constitution and can't be changed or ignored by local anti-constitutional politicians. The Warren court's rulings on the right of privacy really involved "immunities" that states can't abridge – the Fourteenth

Amendment says that. Political and philosophical judgments of the judges weren't behind the Warren decisions; constitutional knowledge was. The controversial rulings by the Warren court concerned subjects not within the authority of elected legislative bodies. Such entities don't have the option of obeying or disregarding the Constitution for political reasons. A three-term attorney general should know that.

Sobran, another supporter of unrestrained government, made similar silly claims as he attacked the court in 1982. He wrote: "... the First Amendment would never have passed if its authors had known that it would eventually be used to circumscribe the freedom of worship and to license pornography."

Sobran was wrong. The court has never used the First Amendment to circumscribe freedom of worship; the judges used it correctly to remind government of all levels that they don't have pietistic power. That protects freedom of worship. The authors of the amendment wanted government out of religion, and that's how the Warren court ruled.

Government isn't a licenser of the press, which means three things: journalists aren't subject to licensing as are physicians, attorneys and hair dressers; the press isn't open to restraint by government; nor is the press compelled to publish what government wants – that also applies to the pornography press. The Fourteenth Amendment passes onto the states the obligation to honor these press freedoms known as "immunities." There's nothing in the Constitution to indicate governments have censorship powers if a publication is obscene, racy or just not to the liking of fans of unrestrained government. Government can control the pornography press through its power to regulate commerce and child pornography through police power – a child is a victim – and commercial power.

Sobran added, "They (the authors) would very likely have torn up the Bill of Rights if they had any idea what tortured logic would one day be used to turn those 10 articles into a mandate for the liberal agenda."

People who understand the authors' purposes know they were concerned with restraining government, which has a tendency to be overzealous. Keeping governments out of all facets of life is why the Bill of Rights was written, and that's how the Warren court interpreted it – limitations on government, which the authors would be proud of. It's tortured logic by Sobran and other advocates of intrusive government to find power for government involvement in religion or publishing when the Constitution specifically forbids such entanglements.

The Bill of Rights authors would probably be appalled by calls for votes on whether to honor minority rights or on religion. They likely would be appalled by those in the mainstream press basking in First Amendment freedom while calling for government regulation for publishing deemed less desirable or an idea that press freedom applies only to an "acceptable" press. The founders wanted government restricted to powers specified or implied in the Constitution, and didn't intend that government could use a universal power. The Fourteenth Amendment extends those restrictions to the states to protect individual liberty; that's why it's the Guardian Amendment.

Critics often try to interpret Supreme Court decisions without knowing what the Constitution says; most haven't studied constitutional law and some may have never read the document. It's important to remember that the judges are attorneys, and the law profession isn't a paragon of clarity with the written word. Attorneys are not accustomed to writing a clear-and-specific statement lest the one penning the clarity should later be required to defend the statement or, worse, challenge it under a different cause. Attorneys express a single thought 12 times with a dozen dissimilar statements; then, should the meaning be too obvious, a half-dozen new phrases are used to present six fresh descriptions of the same concept as if there's a decretum to obfuscate palpable principium. Court followers know a person must analyze a decision to discover one point of law, and that point of law will nearly always concerns government power.

Sobran wrote, "Sensible people, unfortunately, tend not to wind up on the Supreme Court of the United States. Brilliant people do; compassionate people do; honest people do; courageous people do; but not, for some reason, sensible people." That statement is nonsense. Sensible people tend not to wind up writing newspaper columns.

THE FIFTEENTH AMENDMENT (1870)

> *SECTION 1. The right of citizens of the United States to vote shall not be denied or abridged by the United States or by any State on account of race, color, or previous condition of servitude.*
> *SECTION 2. The Congress shall have power to enforce this article by appropriate legislation.*

This amendment is hailed as a breakthrough in promoting race relations following the abolition of slavery, but the amendment is more for show than for practical usage because the right to vote by black Americans could have been secured by other constitutional provisions. The amendment does remove any opportunity for arguing, and arguing definitely would have occurred had Congress or the Supreme Court used other provisions of the

Constitution to assure the vote for blacks. There's nothing in the original Constitution suggesting voting was to be restricted to any specific group. When the Constitution was written, the vote was limited to property-owning males, almost universally white, but that arrangement wasn't incorporated in the document at its creation, nor were any voting qualifications added before this amendment. Prevailing state customs and laws, not constitutionality, determined suffrage both state and federal. Americans could change that suffrage at their will.

There are vague references to voting in the Constitution. Article I, Section 4, says, "The Times, Places and Manner of holding Elections for Senators and Representatives, shall be prescribed in each State by the Legislature thereof; but the Congress may at any time by Law make or alter such Regulations, except as to the Places of chusing Senators." Since senators were chosen by state legislatures instead of popular vote, their selections weren't pertinent to this concern. But Congress was given power to overrule state laws or regulations concerning federal elections of representatives. Congress could have given the federal vote to newly freed blacks – or any other race or minority – under the constitutional provision that it could alter regulations concerning "Manner of holding Elections ..." Once that was done, voting would be a "privilege" of a United States citizen, protectable under the Fourteenth Amendment from state abridgment. The Fourteenth would also permit black – or other – suffrage under the provision that no state could "deny to any person within its jurisdiction the equal protection of the laws." The Rehnquist court used that provision in 1991 to secure voting equality in the election of state judges – judges being considered "representatives."

Until the Fourteenth Amendment was adopted there was no mention that voters must be citizens of the United States or of the states in which they lived. Voter qualifications were left to the states to decide, and the states could have permitted noncitizens to vote, unless prohibited by their constitutions. Congress could have overruled the states on federal elections.

Section 2 of the amendment says, "when the right to vote at any election for (federal and state officials) is denied to any of the male inhabitants of such State, being twenty-one years of age, and citizens of the United States, or in any way abridged, except for participation in rebellion, or other crime, the basis of representation therein shall be reduced in the proportion which the number of such male citizens shall bear to the whole number of male citizens twenty-one years of age in such State." That's interpreted to mean only men 21 or older could vote – that was the suffrage when the amendment was adopted – but that's not what the words say. The words indicate only that representation be reduced if voting privileges are denied.

Voting privileges can be abridged because of participation in rebellion or other crime – race, sex, age are neither rebellion or other crime.

THE SIXTEENTH AMENDMENT (1913)

The Congress shall have power to lay and collect taxes on incomes, from whatever source derived, without apportionment among the several states, and without regard to any census or enumeration.

Many people feel that this amendment has given the federal government an open invitation to their wealth and their incomes. But that isn't true.

In the original Constitution, the federal government would tax states according to populations, and the states would have to tax their inhabitants to raise the money to pay those tax bills. This arrangement would not have protected incomes from taxation because the states could impose an income tax, and there's no assurance states wouldn't have a much heavier tax on incomes than what the federal government now applies. Logic would lead a person to believe taxes would be higher because there would be little accountability – states would plead helplessness from the national government's demand for high taxes and the federal government would remind everyone it was the states taking their money. Most American taxpayers might be better off paying taxes directly to the federal government than indirectly through the states because the states have a history of disdain for the well-being of the people.

The income tax was first imposed by the federal government during the Civil War, and that tax was judged by the Supreme Court in 1881 to be acceptable. But when a peacetime income tax was imposed in the 1890s, the court wouldn't allow it. The two decisions offer an insight into the thinking of some Supreme Court judges because they are reflected in, although not related to, the 1919 opinion written by Justice Holmes that said actions not allowed in peacetime could be constitutionally permitted during war.

The court in 1895 said the income tax was a "direct tax" on individuals (Article I, Section 9, says a "capitation, or other direct Tax" could only be imposed in "Proportion to the Census or Enumeration herein ...") so it was illegal. The ruling indicated a direct (i.e. income) tax could be imposed on each state according to populations, but not directly on an individual taxpayer. The court said each state could "recoup from their own citizens in the most feasible way" what amounts were paid to the federal government. That statement means states could use any tax they wished if that taxation was "the most feasible way" to raise money to pay federal tax bills. Nothing was said in the decision to indicate incomes would be exempt from state taxes, only from federal taxes, so incomes were fair sources of tax revenue for states. The anticonstitutional history of state governments would suggest fairness wouldn't be observed. See the Twenty-Fourth Amendment to see how state and local politicians have viewed fairness in government throughout most of the nation's existence.

Under the original taxing formula, each state would be taxed uniformly by population, not by wealth. The South, with its lower per-capita incomes, would be heavily burdened in relation to Connecticut – with the nation's highest average income – and in relation to other Northeastern and Western states. For example, Connecticut and South Carolina had similar populations in the 1990 census, but, according to the Commerce Department, Connecticut's average per capita income in 1993 was $28,110 while South Carolina's income was $16,923. Under the original method of taxation, both states would have similar tax bills to pay to the national government, but Connecticut would have almost 70 percent more capital at its disposal than would South Carolina. That difference in state wealth would translate into much higher tax bills – as a percentage of income – for South Carolinians. If a Connecticut taxpayer's obligation was 20 percent of income, a South Carolinian would have to surrender close to 35 percent of income. The Sixteenth Amendment has made paying taxes to the federal government much fairer for Southerners and it has not, in any way, raised the level of taxes an individual must pay.

THE SEVENTEENTH AMENDMENT (1913)

The Senate of the United States shall be composed of two Senators from each State, elected by the people thereof, for six years, and each Senator shall have one vote. The electors in each State shall have the qualifications requisite for electors of the most numerous branch of the State legislatures.
(Complete amendment in Appendix.)

This amendment changed the provision in Article I, Section 3, that called for senators to be chosen by the state legislatures. That original concept kept the population detached from the Senate and proved unwise after commercial interests gained too much influence in selection of senators. Those hand-picked politicians went to the United States Senate to represent the concerns of a few special interests, the concerns of the ordinary citizens were ignored. Widespread dissatisfaction with that arrangement where com-

Finishing Touches

mon Americans were excluded led to the adoption of the Seventeenth Amendment.

The original arrangement does explain conditions that continue to exist. The founders envisioned representatives as spokesmen for the states and individuals. Senators were envisioned as representatives of the nation to be concerned with federal interests, not necessarily with local issues. The Constitution incorporates that vision in giving the Senate power to try politicians who have been impeached by the House and to remove convicted offenders from office. The House's power in impeachments is to bring charges, much like a grand jury in a criminal case, but the House has no power to remove an official from office.

The Senate is also to be partners with the president in making treaties and selecting "Ambassadors, other Public Ministers and Consuls, Judges of the supreme Court, and all other Officers of the United States" whose selections aren't specified by Constitution or law. These powers, not shared with the House of Representatives, are truly national in nature and are not to be tampered with by any other governmental body.

THE EIGHTEENTH AMENDMENT (1919)

SECTION 1. After one year from ratification of this article the manufacture, sale, or transportation of intoxicating liquors within, the importation thereof into, or the exportation thereof from the United States and all territory subject to the jurisdiction thereof for beverage purposes is hereby prohibited.
(Complete amendment in Appendix.)

This amendment is regarded as a disaster, even though it did partly accomplish its desired goal. It didn't eliminate problems relating to alcoholic beverages but did reduce consumption substantially. The amendment's failure wasn't in not controlling alcohol, the failure was that the Constitution was used for simple legislation – a misuse. The founders created the Constitution to specify powers, objectives and limitations of government. It was never meant to contain legislation or to control individuals, and using it for simple law demonstrates how far away from the founders' concepts Americans and their politicians have drifted.

Congress has always had power to regulate interstate commerce, and states have always had authority over intrastate commerce, so regulation of alcoholic beverages was always within the authority of lawmakers. There was no need to clutter up the Constitution with nonsense, and this failed experiment should be a lesson not to use the Constitution for simple legislation concerning relatively minor matters such as praying in school or flag-burning protests. The powers to regulate commerce has been present from the beginning of the union, which shows that the United States has never been a land of free enterprise, only of private enterprise; not of free markets, only private markets.

THE NINETEENTH AMENDMENT (1920)

> *The right of citizens of the United States to vote shall not be denied or abridged by the United States or by any State on account of sex. Congress shall have power to enforce this article by appropriate legislation.*

The voting privilege for women could have been secured by other constitutional methods, as it could have been for racial minorities, such as with the equal-protection provision of the Fourteenth Amendment; if interpreted as it is today. But in 1920, the full extent of the Fourteenth Amendment was nowhere defined – it's still not understood by much of the general public – so a constitutional amendment was used.

THE TWENTIETH AMENDMENT (1933)

> *SECTION 1. The terms of the President and Vice President shall end at noon on the 20th day of January, and the terms of Senators and Representatives at noon on the 3d of January, of the years in which such terms would have ended if this article had not been ratified; and the terms of their successors shall then begin.*
> (Complete amendment in Appendix.)

This housekeeping amendment is without controversy. The original Constitution said nothing concerning the beginning or ending of elective terms, only their length, so terms were allowed to begin and end in relationship to the date the Constitution became a legal document establishing the federal government: March 4, 1789. The problem with this arrangement was that there was nothing to prevent legislators from changing the start or end of terms to fit political desires.

This amendment does prevent such things as lengthening a term to increase the time of service that could be used to compute pension plans or other emoluments. For that reason, Americans can rest assured that the Constitution is keeping a figurative eye on the politicians few persons trust in the first place.

THE TWENTY-FIRST AMENDMENT (1933)

SECTION 1. The Eighteenth article of amendment to the Constitution of the United States is hereby repealed.
SECTION 2. The transportation or importation into any State, Territory, or possession of the United States for delivery or use therein of intoxicating liquors, in violation of the laws thereof, is hereby prohibited.
(Complete amendment in Appendix.)

While the Eighteenth Amendment did reduce consumption of alcoholic beverages, it didn't create the paradise its Utopia-seeking creators had sought. Instead, it created several organized-crime problems the nation continues to battle at the end of the century, so it had to be repealed with Section 1 of the Twenty-First Amendment. Section 2 of this amendment only returned power to legislatures where it resided in the first place.

The lessons learned from this experiment with Prohibition should have taught American leaders the folly of amending the Constitution for frivolous matters that can be dealt with in other ways or aren't important enough to be dealt with at all. The United States Constitution should never be allowed to resemble some state constitutions that have been rendered almost meaningless with dozens, if not hundreds, of amendments and which elicit as much reverence as a city's parking ordinances.

THE TWENTY-SECOND AMENDMENT (1951)

SECTION 1. No person shall be elected to the office of President more than twice, and no person who has held the office of President, or acted as President, for more than two years of a term to which some other person was elected President shall be elected to the office of the President more than once.
(Complete amendment in Appendix.)

This is a example of using the Constitution for purely political concerns, and it should be evidence that using the Constitution for political purposes is an abuse of the document. After Democrat Franklin D. Roosevelt broke the unwritten rule that a president voluntarily serve no more than two terms, his political enemies led the crusade during the 1940s for this amendment to prevent individual control of the office only to see it prevent popular Republican President Reagan from seeking a third term in 1988. Conservatives, who wanted the amendment in the 1940s, hated it in the 1980s.

The amendment is little more than another housekeeper having little effect on government, and there's no evidence suggesting this term limitation improved or lessened the conscientiousness or capabilities of presidents. It's only to a few who believe one individual serves as president is there any support for this constitutional principle. People who recognize that a political movement serves as president find little reason to be concerned, one way or the other, with this term limitation on chief executives.

Persons who believe that placing term limitations on representatives and senators would ease their frustrations with government need only to study presidents before and after the Twenty-Second Amendment to determine if term limitation really improves government. If a term limitation hasn't accomplished anything beneficial in the executive branch, there's no reason to think it would do so in the legislative branch. Studying term limits at the state level to see how government improves – if it does – would also be beneficial. Limitations may do little more than provide incentives to built rapport with potential commercial employers with special-interest legislation and to enact looser pension requirements for short-term politicians.

THE TWENTY-THIRD AMENDMENT (1961)

> *SECTION 1. The District constituting the seat of Government of the United States shall appoint in such manner as Congress may direct: A number of electors of President and Vice President equal to the whole number of Senators and Representatives in Congress to which the District would be entitled if it were a State, but in no event more than the least populous State ...*
> (Complete amendment in Appendix.)

This amendment gives voting privileges to District of Columbia residents in presidential elections. The original Constitution specified (Article II) that "Each State shall appoint" electors for president, but it didn't make the same condition for the district to be the seat of government or other territories. That's always been interpreted to mean D.C. voters couldn't vote for president.

D.C. residents also couldn't select local government representatives because Congress was given power (Article I, Section 8) of "exclusive Legislation ... over such District ... as may ... become the Seat of the Government of the United States ..." The provision was that Congress have legislative authority; it didn't provide for federal control of executive or judicial functions. This left the situation somewhat confusing. When the Constitution was written, there was no area set aside to be the capital, so there was no idea how a resident population would regulate a district not yet selected. This is one area in which suffrage probably couldn't be obtained by legislation or court decision, so an amendment was needed to secure the vote for Washingtonians.

THE TWENTY-FOURTH AMENDMENT (1964)

SECTION 1. The right of citizens to vote in any primary or other election for President or Vice President, for electors for President or Vice President, or for Senator or Representative in Congress, shall not be denied or abridged by the United States or any State by reason of failure to pay any poll tax or other tax.
SECTION 2. The Congress shall have power to enforce this article by appropriate legislation.

This amendment was needed to combat the anticonstitutional dispositions of local and state governments, and is a condemnation of claims of "states' rights" concerning elections. Politicians in many states, ever ready to protect their personal interests, used states' rights arguments to exclude numerous American citizens from participation in the operation of the constitutional covenant. The poll tax was designed to keep blacks from voting because few could afford to pay another tax. And it also excluded many whites living in poverty, who were also among those people most needing governmental protection or services. By excluding the poor of all races, privileged white politicians were able to use government to serve themselves. That certainly was a denial of the Constitution's equal-protection principle (Fourteenth Amendment) and, as such, was un-American.

The poll tax (capitation) prohibited in Article I, Section 9, pertained to a levy on voters by the federal government. Such a tax could have been imposed on a state in proportion to the census, but not on individuals. When state officials created poll taxes to exclude the poor and underprivileged, the tax was on individuals. That showed the tax wasn't in accord with "original intent" of the founders.

THE TWENTY-FIFTH AMENDMENT (1967)

SECTION 1. In case of the removal of the President from office or of his death or resignation, the Vice President shall become President
SECTION 2. Whenever here is a vacancy in the office of the Vice

President, the President shall nominate a Vice President who shall take office upon confirmation by a majority vote of both Houses of Congress.
(Complete amendment in Appendix.)

This is another housekeeping amendment adopted because the original Constitution didn't elevate the vice president to the presidency; it said the vice president would discharge the powers and duties of the presidency. That was no problem in 1789, but when the Twenty-Second Amendment limited a president to two terms it became necessary for the vice president to become president, lest one person serve three terms: one as vice president acting as president, if the president died at the onset on a term, and two as the duly-elected president.

The Twenty-Fifth Amendment was carelessly drafted with apparent "sexism" that many persons might conclude restricts the presidency to men. Article II of the Constitution uses "he" or "his" to refer to the president. Amendments 12, 20 and 22 use the word "person," indicating the office was open to both sexes, only to have this amendment revert to "he" and "his." The controversy over sexist language leads many overzealous people to change "chairman" to "chairperson," "salesman" to "salesperson" and "waiters" and "waitresses" to "waitpersons." Use of such exacting language would result in the conclusion that "he" and "his" would restrict Fifth and Sixth Amendment rights and the presidency to men. Therefore, silly-speak – such as waitpersons – must be ignored in order to apply constitutional thought properly. The classical mode of English usage allowed "his" to refer to both male and female when applied in a collective sense. That's how the founders understood the pronoun to apply, but because women weren't involved in government in the 18th century the founders wouldn't have the concept Americans have today about sexist words.

THE TWENTY-SIXTH AMENDMENT (1971)

SECTION 1. The right of citizens of the United States, who are 18 years of age or older, to vote shall not be denied or abridged by the United States or by any State on account of age.
SECTION 2. The Congress shall have power to enforce this article by appropriate legislation.

Like the privilege to vote for racial minorities (Fifteenth Amendment) and women (Nineteenth Amendment), the vote for 18-to-20-year-olds might have been secured by existing powers and constitutional provisions. But by creating these amendments, arguments over interpretation aren't possible, so the amendments haven't been totally unnecessary. The Founding Fathers didn't include voting requirements in the original Constitution because such requirements had nothing to do with giving power to government or restraining government. Voting was to be a "political question"; something that can be decided by legislative action under powers given through the Constitution. The founders weren't concerned with day-to-day governmental operations or the political direction of the nation, those were to be determined by legislation. The founders' main concern was specifying the powers government may use to make those political determinations. Limitations and objectives were secondary concerns. The founders put no political agendas in the Constitution.

THE TWENTY-SEVENTH AMENDMENT (1992)

No law, varying the compensation for the services of the Senators and Representatives, shall take effect, until an election of representatives shall have intervened.

This amendment was proposed in 1789 with what became the Bill of Rights in 1791, but was rejected by the original 13 states because it didn't address individual liberties, the subject of the Bill of Rights. It was subsequently ratified to prevent members of Congress from raising their salaries – without some sort of voter approval – because it provides for an intervening election before a pay raise becomes effective. That gives voters a chance to oust politicians if the pay hike is unpopular. Without this amendment, members of Congress could get a new salary for no longer than two years before being ousted.

The amendment also isn't important because the Constitution had protection against pay-raise abuse by Congress. Article I, section 6, says, "The Senators and Representatives shall receive a Compensation for their Services, to be ascertained by Law, and paid out of the Treasury of the United States." Article I, Section 9, says, "No Money shall be drawn from the Treasury, but in Consequence of Appropriation made by law ..." Article I, Section 7, says law is created by a presidential signature to a bill passed by both houses of Congress. These conditions add up to a provision that no pay raise is legal until the president signs it into law or Congress overrides his (or her) veto. Taxpayers would be protected from outrageous conduct by Congress by the presidential veto.

Chapter 11

MONEY: THE ROOT OF ALL GOVERNMENT

A MUTUAL DEPENDENCY

Monetary wealth is a relative thing for it exists only because government exists, and governments too often exist to serve only those who are possessors of wealth. If there were no government, there would be no wealth because money – the gauge of wealth – is issued by government. That government could not long exist without the means of extracting its creation from the citizenry to fund necessary functions of defense and the general welfare. Most people who derive adequate incomes in a sophisticated-and-advanced civilization would be incapable of maintaining their good fortune should that advanced condition disappear.

Therefore, it's incumbent on citizens with livable incomes to pay taxes to support government because that support provides for the continuance of their earnings. Unfortunately, many people with incomes dependent on the general welfare of society complain the most when taxed to support that general welfare. Business needs consumers affluent enough to purchase, and that requires sustaining the general welfare. Authors, journalists and editors need a literate population, just as computer mavens need a sophisticated society that needs and uses technology. Artists, entertainers and athletes need a society affluent beyond what's needed to maintain life for they live off a nation's excess incomes. Professionals and craftsmen in medicine, law and real estate may need an affluent society more than do the others. Often, these people complain the most that they're punished for success because their government-created money is taxed by government to provide for the general welfare the complainers need for success.

The importance of money to a civilized society is reflected in the Constitution in Article I, Section 8. The Founding Fathers didn't waste time; they got to important matters first. When listing powers for Congress, they didn't dwell on esoteric philosophic concepts or political concerns; they indicated that power to fund government is the most-important power for the first statement in the list of congressional authority is the power to tax ("The Congress shall have Power To lay and collect Taxes, Duties, Imposts and Excises ... "). The second power listed is the power of borrowing. ("To

Money: The Root of All Government

borrow money on the Credit of the United States"). Other explicit constitutional methods of income for government are taking property, including money, as a punishment after a criminal conviction (Fifth Amendment), and imposition of fines (Eighth Amendment) in both criminal and civil cases. Other methods are implied.

Government's other specific functions concerning money are to coin money and regulate its value (Article I, Section 8, paragraph 5). That paragraph empowers the federal government to create and operate mints as needed and to establish the Federal Reserve Board to oversee and regulate the financial condition of the nation. Included in this oversight function would be chartering banks and providing protection by making crimes against banks subject to federal jurisdiction, even though similar crimes against other businesses would be state matters. Congress also has power (Article I, Section 8, paragraph 6) to provide punishment for the counterfeiting of United States coins and securities.

The importance of tax money for government is reflected by the fact one of the Supreme Court's earliest cases (*Hylton v. United States,* 1796) concerned taxes. Another important case (*McCulloch v. Maryland,* 1819) involved the creation of a federal bank and a state's power to tax that bank. In the first case, the court ruled that a $16 federal tax on horse-drawn carriages could be placed on each carriage because such a tax couldn't be extracted from each state according to population. The court said one state might have 100 carriages, another state 1,000, resulting in taxes 10 times higher in the first state if populations were equal. In the second case, a federal bank was allowed under the implied power of Congress to create whatever was needed to establish value of the money that Congress had explicit power to mint and regulate. But the court said Maryland couldn't tax the federal bank, a predecessor to the present Federal Reserve Board, because that would burden or impede constitutional functions exercised by the federal government, which is supreme (Article VI).

States do have some of the same powers as the federal government concerning money and taxes. States can't mint money separate from the national government nor provide punishment for counterfeiters of federal coins and securities, but they can create certificates of value, such as bonds, and can protect those financial instruments with state counterfeiting laws. The Constitution's provision that the federal government may collect money through "Taxes, Duties, Imposts and Excises" isn't permissible for the states in totality. Section 10 of Article I forbids states from imposing duties and imposts on imported and exported goods, without approval of Congress, "except what may be absolutely necessary" for executing inspection laws. Any money collected, above the cost of performing the inspections, is to go to the national Treasury. Section 10 places no similar restrictions on state powers to impose taxes and excises.

Modern Americans need no definitions for the term "taxes," which denotes numerous methods of obtaining funds. The founders, however, felt a need to include other forms of taxes to insure all possible taxation was covered. They specified "duties" in the Constitution, but had to define that term in Hylton. Most of the Supreme Court judges at the time had been signatory founders of the Constitution, so if they had to define the term in 1796, there couldn't have been any agreement on "original intent" of the creators because all involved in government would have known that intent. The court definition said a duty "embraces taxes on stamps, tolls for passage (etc.) and is not confined to taxes on importations only." The Constitution forbids a federal duty (Article I, Section 9) on exports, which is the only explicit limitation on taxing powers in the Constitution, even though there is an implied limitation forbidding governments from taxing each other. There's no constitutional limitation applicable to taxpayers; that's a political issue.

Imposts were also specified in the Constitution but weren't defined. The term allows the government to extend taxes to things that might not be covered by "duties." Excises would apply to commodities that were entirely within internal commerce.

These taxes also indicate – in conjunction with the power to regulate specific types of commerce – that the founders had no designs for a nation with a free-enterprise economy; they envisioned a nation of private enterprise. Failures of the controlled economies of Marxism and the economic anarchy that created the savings-and-loan debacle in the United States show the wisdom in the founders' ideas that commercial interests should not be part of the state, but should be subject to the rule of law, just as are individuals.

The final constitutional method of collecting money is through the disposal of property legally obtained by government, and this method is an implied power. Article IV, Section 3, says, "The Congress shall have Power to dispose of ... Property belonging to the United States." It's this provision that caused some Constitution lovers to be incensed over the Iran-contra scandal during the administration of Ronald Reagan. Administration officials secretly sold military equipment to Iran to raise money to fund guerrilla warfare against the Sandinista government of Nicaragua after Congress refused to subsidize the insurrection. Whether a war in Nicaragua was justified or in the United States' best interest isn't important to the constitutional issue. What's meaningful to constitutional government is that presidents, bureaucrats, military officers or agencies have no power to dispose of any government property on their own initiative. Only Congress has that power – it designates agencies or officials to do the disposing, but law had to be made to sell anything owned by the United States government.

Officials claimed authority to do as the administration wished under the president's duty to conduct foreign policy. The executive branch does have power to conduct foreign policy, but it doesn't have total power over foreign affairs. Foreign policy is reflected in the treaty-making powers (shared by the President and the Senate) and the selection of ambassadors and other officers of the United States (shared by the President and the Senate). The President has sole authority to "receive Ambassadors and other public Ministers." That's conducting foreign policy, but not legislating it.

Nowhere in the Constitution is there a suggestion that the executive branch has authority to negate Congress' power to dispose of United States property. Many people were unconcerned with the Iran-contra affair, even applauded it. Others were concerned with an administration ignoring the law. Few seemed upset that an administration would seize for itself a power specifically belonging to Congress. Taking United States property to sell without legal authority would be ordinary theft. If that was all that was at stake, the years-long investigations costing millions of dollars wouldn't seem to be worth the effort and expense. But the investigations went on because many officials thought the incident was blatant violation of Article IV, Section 3. Such a violation would be un-American subversion.

The power to raise money through legal disposal of government property was first examined *(Ashwander v. Tennessee Valley Authority)* in 1936. A dam, built as an improvement of navigation (power to regulate commerce) included electrical-generating facilities (providing for national defense), was challenged as being outside the powers of the national government. Since the dam and generating facilities were legally created, excess power could be legitimately sold, the court said, because of the power to dispose of government property. That power has been used over the years for government to engage in many activities that some critics think are outside government functions.

QUESTIONABLE PRACTICES

Government isn't a corporation and shouldn't be expected to act as a business. A corporation must eliminate uneconomical practices to remain in business for it would be foolish to continue a practice that would forever lose money and threaten profitability. But a government is often required to continue uneconomical operations because every person is entitled to equality of those services. The Postal Service couldn't ignore small and out-of-the-way communities because income from those locations wasn't adequate for profitable operations. Residents of such locales pay the same postage and are taxed according to the same formula as residents of metropolitan areas and are entitled to the same privileges and government services – profitable or not – because they have the same rights as all other Americans. Congress and state legislatures have power to tax and spend for the general welfare, not to tax and spend to make a profit.

Many people think business practices are unconstitutional, but that would depend on what practices are considered. In the famous 1819 decision *(McCulloch v. Maryland),* Chief Justice John Marshall wrote that while the Constitution didn't list a specific power to create a corporation (the federal bank), it did grant implied authority to carry out explicit powers. That doctrine, plus the powers to dispose of government property and to spend for the general welfare, led to other business practices by the federal government. These include generation of hydroelectric power, selling timber, financing mortgages, lending money for interest and marketing of leases for oil, coal and other minerals. Money obtained from these activities does not come from "Taxes, Duties, Imposts and Excises" nor does it come from the power to "borrow money on the Credit of the United States," but this income is nevertheless legally based on other constitutional provisions.

While one location may benefit from some business activity more than other areas, that wouldn't negate implied power. The Northwest, because of its rugged terrain and broad rivers, receives electricity generated by the Bonneville Power Administration at costs much lower than the rates in the rest of the nation. Those lower rates benefit an aluminum industry that requires considerable electric power for production. Aluminum production and use are beneficial for the entire nation; therefore, they're part of the general welfare. If constitutionality were so strictly interpreted that powers were restricted to those specifically named, little progress could be accomplished. Through some implied money powers, government helps industry prosper.

Government doesn't always use its implied powers wisely. Doctrinaire political interests, trying to operate government like a business, often cause results not beneficial to the general welfare. An example of that occurred during the economic boom of the 1970s and into the early 1980s when timber companies – spurred on by government forecasts – bid up prices at timber auctions to levels that weren't profitable when the economy slowed down early in the Reagan administration.

Money: The Root of All Government

The Seattle Times reported in August 1982 that, "Predicted higher demand for wood products and reduced timber supply resulted in bids on cutting rights for national-forest timber doubling, rising from $200 per thousand board feet in late 1977 to $400 in early 1980. This is the most rapid increase in the 75-year history of selling timber from the national-forest lands."

When the economy slowed and housing demand plunged, the price a timber processor could get for lumber was less than the cost of obtaining the trees. The slowdown threatened the survivability of many companies, forcing government to adopt a plan to buy back some of the uncut timber. The alternative would have been bankruptcy for many companies, which could have resulted in even more lost income for government. To compensate, the Reagan administration embarked on a program to substantially increase the amount of timber harvested; doubling or tripling, in some instances, the amount felled. When overcutting, coupled with environmental concerns, reduced the amount of timber available in the 1990s, bankruptcy closed many sawmills and thousands of workers lost their jobs. (The lumber mill for which this author toiled to finance college and which sustained three generations of his family was one closed in 1994.)

When policies backfire, as did selling national treasures, politicians seek other methods to raise money by any means other than taxes. High deficits and rising unemployment late in 1982 forced the administration to ask Congress for an increase in the gasoline tax, but political doctrine opposing taxes caused the administration to claim it was after a "user fee." The same terminology was used in 1987 when the government sought admission charges at the Statue of Liberty, Valley Forge and numerous other national monuments and attractions. The Constitution doesn't authorize government income from "user fees;" it does authorize revenue from taxes. Honesty requires such fees be called taxes, which they are, or be called unconstitutional.

Taxes don't have to be applied equally and uniformly across the nation. As shown in Chapter 10, there's no specific constitutional command for equality under federal law, and the tax-and-spend clause only requires that "all Duties, Imposts and Excises shall be uniform throughout the United States." A windfall-profits tax on oil companies was declared unconstitutional in 1982 by a federal judge in Wyoming – an oil-producing state – because it exempted newly developed oilfields north of the Arctic Circle. That tax favored operations in Alaska. The decision could have prevented all taxation of those windfall profits, but the Supreme Court unanimously overruled the Wyoming judge because this was a tax on income and that tax doesn't need to be uniform; only duties, imposts and excises do. The court ruled that such an exemption was within the prerogatives of Congress. Such an exemption presumedly promoted the general welfare by encouraging exploration for petroleum.

While using the power to tax and spend for the general welfare can bring benefits that may go unseen to most Americans, abuse of the power often occurs. Politicians at all levels of government use exemptions to benefit friends and campaign contributors, and such misuse could accelerate under term limitations as lame-duck legislators use tax exemptions for special interests as a method of securing executive positions after being forced to retire from government at an early age. That would be a classic example of using government service to serve oneself, and would probably happen more often in populous states where the opportunity to move up to higher offices would be restricted by the number of out-of-time representatives who would have few other positions to contend for.

TAXPAYERS' NONRIGHTS

Some taxpayers seem to think they are protected by "taxpayer rights," but such rights are severely limited or nonexistent. Many persons opposed to abortion and/or "obscene" art railed against government spending for these items in the 1980 and '90s, even though both were legal and spending was done under the authority of general welfare. The protesters couldn't be afforded greater taxpayer rights than allowed in the 1960 and '70s to people who didn't want their tax payments supporting the Vietnam war. Antiwar protesters received little sympathy for their concern about spending tax money on war, and their rights are identical to the rights of antiart and antiabortion protesters.

The concept of taxpayers impacting government spending is like a renter of an apartment claiming a right over money paid as rent. The rent money becomes the property of the apartment owner, who can't be compelled to spend it to satisfy renters' desires, beyond maintenance required by law. Taxpayers have no say over government's spending power other than by voting and protesting, just as renters have no say other than complaining or moving.

Arguments about taxpayer rights affecting government spending were settled in 1923 *(Frothingham V. Mellon* and *Massachusetts v. Mellon)* with the decision that tax money, once received, is the property of the government, not of the taxpayers. The Constitution says Congress has the power to spend the government's money, and may spend it under law as legislators see fit without being challenged with lawsuits and without sharing the duty with anyone else, including the president. Presidents must spend appropriated money because the Constitution doesn't give them authority to overrule Congress on spending. A president must "take care that the Laws be faithfully executed" (Article II, Section 3), and that includes appropriation laws. A president's only constitutional recourse is the veto, as specified in Article I, Section 7. That provision says the president may either accept and sign a bill he (or she) approves or, if the bill is not acceptable, it shall be returned to the chamber in which it originated without the president's signature. Any objection a president has must be registered at that time.

Doctrinaire politicians haven't accepted this clear-and-precise constitutional principle. In arguing for a line-item veto, a Republican functionary, Linda Chavez, wrote in a 1989 USA TODAY guest column: "Congress is in no danger of relinquishing all power of the purse strings by giving the president the line-item veto ... In 1974, the Congress took away the president's right to impound money he didn't want to spend."

Such statements reflect an absence of constitutional understanding. The Constitution specifies in Article I, Section 9, that all appropriations must be by law, and Section 7 says every bill becomes law when signed by the president, but when rejected the entire bill shall be returned to Congress for reconsideration. So, all spending plans begin with bills, not with orders, resolutions or votes. Congress cannot give a line-item veto to the president because it cannot change the constitutional requirement a bill must be rejected in its entirety. The Constitution gives sole power to spend to Congress, and even Congress can't relinquish "power of the purse strings"; that can only be accomplished with a constitutional amendment.

The president, also, never had a constitutional "right" to impound money; the list of presidential powers in Article II nowhere suggests such a power.

Chavez, director of public liaison in the Reagan White House and a Republican candidate for the Senate in 1986, added that, "Forty-three states have conferred line-item veto authority on their governors. What's more, the Congress itself has conferred such authority on territorial governors and on the governors of Puerto Rico, Guam and the Virgin Islands."

These were nonsensical arguments because the constitutional provisions concerning vetoes specify the president of the United States and the Congress of the United States; what various state constitutions or laws stipulate for their governments about line-item vetoes have absolutely no connection with what is specified for the federal government. Territorial rule is covered in Article IV. It says, "The Congress shall have Power to ... make all needful Rules and Regulations respecting the Territory or other Property belonging to the United States." That stipulation treats territorial governors and presidents differently – their powers aren't covered by the same constitutional principles. Congress has interpreted the Article IV provision to mean territorial governors should have powers that are similar to the powers of state governors.

Three consecutive presidents – Ronald Reagan, George Bush and Bill Clinton – called for the line-item veto, and Congress made efforts to give Clinton a form of the line-item veto after the 1994 elections, indicating it's becoming more and more apparent that discovering practicing politicians who understand the Constitution is about as difficult as finding a poet in a Cadillac store.

The only way to get around the requirement that the veto negate all items in a bill is to make each spending item a separate bill. If there were only one item in a bill, the line-item veto would not be needed.

Equality under the taxing-and-spending principle also applies to collecting taxes from individuals. It's human nature for taxpayers to try to resist taxes, and government can tap that desire by providing "loopholes" in tax laws to direct investment into desirable areas which promote the general welfare. But escaping taxation that doesn't contribute to the general welfare hasn't been allowed. The Social Security system is an example.

Many people claim Social Security is unconstitutional because they can't find a specific power to create a retirement plan enumerated in the Constitution. People who understand little about the Constitution or its implied powers assume there can be no retirement fund because one isn't mentioned. Those people are wrong for Congress has the power to tax and spend for the general welfare, that's part of the first enumerated power in Article I, Section 8. Social Security aids the general welfare by providing income to retirees whose spending provides revenue to business, which turns some of that income into additional jobs or younger workers. Encouraging an older employee to retire creates one employment vacancy for a younger worker. Providing retirees with disposable income adds more employment opportunities. One person retired under Social Security adds more than one employment opportunity in the marketplace – that's advancing the general welfare. But this social benefit is often undermined by selfish interests trying to escape taxation imposed on most of the population.

The national Republican Party has often campaigned to make Social Security voluntary, allowing people to drop out if they so desired. The Associated Press reported in 1982 that the conservative Heritage Foundation of Washington, D. C., advocated a policy "to gradually wean workers from the program and allow them to put their payroll taxes into Individual Retirement Accounts and other investments in the private sector." That policy is still being pushed. Social Security has never interfered with the ability to invest in IRAs or other investments by those who can afford independent retirement plans, but it did save many average-income workers from losing their entire retirement to the savings-and-loan debacle or other scams prevalent in American society. Many workers also need their entire income just to survive; they don't have disposable funds for investing. If Social Security payroll taxes weren't withheld, there would be no money available for investing by low-income workers, a fact lost on the privileged minority represented by the Heritage Foundation. And if low-income workers couldn't retire with some income the nation's economy would be weaker.

Many government employees across the nation did leave Social Security, and by 1983, about 227,000 public employees had pulled out before Congress banned the practice. In 1986 the Supreme Court upheld the authority of Congress to prohibit withdrawals. The decision endorsed the principle of equality between employees in the private and public sectors and supported the notion that some persons couldn't evade a general tax just because they didn't want to pay. Antiwar protesters can't voluntarily excuse themselves from tax obligations because they don't agree with a war; they are forced to pay taxes to support a war they despise just as other people pay taxes to finance a war they love. The court decision did support Congress' power to impose a tax – nobody has a special privilege of self-application concerning Congress' powers to tax. But, only Congress has the taxing power. When running for the presidency in 1992, independent candidate Ross Perot said it was up to the people whether or not to raise taxes. He was wrong.

WHEN ALL SEEMS LOST, AMEND

As often happens, when vote-seeking politicians sense an opportunity to capitalize on public dissatisfaction with something politically created, they attempt tried-and-true shenanigans – tampering with the Constitution. So it was with the 1980s-90s budgetary problems. Each political party blamed the other and presidents and Congress exchanged attacks, although these problems were jointly created. Governors waded into the fray by blaming Washington, D. C., for adverse local conditions.

The political "solution" was to advocate a "Balance Budget Amendment." Proponents viewed it as a panacea that would create total fiscal competence where little competence existed before. Opponents dismissed the idea as constitutional clutter that would accomplish nothing because many government officials often ignore the Constitution anyway, and little good would result because the same could be accomplished with existing powers. Critics of the amendment could argue that even the constitutional experts on the Supreme Court have ignored the Constitution on a few rare occasions,.

Initial efforts for the amendment involved states petitioning Congress to call for a constitutional convention under the authority of Article V which says, "Congress ... on the Application of the Legislatures of two-thirds of the several states, shall call a Convention for proposing Amendments ..." When 32 of the required 34 states had called for the convention by early 1982, government officials sensed a danger if a convention was held to alter a document few Americans understand in the first place. It was a similar special convention to amend the Articles of Confederation in 1787 which resulted in destruction of the Articles in favor of the Constitution. The men who met in convention back then understood what a Constitution was all about – many had recently helped create the state constitutions and the Articles of Confederation – and were experienced in making constitutions. The same expertise probably couldn't be found today, so a constitutional convention could be destructive. Critics said there would be no requirement that such a convention be restricted to one amendment.

Proponents of the amendment pointed out that states have balanced-budget requirements in their constitutions. But in the 1980s and early 1990s, many states had to raise taxes to comply with balanced-budget requirements because a national recession – which state taxing and spending couldn't significantly affect – had cut into state income. Governors also complained that the national government imposed expensive mandates on the states while cutting revenue sharing. Included in the mandates were the Americans With Disabilities Act, Fair Labor Standards Act, fair housing standards and efforts to insure clean air, safe drinking water, testing for hazardous materials and protection for endangered species, in addition to several social programs. States had to fund these programs and had to hire thousands of people to administer them. Many of the very people who wanted to move responsibility from the federal government to the states then bewailed the "spending sprees" that the states conducted. States also mandated to counties and cities some obligations without providing funding to pay for them.

Raising taxes to cover a shortfall is something most proponents of the amendment also opposed but that had to be done by the states and this caused many officials to lose re-election bids even though they were only captives of the system. Amendment opponents say raising taxes would

Money: The Root of All Government

occur at the federal level, taking needed consumer disposable income from the economy and encouraging off-budget gimmicks (such as the savings-and-loan rescue) which create additional interest payments without adding economic impetus.

By the summer of 1982, the Reagan administration was firmly behind the proposed amendment, but the administration wanted it to originate in Congress, not in a threatening convention. The proposed amendment passed the Senate but died in the House of Representatives in October of 1982, so Congress made a law (the Gramm-Rudman-Hollings) which was designed to control government spending. It didn't, and was replaced in 1990 by a five-year deficit-reduction law. The deficit continued to grow under that law also, so the amendment was resurrected only to die again in the House in 1992 and again in the Senate in 1994. When Republicans won control of Congress in the 1994 midterm election, the balanced-budget gimmick was back but failed in the Senate in 1995.

Federal taxing and spending are blamed for the nation's budgetary problems – particularly after the 1994 elections when most politicians tried to outdo all other politicians in cutting spending – but, like many political fiascoes, that may be a too-simplistic explanation. Money spent by government can be as beneficial to the economy as money spent by the private sector. The formula for economic health is where and how money is spent, not who does the spending. For example, if a corporation invests several million dollars in construction of an office complex, it gives contracts to local construction firms that purchase building materials from various area suppliers. The construction firms must employ workers, who use their income to purchase from local businesses. Suppliers also employ local residents who spend their earnings close to home. This activity benefits the local economy because it brings in wealth to create jobs which provide taxes for government. If government spent the same amount of money building the same complex, the results to the economy would be essentially the same.

Government has an added advantage in directing spending into areas needing an economic boost and away from areas of an overheated economy, thus promoting economic strength in one area and retarding potential inflation in the second. Government also can spend in a designated industry, boosting fortunes as desired. The American economy will benefit much more if government purchases aircraft built in the United States by Boeing than it would should the private sector spend the same amount to buy from Europe's Airbus Industrie. A government employee is paid with the same money as is a corporate employee and spending by one in local businesses has exactly the same result as spending by the other. Fewer government employees also mean less consumer spending and lower tax receipts.

Cutting government spending or reducing the government work force will have the same effect as corporate cutting and reducing – they can retard the economy and cause recession or, in extreme instances, depression. Reducing government spending could be worse because it could be felt nationwide while corporate austerities might be isolated to limited areas. For these reasons, political rhetoric against government taxing and spending is just rhetoric and does nothing to secure economic health. It amounts to "speaking Sloganese" in quest of votes from a citizenry that feels itself to be abused by taxation.

One type of spending – money paid as interest on borrowed funds – has no worthwhile economic value if the money is immediately lent again to government as soon as it's received by investors; something that happened throughout the 1980s and into the 1990s. Borrowed money also has to be repaid eventually, either with tax money or through more borrowing.

Failure of the Gramm-Rudman effort, which became law at the end of 1985 when the annual deficit was $200 billion, shows the folly of fiscal policy by rhetoric. By the end of 1991, that figure had grown to about $300 billion per annum, a $100 billion increase in the shortfall. Interest payments during the 1985-to-91 period rose from about $150 billion a year to nearly $300 billion, an increase of $150 billion. The figures reflect a $50 billion reduction in noninterest spending – in relationship to government's income – but only worsened the budgetary problems because merely "restraining" spending isn't a solution. These figures from the Congressional Budget Office, the Office of Management and Budget and USA TODAY prove that cutting $50 billion in spending didn't work, the problem is much more complex than spending less because less spending can have more-expensive consequences.

One of the amendment's sponsors, then-Rep. Larry E. Craig, R-Idaho, provided additional statistics in a 1990 USA TODAY guest column that indicated how complex the problem is. He said, "Our national debt has doubled in the last six years ... Interest on that debt alone consumes 54 cents of every tax dollar ... Since 1980, tax receipts have risen from around $500 billion to over $1 trillion, and Congress has spent $1.50 for every additional dollar in tax receipts.

Craig was wrong. Congress hadn't spend $1.50 for every $1 in increased revenues. By Craig's statistics, Congress could only be responsible for spending 46 percent of the $500 billion increase in tax receipts, a $230 billion increase during a decade in which the cost of living increased by about the same percentage. The other $270 billion went to service the

Money: The Root of All Government

debt and cannot be tied entirely to congressional spending because there was little Congress could do to lessen that cost. Debt costs did come down when interest rates fell.

Whining about higher spending is also a false concern. Much of that $230 billion rise couldn't be avoided – an increase in retirements brought on by an economic slowdown or industry forcing retirement onto employees will add to Social Security spending, just as higher unemployment caused by corporations moving manufacturing jobs overseas increases workers' compensation. Government spends billions of dollars cleaning up toxic waste because it refused in the past to regulate commerce or itself to prevent despoiling the environment. That cleanup funding grew in the late 1980s and early 1990s because it was badly needed and could no longer be delayed by politicians ignoring the problem. Out-of-control health-care costs – another area in which Congress has historically refused to act – have also contributed to increased spending. When reduced spending tends to exclude Americans having the least from the general welfare enjoyed by those having the most, it creates a need for additional spending for more police, jails, courts, welfare and other social programs.

Wealth isn't a creation of an individual; it comes from societal cooperation and is maintained through society's governmental functions. Individual fortunes or poverty are determined by who is allowed to tap into a nation's wealth and who is excluded. Historically, minorities were excluded because society wouldn't provide them with the same educations available to the favored majority and commercial enterprises wouldn't allow employment. Such exclusions are at the heart of late 20th-century social problems – especially crime – which require the taxing and spending abhorred by those best served by government.

The concern over the annual deficit is a political issue and it's about something that's really not a deficit at all. The government uses its taxing power to raise most of the money it needs. A small percentage is raised through penalties, sales of resources and energy production, in addition to admission fees at government attractions. The rest comes in through the power to borrow. These methods of raising funds bring in what is needed for spending. There are, of course, some bills that are not paid in a timely fashion. These unpaid bills and anything else done on credit are the real budget deficit – which doesn't amount to much in relationship to the total budget – and are offset by money owed to government but, at the time, uncollected. The money borrowed isn't a real deficit; it's debt. Proposed balanced-budget amendments require that the president and Congress would have to agree on estimated revenues for the coming year, a three-fifths majority would be needed in each house of Congress to approve spending exceeding revenues, and tax increases would need a majority vote of the membership of each house, not just a majority of those voting. Proposed balanced-budget amendments only play games with American taxpayers because they won't do much to secure sound financial health unless they address the borrowing power. The Reagan administration – nor congressional proponents – never tried to restrict government's power to borrow with the amendment because borrowing was used to enrich those the administration represented. Many people, who at one time were adamantly critical of deficit spending, changed their arguments in the 1980s when they saw that a government short by billions of dollars in taxes each year would have to borrow heavily and pay high interest before repaying the principal. The way to profit from this situation was to reduce taxes while raising spending on the military. When taxes were reduced for individuals who did not need the savings for consumer spending, the extra money became investment funds, just as it did for such financial concerns as banks, insurance companies, brokerage firms and mutual funds.

With less tax receipts, government had to sell Treasury bonds, notes and bills – which paid high interest – to attract money away from industrial needs where there is a risk to investments. Institutions and persons with ready cash, made available because of lower taxes, would purchase those financial instruments giving government the same money it would have raised through taxation, but now the money is providing a healthy no-risk return with continuous ownership of the money for the favored few. Investors could get double-digit returns from the Treasury without risking investment cash through the formation of business, which would have created jobs for the middle class and more taxes for government. Investors didn't have to worry about business failure and loss of investment, they got a better return immediately with no risk. The government wouldn't default on loans from its allies; it could merely print money to cover its obligation if it had to. No one ever got a safe return on money paid in taxes, but money used for no-risk investing generates fine profits. Many of the politicians who provided this no-risk investment for a privileged few were also the most-ardent supporters of the balanced-budget amendment.

In 1980 primary campaigning, Bush termed the plan to cut taxes and raise military spending "voodoo economics," but he may have not seen the full picture because there was nothing magical or supernatural about the plan. The huge national debt seems carefully planned and intended as a money-making scheme for the powerful. The budget problem only became an issue when it got out of control and the cycle – borrowing, paying interest, reborrowing that interest payment and then paying more interest on the reborrowed funds – couldn't be halted.

It's for these reasons proposed balanced-budget amendments are nothing more than political metaphors that would do zero about the huge borrowing; they only create political ammunition for one politician to shoot toward another.

Prohibiting politicians from capitalizing on the debt they impose on government would be a good start to the effort to rid the nation of its debtor status. It's not surprising that numerous politicians who instituted into law the economic theories that brought about the huge debt also spent much of the 1980s and '90s loading up on Treasury debt instruments to enhance their incomes, which in turn benefited from lower tax rates. Proposed balanced-budget amendments have never addressed this conflict of interest. And a balanced-budget amendment should be adopted only after the budgetary problems are solved and corrected; it could never solve or correct those problems.

Tax breaks are given to influential concerns on an argument of metaphors that a "rising tide" (the economy) will elevate all the boats in the water. But tax breaks for the privileged to let the savings "trickle down" didn't work because they only lightened the load on the bigger boats. After removing their "cargo," the bigger boats rose because they displaced less water and that caused the support level to fall, not rise. Some positive results can be accomplished with a tax reduction when it is used to create disposable funds to be used to purchase consumer items rather than provide investment funds intended for government borrowing. Tax increases don't harm the economy if they target funds that would normally buy Treasury instruments.

Government isn't without expert knowledge and advice. It employs some of the best-educated people in the world and has access to every university campus and institution, both public and private, for additional genius, as needed. It is incredulous to expect Americans to think budgetary problems were brought about entirely by financial miscalculations of a government having an unlimited supply of economists with Ph.D. credentials and access to million-dollar-a-year executives from prestigious investment firms. If America's universities were in the practice of recalling degrees – especially the Ph.D. (sometimes pronounced phud) – when the holder proves incompetent and should financial firms retrieve bountiful salary and bonuses paid to executives who later establish ineptness, their blunders or manipulations might be less painful to American taxpayers who must pay the bills.

The problem is not taxing. The problem is not spending. The problem is borrowing. The Founding Fathers knew very well that government must tax and spend for the common defense and for the general welfare – that's why such authorizations are the first listed in the powers of Congress. The founders also knew there would be times in which government would have to spend more than it could raise in taxes – that is why the power to borrow is second in the congressional power list. The Founding Fathers – who were the public officials and the most-privileged citizens of their time – probably never envisioned later public officials manipulating these most-important powers for self-enrichment or to provide risk-free returns to the privileged who furnished the financial support by which elected leaders obtained their positions.

The founders probably envisioned that the constitutional powers they created be used with integrity to maintain an arrangement in which everyone would pay a fair share in taxes – rather than by individuals to benefit themselves through the borrowing power – for the common defense and the general welfare because everybody's "Justice ... domestic Tranquility ... and Blessing of Liberty" depend on the co-operation of all in the constitutional covenant.

Chapter 12

OPINIONS AND OTHER BIASES

SEVERAL POINTS OF VIEW

In a modern world in which the thoughts of others are generally ignored, sharing knowledge and philosophies requires an effective method. This draws literate persons to writing. When Herman Melville wished to share his thoughts on the human condition, he wrote *Moby Dick* to demonstrate the folly of man being obsessed with revenge. Oscar Wilde's only novel, *The Picture of Dorian Gray*, ridicules vanity, just as *Brave New World* and *1984* express fear of government that knows no legal limits to its power. Mark Twain's *The Tragedy of Pudd'nhead Wilson* debunks any racist argument one could use trying to justify slavery.

Persons not inclined to the tediousness of composition may choose music or acting, but they often are captive to thoughts of the writer. Others produce documentary films for the Public Broadcasting Service or local outlets. The focus on entertainment blocks any philosophical thoughts a commercial television program may have. For example, many American's were unaware that the popular television comedy "M*A*S*H" carried an antiwar message by portraying its heroes as nonmilitary rebels and its fools as zealous war lovers. Art is too often misunderstood to be effective for expressing thought. The sad fact is that access to forums for expression are too often restricted or nonexistent for the majority of modern Americans. The desire to be heard leads thousands to demonstrate and march in protest. Others burn flags. Many of the unstable shoot.

Creating a book is most satisfying – one can express opinions and biases in a manner not available to the majority. That's why there's a Chapter 12; there must be room for those personal points of view. What seemed to be opinions in the first 11 chapters were really conclusions – real opinions follow.

Some Americans may think the United States is a paragon of freedoms and rights, that they enjoy the most liberty of any society on earth. That's just opinions of a society, for many other nations have similar freedoms and rights. Liberty may be more abundant elsewhere and life may be safer. America's ideals may be more important in their promises than in what has been delivered. Crime, poverty and other social ills attest to that. There is one hard-and-fast truth all Americans must admit – government is the only significant institution existing in this "land of the free" operating on democratic principles. Perhaps that's why government is continually under attack from special interests and antigovernment forces that use government to enrich themselves while arguing for less government for everyone else.

There is no democracy in commerce. Corporate employees have no say in the selection of their leaders. Employees have no rights of free speech, or to petition a corporation for a redress of grievances, nor to due process except what government imposes by law on the business world. Workers have no assurance their abilities or desires concerning career goals will be considered, respected or even acknowledged. Many employees are unhappy with corporate life because they're too often viewed by management as liabilities – salaries are expenses – rather than assets.

Stockholders, likewise, are afforded little democracy in the corporate structure, and often have less choice in the selection of leaders than Soviet voters had under their failed Marxist system. In the Soviet Union, voters were given the option of voting against a candidate if it was unpalatable to vote for that person. That occasionally resulted in a candidate losing an election. In much of corporate America, shareholders may vote for directorial candidates or abstain. They have no say concerning chief executive officers, presidents or others who control the corporation. There's no democratic control for those owning the corporation – owning in name, if not in reality.

There is no democracy in the press. Reporters and copy editors usually have no freedom of the press, that's reserved for those in the offices of editor and publisher. Truth is what management claims it is, and that's readily apparent in innumerable anti-Constitution and anti-Supreme Court diatribes and harangues of thinkless editorials and columns. Most reporters are conscientious and have a serious commitment to fairly and accurately report the news – within their ability to determine what is fair and accurate. Most who edit copy and write headlines try their utmost to see that everything is fair, just and accurate. Impropriety by a reporter or a copy editor is forbidden. Dismissal with no effort at rehabilitating the offending journalist is often the fate of those who invent or purposely distort news. The Washington Post returned a Pulitzer Prize in 1981 because it was won on a fraudulent story concocted for effect. The reporter who presented the story as factual was immediately terminated.

These worthy standards usually don't apply to editors and publishers who use their positions to expound contorted views. An editorial page is intended to present the management's views, but that shouldn't be taken to approve of anti-Constitution proclamations based on ignorance of the document or of court decisions. When journalists argue with the courts or government over freedom-of-the-press issues – such as the New York Times stance in Chapter 8 – they try to excuse themselves from laws applicable to everyone else by claiming to have First Amendment duties and obligations. If there were any such obligations, they would surely include knowing what the Constitution says, so that a court decision could be properly explained instead of having newspapers launch attacks on the Supreme Court for making a sound decision. Another obligation should be to actually read the decision. Journalists ought to be expected to do that and to understand what they've read. Most should be honest enough to state they have never formally studied the Constitution.

A liberal media bias in the United States doesn't exist. "Liberal media" is a catch phrase concocted by special interests and politicians to deflect attention from themselves. Conscientious reporters often uncover truths many biased concerns would like kept secret – or at least slanted to their benefit – so the attempt is made to defame the press by proclaiming a "liberal media" vendetta. Often when a person can't find a bias for a favored position, the assumption is made that there is a bias against that position. The press is used as a scapegoat to campaign against. A weakness of one's position is covered up by claiming a media bias rather than show soundness of what the attacker is supporting. The work force in America's press is undeniable Democratic, but that's true of most work forces with the obvious exception of Wall Street. The decision-making clique of the United States press is overwhelmingly Republican; it is not liberal.

USA TODAY columnist Barbara Reynolds, criticized earlier for not knowing what she was writing about regarding school prayer, correctly chastised executives of her profession for their hypocritical stances. In an April 1991 column, she wrote, "Every year, the media big shots – the American Society of Newspaper Editors – gather to scratch their beards, and crusade to reform Congress, the Pentagon and the courts ... In Boston this week, the ASNE – whose members are 2.5% minority and 10% women, including four black women – released its annual report on minorities. Fifty-one percent of newspapers still hire no minorities; about 95% of top jobs are held by whites – usually males. So news managers generally talk 'cultural diversity' but generally practice newsroom apartheid."

She knew what she was writing about this time and correctly described an industry that is bent on telling others what's proper and right but does not embrace the same principles of propriety. She could have complained that those same news managers brag of being the "engine of democracy," but practice nothing resembling democracy in their operations. Frequently they haven't the faintest idea of what constitutional democracy is all about as indicated by their incessant complaining about the Supreme Court when it applies the Constitution correctly. Unlike constitutional government, where the people are the source of authority, editors and publishers aren't chosen democratically and aren't restrained by internal law emanating from those who are subject to authoritative control. Editors and publishers are often dictatorial and despotic in their operations, and usually do not observe anything resembling a right to petition for grievances or due process.

There is no democracy in religion. No church holds elections to decide which course of belief or interpretation the group is to take. Church leaders claim to be chosen by God, a highly dubious contention considering the behavior of many men of the cloth. Followers often have no say concerning the tenets of the church and must follow the leaders' pronouncements or leave for another congregation or faith where there also is no input or freedom of speech. Members of the congregation often have no right to petition for a redress of grievances – that can be considered anti-God – and what a parishioner thinks or says may have no impact on policy of the leaders. Due process usually means nothing.

There is no democracy in education. While students are encouraged to express independent thought, they do not determine accepted truths. Students are expected to absorb what's taught because all that's known is thought to reside with educators who comprise the established body of authority. The notion is there's no knowledge beyond those qualified as "expert." This is why the legal profession hasn't found "due process of law" described in the Constitution. Law and political-science professors usually don't teach that it's in the Constitution because the Supreme Court hasn't said it's there. The court hasn't said it's in the Constitution because no attorney has argued that it's there. And no attorney has argued it's in the Constitution because law schools don't teach that it's there. Most judicial professionals do follow due process religiously, even though they can't find it described in the Constitution. Reluctance of teachers to embrace undiscovered truths is why additions to knowledge often come from students – usually after ceasing to be institutional students, but often based on concepts formulated while being subjects of the educational process.

There is no democracy in the military or police. If there are any institutions existing in the United States that exemplify the qualities of despotic autocracies so distasteful to the founders, it would be the military and police. But, these two institutions are the ones in which democratic principles would be counterproductive to their missions. They have legitimate reasons to be despotic and autocratic; the others don't.

There was a time when the United States labor movement was democratically based, but that has been undermined in recent years. Unionism has declined and become a minor institution in many areas of the nation, as service-based activities replaced the manufacturing segment of the economy. Many corporations have put some of their operations elsewhere in search of less-expensive and nonunion labor, for fewer government regulations and to escape the cost of health care and other benefits for employees. In areas where unionism hasn't lost out to economic forces, it has aided and abetted its own demise. Widespread corruption by leaders and antidemocratic dealings have combined to convince many workers that unionism wasn't needed. Government has also contributed to the decline by protecting workers' rights by law, thereby lessening a need for unionism.

There are minor groups or co-operatives operating democratically, but their contributions are so minor in the totality of the nation that they wouldn't be considered institutions.

That leaves government as the sole institution of size and influence that still is based on the principles of democracy. Perhaps that is why it is criticized and attacked the most by the aforementioned nondemocratic – in some cases, antidemocratic – social and commercial establishments.

CITIZEN INVOLVEMENT

It's thought and taught that citizen involvement is the most-important aspect of a healthy democratic republic. That contention is a tad amiss and will stay that way until citizens understand the constitutional covenant. Most citizens do little more than vote, and usually they don't know or understand much about the candidates' competence and intentions. Therefore, most elections are decided on concepts having little or nothing to do with government or with the candidates' abilities to administer public affairs competently and efficiently.

Elections are frequently won on the basis of which candidate is viewed as more "patriotic" – whether or not the candidate knows and abides by principles of the Constitution, the only valid patriotism. "Speaking Sloganese" is a favorite campaign tack and has done well for those who concoct the best slogans. Many are the candidates elected on the basis they are "God-fearing Christian family men (or women) who treasure the sanctity of the family and adhere to old-fashioned American values." Others have "met a payroll" – except when they dismiss much of that payroll during economic slumps. Pledges of no taxation are heard too often without any explanation of how government is to maintain the general welfare of society without paying for it. Pictures of candidates in flag factories or riding in military vehicles say nothing about their concern for the constitutional covenant other than it can be ignored in favor of silly manipulation.

There's no evidence that self-proclaimed patriotism was ever the basis for laws that were fair and just for all. Numerous incidents suggest just the opposite has occurred – the classic example were the injustices of the McCarthy era in which thousands of persons were defamed and denied the right to earn livings because they thought differently from a Constitution-hating senator and his un-American allies, all of whom proclaimed themselves "real Americans" and superpatriots.

Fearing God and being devout Christian does nothing to solve the budgetary problems that got out of hand during the 1980s under economic theories of a self-proclaimed God-fearing Christian president. What the sanctity of the family or old-fashioned American values have to do with solving numerous social problems is unknown. In fact, social problems are often ignored on the basis of slogans. Political leaders who have no idea of how to deal with poverty, homelessness or other problems resort to the argument that such social ills should be handled by the family. Old-fashioned values may be fine for nostalgia, but Americans live in a new-fangled world requiring new-fashioned thinking. It's no longer possible to load up the buckboard and head west when the world gets too complicated.

One area of citizen involvement gaining popularity in the latter stages of the 20th century is citizens blaming politicians for all the problems of society, whether they caused those ills or were just unable to eliminate them. Political blunders and embarrassments don't help the politicians either; they just added to the antigovernment feelings of millions of Americans. So when problems seemed to be everywhere by the end of the 1980s, the drive to limit terms of political officeholders was begun. In 1990, voters in California and Oklahoma passed referendums limiting the terms of state lawmakers. Colorado went further and put limitations on its members of Congress to take effect in 2002. Just when term-limitation momentum seemed ready to inundate the nation, voters in Washington state rejected a 1991 limitation initiative that would have applied to state government in addition to Congress. Defeat was attributed mainly to campaigning by Rep. Tom. Foley, the Democratic House speaker from Spokane, who termed the effort unconstitutional.

Other spokesmen helped advance the argument that Washington would lose all its congressional influence – particularly that held by Foley – which would be taken by much dreaded Californians. Limitation opponents said that the parched state to the south has long had its populous eyes on the

Opinions and Other Biases

abundant water sources of the Northwest, so if its politicians gain control of the House of Representatives they could legislate as they wished to pipe the water south. Whether that's true or not is immaterial; it's been Northwest folklore for decades and apparently it swayed the voters so the measure lost 54 to 46 percent.

The editorial-page editor of the Beaumont (Tex.) Enterprise addressed the limitations issue following the defeat by citing Washingtonians' fears. He added, "Other long-term lawmakers, including U.S. Rep. Jack Brooks, D-Tex – who is expected to run next year (1992) for his 20th term in the House of Representatives – say limiting terms is unconstitutional."

The editor then quoted Washington Gov. Booth Gardner as saying voters "are angry. If Congress' response is to do nothing about getting their house in order, we will have term limits back on the ballot again." They were.

It didn't matter that term limitations were on the ballot and the long-term lawmakers were wrong – term limits of members of Congress are not unconstitutional. They may be unwise, unproductive, unlikely and "unpossible." They are not unconstitutional. What was unconstitutional was the method by which term limits were to be obtained. Constitution lovers point quickly to the first line of the Constitution's Article I. It says, "All legislative Powers herein granted shall be vested in a Congress of the United States, which shall consist of a Senate and House of Representatives." That puts all federal lawmaking power in Congress, and nowhere else. The Colorado and Washington referendums, and numerous others that soon followed, were attempts to make law by the citizen-initiative process, which isn't allowed because Article I, Section 7, indicates making law is a legislative power granted to Congress by the Constitution. Article I, Section 8, adds that Congress has power "To make all Laws necessary and proper for carrying into Execution the foregoing Powers, and all other Powers vested by this Constitution in the Government of the United States, or in any Department or Officer thereof." Emphasis should be on "all Laws." Congress is a "Department" of the government and an elected member is an "Officer thereof." One of the "Powers vested by this Constitution" is found in Article I, Section 5, which stipulates "Each House shall be the Judge of ... Qualifications of its own Members ..."

That power to judge qualifications pertains to the idea an electee was to be scrutinized to determine if he or she is eligible for office under the qualifications in the Constitution. Such a judgment can be made only by the Senate regarding senators and by the House for representatives. A citizen initiative can't do it. Colorado's limitations and those later adopted in 22 other states, including Washington on a second attempt, were never destined to be applied. Whether limitation referendums for state officeholders are legal depends on what the state constitutions say; the federal Constitution says nothing on citizen-initiative matters for the states.

The Constitution places some qualifications and limits on members of Congress. It establishes the duration of terms at six years for senators and two years for representatives (Article I) as well as fixing age and residency requirements. It specifies the end of terms to be January 3 (Twentieth Amendment). It also requires that Congress meet at least once every year beginning at noon January 3. The Fourteenth Amendment's Section 3 nullifies the right to be elected to Congress for persons who engaged in insurrection or rebellion against the United States while being an official of the nation or of a state. Any other nullification would also have to be through the Constitution, not referendum.

The modern Congress isn't the same body that existed under the Articles of Confederation. The Constitution created a new Congress just as it created a new government, and all qualifications and duties of elected government officials came into existence through the Constitution. Only a constitutional amendment can alter qualifications on senators and representatives, just as only an amendment can alter the qualifications for a president or for Supreme Court judges. Because amendments must be approved by Congress before being submitted to the states for ratification, the prospects of that occurring are virtually impossible, as proven in 1995 when such an amendment was proposed. It's also unlikely Congress could use the powers of Article I, Section 5 to nullify rights of anyone seeking congressional office.

It should be clear that what was created by the Constitution can only be altered through the Constitution. A term-limitation initiative in order to "return government to the people" is only a gimmick based on sloganeering – it isn't constitutional.

To get around these constitutional stumbling blocks, term-limit proponents attempted to make state laws denying access to the ballot for any veteran officeholder who had served the allotted time. States can't regulate the national government so these laws would have to apply to "persons," and, as shown in Chapter 10, the Fourteenth Amendment prohibits any state law that treats any person differently from the treatment afforded any other person. The length of time someone has served in Congress doesn't negate the designation as a person, so the state term-limitation laws aimed at Congress must be invalid on the grounds they offered unequal treatment.

After the failure of the proposed term-limitation amendment, talk begun in Congress to enact a law to allow the states to limit terms of Congress.

Opinions and Other Biases

Opinion on that is that such a move would be unconstitutional because a mere law from Congress can't negate the superiority of the federal government, as specified in Article VI. Members of Congress should know that.

There may be another reason Colorado voters were the first to fall for an unconstitutional ploy while it took two tries to barely con Washingtonians away from constitutional principles. It could be in the social genes. Colorado, after all, was settled by a pack of pioneer pansies who wimped off the Oregon Trail at the first sign of high ground. Washington grew from a flock of feisty frontier folk who endured the trials and tribulations of traversing what's now Wyoming and Idaho to reach the paradise on the northwest corner of the nation, but who didn't have karmas mellow enough for eligibility to be real Oregonians.

Teasing Coloradans – and Washingtonians – is fine sport; much more pleasant than leading them astray with anticonstitutional deceptions that will only increase frustrations when blatantly unconstitutional referendums are voided in the courts. Some of the frustrations could be eased if only Americans would learn something about American constitutionalism and free themselves from being deceived with slogans and chicanery. A wise nation probably would assess the impacts term limits have had on states before saddling the national government with untried concepts.

DEFENDING THE ACLU

Dislike, distrust or simply an inability to understand the Constitution lead its foes to bizarre conclusions. It isn't popular to publicly attack the Constitution over its principles of limited government and freedom, so other convenient targets must be found and portrayed as threats to "traditional values" and the "principles upon which this nation was founded." In that way, an assault on the Constitution doesn't appear to be un-American.

A convenient scapegoat – in addition to the Supreme Court – is the American Civil Liberties Union (ACLU), and with any attempt to create a scapegoat, distortions are used. As the nation drifted into a political mindset that felt government interference in any area of individual life was permissible – except in the lives of those exercising public power or represented by the power brokers – the ACLU, like the press, served as a target to rail against, but it wasn't just the ACLU attacked; the Constitution was indirectly targeted. So, defense of the ACLU is also defense of the United States Constitution.

Attackers of the ACLU often share a common concern – they endorse government power. Some hold government power directly, others want gov-

THE UN-AMERICANS

ernment power exercised for their benefit. No attackers admit as much in plain language; all hide their positions in anti-ACLU attacks. A favored tactic is to attribute qualities to the attacked group that aren't true. Early in the Reagan administration, advisor and later Attorney General Edwin Meese labeled the ACLU and other similar organizations as "a criminal's lobby" for representing defendants in a few trials having constitutional questions.

The Constitution clearly says that government has no power to deprive a person – criminal or noncriminal – of life, liberty or property without due process of law, and that, as has been shown, requires that all persons must be defended in court whether guilty or innocent. Defending in criminal cases doesn't make defenders "a criminal's lobby," it makes them a "constitutional lobby." But, Meese's criticism was ludicrous because the ACLU seldom takes common criminal cases. It doesn't represent defendants in trials having no constitutional issues; public defenders do that.

Another endorser of unlimited government power – except when it comes to him and those approved by him – was newspaper columnist and television commentator Patrick Buchanan. He composed an anti-ACLU diatribe in 1978 that accused the organization of distorting the Bill of Rights through various court cases. And, like Meese, he totally missed the point with his criticism. Buchanan wrote, "In court civil libertarians have defended the raunchiness of Playboy and the depravity of Hustler and 'Deep Throat' (referring to two magazines and a movie) ... The ACLU had best decide where it draws the line on where freedom ends and intolerable license begins."

Buchanan's attack had nothing to do with the true issue of ACLU actions, and in order to make the attack, he totally ignored reality. The issue wasn't about freedom versus license, and it wasn't about defending raunchiness and depravity. The issue, like all constitutional issues, was whether government has constitutional power to do as it wanted. Buchanan added, "Unless and until the ACLU recognizes there are rational limits upon the freedoms found in the Bill of Rights, it faces a future of ostracism and impotence." Members of the ACLU obviously know there are limits to Bill of Rights freedoms, but they disagree with Buchanan on what those limits are. To the ACLU, limits are placed on constitutional powers, and rights can be restricted only with those powers granted by the people through the Constitution. Dislike by Buchanan or anyone else of racy magazines or sexploitive movies isn't a valid grant of an all-inclusive government power. Portraying the ACLU as an evil organization because it's one of a very few groups in the nation trying to restrict government to its legitimate powers is a sign of an autocratic mind.

Opinions and Other Biases

In an anti-ACLU editorial of December 1978, The Denver Post wrote, "It usually happens about this time of year. Some Grinch-like chapter of the ACLU will clump into courtroom and demand that Christmas be removed from the schools on the theory that the slightest recognition of America's religious heritage is unconstitutional."

That statement is pure fiction regarding both the concerns of the ACLU and America's religious heritage. The ACLU doesn't take a position on Christmas; it's concern is use of government power. As shown in Chapter 9, "no law respecting an establishment of religion" means there's no power to make a law concerning the institution of religion or what that institution has established. Christmas is an establishment (of religion), so government is forbidden to make laws pertaining to it. Santa Claus and candy canes, colorful lights and sleigh bells aren't religious establishments, so civil-rights advocates rarely question them.

The newspaper's reference to America's religious heritage was particularly silly. Many people attribute the founding of America to a band of religious Puritans from England who came to the Western Hemisphere on the Mayflower in 1620. The Pilgrims are also given credit for beginning the semireligious holiday of Thanksgiving. But knowledge of the Puritans shows the ignorance of those citing "America's religious heritage" as a defense of government involvement in religion. This particular corps of Christians refused to celebrate Christmas and banned the practice in areas where it held public power. Puritans forbid the observance of a holiday they considered an evolution from pagan revelries and feasts predating Christ by centuries. Those ancient pagan customs were only in the Northern Hemisphere and were part of the winter solstice celebrations honoring the rebirth of the sun, not the birth of the Son. The pagans thought their celebrating stopped the descent of the sun in the winter sky and caused it to reverse its course.

Throughout the 17th century, the Puritans tried to have Christmas eliminated in all of Scotland, England and New England because of its pagan roots. Acceptance of Christmas in England was one of the reasons they left for the New World. Many religious colonists in the 18th century were nondenominational deists – like Abraham, Isaac and Jacob – in a time when there was little money to be had by sectarian evangelizing. That nondenominationalism often didn't include Christmas. America's heritage contained no government references to religious matters until the Civil War era, four score and seven years after the break from Great Britain. Promoting religion was never part of the national heritage, and the Fourteenth Amendment says it's not to be part of the states' heritages either.

331

THE UN-AMERICANS

The newspaper, knowing nothing of "America's religious heritage," added, "The plain truth is that the U. S. Constitution never forbade religious expression; it only insured its diversity." That, also, is nonsense. The Constitution forbade laws made under powers that don't exit, and it says that government has no power over religion; the Constitution says nothing about insuring religious diversity. Diversity is assured by keeping government completely out of religion. The Constitution says no religious laws, neither incorporating religion into governmental functions as education, nor interfering with it in the individual's domain. The ACLU "Grinches" understand that; constitutional illiterates on newspapers apparently don't.

Using religion as an anti-ACLU club by which to beat on the Constitution invariably brings religionists to the battle. Many television evangelists constantly attack the ACLU for its efforts to keep government out of religion and also assail the public school system for not incorporating religion by claiming that teaching such nonreligious subjects as reading, composition, English, math, science, social studies and history is teaching antireligion. Some claim removing government activity from religion deprives them of their right to exercise religion freely. These attacks usually are conducted in conjunction with pleas that money is needed to fight for the right of free religious practice, but that isn't true. The truth is the ACLU's efforts are to keep government out of religion; to keep religious practice firmly the prerogative of the individual. So, when religionists raise money to oppose the ACLU, they support government intrusion into religion. In short, they oppose freedom of religion and want state involvement in an area which the Constitution expressly forbids government activity – religion. That makes many television preachers un-Americans.

Religionists aren't the only ones who seek to raise money under the argument that keeping government out of religion is undesirable. Politician Gary Bauer, a White House domestic-policy adviser in the Reagan administration, misrepresented court decisions days before Christmas 1994 in an ad in USA TODAY soliciting funds for his Family Research Council's "fight for religious freedom." Bauer's ad said, "Before the Supreme Court began its assault on religious freedom in 1962, Americans enjoyed the Christmas season without fear of landing in court ... We were free to express religious ideas. *But today there is a stifling attitude toward religion, stemming directly from the Court's hostility toward its free exercise.*" Those claims are false. As proven in Chapter 9, the Supreme Court was defending religious freedom in 1962 when it kicked government out of religion, nobody has ever landed in court over religion except government officials, ordering government out of religion made everyone free to express religious ideas, and

Opinions and Other Biases

the court's hostility was toward government in religion, not the free exercise of religion.

One religionist who apparently thinks an absence of government in religion denies religious freedom is Dr. Tim LaHaye, who bills himself as an author, minister and lecturer. In an anti-ACLU publication in the late 1980s, LaHaye wrote, "It is clear that in the next decade, the ACLU and other secularizers of our society will launch the greatest attack on religious freedom, Christianity, traditional moral values, and parental rights in American history. If we sit idly back, they will use the courts against us, as well as our families and our churches, and strip from us the freedoms our founding fathers tried to guarantee us in the U.S. Constitution."

The attack was most comical because the greatest secularizers society has ever known were the men who wrote the Constitution and the Bill of Rights. They secularized government by forbidding religious tests for office holders (Article VI) after purposely leaving out any power over religious matters. The Constitution was secularized further with the First Amendment, which forbids any law relating to religion, and the Fourteenth Amendment, which imposes the same conditions on the states. The "freedoms our founding fathers tried to guarantee us in the U. S. Constitution" are secured by denying government power to dabble in religion. Keeping government out of religion is exactly what the ACLU is trying to accomplish. Keeping government out of religion is precisely what the founders tried to guarantee. Christianity and traditional moral values require truth, and if a person doesn't know the truth, there is an obligation to seek it and keep quiet until it's found. LaHaye hadn't come close to finding truth and may not have tried.

In another anti-ACLU diatribe in 1988, Buchanan wrote, "Traditionally in America, orphanages, adoption agencies, halfway houses, centers for abandoned women, missions for the rehabilitation of drunks and derelicts, were run by religious organizations, from the Methodists and Catholics to the Salvation Army and Chuck Colson's Prison Fellowship. Behind these institutions lay the idea that true 'reform' of the individual, i. e., a man's or woman's 'conversion' from a life of dissolution, must precede his or her becoming a good citizen, and only through such conversions, which are religious in character, can society be transformed. According to ACLU gospel, however, what was traditional in the l9th century is unconstitutional and unAmerican (sic) in the late 20th."

That's more nonsense. Time or activities of private organizations have nothing to do with ACLU efforts, they concern government power. What's done by a church or other religious institution isn't germane to what government does, and if pietistic organizations accomplish their objectives best by religious conversion that's fine because that's their function. Making religious converts isn't a function of the state. Government isn't a church and is devoid of any power to function like a church or to exercise churchly authority. Civil-rights groups never question religiosity of private organizations or how they use doctrine in their work. Civil-rights groups question government attempts at religiosity; they are not concerned with activities of nongovernmental religious organizations.

It's also nonsense to think religion is the only way to become a good citizen. Anticonstitutionalists try any argument and target any scapegoat attempting to get around the constitutional prohibition of a government-religion marriage.

Even people who support the work of the ACLU slightly miss the point at times. Washington Post columnist David Broder wrote a favorable piece in 1981 in which he said: "The ACLU has taken on the mission of protecting in courts and in legislative halls the civil rights and civil liberties of many unpopular people. That guarantees that it will be abused. People support the ACLU only if they think as I do that the Bill of Rights is important enough to defend even in unpopular circumstances."

The focus of ACLU activity shouldn't be considered to be "protecting ... the civil rights and civil liberties of many unpopular people," it should be to prevent unconstitutional governmental intrusion into areas where the state has no power or where the Constitution forbids intrusion. Civil rights and liberties are best protected by government being restricted, as the creators of the Bill of Rights intended, and allowing government to use only the powers in the Constitution, as its founders intended. Preventing government from going too far is protecting Americans' most-precious right, the right to legally resist government – a right never enjoyed in the Marxist Soviet Union or the Nazi Third Reich of Germany or in any other despotic land. By arguing that rights and liberties of unpopular people are protected, civil-libertarians weaken their position, The argument should be that ACLU action is to resist government and force it to obey the law. Most Americans don't care about the rights of unpopular people.

That was illustrated by the 1988 presidential campaigning of George Bush, who attacked his opponent, Michael Dukakis, for his ACLU association. The Bush campaign used such statements as the ACLU did not share "Texas values" or had a "far-out, left-field ideology" or was "out of touch with the American mainstream." Those campaign statements, if true, painted a disturbing picture of America for they suggested "Texas values" weren't close to America's constitutional values of keeping government within legal boundaries. Bush's rhetoric implied obeying the Constitution is a "far-out, left-field" concept, and conveyed the idea that mainstream America is out of touch with constitutional principles. Judging by what Americans hear from political leaders, read in newspaper editorials and columns and from what's preached to them from the pulpit, the conclusion Americans are out of touch with the Constitution and its democratic principles is probably correct.

The ACLU was criticized during the campaign for several stands: one being its opposition to the slogan "In God We Trust" on currency and the other being tax exemptions for churches and other religious organizations. The head of the ACLU said the organization favored removing "God" from money, but it's such an unimportant issue that the group has never contested it. The tax-exemption issue is probably a valid concern because any law giving exemptions to a religious entity just for being religious would require a "law respecting an establishment (institution) of religion." But, as explained in Chapter 9, exemptions can be granted to institutions participating in promotion of the general welfare of society. That includes religious enterprises because to exclude them would also require law "respecting ... religion."

A lawsuit contesting "In God We Trust" on currency or "one nation, under God" in the Pledge of Allegiance wouldn't succeed. (The Supreme Court declined in 1993 to hear a challenge to reciting the Pledge of Allegiance because of its reference to "one nation under God.") The First Amendment right to petition the government for a redress of grievances has long been held to mean someone must be damaged in some way or threatened to be damaged in order to have a grievance. There's no way anyone can be damaged by a slogan on a coin, and the Pledge of Allegiance controversy was settled in 1943 (*West Virginia School Board v. Barnette*, Chapter 7). The issue also involves slogans or mottos, not establishments (of religion). Because of attacks on civil-rights groups, attempts to keep legal limitations on government has become less popular in much of America. But unrestrained government is an evil that constitutionalists will continue to pursue regardless of opposition by self-interests that want to use government to promote their biased concerns.

Opinion says that the American Civil Liberties Union and other civil-rights groups that battle against illegal government action are not "a criminal's lobby," as Meese proclaimed, but politicians, journalists and religionists who distort the work and positions of the ACLU and other civil-rights groups as a method of attacking constitutionalism could well comprise "an un-Americans' lobby."

BAD DECISIONS

Critics of the Supreme Court often dredge up old issues that they think were court mistakes in an attempt to degrade the judiciary or to exalt themselves and their opinions and other biases. The usual anticourt weapon is the infamous Dred Scott decision of 1857. And when wielding this weapon, critics attribute conclusions to the court that were never reached, statements that were never said and a point of law that was never established.

A reporter of the Los Angeles Times-Washington Post News Service wrote in 1981 that, "In 1857, in one of the bleaker moments in its history, the Supreme Court ruled that black slaves and the descendants of slaves were not entitled to the legal protection of the U. S. Constitution." In 1988, TV Guide profiled a Public Broadcasting Service program, *This Honorable Court,* with the statement, " 'the Supreme Court's most disastrous decision,' in the Dred Scott case, upheld the peculiar institution of slavery." In another PBS program, *Visions of the Constitution,* in 1989, a law-school professor said the decision held that blacks were "nonpeople."

All these statements are untrue, although the first is only slightly false. The other two are totally false because the issue before the court was never slavery, whether it was good, bad or evil or if it was acceptable or unjustified. The case never addressed the issue of morality or immorality of slavery. The last statement about blacks being ruled as "nonpeople" was untrue because that simply wasn't said in the decision. The issue was one whether the Constitution gave Congress authority to pass a law known as the Missouri Compromise. The decision never pretended to address those other questions.

From the beginning of constitutional government, abolitionists worked to end slavery in all American states while Southern states were just as determined to retain it. As the nation grew, new states joined as slave or free states causing both sides to be uneasy. Northern abolitionists felt that if too many slave states were in the union it would be impossible to eliminate slavery. Southerners were afraid abolitionist states could outnumber the South, and slavery, which they viewed as vital to their economies, would be outlawed. So Congress compromised on the two positions and passed the 1820 law specifying Maine could be admitted in 1820 as a free state, Missouri as a slave state in 1821 and slavery would be thereafter forbidden in the Louisiana Purchase territory north of 36 degrees 30 minutes latitude, an extension of the border between Missouri and Arkansas.

Scott, a slave of an Army surgeon was taken into the free state of Illinois then into the portion of the Louisiana Purchase where slavery was forbidden. He was then taken back to Missouri where he sued, claiming that residency in a free territory conferred freedom upon him.

The Supreme Court agreed with lower courts that the Missouri Compromise did nothing of the sort and Congress wasn't authorized to pass such legislation. Chief Justice Roger Taney's decision said the Missouri Compromise would dictate citizenship qualifications on residents of all future states and the Constitution didn't give Congress power to do that. The point of law in the Dred Scott decision never endorsed slavery or quality of humanness, it considered only congressional powers under the Constitution.

Taney said in the decision, that blacks weren't included under the word "citizens" in Article IV, Section 2, so they couldn't claim the privileges-and-immunities guarantee imposed on the states by that article. That provision says, "The Citizens of each State shall be entitled to all Privileges and Immunities of Citizens in the several States." Slaves weren't "citizens" because the Constitution gave Congress power in Article I, Section 8, "To establish an uniform Rule of Naturalization," but said nothing about native-born persons; that was left to the states and slave states had decided blacks weren't citizens. Congress couldn't overrule those states without proper authority, the decision said.

On this matter, Taney wrote, "The only two (constitutional) provisions which point to (blacks) treat them as property, and make it the duty of the (national) Government to protect it... The Government of the United States had no right to interfere for any other purpose but that of protecting the rights of the owner, leaving it altogether with the several States to deal with this race, whether emancipated or not, as each State may think justice, humanity, and the interests and safety of society, requires." He added the court couldn't impose a more-liberal interpretation to words of the Constitution "than they were intended to bear when the instrument was framed and adopted ... If any of its provisions are deemed unjust, there is a mode prescribed in the instrument itself by which it may be amended."

The two provision of the Constitution to which Taney referred say (Article I, Section 9), "The Migration or Importation of such Persons as any of the States now existing shall think proper to admit, shall not be prohibited by the Congress prior to the Year one thousand eight hundred and eight, but a tax or duty may be imposed on such Importation, not exceeding ten dollars for each Person." Article VI, Section 2, says, "No Person held to Service or Labor in one State, under Laws thereof, escaping into another, shall in Consequence of any Law or Regulation therein, be discharged from such Service or Labor, but shall be delivered up on Claim of the Party to whom such Service or Labor may be due." These two statements use "persons," and that distinguishes them from the privileges-and-immunities clause that uses "citizens."

Because these were constitutional provisions, any alteration of them had to be by amendment, Taney said, regardless of how moralistic any congressional legislation might be. The chief justice said the legal standings blacks as noncitizens held were determined by what political officials holding power of government decided. Taney wrote, "It is not the province of the court to decide upon the justice or unjustice, the policy or impolicy of these laws. The decision of that question belonged to the political or law-making power; to those who formed the sovereignty and framed the Constitution. The duty of the court is, to interpret the instrument they have framed, with the best lights we can obtain on the subject, and to administer it as we find it, according to its true intent and meaning when it was adopted ..."

On all his points, Taney was technically correct, which makes the decision the greatest monument in American history to the doctrines of "original intent" and "states' rights"; two concepts that refuse to go away no matter how misguided or incorrect they may be. The ruling also incorporated the concept that judges should defer to political bodies.

The charge that the court said blacks are "nonpeople" is not found in Taney's opinion. He wrote blacks "were at that time (creation of the Constitution) considered as a subordinate and inferior class of beings" and "had for more than a century before been regarded as beings of an inferior order ..." While such statements lack the sensitivity and wisdom of modern Americans, nothing in the decision said the Supreme Court felt them, or accepted them, to be true. The words of the decision said those were prevailing perceptions at the time the document governing the nation was created. The court only said that those perceptions had to remain until being changed in the Constitution, and by amending that document, former slaves and their descendants would have "legal protection of the U. S. Constitution." The decision said the federal government wasn't empowered to eliminate this one particular evil some states had imposed; it never endorsed that evil.

The Dred Scott decision was important to the civil-rights gains of the 1960s and '70s because it forced America to focus on the rights of all and on citizenship concerns. It created the Thirteenth, Fourteenth and Fifteenth Amendments, which are at the heart of civil rights. The Fourteenth also protects the civil rights of whites from state subversion. The Dred Scott decision did not cause the Civil War; it would have happened regardless of the decision.

There were two decisions that should surpass the Dred Scott decision as the Supreme Court's "most-disastrous." The 1896 *Plessy v. Ferguson* decision allowed states to inflict evils on some of their citizens or other residents while the 1944 *Korematsu v. United States* decision approved of the federal government imposing an evil. Both should be viewed in a more-critical light than the Dred Scott decision.

In the Korematsu case, the court ruled a presidential order during World War II was enough to incarcerate 120,000 West Coast residents of Japanese descent without concern for loyalty, rights or the constitutional requirement that due process must be used in order to legally deprive a person of liberty. Many persons were also deprived of property because of the confinement. The decision drew its focus from the 1919 case in which Oliver Wendell Holmes said government can do during war what would be unconstitutional in peacetime. The Korematsu decision has never been overruled by a court decision or amendment, but it was repudiated in the late 1980s by congressional apology and promises of a small financial restitution.

The Plessy decision by the court approved the falsely named "separate-but-equal" doctrine. A Louisiana statute of 1890 required railroad companies to provide "equal but separate" accommodations for whites and "colored people" within the state. The law empowered railroad officials to enforce the law and provided punishment for those not obeying segregation orders. When it came before the court, the law was allowed on the rationale that the Fourteenth Amendment's requirement of equality of the laws was intended "to enforce the absolute equality of the two races before the law" (apparently in legal proceedings such as trials) but "could not have been intended to abolish distinctions based upon color, or to enforce social, as distinguished from political equality, or a commingling of the two races upon terms unsatisfactory to either."

The court did say laws needed to be reasonable – not made merely to annoy or harass – and reasonableness could be determined by "reference to the established usages, customs and traditions of the people." Commingling of races was left to social factors and individual desires, the decision said. The court added that racial separation by law doesn't "imply the inferiority of either race" and if such was perceived, it was made by one race or the other, not the law. Separate public schools for whites and blacks in much of the nation including Washington, D. C., and Boston were cited as justification for separate facilities. But those schools were established before the Fourteenth Amendment imposed equal protection of the laws on the states – a fact the court overlooked – and when public schools were so rudimentary they barely existed.

The judges' reasoning sounds good, but the case involved law, not social factors or individual desires, and that law was designed to prevent commingling of the races. By forcing racial segregation, the law denied the individual desires the court said were protected. The only justification that could be made for the decision was that men in 1896 couldn't foresee the psychological evils their ruling would cause. Those evils were understood by 1954 when Plessy was overruled by the *Brown v. Board of Education* decision – an indication that changing social perceptions can alter constitutional meanings and interpretations. The court couldn't anticipate how one ruling concerning public railroad transportation could be used as justification to deprive minority groups of Americans of rights concerning fairness and equality in education, employment, suffrage and political representation, patronage of businesses, use of public facilities and in some instances, of life itself.

The Plessy decision also introduced a concept that strongly persists today and marked a radical change in how politically active people view government. In the nation's first century, the Supreme Court would consider a constitutional power of government and decide accordingly. If there was no power detectable in the Constitution, law or government action was negated and that was the end of the controversy. Plessy was the first major instance in which the court looked only for a constitutional prohibition, and when it could find nothing prohibiting separation of the races, it allowed segregation law to stand even though there was no power to segregate to be found. That marked the first court acceptance of a nonexistent universal power allowing government to do what it wished unless prohibited.

Plessy originated the "strict constructionist" concept held by many politicians who still pretend to find powers authorizing government to impose religion in schools, nationalism rituals, crime by government, and that would allow regulation of political thought or protest, reproductive rights, homosexual love, the arts and entertainment, the press and personal relationships such as prohibiting by law interracial marriages. Strict constructionists replaced "stringent restrictionists" of the first century – Justice Holmes called them "loose constructionists." Restrictionists made a strong reappearance – most noticeably in the Warren Court – to negate use of nonexistent powers in areas of government religion, protest, forced segregation and other inequities, interracial marriage, procreation, nationalism rituals, unpopular political beliefs and some crime by government. Most modern judges seem to retain a strong restrictionist sense of constitutionalism, even though the politicians who select them seek strict constructionists.

Many judges join the Supreme Court as so-called strict constructionists but tend to drift toward a restrictionist philosophy as they become experienced in constitutionalism – judges usually don't determine constitutionality in the lowest courts and follow precedent at higher levels. The Constitution seems to repudiate strict constructionists who would allow a universal power to do anything except what is forbidden. Article I, Section 8, says Congress has power "To make all Laws which shall be necessary and proper for carrying into Execution the foregoing Powers, and all other Powers vested by this Constitution in the Government of the United States, or in any Department or Officer thereof." It's clear by that statement that government can use only "the foregoing Powers" (those in Article I, Section 8, preceding this provision) and "all other Powers" (found or implied in other parts of the Constitution). There are no constitutional powers covering issues listed in the preceding paragraphs.

The Tenth Amendment adds to the repudiation of a universal power by stating that powers are delegated to government by the Constitution, and logic concludes those powers must be detectable in the document. Chief Justice John Marshall – who was an ancillary Founding Father of the Constitution as an important member of the Virginia ratifying convention – said in the famous McCulloch case that government "can exercise only powers granted to it" and "that principle is now universally admitted." If America had real conservatives of the classical nature, they would admit those constitutional statements and court observations and would reject the universal-power approach of strict constructionism that many political conservatives try to use to control the many individual activities mentioned on the previous page.

Strict constructionism seems to be a subversion of Marshall's concept of stringent restrictionism, which that was so prevalent early in the nation's life that no one argued about it. There are three steps to determine the proper constitutionality of any law or action:

– Government must have been given a power through the Constitution by the real creators of the Constitution – the American people. There are many references in the document suggesting a grant of power is absolutely necessary and no references suggesting government can do anything except those things which are forbidden.

– All laws made (or actions taken) must be "necessary and proper." That's been said so many times in so many decisions that it shouldn't be unknown to anyone, especially the politically active. "Necessary" means there must be compelling reasons to make law; a "substantive evil" government has power to prevent, as Justice Holmes explained it. Laws that serve no useful purpose or address no particular evil wouldn't be allowed. The Supreme Court negates laws often because they are so vague there's no way to tell if they're necessary and that vagueness can be used by vindictive government officials to harass people – whether individuals or classes – who are disliked. Many people complain of "too many regulations" on business, but this provision would eliminate unnecessary regulations, if used in court. Proper means laws must be "made in Pursuance" of the Constitution, which conveys the requirement they are to do as the Preamble suggests: "establish Justice, insure domestic Tranquility, provide for the common defence, promote the general Welfare, and secure the Blessing of Liberty to ourselves and our Posterity ..." Laws made for the express purpose of serving oneself or achieving selfish gain for the lawmakers or their allies don't meet these constitutional objectives.

– Laws or government actions may not infringe on privileges and immunities of the individual. This third step is where protection of "constitutional rights" is considered. Judges who would defer to political bodies and protect only rights named in the Constitution without first deciding the first two steps are shortchanging all Americans because that would leave room for a universal government power and for harassing laws and actions. Protecting rights is to be the third consideration of a judge and court, not the only consideration. Protecting only rights found in the Constitution would be nearly impossible because of the Ninth Amendment's reference to other (constitutional) rights "retained by the people." Those retained rights can't be identified by name or title but they exist as surely as those named, and must be protected just as vigorously. That can be done only through the three steps of determining constitutionality. Deferring to political bodies is never done until these three steps are taken and the laws or actions under dispute are judged acceptable.

Motives of legislatures aren't included in these provisions, and nowhere does the Constitution claim that motivation of any legislation is to be considered; any motive is acceptable as long as it uses appropriate power, a law or action is necessary and proper, and doesn't infringe on privileges and immunities. That's why Congress – and state legislatures – can protect individual civil rights by regulating business under the commerce clause or influence actions under the power to tax and spend for the general welfare.

FIXING THE CONSTITUTION

Efforts to change the Constitution began before the document became the guiding law of the new democratic republic. Since the first 12 proposed amendments were introduced shortly after the first Congress began operating in 1789, several thousand other amendments have been proposed, suggested, debated, acted on and tried. The first dozen – 10 of which became the Bill of

Opinions and Other Biases

Rights – were the result of popular demand raised during the ratifying process because many people felt a bill of rights was needed. Many of the unsuccessful thousands of proposals were to promote special or biased interests.

The number of proposed constitutional changes may be impossible to determine; most didn't get very far, and those people who report on such matters don't come close to agreeing on a figure. In 1987, a Boston Globe writer reported, "In two centuries, 2,000 amendments have been proposed to Congress." USA TODAY contradicted that figure in a 1989 editorial, saying, "Amending the Constitution isn't easy. It shouldn't be easy. Of 10,000 changes proposed, only 26, including the Bill of Rights, have been approved." Conservative newspaper columnist James Kilpatrick was capable of finding specific figures for a 1981 column warning of the folly of tinkering with the Constitution. He wrote, "Between 1789 and 1968, when a cumulative count was made, 6,940 resolutions of constitutional amendment were introduced in Congress. Since 1968, there probably have been 2,000 more." Hundreds more – including flag burning, school prayer, balanced budgets – were proposed since then and failed to pass the congressional requirement of two-thirds favorable majority; federal equal rights and statehood for the District of Columbia passed the congressional test but died because they weren't accepted by three fourths of the states. USA TODAY upped the count in 1995 to 10,679 before the failure of the term-limits effort.

The exact number of proposals isn't important; the focus of proposed amendments is. Proposals have been made to lengthen Senate and House terms, abolish the Electoral College for presidential selections, place terms on Supreme Court judges and reduce rights of persons accused of crimes (the falsely accused as well as the guilty), an ever-popular proposal. Add to them proposals allowing members of Congress to hold Cabinet positions – now forbidden by Article I, Section 6 – and set congressional elections only in presidential election years. Some people suggest extending free speech to commercial endeavors – which could negate laws on fraud and false advertising – or including an economic bill of rights, whatever that might turn out to be. An oft-mentioned amendment to outlaw abortion may be too tricky to try – logic says only women could create that measure because only women have procreation rights to be given up to government. Whether a women-only amendment would be valid is unknown.

One of the newer proposals is for an "environmental quality" amendment. USA TODAY quoted a spokesman for the environmental movement as saying in 1990: "We've reached a point where we don't have enough of a guarantee to save our environment. We need a constitutional guarantee. Environmental quality is a basic right for every individual." Environmentalists reportedly had several thousand signatures on petitions calling for an amendment that would say, "Each person has a right to clean air, pure water, productive soils and to the conservation of the natural, scenic, historic, recreational, aesthetic and economic values of America's natural resources."

While the proposal stated noble ideas and valuable concepts, it missed the point because the Constitution isn't to be used to state ideals, values or guarantees; it's a document giving power to government to act in certain defined areas. The proposal said nothing about creating environmental powers so it would do nothing, just as the school-prayer amendment would have been worthless because it didn't give pietistic powers to state governments.

Every environmental right mentioned in the proposal is already in the Constitution; they just aren't detectable to those unfamiliar with the workings of the document. Environmental rights can be found in the Ninth Amendment under the provision that the people retain other rights not listed elsewhere in the Constitution. Those rights are as important as rights of free speech or religion, and only need to be determined if they are privileges or immunities. Whichever they are depends on the powers the government already has. The Constitution's powers to regulate most commerce and to tax and spend for the general welfare would cover environmental issues, making rights for clean surroundings privileges which government has the power and obligation to protect, just as it has the duty to balance them with other persons' privileges. The proposed amendment would never provide for a fair-and-equitable management of the environment that the equal-protection-of-the-law principle now provides. Nor would it protect commercial interests that the necessary-and-proper clause protects. The environmental-quality proposal was little more than "speaking Sloganese."

Dismissing thousands of proposed amendments designed to promote narrow interests or doing nothing more than sloganeering shouldn't be interpreted to mean there's no need to amend the Constitution. It isn't perfect, and wasn't regarded as ideal by those who wrote and ratified it. Many founders voiced the opinion that the Constitution ought to be tried, and if it failed, it failed. They had seen the failure of the Articles of Confederation and they knew they could learn from another failure and try again. They didn't have to try again.

The Constitution shouldn't be used to address every minor inconvenience – it's not be a panacea for every social ill. When proposing amendments, there should be a need for a change and a sense of responsibility, and

Opinions and Other Biases

lacking that, a barrier to more shenanigans. The Republican Party ought not propose amendments until it sheds its self-interest conservatism in favor of the respectable image of classic conservatives – much like the greatest of all conservatives, Oliver Wendell Holmes. Republican efforts on the flag-burning amendment that would have attacked property rights, the school-prayer proposals that only seek votes, the term-limit measure that many politicians voted for knowing it would fail and the balanced-budget schemes that would do nothing to actually balance a budget should serve as disqualifiers. The Democratic Party needn't be barred because it hasn't had an important constitutional idea in decades.

There should be some amendments because there are still some weaknesses in the Constitution. The most-obvious need would be an amendment to clarify the war powers of both Congress and the president. The quibbling before the Persian Gulf war of 1991 showed the need for such an amendment, as have many instances over the years when presidents have misused their commander-in-chief powers to attack other nations.

An amendment might say:

SECTION 1. No declaration of war shall be made by Congress except on approval of three-fourths of the membership of both houses. A declaration of war shall empower Congress to suspend by law those privileges and immunities it deems necessary for prosecuting the war effort, including the privilege of the Writ of Habeas Corpus and the Thirteenth Amendment's prohibition of involuntary servitude. Such suspensions shall terminate at the attainment of the declaration's objective.

SECTION 2. Congress shall authorize unlimited military hostilities upon approval of two-thirds of the members of each house, but such authorization shall not supersede the provisions of Article I, Section 9, Paragraph 2, nor the Thirteenth Amendment.

SECTION 3. Congress shall approve limited military hostilities upon favorable vote by a majority of each house's membership but no privileges or immunities of the people shall be affected.

SECTION 4. Martial obligations by treaty shall be limited to assisting in the defense of the treaty partner or partners as specified by the treaty.

SECTION 5. The right of the people to peacefully protest or legally resist any military action under this article shall be protected by all governments within the United States. Congress shall have power to enforce this provision.

Such an amendment would clarify responsibilities and powers of Congress and the presidency and could go a long way toward preventing a renegade administration from using the armed forces to impose its political biases on other nations when it's prevented from using foreign-affairs powers. The amendment would also replace the flawed War Powers Act of the Vietnam War and Supreme Court decisions saying that government can do in wartime what it can't do in peacetime and that a president can order the imprisonment of an entire ethnic minority without due process or congressional approval. What government could do would be clear.

Another amendment may be needed to cover elections. Such an amendment would be preferable to the term-limitation referendums that are so obviously unconstitutional they should never be taken seriously. The American people have become disillusioned with the political system because of elections won because of financial superiority from special interests, sloganeering having nothing to do with governing, and a built-in incumbency advantage They just don't know what to do about it. A partial solution might be to operate elections on the principles of court trials, where fairness is required. That approach would require government financing in such a manner that elections aren't won or lost mainly on which candidates attract the most special-interest financing. Lavish spending by special interests can't sway votes of jurors or decisions of judges in a trial; it can only provide more-skilled legal practitioners. Outside interests can't claim their speech must be freely allowed in a trial, rather all speech must be approved by an impartial judge who determines its appropriateness to the case being considered. The same principles should be applied to elections to end negative campaigning by special interests which often use distortions, mudslinging and outright lies. Americans need no more lies in campaigns; they need "testimony" fairly judged to be germane to the issues at hand. And they need a rebuttal to accompany each charge a candidate levels at an opponent.

The weakest part of this proposal would be gathering together enough impartial "election judges" to rule on the charges or advertising tactics of candidates and their pertinence to the issues. Perhaps future retired judges could be used to serve that function as a partial requirement for their ample pensions, for they may be as close to impartial as American society can offer. Political parties aren't part of government, so they would have no privileged position in elections that would be open to all candidates and parties who demonstrate a serious effort.

All the fighting, politicking and whining over social issues dominating much of the late 20th century ought to demonstrate the need for an equal-rights amendment receiving another look – not an amendment that applies only to gender, as the one that failed in the early 1980s, but an amendment providing equal application of the law to the sexes, the races, the ages, citizens and legal immigrants.

Opinions and Other Biases

Too much time has been expended and too much animosity has tied up government during arguments about reverse discrimination of affirmative-action civil-rights efforts, set-aside laws, special minority treatment, or compensation for injustices imposed on ancestral groups. When political conservatives cited equality to argue that restitution for past injuries should go only to those who were directly victimized, they missed the point that the equal-protection-of-the-law clause doesn't apply to the national government. If there were a federal equal-rights amendment, set-aside laws and special treatment probably wouldn't be allowed; reverse discrimination wouldn't be permitted. But it was the politically conservative who prevented the first equal-rights amendment from being adopted, so they shouldn't complain about "reverse discrimination" or special treatment.

With a specific provision for equal rights, special treatment for large campaign contributors – if elections continue to be run as they are – or friends of politicians could be negated in the courts. Exemptions from taxes or law might be some of special treatments eliminated if they didn't promote the general welfare. The same fate might befall special exemptions for family, friends and followers should the nation ever again impose a military draft on its citizens.

In defeating the gender-based Equal Rights Amendment, opponents brought to the fore several arguments, many of which were silly. The same silliness would probably occur in any future attempt at equal rights. One argument was the amendment would legalize homosexual marriages – that's nonsense. A second was that the judiciary would impose unisex toilets on the public – that's doubly nonsensical.

A usually level-headed conservative, Kevin Phillips, rejoicing in the ERA's 1982 defeat, wrote in a newspaper column distributed by King Features Syndicate, "As a lawyer and amateur historian, I found the late and unlamented 'Equal Rights Amendment' to the U. S. Constitution unappealing on precisely those two dimensions. Had we chosen to insert a simple, rigid sexual equality mandate into the U. S. Constitution, who knows what it would have become in the hands of the same federal judiciary that has managed to torture the requirement for equal protection of the laws for all races into a mandate for crosstown busing ..."

Phillips added that, "when it comes to service in the armed forces or in the police, equality of the sexes never really was possible." He concluded with, "On most dimensions, I think the trend to equality between the sexes will continue. But fortunately, there isn't going to be any constitutional mandate to apply that equality to bayonet practice, police SWAT teams or fire department rescue squads."

THE UN-AMERICANS

Phillips' argument is comical for one important reason: all of these issues except "bayonet practice," are addressed by an equal-rights amendment that already exists in the U. S. Constitution. That amendment is the Fourteenth Amendment. It became part of the Constitution in 1868 and it says, "No State shall ... deny to any person within its jurisdiction the equal protection of the laws." Those words acknowledge equal rights under state jurisdiction for all races, for male and female, for the young and the old, for the citizen and the alien and for legal and illegal residents. As a lawyer, Phillips should have recognized the equal-rights aspect of our Guardian Amendment.

In the nearly one and a third centuries the Fourteenth Amendment has addressed equal rights, the dreaded "federal judiciary" has never managed "to torture the requirement for equal protection of the laws" to mandate police SWAT teams or fire department rescue squads be balanced between the sexes. The judiciary has never said or implied the Fourteenth Amendment mandates that states provide legalization for homosexual marriages. These issues fall under the equal-rights mandate required of state and local governments, and if the issues were to be applied as Phillips and other ERA foes suggested, the Fourteenth would have been used to do that.

The proposed federal Equal Rights Amendment that failed in 1982 would have applied only to federal matters – i.e. bayonet practice, and that's moot because the draft contravenes the Thirteenth Amendment, except when privileges and immunities are revoked, which means equal rights wouldn't have to be observed in war conditions. Justice Holmes said government doesn't have to respect certain rights while conducting a war because of the severity of the situation, and that's still the law of the land. What happens with bayonet practice during peacetime is immaterial. Crosstown busing was approved, not mandated, because without it, school officials would be allowed to exercise unconstitutional powers of inequality. Inequality is the only alternative to integration, so nothing was tortured.

The claim that courts would use the Equal Rights Amendment to mandate unisex public restrooms isn't even acceptable as coming from human intelligence; it's utterly ridiculous. The majority of the public restrooms in this nation fall under state jurisdiction, which is governed by the Fourteenth Amendment. Those facilities are in state, city and county office buildings; in parks, museums and along public thoroughfares; in all schools, universities and colleges; in athletic stadiums and arenas; and in commerce where there's local concern – that means the structures in which businesses is conducted – because they all fall under a state's building codes. There's never been an attempt to mandate unisex restrooms in these facilities, and there's never been a judicial decision even approximating such a conclusion.

Opinions and Other Biases

The courts would never apply a unisex-toilet standard, and the judges know very well they couldn't for three very valid reasons:

– As stated, the issue falls under the Fourteenth Amendment, and what that amendment hasn't required of state or local governments a federal equal-rights provision wouldn't require. It would apply to federal concerns.

– Laws made under a mandate for equal rights are required by the Constitution to be "necessary and proper." There's no necessity for unisex restrooms, and to most people they would be improper.

– To sue for a redress of grievance under the First Amendment, a person must have suffered an injury or be threatened with injury. If there's no damage, there's no right to bring a court challenge to any condition or law There's no possible way a person would be damaged by using public restroom facilities designated for a single sex. Great damage was proven in separation of the races because minorities were cheated in many areas and psychologically harmed by the laws. No such condition exists, or could exist, because of separate restrooms, and such separation couldn't impact an entire class of people as did forced racial segregation. It seems impossible for any court to ever hear a unisex-toilet case, and honest people will admit that.

Phillips was in error in thinking an equal-rights mandate was to create equality of individuals; that's not the purpose. The objective is that laws apply equally to all and no one suffers discrimination because of the law. The Fourteenth Amendment's equal-rights provision didn't – and couldn't – impose an equality of intelligence on those fearing unisex toilets; it would be impossible to raise that mindset to functional human levels.

OPPOSITION AND CONFUSION

Just as efforts to change the Constitution predate the document, so does opposition to it and confusion about it. The creators of the constitutional covenant had little confusion, but many people who serve under it today have considerable addlement; that should be obvious by now. Opposition to the Constitution has been continual since the beginning and it remains strong today; it just isn't advertised as opposition. Opponents would prefer to see the document ignored so their political objectives would be promoted, and the Supreme Court is attacked as hostile to the Constitution when it doesn't ignore the document. People who don't understand the document talk about concepts that are not pertinent to constitutional government or are simply wrong. Arguing for states' rights, ancient roots, God's law, original intent and a higher or natural law are a few examples. Opposition to the Constitution was certainly known by the framers; Alexander Hamilton addressed the issue in the first of the newspaper articles that became The Federalist Papers. He wrote:

"Among the most formidable of the obstacles which the new Constitution will have to encounter may readily be distinguished (by) the obvious interest of a certain class of men in every State to resist all changes which may hazard a diminution of the power, emolument, and consequence of the offices they hold under the State establishments; and the perverted ambition of another class of men, who will either hope to aggrandize themselves by the confusions of their country, or will flatter themselves with fairer prospects of elevation from the subdivision of the empire into several partial confederacies than from its union under one government."

If put in modern terminology, Hamilton's statement was that there were state and local politicians who would prefer the federal government be weak or nonexistent so states would retain most or all government authority. In that way, those politicians would be important persons in governing or controlling society, and they didn't want their important-and-powerful political state positions lessened by the Constitution and would work to create obstacles to constitutionalism in order to retain authority and privileges.

Hamilton's second point was that special interests would prefer to have most government authority remain with the states, rather than go to a federal government, because state and local policies would be easier to control or influence than would national policies. By keeping government power at local levels, special interests would have an easier time exalting themselves in social importance. It seems special interests control the federal government now, but they need less effort to influence lower governments.

Similar anticonstitutional arguments are common today as calls repeatedly go out to return most government authority to the states and cities. But often those concerns cover ulterior motives by people who have great power and influence at the city level. They lose much of that prestige at the state level and may have none in Washington, D. C. It's in their best interests to have decision-making authority and government control where they have the greatest influence on the people exercising governmental power. Results of such influence were presented in Chapter 4's "States' Wrongs, Not Rights" detailing anticonstitutional records of state and local governments.

Those records and America's descent into constitutional apostasy can be demonstrated by figures compiled by Prof. Lawrence Baum for his book, *The Supreme Court*. From the beginning of the nation until 1899 (110 years), 23 federal laws were found to be unconstitutional. In the years from 1900 until 1978, another 82 were voided. There were 176 state and local laws overturned in the first 110 years of the union; 831 in the following 79

Opinions and Other Biases

years. Of those 1,007 state and local laws found unconstitutional, only 58 occurred before 1868, the year the Fourteenth Amendment was adopted to protect civil rights from state subversion. States' records under the Fourteenth Amendment show the utter disregard local politicians have had for constitutional limitations to their power and authority.

Not much has changed in two centuries, as demonstrated by repeated pontificating against Washington, D. C., and in favor of local authority. About the only change is that special interests no longer are restricted to the "men" Hamilton wrote about. Now many women are trying to exercise special-treatment influence. Special interests threatening equality of the races or sexes; freedoms of speech, religion, press; privileges and immunities; or fairness under the laws can be restrained by the Supreme Court and other responsible courts. Confusion over the Constitution's principles is another matter; courts can't force the American public to understand those tenets.

Many people, unable to comprehend constitutional government, try to take their frustration out on justices. In 1982, a man physically attacked Supreme Court Judge Byron White, who was about to speak before the Utah Bar Association in Salt Lake City. The attacker reportedly used that occasion to vent anger over "pornography and busing." A bullet was fired into the Washington, D. C., apartment of Judge Harry Blackmun in 1985. Blackmun had received many death threats and hate mail from abortion foes – apparently not prolife types – after the *Roe v. Wade* decision. In 1982, the police providing security for the court building in Washington were armed as crime increased. Security also was increased following the shooting into Blackmun's apartment.

One newspaper, The Tacoma (Wash.) News Tribune, editorializing on the increased police security in 1982, said that the public "remembers too many Supreme Court decisions that have emphasized criminals' rights and not the rights of citizens to defend themselves." That's not quite true. The public only remembers what the news industry reported about Supreme Court decisions, and no Supreme Court decision ever emphasized criminals' rights or degraded rights of citizens to defend themselves. All decisions emphasized the legal role of government in the criminal-justice process. In short, court decisions address government power, not criminal rights or rights of self-defense. Frustrations that Americans feel about Supreme Court decisions can be attributed mostly to a news industry that is unable to report accurately what it doesn't understand, and especially to editorialists and columnists who distort the Constitution and court decisions to advance their political opinions and other biases.

A lack of constitutional understanding was demonstrated in a 1989 guest column in USA TODAY when novelist and screenwriter Jesse Hill Ford proposed getting public education "back to basics." For a safe academic atmosphere, he proposed:

"And while we are about the work of restoring order in the classroom, I have another suggestion: striking a teacher must be made a federal offense. Teachers deserve the same respect and protection now afforded postal workers."

Teaching elementary constitutional principles to people who write newspaper columns might be a better idea, because they should learn that federal authority can't cover any activity. Federal offenses can exist only in those areas put under federal control by the Constitution – legislative control of public education definitely isn't one of those; it's one of those powers "reserved to the States" as Article I, Section 10, suggests and the Tenth Amendment says. People who have been given access to the public domain in which to air their views have a special obligation accompanying that privilege: they should know what they're writing and talking about.

Perhaps the greatest ignorance of the Constitution is demonstrated by the recent growth of so-called "citizen militias" in about half the states of the country. These groups have been formed mainly to prepare for revolution against the federal government in a nation where the federal government has been the greatest protector of militia members' freedoms. This hatred of the federal government which, as shown, predates the Constitution comes mainly from the extreme right; the same political force that opposed the Revolutionary War, opposed the Constitution, opposed freeing of the slaves and opposed civil rights for all Americans. But extremists have been helped in forming a hatred of the finest political system in the history of the world.

They have been aided and abetted by political parties and politicians who repeatedly gain elective office with anti-Constitution campaigns (such as pandering to racial, religious and sexual intolerance), who are anti-Supreme Court and antigovernment or appeal to anti-immigrant fervor.

They have been aided and abetted by persons who subvert our constitutional principles while holding government positions then claim to be "patriots."

They have been aided and abetted by talk-radio hosts who have grown rich and famous by assailing our constitutional doctrines and who serve as spokesmen for organizations and people who detest our principles of liberty for all, equality, human rights, due process, superiority of the national government, separation of church and state, restraint of police or regulation of commerce.

They have been aided and abetted by special-interest groups that distort the Constitution or laws to justify their biased positions, such as those who have misrepresented the Second Amendment to claim that it says something it doesn't say.

They have been aided and abetted by religionists who sermonize against court and Constitution because both prohibit government involvement in religion.

They have been aided and abetted by book publishers who fill their print lists with tomes by celebrities, criminals and subversives and with works that denigrate the United States.

They have been aided and abetted by journalists – plus editors and publishers who print them – who use their privileged positions to wage political attacks on constitutional principles or perfectly accurate court decisions.

None of these groups caused fanatics to bomb the Alfred P. Murrah Federal Office Building in Oklahoma City in April of 1995, but all of them have contributed to poisoning the well one drop at a time over a prolonged period with antigovernment posturing that has turned the nation into a battlefield where American assails American.

The media – newspapers, magazines, book publishers, radio and television – provide a direct link between the American people and the Supreme Court, which is the most-important institution promoting constitutional understanding. But many in the media are abdicating their responsibilities. Instead they are promoting personal interests or attempting to cover their ignorance by pretending to know what the Constitution says.

Many politicians know little of constitutional government; they know political survival. At times they campaign against constitutional principles to pander to an electorate that often knows less about constitutionalism.

The legal community – including Supreme Court judges – lacks communicative skills, except in a few uncommon instances, and that makes understanding of decisions rare. Reporters and editors who don't understand the Constitution rely on judges' written decisions, which they also don't understand.

Schools could teach constitutionalism, but education officials obviously don't understand the Constitution or Supreme Court rulings, as shown in Chapter 9 (religion) and Chapter 10 (equal protection of the laws). Schools have to be careful to teach objectively and not resort to indoctrination. Educators who still try to incorporate pietistic practices in education or attempt to prevent students' personal religious activities certainly aren't ready to teach constitutionalism; they don't understand it. They won't be ready to teach constitutionalism until they cease unconstitutional activities and understand why those activities are forbidden.

But persons in all four groups have an obligation to seek accuracy and should read the Constitution occasionally to see what it really says. Pretending to be constitutionally knowledgeable when knowing little or nothing is dishonest and promotes un-American concepts. Until this "ignorant quartet" (the press, politics, education and the law) learns the constitutional principles on which the nation was founded, or learns to communicate those principles, the nation will endure subversions such as religion by government, use of nonexistent powers, government crime, citizen initiatives creating subversive laws and bigotry by some state officials or employees.

While these are serious un-American practices, there are two greater problems; remaining totally ignorant of the Constitution and serving government in order to profit allies, friends and self. These problems must be corrected if the United States is to extend its constitutional principles to the rest of the world. Trying to Americanize the world, which has accelerated since the collapse of Marxism, is a worthwhile effort. The constitutional democratic republic has much to offer people and nations never before blessed with the knowledge that government must also obey laws or that people have a right to resist the state.

Of the five forms of government – theocracy, aristocracy, autocracy, militocracy and democracy – only democracy admits to those principles. While no democratic republic has as yet attained total obedience to law, each Supreme Court decision – except the rare mistake – is another step in that direction, perhaps leading to that Eden mankind is required to rediscover. Until that paradise is found, the world undergoing Americanization has one reality to serve as a manmade salvation: democratic republics don't wage war against each other – the United States Civil War put an end to that.

To keep what freedoms Americans have, or to extend them to others, it's important to understand the document that provides for liberties by restricting government. Calling for those restrictions to be removed for any reason – be it for selfish gain or lack of knowledge about the Constitution – and placing personal opinions and other biases above the social covenant is a form of un-Americanism shared by nearly all Americans.

Teaching others to be Americanized is fine, but there should also be an effort to Americanize the U. S. of America first, which can be done after admitting one truth. That truth is suggested by distorting a view of the swampland sage the late cartoonist Walt Kelly provided in "intellectual sections" of most Sunday newspapers. It can be expressed by slightly misquoting the great Pogo Possum, "We have met the anticonstitutional un-Americans, and they is us."

Appendix

Constitution of the United States of America

We the People of the United States of America, in order to form a more perfect Union, establish Justice, insure domestic Tranquility, provide for the common defence, promote the general Welfare, and secure the Blessing of Liberty to ourselves and our Posterity, do ordain and establish this CONSTITUTION for the United States of America.

ARTICLE I
SECTION 1. All legislative Powers herein granted shall be vested in a Congress of the United States, which shall consist of a Senate and House of Representatives.

SECTION 2. The House of Representatives shall be composed of Members chosen every second Year by the People of the several States, and the Electors of each State shall have the Qualifications requisite for Electors of the most numerous Branch of the State Legislature.

No Person shall be a Representative who shall not have attained to the Age of twenty five Years, and been seven Years a citizen of the United States, and who shall not when elected, be an Inhabitant of that State in which he shall be chosen.

[Representation and direct Taxes shall be apportioned among the several States which may be included within this Union, according to their respective Numbers, which shall be determined by adding to the whole Number of free Persons, including those bound to Service for a term of Years, and excluding Indians not taxed, three fifths of all other Persons.] The actual Enumeration shall be made within three Years after the first Meeting of the Congress of the United States, and within every subsequent Terms of ten Years, in such Manner as they shall by Law direct. The Number of Representatives shall not exceed one for every thirty Thousand, but each State shall have at Least one Representative; and until such enumeration shall be made, the State of New Hampshire shall be entitled to chuse three, Massachusetts eight, Rhode-Island and Providence Plantations one, Connecticut five, New-York six, New Jersey four, Pennsylvania eight, Delaware one, Maryland six, Virginia ten, North Carolina five, South Carolina five, and Georgia three.

When vacancies happen in the Representation from any State, the Executive Authority thereof shall issue Writs of Election to fill such Vacancies.

The House of Representatives shall chuse their Speaker and other Officers; and shall have the sole Power of Impeachment.

SECTION 3. The Senate of the United States shall be composed of two Senators from each State, chosen by the Legislature thereof, for six Years; and each Senator shall have one Vote.

Immediately after they shall be assembled in Consequence of the first Election, they shall be divided as equally as may be into three Classes. The Seats of the Senators of the first Class shall be vacated at the Expiration of the second Year, of the second Class at the Expiration of the fourth Year, and of the third Class at the Expiration of the sixth Year, so that one third may be chosen every second Year; and if Vacancies happen by Resignation, or otherwise, during the Recess of the Legislature of any State, the Executive thereof may make temporary Appointments until the next Meeting of the Legislature, which shall then fill such Vacancies.

No Person shall be a Senator who shall not have attained to the Age of thirty Years, and been nine Years a Citizen of the United States, and who shall not, when elected, be an Inhabitant of that State for which he shall be chosen.

The Vice President of the United States shall be President of the Senate, but shall have no Vote, unless they be equally divided.

The Senate shall chuse their other Officers, and also a President pro tempore, in the absence of the Vice President, or when he shall exercise the Office of President of the United States.

The Senate shall have the sole Power to try all Impeachments. When sitting for that Purpose, they shall be on Oath or Affirmation. When the President of the United States is tried, the Chief Justice shall preside: And no Person shall be convicted without the Concurrence of two thirds of the Members present.

Judgment in Cases of Impeachment shall not extend further than to removal from Office, and disqualification to hold and enjoy any Office, of honor, Trust or Profit under the United States: but the Party convicted shall nevertheless be liable and subject to Indictment, Trial, Judgment and Punishment, according to Law.

SECTION 4. The Times, Places and Manner of holding Elections for Senators and Representatives, shall be prescribed in each State by the Legislature thereof; but the Congress may at any time by Law make or alter such Regulations, except as to the Places of chusing Senators.

The Congress shall assemble at least once every Year, and such

Constitution of the United States

Meeting shall be on the first Monday in December, unless they shall by Law appoint a different Day.

SECTION 5. Each House shall be the Judge of the Elections, Returns and Qualifications of its own Members, and a Majority of each shall constitute a Quorum to do Business; but a smaller Number may adjourn from day to day, and may be authorized to compel the Attendance of absent Members, in such Manner, and under such Penalties as each House may provide.

Each House may determine the Rules of its Proceedings, punish its Members for disorderly Behavior, and, with the Concurrence of two thirds, expel a Member.

Each House shall keep a Journal of its Proceedings, and from, time to time publish the same, excepting such Parts as may in their Judgment require Secrecy; and the Yeas and Nays of the Members of either House on any question shall, at the Desire of one fifth of those Present, be entered on the Journal.

Neither House, during the Session of Congress, shall, without the Consent of the other, adjourn for more than three days, nor to any other Place than that in which the two Houses shall be sitting.

SECTION 6. The Senators and Representatives shall receive a Compensation for their Services, to be ascertained by Law, and paid out of the Treasury of the United States. They shall in all Cases, except Treason, Felony and Breach of the Peace, be privileged from Arrest during their Attendance at the Session of their respective Houses, and in going to and returning from the same; and for any Speech or Debate in either House, they shall not be questioned in any other Place.

No Senator or Representative shall, during the time for which he was elected, be appointed to any civil Office under the Authority of the United States, which shall have been created, or the Emoluments whereof shall have been encreased during such time; and no Person holding any Office under the United States, shall be a Member of either House during his Continuance in Office.

SECTION 7. All Bills for raising Revenue shall originate in the House of Representatives; but the Senate may propose or concur with Amendments as on other Bills.

Every Bill which shall have passed the House of Representatives and the Senate, shall, before it becomes a Law, be presented to the President of the United States; If he approve he shall sign it, but if not he shall return it, with his Objections to that House in which it shall have originated, who shall enter the Objections at large on their Journal, and proceed to reconsider it. If after such Reconsideration two thirds of that House shall agree to pass the Bill, it shall be sent, together with the Objections, to the other House, by which it shall like-

Constitution of the United States

wise be reconsidered, and if approved by the two thirds of that House, it shall become a Law. But in all such Cases the Votes of both Houses shall be determined by Yeas and Nays, and the Names of the Persons voting for and against the Bill shall be entered on the Journal of each House respectively. If any Bill shall not be returned by the President within ten Days (Sundays excepted) after it shall have been presented to him, the Same shall be a law, in like Manner as if he had signed it, unless the Congress by their Adjournment prevent its Return, in which case it shall not be a Law.

Every Order, Resolution, or Vote to which the Concurrence of the Senate and House of Representatives may be necessary (except on a question of Adjournment) shall be presented to the President of the United States; an before the Same shall take Effect, shall be approved by him, or being disapproved by him, shall be repassed by two thirds of the Senate and House of Representatives, according to the Rules and Limitations prescribed in the Case of a Bill.

SECTION 8. The Congress shall have Power To lay and collect Taxes, Duties, Imposts and Excises, to pay the Debts and provide for the common Defence and general Welfare of the United States; but all Duties, Imposts and Excises shall be uniform throughout the United States;

To borrow Money of the credit of the United States;

To regulate Commerce with foreign Nations, and among the several States, and with the Indian Tribes;

To establish an uniform Rule of Naturalization, and uniform Laws on the subject of Bankruptcies throughout the United States;

To coin Money, regulate the Value thereof, and of foreign Coin, and fix the Standard of Weights and Measures;

To provide for the Punishment of counterfeiting the Securities and current Coin of the United States;

To establish Post Offices and post Roads;

To promote the Progress of Science and useful Arts, by securing for limited Times to Authors and Inventors the exclusive Right to their respective Writings and Discoveries;

To constitute Tribunals inferior to the Supreme Court;

To define and punish Piracies and Felonies committed on the high Seas, and Offenses against the Law of Nations;

To declare War, grant Letters of Marque and Reprisal, and make Rules concerning Captures on Land and Water;

To raise and support Armies, but no Appropriation of Money to that Use shall be for a longer Term than two Years;

To provide and maintain a Navy;

To make Rules for the Government and Regulation of the land and naval Forces;

To provide for calling forth the Militia to execute the Laws of the

Constitution of the United States

Union, suppress Insurrections and repel Invasions;

To provide for organizing, arming, and disciplining, the Militia, and for governing such Part of them as may be employed in the Service of the United States, reserving to the States respectively, the Appointment of the Officers, and the Authority of training the Militia according to the discipline prescribed by Congress;

To exercise exclusive Legislation in all Cases whatsoever, over such District (not exceeding ten Miles square) as may, by Cession of particular States, and the acceptance of Congress, become the Seat of the Government of the United States, and to exercise like Authority over all Places purchased by the Consent of the Legislature of the State in which the Same shall be, for the Erection of Forts, Magazines, Arsenals, dock-Yards, and other needful Buildings; – And

To make all Laws which shall be necessary and proper for carrying into Execution the foregoing Powers, and all other Powers vested by this Constitution in the Government of the United States, or in any Department or Officer thereof.

SECTION 9. The Migration and Importation of such Persons as any of the states now existing shall think proper to admit, shall not be prohibited by the Congress prior to the Year one thousand eight hundred and eight, but a tax or duty may be imposed on such Importation, not exceeding ten dollars for each Person.

The Privilege of the Writ of Habeas Corpus shall not be suspended, unless when in Cases of Rebellion or Invasion the public Safety may require it.

No Bill of Attainder, or ex post facto Law shall be passed.

No capitation, or other direct, Tax shall be laid, unless in Proportion to the Census or Enumeration herein before directed to be taken.

No Tax or Duty shall be laid on Articles exported from any State.

No Preference shall be given by any Regulation of Commerce or Revenue to the Ports of one State over those of another: nor shall Vessels bound to, or from, one State, be obliged to enter, clear, or pay Duties in another.

No Money shall be drawn from the Treasury, but in Consequence of Appropriations made by Law; and a regular Statement and Account of the Receipts and Expenditures of all public Money shall be published from time to time.

No Title of Nobility shall be granted by the United States: And no Person holding any Office of Profit or Trust under them, shall, without the Consent of the Congress, accept of any present, Emolument, Office, Title, of any kind whatever, from any King, Prince, or foreign State.

SECTION 10. No State shall enter into any Treaty, Alliance, or Confederation; grant Letters of Marque and Reprisal; coin Money; emit Bills of Credit; make any Thing but gold and silver Coin a Tender in

Constitution of the United States

payment of Debts; pass any Bill of Attainder, ex post facto Law, or Law impairing the Obligation of Contracts, or grant any Title of Nobility.

No State shall, without the Consent of the Congress, lay any Imposts or Duties on Imports or Exports, except what may be absolutely necessary for executing its inspection Laws: and the net Produce of all Duties and Imposts, laid by any State on Imports or Exports, shall be for the Use of the Treasury of the United States; and all such Laws shall be subject to the Revision and Control of the Congress.

No State shall, without the Consent of Congress, lay any Duty of Tonnage, keep Troops, or Ships of War in time of Peace, enter into any Agreement or Compact with another State, or with a foreign Power, or engage in War, unless actually invaded, or in such imminent Danger as will not admit of delay.

ARTICLE II

SECTION 1. The executive Power shall be vested in a President of the United States of America. He shall hold his Office during the Term of four years, and, together with the Vice President, chosen for the same Term, be elected, as follows

Each State shall appoint, in such Manner as the Legislature thereof may direct, a Number of Electors, equal to the whole Number of Senators and Representatives to which the State may be entitled in the Congress: but no Senator or Representative, or Person holding an Office of Trust or Profit under the United States, shall be appointed an Elector.

[The Electors shall meet in their respective States, and vote by Ballot for two Persons, of whom one at least shall not be an Inhabitant of the same State with themselves. And they shall make a List of all the Persons voted for, and the Number of Votes for each; which List they shall sign and certify, and transmit sealed to the Seat of the Government of the United States, directed to the President of the Senate. The President of the Senate shall, in the Presence of the Senate and House of Representatives, open all the Certificates, and the Votes shall then be counted. The Person having the greatest Number of Votes shall be the President, if such Number be a Majority of the whole Number of Electors appointed; and if there be more than one who have such Majority, and have an equal Number of Votes, then the House of Representatives shall immediately chuse by Ballot one of them for President; and if no Person have a Majority, then from the five highest on the List the said House shall in like Manner chuse the President. But in chusing the President, the Votes shall be taken by States, the Representation from each State having one Vote; A quorum for this Purpose shall consist of a Member or Members from two thirds of the

Constitution of the United States

States, and a Majority of all the States shall be necessary to a Choice. In every Case, after the Choice of the President, the Person having the greatest Number of Votes of the Electors shall be the Vice President. But if there should remain two or more who have equal Votes, the Senate shall chuse from them by Ballot the Vice President.]

The Congress may determine the Time of chusing the Electors, and the Day on which they shall give their Votes; which Day shall be the same throughout the United States.

No Person except a natural born Citizen, or a Citizen of the United States, at the time of the Adoption of this Constitution, shall be eligible to the Office of President; neither shall any Person be eligible to that Office who shall not have attained to the Age of thirty five Years, and been fourteen Years a Resident within the United States.

In Case of the Removal of the President from Office, or of his Death, Resignation, or Inability to discharge the Powers and Duties of the said Office, the Same shall devolve on the Vice President, and the Congress may by Law provide for the Case of Removal, Death, Resignation or Inability, both of the President and Vice President, declaring what Officer shall then act as President and such Officer shall act accordingly, until the Disability be removed, or a President be elected.

The President shall, at stated Times, receive for his Services, a Compensation, which shall neither be encreased nor diminished during the Period for which he shall have been elected, and he shall not receive within that Period any other emolument from the United States, or any of them.

Before he enter on the Execution of his Office, he shall take the following Oath of Affirmation: – "I do solemnly swear (or affirm) that I will faithfully execute the Office of President of the United States, and will to the best of my Ability, preserve, protect and defend the Constitution of the United States."

SECTION 2. The President shall be Commander in Chief of the Army and Navy of the United States, and of the Militia of the several States, when called into actual Service of the United States; he may require the Opinion, writing, of the principal Officer in each of the executive Departments, upon any Subject relating to the Duties of their respective Offices, and he shall have Power to Grant Reprieves and Pardons for Offenses against the United States, except in Cases of Impeachment.

He shall have Power, by and with the Advice and Consent of the Senate, to make Treaties, providing two thirds of the Senators present concur; and he shall nominate, and by and with the Advice and Consent of the Senate, shall appoint Ambassadors, other public Ministers and Consuls, Judges of the supreme Court, and all other Officers of the United States, whose Appointments are not herein otherwise provided for, and which shall be established by Law; but the Congress may by Law vest the Appointment of such inferior Officers, as they think proper, in the President alone, in the Courts of Law, or in the Heads of Departments.

The President shall have Power to fill up all Vacancies that may happen during the Recess of the Senate, by granting Commissions which shall expire at the End of the next Session.

SECTION 3. He shall from time to time give to the Congress Information of the State of the Union, and recommend to their Consideration such Measures as he shall judge necessary and expedient; he may, on extraordinary Occasions, convene both Houses, or either of them, and in Case of Disagreement between them, with Respect to the Time of Adjournment, he may adjourn them to such Time as he shall think proper; he shall receive Ambassadors and other public Ministers; he shall take Care that the Laws be faithfully executed, and shall Commission all the Officers of the United States.

SECTION 4. The President, Vice President and all civil Officers of the United States, shall be removed from Office on Impeachment for, and Conviction of, Treason, Bribery, or other high Crimes and Misdemeanors.

ARTICLE III

SECTION 1. The judicial Power of the United States, shall be vested in one supreme Court, and in such inferior Courts as the Congress may from time to time ordain and establish. The Judges, both of the supreme and inferior Courts, shall hold their Offices during good Behaviour, and shall, at stated Times, receive for their Services, a Compensation, which shall not be diminished during their Continuance in Office.

SECTION 2. The judicial Power shall extend to all Cases, in Law and Equity, arising under this Constitution, the Laws of the United States, and Treaties made, or which shall be made, under their Authority;-to all Cases affecting Ambassadors, other public Ministers and Consuls; – to all Cases of admiralty and maritime Jurisdiction; – to Controversies to which the United States shall be a Party; – to Controversies between two or more States; – between a State and Citizens of another State; – between Citizens of different States; – between Citizens of the same State claiming Lands under Grants of different states, and between a State, or the Citizens thereof, and foreign States, Citizens or Subjects.

In all Cases affecting Ambassadors, other public Ministers and Consuls, and those in which a State shall be Party, the supreme Court shall have original Jurisdiction. In all other Cases before mentioned, the supreme Court shall have appellate Jurisdiction, both as to Law and Fact, with such Exceptions, and under such Regulations as the Congress shall make.

The Trial of all Crimes, except in Cases of Impeachment, shall be by Jury; and such Trial shall be held in the State where the said Crimes shall have been committed; but when not committed within any State, the Trial shall be at such Place or Places as the Congress may by Law have directed.

SECTION 3. Treason against the United States, shall consist only in levying War against them, or adhering to their Enemies, giving them Aid and Comfort. No Person shall be convicted of Treason unless on the Testimony of two Witnesses to the same overt Act, or on Confession in open Court.

The Congress shall have Power to declare the Punishment of Treason, but no Attainder of Treason shall work Corruption of Blood, or Forfeiture except during the lifetime of the Person attainted.

ARTICLE IV

SECTION 1. Full Faith and Credit shall be given in each State to the public Acts, Records, and judicial Proceedings of every other State. And the Congress may by general Laws prescribe the Manner in which such Acts, Records and Proceedings shall be proved, and the Effect thereof.

SECTION 2. The Citizens of each State shall be entitled to all Privileges and Immunities of Citizens in the several States.

A Person charged with Treason, Felony, or other Crime, who shall flee from Justice, and be found in another State, shall on Demand of the executive Authority of the State from which he fled, be delivered up, to be removed to the State having Jurisdiction of the Crime.

No Person held to Service or Labour in one State, under the Laws thereof, escaping into another, shall, in Consequence of any Law or Regulation therein, be discharged from such Service or Labour, but shall be delivered up on Claim of the Party to whom such Service or Labour may be due.

SECTION 3. New States may be admitted by the Congress into this Union; but no new State shall be formed or erected within the Jurisdiction of any other State; nor any State be formed by the Junction of two or more States, or Parts of States, without the Consent of the Legislatures of the States concerned as well as of the Congress.

The Congress shall have Power to dispose of and make all needful Rules and Regulations respecting the Territory or other Property belonging to the United States; and nothing in this Constitution shall be so construed as to Prejudice any Claims of the United States, or of any particular State.

Constitution of the United States

SECTION 4. The United States shall guarantee to every State in this Union a Republican Form of Government, and shall protect each of them against Invasion; and on Application of the Legislature, or of the Executive (when the Legislature cannot be convened) against domestic Violence.

ARTICLE V

The Congress, whenever two-thirds of both Houses shall deem it necessary, shall propose Amendments to this Constitution, or, on the Application of the Legislatures of two thirds of the several States, shall call a Convention for proposing Amendments, which, in either Case, shall be valid to all Intents and Purposes, as Part of this Constitution, when ratified by the Legislatures of three-fourths of the several States, or by Conventions in three-fourths thereof, as the one or the other Mode of Ratification may be proposed by the Congress; Provided that no Amendment which may be made prior to the Year One thousand eight hundred and eight shall in any Manner affect the first and fourth Clauses in the Ninth Section of the first Article; and that no State, without its Consent, shall be deprived of its equal Suffrage in the Senate.

ARTICLE VI

All Debts contracted and Engagements entered into, before the Adoption of this Constitution, shall be valid against the United States under this Constitution, as under the Confederation.

This Constitution, and the Laws of the United States which shall be made in Pursuance thereof; and all Treaties made, or which shall be made, under the Authority of the United States, shall be the supreme Law of the Land; and the Judges in every State shall be bound thereby, any Thing in the Constitutions or Laws of any State to the Contrary notwithstanding.

The Senators and Representatives before mentioned, and the Members of the several State Legislatures, and all executive and judicial Officers, both of the United States and of the several States, shall be bound by Oath or Affirmation, to support this Constitution; but no religious Test shall ever be required as a Qualification to any Office or public Trust under the United States.

ARTICLE VII

The Ratification of the Conventions of nine States, shall be sufficient for the Establishment of this Constitution between the States so ratifying the Same. Done in Convention by the Unanimous Consent of the States present the Seventeenth Day of September in the Year of

Constitution of the United States

our Lord one thousand seven hundred and Eighty seven and of the Independence of the United States of America the Twelfth. In Witness whereof We have hereunto subscribed our Names.

Attest: WILLIAM JACKSON,
Secretary

Go. WASHINGTON
Presd't and deputy from Virginia

Delaware
   Geo: Read
   John Dickinson
   Jaco: Broom
   Gunning Bedford jun
   Richard Bassett

Maryland
   James McHenry
   Danl Carroll
   Dan: of St. Thos Jenifer

Virginia
   John Blair
   James Madison, Jr.

No. Carolina
   Wm Blount
   Richd Dobbs Spaight
   Hu Williamson

So. Carolina
   J. Rutledge
   Charles Cotesworth Pinckney
   Charles Pinckney
   Pierce Butler

Georgia
   William Few
   Abr Baldwin

New Hampshire
   John Langdon
   Nicholas Gilman

Massachusetts
   Nathaniel Gorham
   Rufus King

Connecticut
   Wm Saml Sherman
   Roger Sherman

New York
   Alexander Hamilton

New Jersey
   Wil: Livingston
   David Brearley
   Wm. Paterson
   Jona: Dayton

Pennsylvania
   B. Franklin
   Thomas Mifflin
   Robt. Morris
   Geo. Clymer
   Thos. Fitzsimons
   Jared Ingersoll
   James Wilson
   Gouv Morris

(Articles in addition to, and Amendment of the Constitution of the United States of America, proposed by Congress, and ratified by the Legislatures of the several States, pursuant to the fifth Article of the Original Constitution.)

The Conventions of a number of the States having, at the time of their adopting the Constitution, expressed a desire, in order to prev-

Constitution of the United States

ent misconstruction or abuse of its powers, that further declaratory and restrictive clauses should be added: And as extending the ground of public confidence in the Government, will best insure the beneficent ends of its institution:

Resolved, by the SENATE and HOUSE of REPRESENTATIVES of the UNITED STATES of AMERICA in Congress assembled, two thirds of both Houses concurring. That the following Articles be proposed to the Legislatures of the several States, as Amendments to the Constitution of the United States; all or any of which articles, when ratified by three fourths of the said Legislatures, to be valid to all intents and purposes, as part of the said Constitution, viz.

AMENDMENT I (1791)

Congress shall make no law respecting an establishment of religion, or prohibiting the free exercise thereof; or abridging the freedom of speech, or of the press; or the right of the people peaceably to assemble, and to petition the Government for a redress of grievances.

AMENDMENT II (1791)

A well regulated Militia, being necessary to the security of a free State, the right of the people to keep and bear Arms, shall not be infringed.

AMENDMENT III (1791)

No Soldier shall, in time of peace, be quartered in any house, without the consent of the owner, nor in time of war, but in a manner to be prescribed by law.

AMENDMENT IV (1791)

The right of the people to be secure in their persons, houses, papers, and effects, against unreasonable searches and seizures, shall not be violated, and no Warrants shall issue, but upon probable cause, supported by Oath or affirmation, and particularly describing the place to be searched, and the persons or things to be seized.

AMENDMENT V (1791)

No person shall be held to answer to a capital, or otherwise infamous crime, unless on a presentment or indictment of a grand jury, except in cases arising in the land or Naval forces, or in the Militia, when in actual service in time of War or public danger; nor shall any person be subject for the same offence to be twice put in jeop-

Constitution of the United States

ardy of life or limb; nor shall be compelled in any criminal case to be a witness against himself, nor be deprived of life, liberty, or property, without due process of law; nor shall private property be taken for public use, without just compensation.

AMENDMENT VI (1791)

In all criminal prosecutions, the accused shall enjoy the right to a speedy and public trial, by an impartial jury of the State and district wherein the crime shall have been committed, which district shall have been previously ascertained by law, and to be informed of the nature and cause of the accusation; to be confronted with the witnesses against him; to have compulsory process for obtaining witnesses in his favor, and to have the assistance of counsel for his defence.

AMENDMENT VII (1791)

In suits of common law, where the value in controversy shall exceed twenty dollars, the right of trial shall be preserved, and no fact tried by a jury, shall be otherwise re-examined in any Court of the United States, than according to the rules of the common law.

AMENDMENT VIII (1791)

Excessive bail shall not be required, nor excessive fines imposed, nor cruel and unusual punishments inflicted.

AMENDMENT IX (1791)

The enumeration in the Constitution, of certain rights, shall not be construed to deny or disparage others retained by the people.

AMENDMENT X (1791)

The powers not delegated to the United States by the Constitution, nor prohibited by it to the States, are reserved to the States respectively, or to the people.

(Articles in addition to the Constitution and the Bill of Rights, proposed by Congress and ratified by the legislatures of the states, as specified in the fifth article of the original Constitution.)

AMENDMENT XI (1795)

The Judicial power of the United States shall not be construed to extend to any suit in law and equity, commenced or prosecuted against one of the United States by Citizens of another State, or by Citizens or Subjects of any Foreign State.

AMENDMENT XII (1804)

The Electors shall meet in the respective states and vote by ballot for President and Vice-President, one of whom, at least, shall not be an inhabitant of the same state with themselves; they shall name in their ballots the person voted for as President, and in distinct ballots the person voted for as Vice President, and they shall make distinct lists of all persons voted for as President, and of all persons voted for as Vice-President, and of the number of votes for each, which lists they shall sign and certify, and transmit sealed to the seat of the government of the United States, directed to the President of the Senate; – The President of the Senate shall, in the presence of the Senate and the House of Representatives, open all the certificates and the votes shall then be counted; – The person having the greatest number of votes for President, shall be the President, if such number be a majority of the whole number of Electors appointed; and if no person have such majority, then from the persons having the highest numbers not exceeding three on the list of those voted for as President, the House of Representatives shall choose immediately, by ballot, the President. But in choosing the President, the votes shall be taken by states, the representation from each state having one vote; a quorum for this purpose shall consist of a member or members from two-thirds of the states, and a majority of all states shall be necessary to a choice. And if the House of Representatives shall not choose a President whenever the right of choice shall devolve upon them, before the fourth day of March next following, then the Vice-President shall act as President, as in the case of the death or other constitutional disability of the President; – The person having the greatest number of votes as Vice-President, shall be the Vice President, if such number be a majority of the whole number of Electors appointed, and if no person have a majority, then from the two highest numbers on the list, the Senate shall choose the Vice-President; a quorum for the purpose shall consist of two-thirds of the whole number of Senators, and a majority of the whole number shall be necessary to a choice. But no person constitutionally ineligible to the office of President shall be eligible to that of Vice-President of the United States.

AMENDMENT XIII (1865)

SECTION 1. Neither slavery nor involuntary servitude, except as a punishment for crime whereof the party shall have been duly convicted, shall exist within the United States, or any place subject to their jurisdiction.

SECTION 2. Congress shall have power to enforce this article by appropriate legislation.

Constitution of the United States

AMENDMENT XIV (1868)

SECTION 1. All persons born or naturalized in the United States, and subject to the jurisdiction thereof, are citizens of the United States and of the State wherein they reside. No State shall make or enforce any law which shall abridge the privileges and immunities of citizens of the United States; nor shall any State deprive any person of life, liberty, or property, without due process of law; nor deny to any person within its jurisdiction the equal protection of the laws.

SECTION 2. Representatives shall be apportioned among the several States according to their respective numbers, counting the whole number of persons in each State, excluding Indians not taxed. But when the right to vote at any election for the choice of electors for President and Vice President of the United States, Representatives in Congress, the Executive and Judicial officers of a State, or the members of the Legislature thereof, is denied to any of the male inhabitants of such State, being twenty-one years of age, and citizens of the United States, or in any way abridges, except for participation in rebellion, or other crime, the basis of representation therein shall be reduced in the proportion which the number of such male citizens shall bear to the whole number of male citizens twenty-one years of age in such State.

SECTION 3. No person shall be a Senator or Representative in Congress, or elector of President and Vice President, or hold any office, civil or military, under the United States, or under any State, who, having previously taken an oath, as a member of Congress, or as an officer of the United States, or as a member of any State legislature, or as an executive or judicial officer of any State, to support the Constitution of the United States, shall have engaged in insurrection or rebellion against the same, or given aid and comfort to the enemies thereof. But Congress may by vote of two-thirds of each House remove such disability.

SECTION 4. The validity of the public debt of the United States, authorized by law, including debts incurred for payment of pensions and bounties for services in suppression insurrection or rebellion, shall not be questioned. But neither the United States nor any State shall assume or pay any debt or obligation incurred in aid of insurrection or rebellion against the United States, or any claim for the loss or emancipation of any slave; but all such debts, obligations and claims shall be held illegal and void.

SECTION 5. The Congress shall have power to enforce, by appropriate legislation, the provisions of this article.

AMENDMENT XV (1870)

SECTION 1. The right of citizens of the United States to vote shall not be denied or abridged by the United States or by any State on account of race, color, or previous condition of servitude.

SECTION 2. The Congress shall have power to enforce this article by appropriate legislation.

AMENDMENT XVI (1913)

The Congress shall have power to lay and collect taxes on incomes, from whatever source derived, without apportionment among the several States, and without regard to any census or enumeration.

AMENDMENT XVII (1913)

The Senate of the United States shall be composed of two Senators from each State, elected by the people thereof, for six years; and each Senator shall have one vote. The electors in each State shall have the qualifications requisite for electors of the most numerous branch of the State legislature.

When vacancies happen in the representation of any State in the Senate, the executive authority of such State shall issue writs of election to fill such vacancies: Provided, That the legislature of any State may empower the executive thereof to make temporary appointments until the people fill the vacancies by election as the legislature may direct.

This amendment shall not be construed as to effect the election or term of any Senator chosen before it becomes valid as part of the Constitution.

AMENDMENT XVIII (1919)

SECTION 1. After one year from the ratification of this article the manufacture, sale, or transportation of intoxicating liquors within, the importation thereof into, or the exportation thereof from the United States and all territory subject to the jurisdiction thereof for beverage purposes is hereby prohibited. SECTION 2. The Congress and the several States shall have concurrent power to enforce this article by appropriate legislation. SECTION 3. This article shall be inoperative unless it shall have been ratified as an amendment to the Constitution by the legislatures of the several States, as provided in the Constitution, within seven years from date of the submission hereof to the States by the Congress.

Constitution of the United States

AMENDMENT XIX (1920)

The right of citizens of the United States to vote shall not be denied or abridged by the United States or any State on account of sex.

Congress shall have power to enforce this article by appropriate legislation.

AMENDMENT XX (1933)

The terms of the President and Vice President shall end at noon on the 20th day of January, and the terms of Senators and Representatives at noon on the 3d day of January, of the years in which such terms would have ended if this article had not been ratified; and the terms of their successors shall then begin.

SECTION 2. The Congress shall assemble at least once in every year, and such meeting shall begin at noon on the 3d day of January, unless they shall by law appoint a different day.

SECTION 3. If, at the time fixed for the beginning of the term of the President, the President elect shall have died, the Vice President elect shall become President. If a President shall not have been chosen before the time fixed for the beginning of his term, or if the President elect shall have failed to qualify, then the Vice President elect shall act as President until a President shall have qualified; and the Congress may by law provide for the case wherein neither President nor a Vice President elect shall have qualified, declaring who shall then act as President, or the manner in which one who is to act shall be selected, and such person shall act accordingly until a President or Vice President shall have qualified.

SECTION 4. The Congress may by law provide for the case of the death of any of the persons from whom the House of Representatives may choose a President whenever the right of choice shall have devolved upon them, and for of the death of any of the persons from whom the Senate may choose President whenever the right of choice shall devolve upon them.

SECTION 5. Sections 1 and 2 shall take effect on the 15th day of October following the ratification of this article.

SECTION 6. This article shall be inoperative unless it shall have been ratified as an amendment to the Constitution by the legislatures of three-fourths the several States within seven years from the date of its submission.

AMENDMENT XXI (1933)

SECTION 1. The eighteenth article of amendment to the Constitution of the United States is hereby repealed.

SECTION 2. The transportation or importation into any State, Territory, or possession of the United States for delivery or use therein of intoxicating liquors, in violation of the laws thereof, is hereby prohibited.

SECTION 3. This article shall be inoperative unless it shall have been ratified as an amendment to the Constitution by conventions in the several States, as provided in the Constitution, within seven years from the date of submission hereof to the States by the Congress.

AMENDMENT XXII (1951)

SECTION 1. No person shall be elected to the office of the President more than twice, and no person who has held the office of President, or acted as President, for more than two years of a term to which some other person was elected President shall be elected to the office of the President more than once. But this Article shall not apply to any person holding the office of President when this Article was proposed by the Congress, and shall not prevent any person who may be holding the office of President, or acting as President, during the term within which this Article becomes operative from holding the office of President, or acting as President during the remainder of such term.

SECTION 2. This article shall be inoperative unless it shall have been ratified as an amendment to the Constitution by the legislatures of three fourths of the several States within seven years from the date of its submission to the States by the Congress

AMENDMENT XXIII (1961)

SECTION 1. The District constituting the seat of Government of the United States shall appoint in such manner as the Congress may direct: A number of electors of President and Vice President equal to the whole number of Senators and Representatives in Congress to which the District would be entitled if it were a State, but in no event more than the least populous State; they shall be in addition to those appointed by the States, but they shall be considered for the purpose of the election of President and Vice President, to be electors appointed by a State; and they shall meet in the District and perform such duties as provided by the twelfth article of amendment.

SECTION 2. The Congress shall have power to enforce this article by appropriate legislation.

AMENDMENT XXIV (1964)

SECTION 1. The right of citizens of the United States to vote in any primary or other election for President or Vice President, for electors for President or Vice President, or for Senator or Representative in Congress shall not be denied or abridged by the United States or any

Constitution of the United States

State by reason of failure to pay any poll tax or other tax.
SECTION 2. The Congress shall have power to enforce this article by appropriate legislation.

AMENDMENT XXV (1967)

SECTION 1. In case of removal of the President from office or of his death or resignation, the Vice President shall become President.

SECTION 2. Whenever there is a vacancy in the office of Vice President, the President shall nominate a Vice President who shall take office on confirmation by a majority vote of both Houses of Congress.

SECTION 3. Whenever the President transmits to the President pro tempore of the Senate and the Speaker of the House of Representatives his written declaration that he is unable to discharge the powers and duties of his office, and until he transmits to them a written declaration to the contrary, such powers and duties shall be discharged by the Vice President as Acting President.

SECTION 4. Whenever the Vice President and a majority of either the principal officers of the executive departments or of such other body as Congress may by law provide, transmit to the President pro tempore of the Senate and the Speaker of the House of Representatives their written declaration that the President is unable to discharge the powers and duties of his office, the Vice President shall immediately assume the powers and duties of the office as Acting President.

Thereafter, when the President transmits to the President pro tempore of the Senate and the Speaker of the House of Representatives his written declaration that no inability exists, he shall resume the power and duties of his office unless the Vice President and a majority of either the principal officers of the executive department or of such other body as Congress may by law provide, transmit within four days to the President pro tempore of the Senate and the Speaker of the House of Representatives their written declaration that the President is unable to discharge the powers and duties of his office. Thereupon Congress shall decide the issue, assembling within forty-eight hours for that purpose if not in session. If the Congress, within twenty-one days after receipt of the latter written declaration, or, if Congress is not in session, within twenty-one days after Congress is required to assemble, determines by two-thirds vote of both Houses that the President is unable to discharge the powers and duties of his office, the Vice President shall continue to discharge the same as Acting President; otherwise the President shall resume the power and duties of his office.

AMENDMENT XXVI (1971)

SECTION 1. The right of citizens of the United States, who are 18 years of age or older, to vote shall not be denied or abridged by the United States or by any State on account of age.

SECTION 2. The Congress shall have power to enforce this article by appropriate legislation.

AMENDMENT XXVII (1992)

No law, varying the compensation for the services of the Senators and Representatives, shall take effect, until an election of Representatives shall have intervened.

INDEX

Adams, Brock, 120, 123
Alabama, 49, 223, 224, 225, 232, 238
   Education Association, 223
Alaniz, Delia, 128, 129
Alaska, 204, 309
Alexander, Dan C. Jr., 218
American Broadcasting Company, 120, 121, 163
American Center for Law and Justice-Atlanta, 245
American Civil Liberties Union (ACLU), 172, 173, 202, **329-35**
American Ex-Prisoners of War, 144
American Federation of Police, 144
American Legion, 144
American Medical Association, 273
American Society of Newspaper Editors, 323
American Veterans of World War II, Korea, Vietnam, 144
Arizona, 258, 288
Arkansas, 246,336
Armstrong, William, 31
Ashwander v. Tennessee Valley Authority, 307
Articles of Confederation, 12, 38, 107, 160, 314, 328, 344
Aryan Nations, the, 65, 253
Associated Press, the, 41, 42, 51, 63, 223, 242, 245, 248, 312

Baker, Jim, 182
Baltimore Sun, the, 273
Bambi, 179
Barry, Marion, 149
Bauer, Gary, 332
Baum, Lawrence, 83, 350
Beaney, William M., 111
Beauharnais v. Illinois, 163
Beaumont (Tex.) Enterprise, the, 327
Bill of Rights, the, **155-217**
Bingham, John A.,50, 266
Birmingham, Ala., 177, 290
Black, Hugo, 159, 208, 227, 228
Blackmun, Harry, 58, 142, 268, 269, 351
Blinded Veterans Association, 144
Bob Jones University, 250, 251, 252, 253
Bonneville Power Administration, 308
Boone, Pat, 226
Bork, Robert, **51-6,** 96, 97, 140 156
Boston, 248, 284, 323, 339
Boston Globe, the, 343
Bowers v. Hardwick, 270
Brandeis, Louis, 39, 40
Brennan, William, 58, 203, 235
Broder, David, 334

Brooklyn, 204
Brooks, Jack, 327
Brown v. Board of Education, 81, 102, 178, 283, 340
Bryant, William B., 149
Buchanan, Patrick, 252, 291, 330, 333
Buckley, William F., 173, 174
Buffalo, 159
Burger, Warren, 60, 212, 251, 252, 276, 291
Burr, Aaron, 77, 262
Bush, George, 62, 63, 99, 118, 119, 121, 122, 123, 124, 135, 137, 138, 144, 145, 152, 178, 182, 262,312, 318, 334, 335
   administration, 192
Butler, Richard, 65, 66, 67

California, 49, 185, 203, 205, 243, 267, 287, 288, 289, 290, 326
Canada, 72, 125, 130, 132, 214
Cantwell v. Connecticut, 136, 250
Carter, Jimmy, 6, 116, 262
Catholic Wars Veterans, USA, Inc., 144
Cathy, 168
Center for Judicial Studies, 48
Central Intelligence Agency, 63
Charlotte, N. C., 284
Charter of Liberties, 21
Chavez, Linda, 311
Chicago, 52, 80, 171, 173, 202
   University of, 51
Chicago Tribune, the, 283
Christmas, 239, **246-9,** 255, 258, 331, 332
Church of Christ, 240
Church of Jesus Christ, Christian, 65, 253
Citizens Committee for the Right to Keep and Bear Arms, 180, 182
Civil War, the, 85, 94, 247, 260, 261, 264, 267, 295, 331, 338, 353
Clarion-Ledger, the, 196
Cleveland, Grover, 247
Clinton, Bill, 178, 262, 312
Coffey, Shelby, 14
Coke, Sir Edward,104
Collin, Francis Joseph, 171, 172
Colorado, 186, 326, 327, 329
   Court of Appeals, 105, 106
   Supreme Court, 281
Columbia Broadcasting System, 162
Confederate States of America, 94
Confirmatio Cartarum, 21
Connecticut, 54, 208, 296
Continental Congress, 12, 145
Constitutional Convention, 32, 103, 155, 157
Constitutional Patriots, 131, 133
Craig, Larry, 316
Cromwell, Oliver, 28
Cruzan, Nancy, 216, 271

INDEX

Daily Oklahoman, the, 2
Dallas, 139, 144, 215
Decker, Bernard, 172
Declaration of Independence, 11, 12, 65, 96, 2217
Democratic Party, the, 6, 345
Denniston, Lyle, 273
Denver, 243, 246
Denver Post, the, 10, 14, 41, 45, 72, 106, 114, 168, 186, 195, 245, 247, 264, 265, 331
DiBacco, Thomas, 273
Disabled American Veterans, 144
Dole, Robert, 144
Doonesbury, 169
Douglas, William O., 40, 161, 163
Dr. Bonham Case, 104
Dred Scott decision, 45, 93, 108, 222, 336, 337, 338, 339
Dukakis, Michael, 62, 64, 135, 334

Eagle Forum, the, 138, 145, 212, 229, 249, 258
Eighteenth Amendment, **297**
Eighth Amendment, **201-6**
   cruel and unusual punishments 201-6
   capital punishment 202-3
   excessive bail and fines 201
Eleventh Amendment, **261-2**
Ellis, Tottie, 138, 229, 249
Engel v. Vitale, 222, 223, 226, 227, 228
Environmental Protection Agency, 99
Epling, Miles S., 144, 146
Equal Rights Amendment, 41, 257, 289, 347, 348
Evers, Medgar, 196
Exclusionary Rule, the, 149, 150, 186

Falwell, Jerry, 225, 226, 257, 258, 276
Farber, Myron A., 166, 168, 187
Federal Bureau of Investigation, 63, 65, 100, 1485
Federalist Papers, the, 31, 32, 38, 48, 49, 68, 72, 90, 104, 254, 350
Fein, Bruce, 52, 96, 99
Fifteenth Amendment, **293-5**
Fifth Amendment, **188-93**
   double jeopardy, 189-90
   due process of law, 190-2
   grand-jury indictment, 189
   self-incrimination, 190-2
   private property, 192
First Amendment, **159-79**
   freedom of assembly, 170-5
   freedom to petition, 175-9
   freedom of the press, 163-70
   freedom of religion, 218-59
   freedom of speech, 159-63

Fitzgerald, Randy, 287
Florida, 36, 47, 79, 80, 204, 229, 232, 243, 287
Florida Today, 79
Foley, Tom, 326
Ford, Jesse Hill, 145, 351
Fourteenth Amendment, **265-93**
   due process, 277-80
   equal protection, 280-90
   privileges & immunities, 267-77
Fourth Amendment, **184-8**
   probable cause, 184-5
   searches and seizures, 184-8
Frankfurter, Felix, 38, 57, 136, 137
Franklin, Benjamin, 46, 47
Fraternal Order of Police, 144
Freedom of Information Act, 63
Frothingham v. Mellon, 310
Furman v. Georgia, 203

Gannett Corp., 13, 79, 80
Gannett v. DePasquale, 195
Gardner, Booth, 128, 129, 327
Garn, Jake, 273, 274
Georgia, 232, 242, 269, 270
Germany, Nazi, 32, 53, 71, 72, 137, 169, 334
Gingrich, Newt, 228
Ginsburg, Ruth Bader, 2
Goldwater, Barry, 258
Gorton, Slade, 291
Gorsuch, Anne, 99
Gottlieb, Alan M., 182
Graham, Billy, 225, 241, 242, 258
Gramm-Rudman-Hollings Bill, 315, 316
Gregg v. Georgia, 203
Guardian Angels, the, 130, 214, 215
Gun Owners of America, the, 180

Halbrook, Stephen, 180
Halloween, 255
Hamilton Alexander, 31, 38, 39, 66, 68, 77, 88, 104, 155, 156, 157, 207, 254, 349, 350, 351
Harkin, Tom, 120, 123
Hartford, Conn., 284
Hatch, Orrin, 41
Hearst, William R. Jr., 119, 120, 122, 123
Helms, Jesse, 64, 65, 90, 114, 115, 116, 222, 224,
Heritage Foundation, the, 63, 96, 312, 313
Hollings, Ernest F., 222, 224
Holmes, Oliver Wendell, 17, 18, 21, 39, 40, 59, 65, 80, 83, 94, 125, 135, 143, 160, 161, 264, 295, 339, 340, 341, 345, 348
Hoover, J. Edgar, 65, 100
House of Commons, 27

INDEX

Howard University, 290
Huffington, Michael, 289
Hurtado v. California, 278
Hylton v. United States, 305, 306

Idaho, 4, 65, 253, 281, 329
Illinois, 80, 171, 288, 336
   Appellate Court, 172
   Supreme Court, 172
   University of, 121
Indiana, 277
Internal Revenue Service (IRS), 39, 77, 250, 251, 252, 253
International Anti-Euthanasia Task Force, 41
Iowa, 243
Iran-contra, 13, 85, 86, 88, 98, 99, 148, 188, 306, 307
Iwo Jima Memorial, 144

Jackson, Miss., 196
James, Fob, 223
Janklow, Bill, 248
Jay, John, 31, 49, 66, 72, 73, 74, 80, 81, 82, 90, 102, 111, 128, 134, 148, 206, 207, 209, 221, 254, 270
Jefferson, Thomas, 12, 17, 96, 120, 154, 173, 221, 254, 262, 263
Jehovah's Witnesses, 135, 136, 176, 240
Jewish Anti-Defamation League, 172
Johnson, Lyndon, 120, 122, 285
Justice Department, 52, 53, 116, 117, 182

Kennedy, Anthony, 56, **57-9**, 80, 81, 143
Kennedy, Edward, 120, 121, 123, 124
Kentucky, 240, 143
Kevorkian, Jack, 217
Kilpatrick, James, 116, 223, 224, 251, 252, 283, 343
King Features Syndicate, 347
King, Martin Luther Jr., 64
Knight-Ridder News Service, 157, 183, 192, 205
Korematsu v. United States, 339
Ku Klux Klan, 253

LaHaye, Tim, 333
Lee Robert E., 267
LaPierre, Wayne, 182
Limbaugh, Rush, 220
Lincoln, Abraham, 74
Locke, John, 17, 35, 142
Lofton, John, 270
Logan, Utah, 223
Los Angeles, 189

Los Angeles Times, the, 12, 14, 78, 81, 157, 202
Los Angeles Times Syndicate, 144, 249
Los Angeles Times-Washington Post News Service, 336
Louisiana, 14, 236, 246, 339
Louisiana Purchase, 336

Madison, James, 31, 32, 49, 66, 72, 104, 157, 159,, 160, 164, 181, 183, 191, 207, 209, 219, 254
Magna Charta, 21, 176, 191
Maine, 336
Marshall, John, 9, 11, 29, 30, 44, 48, 61, 145, 269, 308, 341
Marshall, Thurgood, 40, 203
Martin, Lynn, 138
Martin v. Wilks, 177
Maryland, 230, 270, 305
Marxism, 6, 19, 20, 151, 161, 306, 354
Mason, Alpheus Thomas, 111
Massachusetts, 29, 41, 62, 66, 135
Massachusetts v. Mellon, 310
McCarthy, Joseph, 63, 160, 189, 326
McCulloch v. Maryland, 29, 30, 48, 269, 305, 308
McDonald, Larry, 63, 67
McKenna, Joseph, 202
Meese, Edwin, 49, 50, 197, 330, 335
Mencken, H. L., 16
Michigan, 205, 217, 243, 272
Military Order of the Purple Heart, 144
Minersville School District v. Gobitis, 135, 136, 138, 220
Minnesota, 108
Miranda v. Arizona, 197
Mississippi, 108, 196, 225, 229, 255
Missouri, 17, 74, 75, 79, 125, 215, 216, 271, 275, 336, 337
Missouri Compromise, the, 336, 337
Missouri v. Holland, 125
Mobile (Ala.) County School Board, 218
Montgomery, Ala., 232
Moral Majority, the, 274
Morris, Gouverneur, 191
Muller, Herbert J., 33, 34
Murray's Lessee v. Hoboken Land and Development, 191

National Association of Chiefs of Police, 144
National Broadcasting Company, 256
National Endowment for the Arts, 91
National Guard, the, 109, 181
National Legal Foundation, 227, 238
National Organization for Women, 211
National Rifle Association, 180, 182

377

INDEX

National Right-to-Life Committee, 274
National Socialist Party of America, 171
Nebraska, 267
Neier, Aryeh, 174
Newark, N. J., 214
New Hampshire, 15, 110
Newhouse News Service, 63
New Jersey, 66, 166, 168
New Mexico, 223
New Orleans, 246
Newsday, 101
New York state, 66, 223, 224, 227, 229, 233, 262, 267, 291
New York City, 52, 130, 214, 215, 229, 256, 273
New York Times, the, 58, 62, 113, 166, 187, 267, 284, 323
Nineteenth Amendment, **298**
Ninth Amendment, **206-8**
Nixon, Richard, 100, 123, 126, 148, 168
  administration, 52, 62, 148
North Carolina, 36, 242
North, Oliver, 13, 85, 86, 87, 88, 99
Notson, Robert C., 233, 234, 235

O'Connor, Sandra D., 40, 47, 49, 139, 274, 275
O'Hair, Madalyn Murry, 226, 227, 229, 230
Ohio, 50, 108, 243, 266
  State University, 83
  University of Steubenville, 41
Oklahoma, 108, 326
Oklahoma City, 2, 352
Omaha, Neb., 244
Oregon, 77, 79, 136, 204, 217, 281,
  University of, 204
Oregon v. Smith, 77

Paralyzed Veterans of America, 144
Paterson, William, 29, 30
Pawtucket, R. I., 248
Pelosi, Nancy, 99
Pennsylvania, 66, 136, 191, 230, 243, 262, 275
Pensacola, Fla., 276
Permoli v. First Municipality, 246
Perot, Ross, 313
Phillips, Kevin, 347, 348, 349
Picket, David, 144
Pledge of Allegiance, the, 4, 31, 62, 64, 135, 138, 142, 335
Plessy v. Ferguson, 338, 339, 340
Pogo Possum, 354
Polish Legion of American Veterans, 144
Portland (Ore.) Oregonian, the, 233
Powell, Lewis, 270

Pratt, Larry, 180, 181, 182
Pro-Life Action League, 272
Public Broadcasting Service (PBS), 44, 91, 321, 336, 327

Quayle, Dan, 169

Reader's Digest, 286, 287
Reagan, Ronald, 49, 51, 56, 61, 63, 97, 116, 124, 148, 149, 226, 227, 228, 258, 262, 274, 286, 299, 311, 312
  administration, 50, 57, 62, 85, 99, 113, 152, 192, 197, 222, 275, 285, 289, 306, 308, 309, 315, 318, 330, 332
Rehnquist, William, 75, 139, 140, 216, 218, 219, 271, 291, 294
Religious Freedom Restoration Act, 78
Reporters Committee for Freedom of the Press, 185

Republican Party, the, 6, 31, 168, 256, 312, 345
Revolutionary War, the, 10, 131, 183, 245, 2660
Reynolds, Barbara, 227, 229, 323
Richmond, Va., 285
Robertson, Pat, 225, 257
Rochester, N. Y., 217
Rocky Mountain News, the, 168, 246
Roe v. Wade, 4, 271, 273, 275, 351
Rooney, Andy, 162, 163
Roosevelt, Franklin D., 113, 300
Rowan, Carl T., 40
Rust v. Sullivan, 275

Sacramento, Calif., 57
Safire, William, 62
Salt Lake City, 351
San Francisco, 215, 284
Sattler, H. Vernon, 220
Scalia, Antonin, 6, 7, 26, 35, 37, 39, 40, 50, 62, 65, 67, 84, 88, 98, 133, 138, 143, 157, 205, 286, 289
Scarsdale, N. Y., 248
Schlafly, Phyllis, 145, 258
Scheidler, Joseph M., 272
Schenck v. United States, 160
Schott, Marge, 163
Scowcroft, Brent, 121
Scripps-Howard News Service, 140
Seattle, 91, 139, 142, 153, 204, 214, 269, 284, 291
Seattle Post-Intelligencer, the, 31, 120, 268
Seattle Times, the, 41, 157, 309
Second Amendment, **179-83**
Second Amendment Foundation, 180, 182
Seventeenth Amendment, **296-7**

INDEX

Seventh Amendment, **199-201**
Simpson, Alan, 165
Sixteenth Amendment, **295-6**
Sixth Amendment, **193-9**
  assistance of counsel, 198-9
  compulsory process, 187
  impartial jury, 196-7
  public trial, 194-6
Skokie, Ill., 171, 172, 173, 174, 175, 200
Skolrood, Robert K., 238
Sliwa, Curtis, 214
Smith, William French, 113
Sobran, Joseph, 274, 292, 293
Social Security, 89, 250, 287, 312, 313, 317
South Carolina, 296
South Dakota, 246, 248
Southeast Asia Treaty Organization, 123
Sovereignty Commission, 196
Sowell, Thomas, 140, 141, 198
Stevens, John Paul, 139
Stewart, Potter, 59, 218, 219
St. Louis Post Dispatch, the, 157, 205
Sunday Closing Laws Cases, 255
Supreme Court Reporter, the, 228
Swann v. Mecklenburg Board of Education, 283

Tacoma (Wash.) News Tribune, the, 12, 351
Taney, Roger, 337, 338
Ten Commandments, the, 233, 240, 276
Tennessee, 231, 236, 243
Tenth Amendment, **208-17**
Texas, 4, 139, 140, 287, 288, 334
Third Amendment, **183-4**
Thirteenth Amendment, **263-5**
Thomas, Cal, 143, 249, 274
Thumper, 179
Thurmond, Strom, 82, 83, 84
Todd, Terry, 212
Truman, Harry, 119, 120, 122
Tsongas, Paul, 41
TV Guide, 336
Twelfth Amendment, **262-3**
Twentieth Amendment, **298-9**
Twenty-Fifth Amendment, **301-2**
Twenty-First Amendment, **299**
Twenty-Fourth Amendment, **301**
Twenty Second Amendment, **299-300**
Twenty-Seventh Amendment, **303**
Twenty-Sixth Amendment, **302-3**
Twenty-Third Amendment, **300-1**

Unification Church, the, 256

Union of Soviet Socialist Republics
  (Soviet Union), 5, 24, 32, 53, 72, 124, 176, 177,
  190, 240, 322, 334
United Press International, 168, 185
United States Jaycees, 144
United States v. Miller, 181
University of California Regents v. Bakke, 286
USA TODAY,13, 14, 15, 16, 17, 41, 59, 60, 74, 75,
  76, 79, 86, 121, 143, 144, 153, 162, 163, 168,
  179, 197, 226, 227, 228, 229, 232, 257, 273,
  316, 332, 343
Utah, 41
  Bar Association, 351
  Supreme court, 203

Veterans of Foreign Wars, 144
Viguerie, Richard, 274
Virginia, 36, 227, 238, 243, 270
  Ratifying Convention, 30, 341
  Constitution, 30, 157

Warner, John, 120
War Powers Act, 126, 346
Warren Court, the, 113, 291, 292, 340
Warren, Earl, 202, 291
Warrensford, Don, 79
Washington, D. C., 35, 48, 53, 63, 135, 144, 149,
  196, 288, 290, 312, 313, 339, 350, 351
Washington, George, 103
Washington Post, the, 322, 334
Washington state, 6, 31, 117, 128, 129, 281, 326,
  327, 328, 329
  Supreme Court, 41
Watergate, 52, 100, 148, 168, 188
Webster, Daniel, 29, 30
Webster v. Reproductive Health Services, 275
West Virginia Board of Education v. Barnette, 135, 137, 138, 335
White, Byron, 136, 1666, 186, 269, 351
Wichita, Kan., 178, 276
Wicker, Tom, 113
Wickham, DeWayne, 80
Wilkie, J. C., 274
Will, George, 41, 59, 119, 123, 142, 159, 288
Wilson, Pete, 288
Wisconsin, 270
Wosik, Joseph, 171
Wyoming, 289, 309, 329

Yale University, 51

Zurcher v. Stanford Daily, 185

ACKNOWLEDGEMENT

Special thanks go to Linda Hinthorne-King and her assistant, Christopher Johnson, for their assistance in eliminating errors, straightening syntax and polishing prose so this book can be presented to the American public in readable condition.

JK 34 .B627 1995